Judi Dench

Contents

References

Article Licenses

Judi Dench

Dame Judith Olivia "Judi" Dench, CH, DBE, FRSA (born 9 December 1934) is an English film, stage and television actress.

Dench made her professional debut in 1957 with the Old Vic Company. Over the following few years she played in several of William Shakespeare's plays in such roles as Ophelia in Hamlet, Juliet in Romeo and Juliet and Lady Macbeth in Macbeth. She branched into film work, and won a BAFTA Award as Most Promising Newcomer, however most of her work during this period was in theatre. Not generally known as a singer, she drew strong reviews for her leading role in the musical Cabaret in 1968.

During the next two decades, she established herself as one of the most significant British theatre performers, working for the National Theatre Company and the Royal Shakespeare Company. In television, she achieved success during this period, in the series A Fine Romance from 1981 until 1984 and in 1992 began a continuing role in the television romantic comedy series As Time Goes By.

Her film appearances were infrequent until she was cast as M in GoldenEye (1995), a role she has played in each James Bond film since. She received several notable film awards for her role as Queen Victoria in Mrs. Brown (1997), and has since been acclaimed for her work in such films as Shakespeare in Love (1998), Chocolat (2000), Iris (2001), Mrs Henderson Presents (2005) and Notes on a Scandal (2006), and the television production The Last of the Blonde Bombshells (2001).

Regarded by critics as one of the greatest actresses of the post-war period, and frequently named as the leading British actress in polls, Dench has received many award nominations for her acting in theatre, film and television; her awards include ten BAFTAs, seven Laurence Olivier Awards, two Screen Actors Guild Awards, two Golden Globes, an Academy Award, and a Tony Award.

She was married to the actor Michael Williams from 1971 until his death in 2001. They are the parents of the actress Finty Williams.

Personal life

Dench was born in Heworth, York, England, the daughter of Eleanora Olave (née Jones), a native of Dublin, and Reginald Arthur Dench, a doctor who met Judi's mother while studying medicine at Trinity College.[1] Dench was raised a Methodist until, at age 13, she attended The Mount School, a Quaker Public Secondary school in York, becoming a Quaker.[2][3] Her brothers, one of whom is actor Jeffery Dench, were born in Tyldesley, Yorkshire.[2][3] Notable relatives also include her niece, Emma Dench, a Roman historian and professor previously at Birkbeck, University of London, and currently at Harvard University, Cambridge, Massachusetts.[4]

In 1971, Dench married British actor Michael Williams and they had their only child, Tara Cressida Williams, known professionally as Finty Williams, on 24 September 1972.

Dench and her husband starred together in several stage productions, and the Bob Larbey British television sitcom, A Fine Romance (1981–84). Michael Williams died from lung cancer in 2001, aged 65.

Career

In Britain, Dench has developed a reputation as one of the greatest actresses of the post-war period, primarily through her work in theatre, which has been her forte throughout her career. She has more than once been named number one in polls for Britain's best actress.[5][6]

Early years

Through her parents, Dench had regular contact with the theatre. Her father, a physician, was also the GP for the York Theatre, and her mother was its wardrobe mistress.[7] Actors often stayed in the Dench household. During these years, Judi was involved on a non-professional basis in the first three productions of the modern revival of the York Mystery Plays in the 1950s. In 1957, in one of the last productions in which she appeared during this period, she played the role of the Virgin Mary, performed on a fixed stage in the Museum Gardens.[8] Though she initially trained as a set designer, she became interested in drama school as her brother Jeff attended the Central School of Speech and Drama.[9] She applied and was accepted, where she was a classmate of Vanessa Redgrave, graduating with a first class degree in drama and four acting prizes, one being the Gold Medal as Outstanding Student.[10]

In September 1957, she made her first professional stage appearance with the Old Vic Company, at the Royal Court Theatre, Liverpool, as Ophelia in Hamlet, then her London debut in the same production at the Old Vic. She remained a member of the company for four seasons, 1957–1961, her roles including Katherine in Henry V in 1958 (which was also her New York debut) and as Juliet in Romeo and Juliet in October 1960, directed and designed by Franco Zeffirelli. During this period, she toured the United States and Canada, and appeared in Yugoslavia and at the Edinburgh Festival.

She joined the Royal Shakespeare Company in December 1961 playing Anya in The Cherry Orchard at the Aldwych Theatre in London, and made her Stratford-upon-Avon debut in April 1962 as Isabella in Measure for Measure. She subsequently spent seasons in repertory both with the Nottingham Playhouse from January 1963 (including a West African tour as Lady Macbeth for the British Council), and with the Oxford Playhouse Company from April 1964. That same year she made her film debut in The Third Secret.

Prominence

In 1968, she was offered the role of Sally Bowles in the musical Cabaret. As Sheridan Morley later reported: "At first she thought they were joking. She had never done a musical and she has an unusual croaky voice which sounds as if she has a permanent cold. So frightened was she of singing in public that she auditioned from the wings, leaving the pianists alone on stage".[11] But when it opened at the Palace Theatre in February 1968, Frank Marcus, reviewing for Plays and Players, commented that: "She sings well. The title song in particular is projected with great feeling."

After a long run in Cabaret, she rejoined the RSC making numerous appearances with the company in Stratford and London for nearly twenty years, winning several best actress awards. Among her roles with the RSC, she was the Duchess in John Webster's The Duchess of Malfi in 1971. In the Stratford 1976 season, and then at the Aldwych in 1977, she gave two comedy performances, first in Trevor Nunn's musical staging of The Comedy of Errors as Adriana, then partnered with Donald Sinden as Beatrice and Benedick in John Barton's "British Raj" revival of Much Ado About Nothing. As Bernard Levin wrote in The Sunday Times: "...demonstrating once more that she is a comic actress of consummate skill, perhaps the very best we have."[12]

But one of her most notable achievements with the RSC was her performance as Lady Macbeth in 1976. Nunn's acclaimed production of Macbeth was first staged with a minimalist design at The Other Place theatre in Stratford. Its small round stage focused attention on the psychological dynamics of the characters, and both Ian McKellen in the title role, and Dench, received exceptionally favourable notices. "If this is not great acting I don't know what is", wrote Michael Billington in The Guardian. "It will astonish me if the performance is matched by any in this actress's generation", commented J C Trewin in The Lady. The production transferred to London, opening at the Donmar Warehouse in September 1977, and was adapted for television, later released on VHS and DVD. Dench won the SWET Best Actress Award in 1977.

In 1989 she was cast as Pru Forrest, the long-time silent wife of Tom Forrest, in the BBC soap opera The Archers on its 10,000th edition.[13]

She had a romantic role in the BBC television film Langrishe, Go Down (1978), with Jeremy Irons and a screenplay by Harold Pinter from the Aidan Higgins novel, directed by David Jones, in which she played one of three spinster sisters living in a fading Irish mansion in the Waterford countryside.

Dench made her debut as a director in 1988 with the Renaissance Theatre Company's touring season, Renaissance Shakespeare on the Road, co-produced with the Birmingham Rep, and ending with a three month repertory programme at the Phoenix Theatre in London. Dench's contribution was a staging of Much Ado About Nothing, set in the Napoleonic era, which starred Kenneth Branagh and Samantha Bond as Benedick and Beatrice. In the same season, Geraldine McEwan and Derek Jacobi also made their directorial debuts.

She has made numerous appearances in the West End including the role of Miss Trant in the 1974 musical version of The Good Companions at Her Majesty's Theatre. In 1981, Dench was due to play the title role of Grizabella in the original production of Cats, but was forced to pull out due to a torn Achilles tendon, leaving Elaine Paige to play the role.[14] She has acted with the National Theatre in London where, in September 1995, she played Desiree Armfeldt in a major revival of Stephen Sondheim's A Little Night Music, for which she won an Olivier Award.

Popular success

In 1995, she took over the role of M (James Bond's boss) with the James Bond film series, starting with GoldenEye replacing Robert Brown. She is the only actor from Pierce Brosnan's Bond films to remain in the franchise. She has appeared in Casino Royale (2006) and its direct sequel Quantum of Solace (2008).

She has won multiple awards for performances on the London stage, including a record six Laurence Olivier Awards. She also won the Tony Award for her 1999 Broadway performance in the role of Esme Allen in David Hare's Amy's View. Alongside her numerous award winning performances, she has also managed to take on the role of Director for a number of stage productions. Dench won the Academy Award for Best Supporting Actress as Elizabeth I in the film Shakespeare in Love.

Judi Dench has frequently appeared with her close friend Geoffrey Palmer. They co-starred in the series As Time Goes By, where she played Jean Pargetter, becoming Jean Hardcastle after she married Lionel Hardcastle. The program spanned nine seasons. They also worked together on the films Mrs. Brown and Tomorrow Never Dies, both filmed in 1997. Dench has also lent her voice to many animated characters, narrations, and various other voice work. She plays the role of "Miss Lilly" in the children's animated series Angelina Ballerina (alongside her daughter, Finty Williams, as the voice of Angelina) and as Mrs. Calloway in the Disney animated film Home on the Range. She has narrated various classical music recordings (notably Mendelssohn's A Midsummer Night's Dream, and Britten's Canticles-The Heart of the Matter), and has appeared in numerous BBC radio broadcasts as well as commercials. Her many television appearances include lead roles in the series A Fine Romance and As Time Goes By. In the U.S., As Time Goes By has been repeated on PBS and on BBC America.

Recent years

Dench returned to the West End stage in April 2006 in Hay Fever alongside Peter Bowles, Belinda Lang and Kim Medcalf. She finished off 2006 with the role of Mistress Quickly in the RSC's new musical The Merry Wives, a version of The Merry Wives of Windsor.[15]

Dench's more recent film career has garnered six Academy Award nominations in nine years for Mrs. Brown in 1997; her Oscar-winning turn as Elizabeth I in Shakespeare in Love in 1998; for Chocolat in 2000; for the lead role of writer Iris Murdoch in Iris in 2001 (with Kate Winslet playing her as a younger woman); for Mrs Henderson Presents (a romanticised history of the Windmill Theatre) in 2005; and for 2006's Notes on a Scandal, a film for which she received critical acclaim, including Golden Globe, Academy Award, BAFTA and Screen Actors Guild nominations.

In 2007 the BBC issued The Judi Dench Collection, DVDs of eight television dramas: Talking to a Stranger quartet (1966), Keep an Eye on Amélie (1973), The Cherry Orchard (1981), Going Gently (1981), Ghosts (with Kenneth Branagh and Michael Gambon, 1987), Make and Break (with Robert Hardy, 1987), Can You Hear Me Thinking? (co-starring with her husband, Michael Williams, 1990) and Absolute Hell (1991).[16]

Dench, as Miss Matty Jenkins, co-starred with Eileen Atkins, Michael Gambon, Imelda Staunton and Francesca Annis, in the BBC One five-part series Cranford. The series began transmission in the UK in November 2007, and on the BBC's U.S. producing partner station WGBH (PBS Boston) in spring 2008.

Dench became the voice for the narration for the updated Walt Disney World Epcot attraction Spaceship Earth in February 2008.

In February 2008, she was named as the first official patron of the York Youth Mysteries 2008, a project to allow young people to explore the York Mystery Plays through dance, film-making and circus. This culminated on 21 June with a day of city centre performances in York.

She worked on the 22nd Bond adventure Quantum Of Solace and reprised her role as M.

She is interested in horse racing and in partnership with her chauffeur Bryan Agar owns a four-year-old horse, "Smokey Oakey", who won the 2008 Brigadier Gerard Stakes.[17]

She returned to the West End from 13 March-23 May 2009 playing Madame de Merteuil in Yukio Mishima's Madame De Sade, directed by Michael Grandage as part of the Donmar season at Wyndham's Theatre. A year later Dench renewed her collaboration with Sir Peter Hall at the Rose Theatre in Kingston upon Thames in A Midsummer Night's Dream which opened in February 2010, when she played Titania as Elizabeth I of England in her later years: Queen of the Forest of Arden. On July 31st 2010, Dame Judi performed Send in the Clowns at a special celebratory Promenade Concert from The Royal Albert Hall as part of the Proms Season, in honour of composer Stephen Sondheim's 80th Birthday, the entire concert in honour of his music.[18][19]

Public life

Dench was appointed an Officer of the Order of the British Empire in 1970[20] and promoted to Dame Commander of the order in 1988.[21] She was appointed a Member of the Order of the Companions of Honour in 2005.[22]

Dench is a patron of The Leaveners, Friends School Saffron Walden and the Archway Theatre, Horley, UK. She became president of Mountview Academy of Theatre Arts in London in 2006,[23] taking over from Sir John Mills, and is also president of the Questors Theatre. In May 2006, she became an Honorary Fellow of the Royal Society of Arts. She is also patron of Ovingdean Hall School, a special day and boarding school for the deaf and hard of hearing in Brighton and Vice President of The Little Foundation.

Dench is an Honorary Fellow of Lucy Cavendish College, Cambridge. In 1996 she was awarded an Honorary Doctorate (D.Univ) from Surrey University[24] and in 2000-2001 she received an Honorary DLitt from Durham University. On 24 June 2008, she was honoured by the University of St Andrews, receiving the honorary degree of Doctor of Letters (D.Litt) at the university's graduation ceremony.[25]

Dench has worked with the non-governmental indigenous organization, Survival International, campaigning in the defence of the tribal people, the Bushmen of Botswana and the Arhuaco of Colombia. She made a small supporting video saying the Bushmen are victims of tyranny, greed and racism.[26][27]

On 22 July 2010, Dench was awarded an honorary degree of Doctor of Letters (DLitt) by Nottingham Trent University.[28]

Filmography

Year Film Role Notes
1964 The Third Secret Miss Humphries
1965 Four in the Morning Wife[29] BAFTA Award for Most Promising Newcomer to Leading Film Roles
A Study in Terror Sally
He Who Rides a Tiger Joanne
1968 A Midsummer Night's Dream Titania
1973 Luther Katherine
1974 Dead Cert Laura Davidson
1978 Langrishe, Go Down Imogen Langrishe (BBC TV film)
1985 The Angelic Conversation (narrator)
Wetherby Marcia Pilborough Nominated — BAFTA Award for Best Actress in a Supporting Role
A Room with a View Eleanor Lavish BAFTA Award for Best Actress in a Supporting Role
1987 84 Charing Cross Road Nora Doel Nominated — BAFTA Award for Best Actress in a Supporting Role
1988 A Handful of Dust Mrs. Beaver BAFTA Award for Best Actress in a Supporting Role
1989 Henry V Mistress Quickly
Behaving Badly Bridget Mayor Channel 4 television serial
1995 Jack and Sarah Margaret
GoldenEye M
1996 Hamlet Hecuba
1997 Mrs. Brown Queen Victoria BAFTA Award for Best Actress in a Leading Role
BAFTA Scotland Award for Best Actress in a Film
Golden Globe Award for Best Actress – Motion Picture Drama
Chicago Film Critics Association Award for Best Actress
London Film Critics Circle Award for British Actress of the Year
Online Film Critics Society Award for Best Actress
Satellite Award for Best Actress – Motion Picture Drama
Nominated — Academy Award for Best Actress

Nominated — Screen Actors Guild Award for Outstanding Performance by a Female Actor in a Leading Role
Tomorrow Never Dies M
1998 Shakespeare in Love Queen Elizabeth Academy Award for Best Supporting Actress
BAFTA Award for Best Actress in a Supporting Role
Kansas City Film Critics Circle Award for Best Supporting Actress
National Society of Film Critics Award for Best Supporting Actress
Nominated — Chlotrudis Award for Best Supporting Actress
Nominated — Golden Globe Award for Best Supporting Actress – Motion Picture
Nominated — Screen Actors Guild Award for Outstanding Performance by a Female Actor in a Supporting Role
1999 Tea with Mussolini Arabella
The World Is Not Enough M
2000 Into the Arms of Strangers: Stories of the Kindertransport (narrator) (documentary)
The Last of the Blonde Bombshells Elizabeth British Academy Television Award for Best Actress
Golden Globe Award for Best Actress – Miniseries or Television Film
Nominated — Emmy Award for Outstanding Lead Actress – Miniseries or a Movie
Nominated — Screen Actors Guild Award for Outstanding Performance by a Female Actor in a Miniseries or Television Movie
Chocolat Armande Voizin Screen Actors Guild Award for Outstanding Performance by a Female Actor in a Supporting Role
Nominated — Academy Award for Best Supporting Actress
Nominated — BAFTA Award for Best Actress in a Supporting Role
Nominated — Golden Globe Award for Best Supporting Actress – Motion Picture
Nominated — Satellite Award for Best Supporting Actress – Motion Picture
2001 Iris Iris Murdoch BAFTA Award for Best Actress in a Leading Role
London Film Critics Circle Award for British Actress of the Year
Nominated — Academy Award for Best Actress
Nominated — Golden Globe Award for Best Actress – Motion Picture Drama
Nominated — Phoenix Film Critics Society Award for Best Actress
Nominated — Screen Actors Guild Award for Outstanding Performance by a Female Actor in a Leading Role
Nominated — Satellite Award for Best Actress – Motion Picture Drama
The Shipping News Agnis Hamm Nominated — BAFTA Award for Best Actress in a Supporting Role
Nominated — Screen Actors Guild Award for Outstanding Performance by a Female Actor in a Supporting Role
2002 The Importance of Being Earnest Lady Bracknell
Die Another Day M
2002-05 Angelina Ballerina Miss Lilly (voice)
2003 Bugs! (narrator) (short subject)
2004 Home on the Range Mrs. Caloway (voice)
The Chronicles of Riddick Aereon
Ladies in Lavender Ursula Widdington
2005 Pride & Prejudice Lady Catherine de Bourgh
Mrs Henderson Presents Mrs. Laura Henderson St. Louis Gateway Film Critics Association Award for Best Actress
Nominated — Academy Award for Best Actress
Nominated — BAFTA Award for Best Actress in a Leading Role
Nominated — British Independent Film Award for Best Actress
Nominated — Broadcast Film Critics Association Award for Best Actress
Nominated — Golden Globe Award for Best Actress – Motion Picture Musical or Comedy

Nominated — London Film Critics Circle Award for British Actress of the Year
Nominated — Screen Actors Guild Award for Outstanding Performance by a Female Actor in a Leading Role
Nominated — Satellite Award for Best Actress – Motion Picture Musical or Comedy
2006 The Magic Roundabout (narrator)
Casino Royale M Nominated — National Movie Award for Best Actress
Notes on a Scandal Barbara Covett British Independent Film Award for Best Actress
Evening Standard British Film Award for Best Actress
Nominated — Academy Award for Best Actress
Nominated — BAFTA Award for Best Actress in a Leading Role
Nominated — Broadcast Film Critics Association Award for Best Actress
Nominated — Chicago Film Critics Association Award for Best Actress
Nominated — Golden Globe Award for Best Actress – Motion Picture Drama
Nominated — London Film Critics Circle Award for Best Actress
Nominated — London Film Critics Circle Award for British Actress of the Year
Nominated — Online Film Critics Society Award for Best Actress
Nominated — Screen Actors Guild Award for Outstanding Performance by a Female Actor in a Leading Role
Nominated — Satellite Award for Best Actress – Motion Picture Drama
2007 Go Inside to Greet the Light (narrator)
2008 Quantum of Solace M
2009 Rage Mona Carvell
Nine Liliane La Fleur Satellite Award for Best Cast – Motion Picture
Nominated — Broadcast Film Critics Association Award for Best Cast
Nominated — Screen Actors Guild Award for Outstanding Performance by a Cast in a Motion Picture
Nominated — Washington D.C. Area Film Critics Association Award for Best Ensemble
2011 Jane Eyre Mrs. Fairfax Filming
My Week with Marilyn Dame Sybil Thorndike Filming
? Bond 23 M postponed

She has also lent her likeness and voice for the role of M in James Bond video games:

* Everything or Nothing
* GoldenEye: Rogue Agent
* Quantum of Solace
* GoldenEye 007
* Blood Stone

Theatre work

Source: "Judi Dench: With a Crack in her Voice" by John Miller
As an actress

St Mary's Abbey

* 1957

York Mystery Plays - Virgin Mary

Old Vic Company

* 1957

Hamlet - Ophelia
Measure for Measure - Juliet
A Midsummer Night's Dream - First Fairy

* 1958

Twelfth Night - Maria (also USA tour)
Henry V - Katharine (also USA tour)

* 1959

The Double Dealer - Cynthia
As You Like It - Phebe
The Importance of Being Earnest - Cecily
The Merry Wives of Windsor - Anne Page

* 1960

Richard II - Queen
Romeo and Juliet - Juliet (also Venice Festival)
She Stoops to Conquer - Kate Hardcastle
A Midsummer Night's Dream - Hermia

Also walk-on roles in King Lear and Henry VI[disambiguation needed])

Royal Shakespeare Company RSC

* 1961

The Cherry Orchard - Anya, Aldwych Theatre

* 1962

Measure for Measure - Isabella, Stratford
A Midsummer Night's Dream - Titania, Stratford
A Penny for a Song - Dorcas Bellboys, Aldwych

Nottingham Playhouse Company

* 1963

Macbeth - Lady Macbeth (also West Africa tour)
Twelfth Night - Viola (also West Africa tour)
A Shot in the Dark - Josefa Lautenay, Lyric Theatre

The Oxford Playhouse Company

* 1964

Three Sisters - Irina
The Twelfth Hour - Anna

* 1965

The Alchemist - Dol Common
Romeo and Jeannette - Jeannette
The Firescreen - Jacqueline

Nottingham Playhouse Company

* 1965

Measure for Measure - Isabella
Private Lives - Amanda

* 1966

The Country Wife - Margery Pinchwife
The Astrakhan Coat - Barbara
St Joan - Joan

Oxford Playhouse Company

* 1966

The Promise - Lika
The Rules of the Game - Silia

* 1967

The Promise - Lika, Fortune Theatre

Palace Theatre

* 1968

Cabaret - Sally Bowles

RSC

* 1969

The Winter's Tale - Hermione and Perdita, Stratford
Women Beware Women - Bianca, Stratford
Twelfth Night - Viola, Stratford

* 1970

London Assurance - Grace Harkaway, Aldwych
Major Barbara - Barbara Undershaft, Aldwych

* 1971

The Merchant of Venice - Portia, Stratford
The Duchess of Malfi - Duchess, Stratford
Toad of Toad Hall - Fielfmouse, Stoat and Mother Rabbit, Stratford

No Company

* 1973

Context to Whisper - Aurelia, Royal, York
Fanfare - Royal Opera House (with Laurence Olivier)
The Wolf - Vilma, Oxford Playhouse (also at Apollo, Queen's & New London)

West End

* 1974

The Good Companions - Miss Trant, Her Majesty's

* 1975

The Gay Lord Quex - Sophy Fullgarney, Albery

RSC

* 1975

Too True to Be Good - Sweetie Simpkins, Aldwych

* 1976

Much Ado About Nothing - Beatrice, Stratford
Macbeth - Lady Macbeth, Stratford (also Donmar Warehouse and Young Vic)
The Comedy of Errors - Adriana, Stratford
King Lear - Regan, Stratford

* 1977

Pillars of the Community - Lona Hessel, Aldwych

* 1978

The Way of the World - Millamant, Aldwych

* 1979

Cymbeline - Imogen, Stratford

* 1980

Juno and the Paycock - Juno Boyle, Aldwych

No Company

* 1981

A Village Wooing - Young Woman, New End

National Theatre

* 1982

The Importance of Being Earnest - Lady Bracknell, Lyttleton
A Kind of Alaska - Deborah, Cottesloe

* 1983

Pack of Lies - Barbara Jackson, Lyric

RSC

* 1984

Mother Courage - Mother Courage, Barbican
Waste Amy O'Connell, Barbican and Lyric

West End

* 1986

Mr and Mrs Nobody - Carrie Pooter, Garrick

National Theatre

* 1987

Antony and Cleopatra - Cleopatra, Olivier
Entertaining Strangers - Sarah Eldridge, Cottesloe

* 1989

Hamlet - Gertrude, Olivier

RSC

The Cherry Orchard - Ranevskaya, Aldwych

* 1991

The Plough and the Stars - Bessie Burgess, Young Vic

National Theatre

* 1991

The Sea - Mrs Rafi, Lyttleton

* 1992

Coriolanus - Volumnia, Chichester

Royal Shakespeare Company

* 1992

The Gift of the Gorgon - Helen Damson, Barbican and Wyndham's

National Theatre

* 1994

The Seagull - Arkadina, Olivier

* 1995

Absolute Hell - Christine Foskett, Lyttleton
A Little Night Music - Desirée Armfeldt, Olivier

* 1997

Amy's View - Esmé, Lyttleton

* 1998

Amy's View - Esmé, Aldwych

West End and Broadway

* 1998

Filumena - Filumena, Piccadilly

* 1999

Amy's View - Esmé, Barrymore, New York

* 2001

The Royal Family - Fanny Cavendish, Theatre Royal Haymarket

* 2002

The Breath of Life - Frances, Theatre Royal Haymarket

RSC

* 2003

All's Well That Ends Well - The Countess, Stratford and Gielgud

West End

* 2006

Hay Fever - Judith Bliss, Theatre Royal Haymarket

RSC

* 2006

The Merry Wives - The Musical - Mistress Quickly, Stratford

Donmar Warehouse

* 2009

Madame de Sade - Madame de Montreuil, Donmar at Wyndham's

Rose Theatre, Kingston

* 2010 A Midsummer Night's Dream - Titania (as Elizabeth I, Queen of the Forest of Arden)

Open Air Theatre, Regent's Park

* 2010 Into The Woods - Stephen Sondheim - Voice of The Giant

As a director

* 1988 - Much Ado About Nothing, Renaissance Theatre Company
* 1989 - Look Back in Anger - Renaissance Theatre Company
* 1989 - Macbeth - Central School of Speech and Drama
* 1991 - The Boy from Syracuse, Regent's Park Open Air Theatre
* 1993 - Romeo and Juliet, Regent's Park Open Air Theatre

Discography

* Cabaret (1968), Original London cast album CBS (1973)
* The Good Companions (1974), Original London cast recording (1974)
* A Midsummer Night's Dream (1995); from Felix Mendelssohn as Recitant. Conducted by Seiji Ozawa
* A Little Night Music (1995) by Stephen Sondheim, Royal National Theatre Cast

---

* Nine (2009) Original Motion Picture Soundtrack

Awards and nominations

Theatre

Awards

* 1977: Laurence Olivier Award for Best Actress in a Revival – Macbeth
* 1980: Evening Standard Award for Best Actress – Juno and the Paycock
* 1980: Laurence Olivier Award for Best Actress in a Revival – Juno and the Paycock
* 1982: Critics' Circle Theatre Award for Best Actress – The Importance of Being Earnest and A Kind of Alaska
* 1982: Evening Standard Award for Best Actress – The Importance of Being Earnest and A Kind of Alaska
* 1984: Laurence Olivier Award for Best Actress in a New Play – Pack of Lies
* 1987: Critics' Circle Theatre Award for Best Actress – Antony and Cleopatra
* 1987: Evening Standard Award for Best Actress – Antony and Cleopatra
* 1987: Laurence Olivier Award for Best Actress – Antony and Cleopatra
* 1996: Laurence Olivier Award for Best Actress – Absolute Hell
* 1996: Laurence Olivier Award for Best Actress in a Musical or Entertainment – A Little Night Music
* 1997: Critics' Circle Theatre Award for Best Actress – Amy's View
* 1999: Tony Award for Best Performance by a Leading Actress in a Play – Amy's View
* 2004: Laurence Olivier Award: Special Award for Outstanding Contributions to British Theatre

Television

Awards

* 1967: BAFTA Television Award for Best Actress - Talking to a Stranger[30]
* 1982: British Television Academy Award for Best Light Entertainment Performance - A Fine Romance, Going Gently and The Cherry Orchard
* 1982: Broadcast Press Guild Award for Best Actress - A Fine Romance
* 1985: British Television Academy Award for Best Light Entertainment Performance - A Fine Romance
* 2001: British Academy Television Award for Best Actress - The Last of the Blonde Bombshells
* 2001: Golden Globe Award for Best Actress - Miniseries or Television Film - The Last of the Blonde Bombshells

Nominations

* 1983: British Television Academy Award for Best Light Entertainment Performance - A Fine Romance
* 1984: British Academy Television Award for Best Actress - Saigon: Year of the Cat
* 1984: British Television Academy Award for Best Light Entertainment Performance - A Fine Romance
* 1990: British Academy Television Award for Best Actress - Behaving Badly
* 1998: British Television Academy Award for Best Comedy Performance - As Time Goes By
* 2001: American Comedy Award for Funniest Female Performer in a TV Special - The Last of the Blonde Bombshells
* 2001: Emmy Award for Outstanding Lead Actress - Miniseries or a Movie - The Last of the Blonde Bombshells
* 2001: Screen Actors Guild Award for Outstanding Performance by a Female Actor in a Miniseries or Television Movie - The Last of the Blonde Bombshells
* 2008: British Academy Television Award for Best Actress - Cranford
* 2008: Emmy Award for Outstanding Lead Actress - Miniseries or a Movie - Cranford
* 2008: Golden Globe Award for Best Actress - Miniseries or Television Film - Cranford

* 2008: Satellite Award for Best Actress - Miniseries or Television Film - Cranford
* 2010: Emmy Award for Outstanding Lead Actress - Miniseries or a Movie - Return to Cranford

References

1. Staff writers (6 September 2002). "The Importance of Dame Judi". BBC News. http://news.bbc.co.uk/2/hi/in_depth/uk/2000/newsmakers/2241129.stm. Retrieved 2009-02-16.
2. a b Michael Billington (12 September 2005). "Please God, not retirement". The Guardian. http://film.guardian.co.uk/oscars2006/story/0,,1699880,00.html. Retrieved 2009-02-16.
3. a b Michael Billington (23 March 1998). "Judi Dench: Nothing like the Dame". The Guardian. http://film.guardian.co.uk/Feature_Story/Guardian/0,,44053,00.html. Retrieved 2009-02-16.
4. "Emma Dench". Harvard Magazine. March–April 2010. http://harvardmagazine.com/2010/03/emma-dench. Retrieved 11 September 2010.
5. "Hopkins and Dench named best British actors". The Guardian. 18 August 2005. http://film.guardian.co.uk/news/story/0,12589,1551503,00.html. Retrieved 2006-12-29.
6. "Connery and Dench Top Legend Poll". Time Out Group. 25 February 2005. http://www.timeout.com/film/news/303/connery-and-dench-top-legend-poll.html. Retrieved 2006-12-29.
7. http://www.talktalk.co.uk/entertainment/film/biography/artist/judi-dench/biography/61?page=1
8. "Dame Judi speaks up for Mystery Plays". HoldTheFrontPage.co.uk. 18 September 2003. http://www.holdthefrontpage.co.uk/CAMPAIGNS/2003/09sep/030918judi.shtml. Retrieved 2006-12-29.
9. http://www.talktalk.co.uk/entertainment/film/biography/artist/judi-dench/biography/61?page=2
10. http://www.talktalk.co.uk/entertainment/film/biography/artist/judi-dench/biography/61?page=3
11. Sheridan Morley (1986). The great stage stars: distinguished theatrical careers of the past and present. London: Angus & Robertson. ISBN 978-020714970-2.
12. Robert Tanitch (2007). London stage in the 20th century. London: Haus Publishing. ISBN 978-190495074-5.
13. "The Archers Backstage". BBC Online. http://www.bbc.co.uk/radio4/archers/backstage/14000.shtml. Retrieved 6 August 2010.
14. Staff writers (15 January 2002). "Record-breaking Cats bows out". BBC News. http://news.bbc.co.uk/1/hi/entertainment/showbiz/1761508.stm. Retrieved 2009-02-16.
15. "Merry Wives – The Musical". Royal Shakespeare Company. http://www.rsc.org.uk/WhatsOn/3537.aspx. Retrieved 2006-12-29.
16. Philip Fisher (2007). "Reviews: Absolute Hell". British Theatre Guide. http://www.britishtheatreguide.info/reviews/DVD-jdenchabshell-rev.htm.
17. "Dame Judi Dench lands Brigadier Gerard Stakes with Smokey Oakey". This is London. The Evening Standard. 29 May 2008. http://www.thisislondon.co.uk/sport/article-23488432-details/Dame+Judi+Dench+lands+Brigadier+Gerard+Stakes+with+Smokey+Oakey/article.do. Retrieved 2009-02-16.
18. White, Lesley (2010-02-14). "Peter and Judi play a Tug of Love". Sunday Times. http://entertainment.timesonline.co.uk/tol/arts_and_entertainment/stage/theatre/article7021949.ece.
19. "About the Rose". The Rose Theatre. http://www.rosetheatrekingston.org/about-us. Retrieved 2009-10-22.
20. London Gazette: (Supplement) no. 45117, p. 6374, 5 June 1970.
21. London Gazette: (Supplement) no. 51171, p. 7, 31 December 1987..
22. London Gazette: (Supplement) no. 57665, p. 4, 11 June 2005.
23. "Dench is appointed Mountview president". The Stage (London): p. 6. 2006-03-30. ISSN 0038-9099.
24. "Doctor of the University". http://portal.surrey.ac.uk/calendar/hongrads/01doctor.jsp. Retrieved 2010-01-01.
25. "Distinguished actress to be honoured by University". University of St Andrews. 21 May 2008. http://www.st-andrews.ac.uk/news/Title,21556,en.html. Retrieved 2009-02-16.
26. "Journalists need to leave the Stone Age". The Independent. 2006-01-23. http://www.independent.co.uk/news/media/journalists-need-to-leave-the-stone-age-524213.html. Retrieved 2009-07-18.
27. "News & Media". Survival International. http://www.survival-international.org/news/video. Retrieved 2009-07-18. [dead link]

28. Stars of stage and screen among honorary graduates of Nottingham Trent University
29. Called Judy by her husband in the film, but imdb refers to the character by this name.
30. British Theatre Guide review

My Week with Marilyn

My Week with Marilyn is an upcoming British drama film directed by Simon Curtis and starring Emma Watson, Michelle Williams, Dominic Cooper and Kenneth Branagh. Based on the book by Colin Clark, it depicts the making of the 1957 film *The Prince and the Showgirl* which starred Marilyn Monroe and Laurence Oliver. In particular it focuses on the difficult interactions between the film's two stars. It began filming in September 2010.[1]

Cast

- Emma Watson ... Lucy
- Michelle Williams ... Marilyn Monroe
- Dominic Cooper ... Milton Greene
- Eddie Redmayne ... Colin Clark
- Kenneth Branagh ... Sir Laurence Olivier
- Julia Ormond ... Vivien Leigh
- Judi Dench ... Dame Sybil Thorndike
- Derek Jacobi ... Sir Owen Morshead
- Miranda Raison ... Vanessa
- Pete Noakes ... Clapper Loader
- Zoe Wanamaker ... Paula Strasberg

References

[1] http://www.dailymail.co.uk/tvshowbiz/article-1314729/Emma-Watson-Whats-happened-Harry-Potters-Hermione.html

External links

- *My Week with Marilyn* (http://www.imdb.com/title/tt1655420/) at the Internet Movie Database

Jane Eyre (2011 film)

Jane Eyre	
Directed by	Cary Fukunaga
Produced by	Alison Owen Paul Trijbits
Written by	Novel: Charlotte Brontë Screenplay: Moira Buffini
Starring	Mia Wasikowska Michael Fassbender Jamie Bell Judi Dench Holliday Grainger Sally Hawkins Tamzin Merchant Imogen Poots Jayne Wisener
Cinematography	Adriano Goldman
Distributed by	Focus Features
Release date(s)	March 11, 2011
Language	English

Jane Eyre is an upcoming film directed by Cary Fukunaga and starring Mia Wasikowska and Michael Fassbender. The screenplay is written by Moira Buffini based on the 1847 novel of the same name by Charlotte Brontë. The film is set for release on March 11, 2011.

Production

Writing

The film is a co-production between BBC Films, Focus Features and Ruby Films.[1] The script by Moira Buffini appeared on the 2008 Brit List, a film-industry-compiled list of the best unproduced screenplays in British film.[2] The adaptation is expected to stick closely to the book.[3] However, the character of Blanche Ingram is less conniving than in the novel.[4]

Filming

In October 2009, it was announced that Cary Fukunaga would direct the adaptation.[5] The adaptation will play up the Gothic elements of the classic novel.[6] Fukunaga stated, "I've spent a lot of time rereading the book and trying to feel out what Charlotte Brontë was feeling when she was writing it. That sort of spookiness that plagues the entire story... there's been something like 24 adaptations, and it's very rare that you see those sorts of darker sides. They treat it like it's just a period romance, and I think it's much more than that."[7]

Principal photography began on March 22, 2010 and concluded in mid-May.[1] [8] [9] Filming locations include London and various locations in Derbyshire, including Chatsworth, Haddon Hall, Derbyshire Dales, Froggatt, and Fox House (Sheffield).[1] [10] [11]

Release

Focus Features holds worldwide distribution rights.[12] *Jane Eyre* will open in selected cities on March 11, 2011.[13]

Cast

In November 2009 it was revealed that Mia Wasikowska would star as the title character and Michael Fassbender as Edward Rochester.[6] Jamie Bell, Judi Dench, Sally Hawkins, Imogen Poots, Holliday Grainger and Tamzin Merchant also joined the cast.[12] [14]

- Mia Wasikowska as Jane Eyre
- Michael Fassbender as Edward Rochester
- Jamie Bell as St. John
- Judi Dench as Mrs. Fairfax
- Holliday Grainger as Diana Rivers
- Sally Hawkins as Mrs. Reed
- Tamzin Merchant as Mary Rivers
- Imogen Poots as Blanche Ingram
- Jayne Wisener as Bessie Lee
- Amelia Clarkson as Young Jane Eyre
- Freya Parks as Helen Burns
- Rosie Cavaliero as Grace Poole
- Harry Lloyd as Richard Mason

References

[1] "Michael Fassbender Finds his 'Jane Eyre'" (http://www.iftn.ie/?act1=record&aid=73&rid=4282933&tpl=archnewshome&only=1&force=1). *Irish Film and Television Network.* March 12, 2010. . Retrieved March 18, 2010.

[2] Thomas, Archie (October 3, 2008). "Brit List brings scripts to light" (http://www.variety.com/article/VR1117993429.html?categoryid=2523&cs=1). *Variety* (Reed Business Information). . Retrieved April 8, 2010.

[3] Hoyle, Ben (April 24, 2010). "Brooding Brontës replace Austen as 'bonnet drama' returns" (http://entertainment.timesonline.co.uk/tol/arts_and_entertainment/film/article7106879.ece). *timesonline.co.uk.* . Retrieved April 27, 2010.

[4] Buchanan, Kyle (May 17, 2010). "The Verge: Imogen Poots" (http://www.movieline.com/2010/05/the-verge-imogen-poots.php?page=all). *Movieline.com.* . Retrieved May 21, 2010.

[5] Jaafar, Ali (October 20, 2009). "Fukunaga near 'Jane Eyre' redo" (http://www.variety.com/article/VR1118010174.html?categoryid=3768&cs=1). *Variety (magazine).* . Retrieved March 18, 2010.

[6] Jaafar, Ali (November 19, 2009). "Wasikowska in talks for 'Jane Eyre'" (http://www.variety.com/article/VR1118011645.html?categoryId=2431&cs=1). *Variety (magazine).* . Retrieved March 18, 2010.

[7] Buchanan, Kyle (March 10, 2010). "Director Cary Fukunaga on the 'Darker Sides' of His Upcoming Jane Eyre" (http://www.movieline.com/2010/03/cary-fukunaga-on-jane-eyre.php). *Movieline.* . Retrieved March 18, 2010.

[8] "Production begins on Jane Eyre" (http://www.bbc.co.uk/pressoffice/pressreleases/stories/2010/03_march/19/jane.shtml). *BBC.* March 19, 2010. . Retrieved May 21, 2010.

[9] "New BBC One drama, Helena Bonham Carter and Freddie Highmore star in Toast" (http://www.bbc.co.uk/pressoffice/pressreleases/stories/2010/05_may/21/toast.shtml). *BBC.* May 21, 2010. . Retrieved May 21, 2010.

[10] "Top actors heading here to shoot new Jane Eyre movie" (http://www.thisisderbyshire.co.uk/news/actors-heading-shoot-new-Jane-Eyre-movie/article-1977825-detail/article.html). *Derby Telegraph.* April 7, 2010. . Retrieved April 8, 2010.

[11] Dawes, Martin (March 24, 2010). "It's not Lark Rise to Grindleford!" (http://www.thestar.co.uk/diary/ASIDELINES--It39s-not-Lark.6175235.jp). *thestar.co.uk.* . Retrieved April 8, 2010.

[12] "Production begins on Jane Eyre" (http://www.bbc.co.uk/pressoffice/pressreleases/stories/2010/03_march/19/jane.shtml). March 19, 2010. . Retrieved March 19, 2010.

[13] "Focus Confirms Dates for Four Movies in 2011" (http://www.comingsoon.net/news/movienews.php?id=66404). *ComingSoon.net.* May 26, 2010. . Retrieved May 26, 2010.

[14] Kit, Borys (February 10, 2010). "'Jane Eyre' adaptation attracts cast" (http://www.hollywoodreporter.com/hr/content_display/world/news/e3iafcbd501634f9b088c74f2e93db59c12). *Hollywood Reporter.* . Retrieved March 18, 2010.

External links

- Official Facebook page (http://www.facebook.com/JaneEyreMovie)
- *Jane Eyre* (http://www.imdb.com/title/tt1229822/) at the Internet Movie Database

Nine (film)

Nine	
 Theatrical release poster	
Directed by	Rob Marshall
Produced by	• Rob Marshall • Marc Platt • Harvey Weinstein • Bob Weinstein • John DeLuca • Maury Yeston
Written by	• Michael Tolkin • Anthony Minghella
Starring	• Daniel Day-Lewis • Marion Cotillard • Penélope Cruz • Judi Dench • Fergie • Kate Hudson • Nicole Kidman • Sophia Loren
Music by	• Andrea Guerra • Maury Yeston
Cinematography	Dion Beebe
Editing by	• Claire Simpson • Wyatt Smith
Studio	• Relativity Media • Lucamar Productions

Distributed by	The Weinstein Company
Release date(s)	December 18, 2009 (United States) January 15, 2010 (Italy)
Running time	118 minutes
Country	• United States • Italy
Language	• English • Italian
Budget	$80 million[1]
Gross revenue	$53,902,165[1]

Nine is a 2009 musical-romantic film directed and produced by Rob Marshall. The screenplay, written by Michael Tolkin and Anthony Minghella,[2] is based on Arthur Kopit's book for the 1982 musical of the same name, which was itself suggested by Federico Fellini's semi-autobiographical film *8½*. Maury Yeston composed the music and wrote the lyrics for the songs.

The film premiered in London and was released in the United States on December 18, 2009, in New York City and Los Angeles, with a wide release on December 25, 2009.[3]

The principal cast consists of Academy Award winners Daniel Day-Lewis, Judi Dench, Nicole Kidman, Marion Cotillard, Penélope Cruz, Sophia Loren, Academy Award nominee Kate Hudson, and Grammy Award winner Fergie.

Despite mixed to negative reviews, *Nine* was nominated for four Academy Awards: Best Supporting Actress (Penélope Cruz), Best Art Direction (John Myhre (AD), Gordon Sim (SD)), Best Costume Design (Colleen Atwood) and Best Original Song ("Take It All" Music and Lyrics by Maury Yeston).

Plot

Guido Contini (Daniel Day Lewis) is a gifted Italian filmmaker who, at the age of fifty, has developed writer's block and urges all the women in his life, alive and dead, to help him with it - his mind wanders to his unfinished set, where dozens of dancers and the film's leading ladies appear – first Claudia Jenssen (Nicole Kidman), his leading lady; then Luisa (Marion Cotillard), his wife; Carla (Penelope Cruz), his mistress; Lilli (Judi Dench), his costume designer; his beloved Mamma (Sophia Loren); Stephanie (Kate Hudson), an American fashion journalist from *Vogue*; and finally Saraghina (Fergie), a prostitute from his childhood; ("*Overture Delle Donne*"). It is 1965, and at the famous Cinecittà movie studios, in Rome, 'everyone has questions for Signor Contini.'

At a press conference at the Hotel Excelsior on the Via Veneto, he's charming and colorful, avoiding any clear answer on his new movie - his ninth with producer, Dante (Ricky Tognazzi), - tentatively entitled "*Italia*". Here he meets Stephanie, a *Vogue* fashion journalist, whom he begins a flirtation with. Escaping the biting probes of the reporters, he creates an elaborate fantasy, which becomes ("*Guido's Song*") where he explains that he wishes he was young and energetic once again, since his talent was better then.

He escapes the press conference, the reporters and his producer and arrives at the Bellavista Spa Hotel. While being examined by the doctor, he receives a call from Carla, his mistress ("*A Call from the Vatican*"). She describes her desire for him, as he excitedly listens on the other end. She arrives at the spa, expecting to share his suite, but is upset to find that she's staying in a shabby pensione by the train station. Meanwhile, Guido learns that a Cardinal is also staying at his hotel and tells the cardinal's assistant to arrange a meeting.

However, Dante soon arrives at the spa and escorts Contini to a banquet hall where the entire production team is assembled to help him prepare for his film. He sees Lilli, his costume designer, and begs for inspiration, while criticizing the costume she's in the middle of making as not being something an Italian woman would wear. She reminds him of Luisa's birthday the previous day and disagrees, saying that it reminds her of Folies Bergères, a Parisian music hall that featured showgirls, where she 'learnt her art' ("*Folies Bergères*").

The Cardinal agrees to meet him and advises him to lead a more moral life and look to his youth for inspiration. Guido's thoughts lead him to remembering Saraghina, a prostitute whom he and his friends paid to teach them the art of love and sex ("*Be Italian*"). Young Guido is caught by his school teachers/priests and whipped by his principal. He awakens on top of Carla, in a fit of anxiety and abruptly leaves to meet his production team for dinner. She wants to come, but he vehemently refuses, reminding her that they don't want to hurt either of their spouses.

At dinner, he's happily surprised to see Luisa, who has come at Lilli's request. He embraces her and wishes her a happy birthday, promising that when she returns home, thee house will be filled with flowers. She sits, and the young priest from earlier, who recognizes her as one of Guido's earlier actresses, joins the table. In song, Luisa explains how she's become a different woman to be Guido's wife, abandoning her acting career to be at his side ("*My Husband Makes Movies*"). She then notices Carla entering the restaurant and immediately leaves, saying she feels tired. Guido doesn't understand why and follows her, asking what's happened. She ignores him and when he returns to the restaurant and sees Carla, he finally understands. He demands that Carla go back to the pensione, and she leaves, heartbroken.

When Guido goes to the suite to try to smooth things over, Luisa refuses to listen. He goes to the lobby and meets Stephanie, who has tracked him down. Guido and Stephanie continue to flirt, and she describes her love for his movies and how fashionable he makes everything seem ("*Cinema Italiano*"). She leaves her room key in his pocket. While in her room, watching her undress, he realizes how much he cares for his wife and leaves. He returns to the suite and promises that he's done with cheating. Luisa embraces him, but he's called away to help Carla, who's overdosed on pills. The doctor comments how reckless and immoral Guido is, which Guido doesn't contest. He stays with Carla until her husband arrives. He returns to the hotel to find that Luisa has left and the crew has returned to Rome to begin filming.

His mother returns to him to advise him to repair his life ("*Guarda La Luna*"). He calls Luisa from the studio to beg her to come to the screen testing that evening. She hangs up without response. He arrives at the set to film shots of Claudia in her costumes. She does a few takes, but leaves, saying she'll return when she reads the script. Guido agrees that that's fair and drives her away. They're followed by paparazzi, but he manages to lose them. Claudia realizes that there is no script and they take a walk. She asks him what he wants the film to be about and his description closely resembles his own ordeal: a man lost and in love with so many women. When they stop to rest, she tells him that she loves him but he is unable to love her ("*Unusual Way*"). Claudia tells him he doesn't see the real her, only the movie star he has created for the masses. She leaves.

He returns to review screen tests of new actresses and keeps looking to the back to see if Luisa has arrived. He's relieved when she finally does. She watches and is heartbroken to see him say something in a clip to an actress that he'd said to her when they first met. When everyone leaves, she explains to him that he's reminded her that she's not special, just another link in the chain and leaves him ("*Take It All*").

He finally comes to terms with his mental block ("*I Can't Make This Movie*"), realizing that he's lost everything: his wife, his muse, his talent, and has nothing to make the movie. He apologizes to the staff that there was never a movie, just an idea, and has the set destroyed before leaving Rome.

Two years later, Guido is in a café in Anguillara looking at an advertisement for a play starring Luisa. He waits outside the theatre that night, and watches her leave with a man. He walks with Lilli a few days later and tries to find more information about her. Lilli tells him that she's not going be to be the middle-man for them, implying that Luisa asks for him as well. She asks if he will ever make a movie again. He says that he won't because he wouldn't know what to make, except a movie about a man trying to win back his wife. Lilli says that that's a good start and the costumes won't be too bad either.

Guido returns to his element, passionate about a story once more. As he speaks with his actors about the scene, his nine-year-old self (Giuseppe Spitaleri) gathers the cast of Guido's life together. As Guido takes his place in the director's chair, the cast of Guido's life assemble on the scaffolding behind him, culminating with the arrival of his mother and nine-year-old Guido running to sit on the older Guido's lap ("*Finale*"). Luisa arrives without being seen and watches in that background, happy to see Guido back to his old self. She smiles as he is raised on a crane and calls, "Action!"

Cast

- Daniel Day-Lewis as Guido Contini
- Marion Cotillard as Luisa Contini (née Acari)
- Penélope Cruz as Carla Albanese
- Judi Dench as Lilli La Fleur
- Nicole Kidman as Claudia Jenssen
- Kate Hudson as Stephanie Necrophorus
- Fergie as Saraghina
- Sophia Loren as Mamma Contini
- Ricky Tognazzi as Dante, Guido's producer
- Giuseppe Spitaleri as young Guido Contini
- Andy Pessoa as Italian boy
- Max Procaccini as The Business Man

Production

Development

On April 12, 2007, *Variety* announced Rob Marshall would direct a feature film adaptation of *Nine* for The Weinstein Company. Marshall had previously directed *Chicago* for the Weinsteins while they were still at Miramax. The film was co-produced by Marshall's own production company, Lucamar Productions.

In 2008, a short "teaser" for the film was featured in an episode of the Food Network show, *Barefoot Contessa*, with the host, Ina Garten, making breakfast and lunch for her friends, producers John DeLuca and Rob Marshall, as they edited their new film, at the end being a "preview" of their film for the host to see in appreciation.

In December 2009, the film contracted the soap operas *One Life to Live* and *General Hospital* for advertising purposes. The former featured two of the characters watching one of the film's trailers on the Internet on a YouTube-esque website, and there were subtle setting alterations performed for the latter, including movie posters on the walls of various public places.

Casting

On April 4, 2008, it was reported that Nicole Kidman had replaced Catherine Zeta-Jones in the role of Claudia Jenssen, who turned down the role when director Marshall refused to expand the role for the film. The film was Kidman's first big-screen musical since *Moulin Rouge!*. After Catherine Zeta-Jones' departure, Anne Hathaway was auditioned for the role, but was turned down.[4]

On May 14, 2008, *Variety* reported Daniel Day-Lewis was in talks to star in the film as Guido Contini, the film's lead character,[5] after Javier Bardem dropped out due to exhaustion. Later, it was reported Day-Lewis sent producers a video of him singing and shocked them with his voice. On May 19, 2008, *People* reported the actor had landed the role.[6] Antonio Banderas, who had starred in the Broadway revival said he was "disappointed" at not being cast, said that the trailer to the film looked great and only wished the "best" for everyone involved.[7]

Variety also reported that Penélope Cruz auditioned for the role of Claudia, but was cast as Carla, and that Marion Cotillard auditioned for Lili, but was cast as Luisa, and that Kate Hudson had also been cast in a role created specifically for her which had not been featured in the Broadway show.[8] On July 18, 2008, *People* reported Fergie had been cast as Saraghina.[9]

Katie Holmes auditioned for the role of Carla Albanese and Demi Moore auditioned for the role of Luisa Contini, but both failed to win those roles. Barbra Streisand was considered for the role of Lilli, but the role went to Judi Dench.[10]

Filming

Day-Lewis studied Italian for his role and frequently spoke the language in and out of character. According to music supervisor Matt Sullivan, "One day during shooting at London's Shepperton Studios, "Rob and I got called into Daniel's dressing room, which was designed as a 1960s film director's office," says Sullivan. 'He's smoking a cigarette, in full outfit and in character, and he's telling us how he would like to see this number that he's performing. And he's talking to us as Guido Contini. It was a really surreal experience.' "[8]

Rehearsals for the film began in August 2008, the songs were then subsequently recorded in late September and filming commenced in October at Shepperton Studios, London. The film had been set to shoot in Toronto, though once Day-Lewis signed on, the production then moved to London.[11] Further filming took place in Italy, and at Cinecittà Film Studios.[12]

Nine's schedule required Kidman to begin rehearsals just four weeks after giving birth to her daughter.

The teaser trailer for the film was released on May 14, 2009.

Soundtrack

The soundtrack was released by Geffen Records, on December 22.[13] It peaked at number twenty-six on the Billboard 200. It also peaked at number three on the Polish Albums Chart[14] and at number nine on the Greek Albums Chart.[15]

Variety confirmed that three new songs had been created for the film by original Broadway composer Maury Yeston and were not included in the original stage score. They were:

1. *Guarda La Luna* (Look at the Moon), a lullaby sung by Sophia Loren as Mamma. Yeston tailored this song specifically for Loren's voice, though he based the melody on the song *Waltz from Nine* from the Broadway score.
2. *Cinema Italiano*, a number which Kate Hudson performs as Stephanie. This has "a retro feel" with "elements of '60s pop" that demonstrate how important Italian cinema was in that era and to illustrate the shallowness and vanity of Stephanie.
3. *Take It All*, originally written as a trio for Claudia, Carla, and Luisa, but, just before shooting, rearranged as a solo for Luisa, according to music supervisor Matt Sullivan.[8]

Tracklist

#	Title	Singer	Character	Time
1.	"Overture Delle Donne"	Female Ensemble		4:07
2.	"Guido's Song"	Daniel Day-Lewis	Guido Contini	3:41
3.	"A Call from the Vatican"	Penélope Cruz	Carla Albanese	3:40
4.	"Folies Bergères"	Judi Dench	Lilli La Fleur	4:42
5.	"Be Italian"	Fergie	Saraghina	4:12
6.	"My Husband Makes Movies"	Marion Cotillard	Luisa Contini	4:48
7.	"Cinema Italiano"	Kate Hudson	Stephanie Necrophorus	3:13
8.	"Guarda La Luna"	Sophia Loren	Mamma Contini	3:10
9.	"Unusual Way"	Nicole Kidman	Claudia Jenssen	3:26
10.	"Take It All"	Marion Cotillard	Luisa Contini	3:03
11.	"I Can't Make This Movie"	Daniel Day-Lewis	Guido Contini	2:11
12.	"Finale"	Orchestra		3:35

Bonus tracks

#	Title	Singer	Time
13.	"Quando Quando Quando"	Fergie feat. will.i.am	3:15
14.	"Io Bacio... Tu Baci"	The Noisettes	3:24
15.	"Cinema Italiano (The Ron Fair Remix)"	Kate Hudson	3:25
16.	"Unusual Way"	Griffith Frank	3:42
17.	"Cinema Italiano (The Ron Fair Remix Club Version)" Amazon mp3 Store Only	Kate Hudson	3:26
18.	"Be Italian (Club Version)" (iTunes Store Only)	Fergie	2:48

Cut songs

Title	Character(s)
"Germans at the Spa"	Company
"Not Since Chaplin"	Company
"Only with You"	Guido
"The Script"	Guido
"Nine"	Mamma
"Ti Voglio Bene"	Saraghina
"The Bells of St. Sebastian"	Guido, Little Guido
"A Man Like You"	Guido, Claudia
"Contini Submits"	Guido
"The Grand Canal" (Every Girl in Venice/Amor/Only You/Finale)	Guido, Claudia, Lilli, Luisa, Stephanie, Carla, Mamma, Company
"Simple"	Carla
"Be on Your Own"	Luisa
"Getting Tall"	Little Guido
Reprises	Guido, Little Guido, Luisa

Reception

The film received generally mixed reviews. Review aggregate Rotten Tomatoes reports that 37% of critics have given the film a positive review based on 182 reviews, with an average score of 5/10. The critical consensus is: *It has a game, great-looking cast, led by the always worthwhile Daniel Day-Lewis, but Rob Marshall's Nine is chaotic and curiously distant.*[16] While *Nine* wasn't a critical hit, Marion Cotillard's performance was greatly praised, as was Penélope Cruz's. Despite less than favorable reception, it received four nominations for the 82nd Academy Awards and has received other notable awards and nominations.

On June 13, 2010, at the Tony Awards, host Sean Hayes slighted the film when introducing Antonio Banderas, who portrayed Guido in the 2003 Broadway revival. Hayes said, "Our next presenter has uncanny instincts. He got a Tony nomination for the Broadway production of *Nine* and he avoided the film version of *Nine*."[17]

Awards and nominations

Awards			
Award	**Category**	**Recipient(s)**	**Outcome**
Academy Awards	Academy Award for Best Supporting Actress	Penélope Cruz	Nominated
	Academy Award for Best Art Direction	John Myhre and Gordon Sim	Nominated
	Academy Award for Best Costume Design	Colleen Atwood	Nominated
	Academy Award for Best Original Song ("Take It All")	Maury Yeston	Nominated
British Academy of Film and Television Arts Awards			
	BAFTA Award for Best Makeup and Hair	Peter King	Nominated

Broadcast Film Critics Association Awards	Best Film	*Nine*	Nominated
	Best Supporting Actress	Marion Cotillard	Nominated
	Best Acting Ensemble	Daniel Day-Lewis, Marion Cotillard, Sophie Loren, Judi Dench, Nicole Kidman, Penélope Cruz, Fergie and Kate Hudson	Nominated
	Best Cinematography	Dio Beebe	Nominated
	Best Art Direction	John Myhre and Gordon Sim	Nominated
	Best Editing	Claire Simpson and Wyatt Smith	Nominated
	Best Costume Design	Coleen Atwood	Nominated
	Best Makeup	Peter King	Nominated
	Best Sound		Nominated
	Best Song ("Cinema Italiano")	Maury Yeston	Nominated
Detroit Film Critics Society Awards 2009	Best Supporting Actress	Marion Cotillard	Nominated
Golden Globe Awards	Best Motion Picture – Musicalor Comedy	*Nine*	Nominated
	Best Original Song ("Cinema Italiano")	Maury Yeston	Nominated
	Best Actor – Motion Picture Musical or Comedy	Daniel Day-Lewis	Nominated
	Best Actress – Motion Picture Musical or Comedy	Marion Cotillard	Nominated
	Best Supporting Actress – Motion Picture	Penélope Cruz	Nominated

Award	Category	Nominee	Result
Satellite Awards	Best Motion Picture – Comedyor Musical	*Nine*	Won
	Best Director	Rob Marshall	Nominated
	Best Actress – Comedy or Musical	Marion Cotillard	Nominated
	Best Actor – Comedy or Musical	Daniel Day-Lewis	Nominated
	Best Supporting Actress – Motion Picture	Penélope Cruz	Nominated
	Best Cinematography	Dion Beebe	Won
	Best Costume Design	Colleen Atwood	Nominated
	Best Film Editing	Claire Simpson and Wyatt Smith	Nominated
	Best Original Song ("Cinema Italiano")	Maury Yeston	Nominated
	Best Sound (Mixing and Editing)		Nominated
	Best Cast – Motion Picture	Daniel Day-Lewis, Marion Cotillard, Sophie Loren, Judi Dench, Nicole Kidman, Penélope Cruz, Fergie and Kate Hudson	Won
	Ten Best Films of 2009	*Nine*	Won
Screen Actors Guild Awards	Outstanding Performance by a Cast in a Motion Picture	*Nine* (Daniel Day-Lewis, Marion Cotillard, Sophie Loren, Judi Dench, Nicole Kidman, Penélope Cruz, Fergie and Kate Hudson)	Nominated
	Outstanding Performance by a Female Actor in a Supporting Role	Penélope Cruz	Nominated
St. Louis Gateway Film Critics Association Awards	Best Supporting Actress	Marion Cotillard	Nominated
	Best Cinematography	Dion Beebe	Won
	Best Music		Won
Washington D.C. Area Film Critics Association	Best Art Direction	John Myhre and Gordon Sim	Won

Home media

Nine was released on DVD and Blu-ray May 4, 2010. The DVD featured an audio commentary by director Rob Marshall and producer John DeLuca, 8 featurettes, and 3 music videos. The Blu-ray Disc included all the DVD extras including another featurette and a Screen Actors Guild Q&A.[18]

References

[1] "Nine (2009) Box Office" (http://www.boxofficemojo.com/movies/?id=nine.htm). Box Office Mojo. . Retrieved 2010-02-14.

[2] http://www.imdb.com/title/tt0875034/fullcredits#writers

[3] Hernandez, Ernio (2008-01-23). "Work Resumes on Script for Rob Marshall's *Nine* Film" (http://www.playbill.com/news/article/114520.html). *Playbill News* (Playbill). . Retrieved 2008-08-07.

[4] "Kidman and Dench Rumored To Star In 'Nine'" (http://www.broadwayworld.com/viewcolumn.cfm?colid=26669). *broadwayworld.com*. Wisdom Digital Media. 2008-04-04. . Retrieved 2008-08-07.

[5] Fleming, Michael (2008-05-14). "Daniel Day-Lewis eyes 'Nine' role" (http://www.variety.com/article/VR1117985677.html?categoryid=1236&cs=1). *Variety Los Angeles* (Variety). . Retrieved 2008-08-07.

[6] Silverman, Stephen M (2008-05-19). "Daniel Day-Lewis Lands *Nine* Role" (http://www.people.com/people/article/0,,20201089,00.html). *People*. Time Inc.. . Retrieved 2008-08-07.

[7] "Antonio Banderas and Laura Linney; Interview for 'The Other Man'" (http://www.youtube.com/watch?v=XWR32LTJ9wE&feature=related). Youtube.com. 2009-09-03. . Retrieved 2010-06-04.

[8] By (2009-08-24). "Oscar winners abound in 'Nine' – Entertainment News, Music for Screens: Summer '09, Media" (http://www.variety.com/article/VR1118007662.html?categoryId=3703&cs=1). Variety. . Retrieved 2010-01-12.

[9] Tapper, Christina (2008-07-30). "Fergie to Play a Prostitute in the Movie Musical *Nine*" (http://www.people.com/people/article/0,,20215725,00.html). *People*. Time Inc.. . Retrieved 2008-08-07.

[10] "Katie Holmes and Demi Moore Audition for 'Nine' Film 2007/07/01" (http://broadwayworld.com/article/Katie_Holmes_and_Demi_Moore_Audition_for_Nine_Film_20070701). Broadwayworld.com. 2007-07-01. . Retrieved 2010-01-12.

[11] Bamigboye, Baz (2008-06-26). "BAZ BAMIGBOYE on Gillian Anderson, Nicole Kidman, Roman Polanski and much more... | Mail Online" (http://www.dailymail.co.uk/tvshowbiz/article-1029830/BAZ-BAMIGBOYE-Gillian-Anderson-Nicole-Kidman-Roman-Polanski-.html). London: Dailymail.co.uk. . Retrieved 2010-01-12.

[12] "Nicole Kidman and Daniel Day-Lewis take a spin in the Eternal City, dodging the Sixties-style paparazzi | Mail Online" (http://www.dailymail.co.uk/tvshowbiz/article-1131451/Nicole-Kidman-Daniel-Day-Lewis-spin-Eternal-City-dodging-Sixties-style-paparazzi.html). London: Dailymail.co.uk. 2009-01-29. . Retrieved 2010-01-12.

[13] ""Nine" Soundtrack Will Hit Stores in December" (http://www.playbill.com/news/article/134112- Nine Soundtrack_Will_Hit_Stores_in_December#). Playbill.com. 2009-10-26. . Retrieved 2010-01-12.

[14] "OLIS – Official Retail Sales Chart" (http://olis.onyx.pl/listy/index.asp?lang=en). ZPAV. . Retrieved February 22, 2010.

[15] "Top 50 Ξένων Αλμπουμ" (http://www.ifpi.gr/chart01.htm) (in Greek). IFPI Greece. . Retrieved January 29, 2010.

[16] "Nine (2009)" (http://www.rottentomatoes.com/m/nine_2009/). *IGN Entertainment*. Rotten Tomatoes. . Retrieved 2010-06-11.

[17] http://www.dnainfo.com/20100614/midtown-west-hells-kitchen/hollywood-steals-broadways-spotlight-during-colorful-tony-awards

[18] "Nine (US – DVD R1" (http://www.dvdactive.com/news/releases/nine.html). DVDActive. . Retrieved 2010-03-13.

External links

- Official website (http://nine-movie.com)
- *Nine* (http://www.imdb.com/title/tt0875034/) at the Internet Movie Database
- *Nine* (http://www.allmovie.com/work/394509) at Allmovie
- *Nine* (http://www.boxofficemojo.com/movies/?id=nine.htm) at Box Office Mojo
- *Nine* (http://www.rottentomatoes.com/m/nine_2009/) at Rotten Tomatoes
- *Nine* (http://www.metacritic.com/film/titles/nine) at Metacritic
- Official Maury Yeston Website (http://www.mauryyeston.com)

Rage (2009 film)

Film poster

Rage	
Directed by	Sally Potter
Produced by	Andrew Fierberg, Christopher Sheppard
Written by	Sally Potter
Starring	Jude Law Judi Dench Dianne Wiest Steve Buscemi John Leguizamo Lily Cole
Cinematography	Steven Fierberg
Editing by	Daniel Goddard
Distributed by	- USA - Cinetic Media - International - 6Sales
Release date(s)	2009
Running time	98 minutes
Language	English

Rage is a 2009 film written and directed by Sally Potter starring Jude Law and Judi Dench. The filmmakers said that the film created a new genre in filmmaking, called *naked cinema*.[1]

Press releases

"The film is a bitterly funny exposé of the inner lives of individuals working at a New York fashion house – as if shot by a schoolboy on his cellphone camera - over seven days in which an accident on the runway becomes a murder investigation."[2]

"The world's first multi-venue interactive premiere, broadcast live by satellite from London's BFI Southbank to dozens of cinemas across the UK and Europe. You can be part of the satellite broadcast of the Q&A after the film, sending your questions by Skype video and SMS direct from your local cinema live to director Sally Potter and members of the RAGE cast, including Jude Law, Eddie Izzard and Lily Cole.

RAGE: a schoolboy uses his cellphone camera to shoot intimate interviews with people working at a New York fashion house and secretly posts them on the internet. Result: a bitterly funny expose of an industry in crisis, during a week in which an accident on the runway becomes a murder investigation, and denial leads to devastation."[3]

"The filmmakers have partnered with Babelgum for the film's release, which will see RAGE simultaneously available on mobile, online, digital screens and DVD."[4]

Potter said:

> *"With Rage, I want us all to laugh about beauty and success, disappointment and failure."*[5]

"Part of the subject matter of Rage is the ugly use of beauty in the pursuit of profit. Drugged by marketing, sapped by fear of aging, conned by the cult of celebrity ... image becomes all."[6]

Cast

- Jude Law as Minx
- Steve Buscemi as Frank
- Judi Dench as Mona Carvell
- John Leguizamo as Jed
- Dianne Wiest as Miss Roth
- Eddie Izzard as Tiny Diamonds
- Riz Ahmed as Vijay
- Bob Balaban as Mr. White
- Lily Cole as Lettuce Leaf
- Patrick J. Adams as Dwight Angel
- David Oyelowo as Homer
- Adriana Barraza as Anita de Los Angeles
- Simon Abkarian as Merlin
- Jakob Cedergren as Otto

World premiere and release dates

The film premiered at the 2009 Berlin International Film Festival and was nominated for the Golden Berlin Bear.[7] [8] [9]

The DVD was released on September 22, 2009 in the US, respectively September 28, 2009 in the UK. A special edition version of the DVD was released through the official *Rage* website.

Babelgum premiered the film on mobile phones and internet at the same time as the cinema and DVD release. Babelgum released *Rage* in the UK, North America, Australia, Italy, France, Germany and Spain.[10] [11] [12]

Rage is the world's first feature film to debut on mobile phones. The movie will be shown in seven episodes beginning on September 21, 2009. The online screening began on Monday, September 28, 2009.[13]

Rage had its New York screen premiere on September 21, 2009 at "The Box".[14]

References

[1] *"Rage" strips down at Berlin* (http://www.reuters.com/news/video?newsChannel=entertainmentNews&videoId=98469), at Reuters, accessed May 7, 2009
[2] *Rage announced in Cannes* (http://www.sallypotter.com/node/153) at *sallypotter.com*, submitted on May 5, 2008, accessed November 4, 2008
[3] (http://ragethemovie.com/screenings) posted September 14, 2009
[4] (http://ragethemovie.com/mobile), submitted on September 14, 2009
[5] Anne Thompson /John Hopewell, *Sally Potter film stars Law, Dench* (http://www.variety.com/index.asp?layout=festivals&jump=story&id=1061&articleid=VR1117985859&cs=1) at Variety, posted May 16, 2008, accessed October 10, 2008
[6] *Beauty* (http://www.sallypotter.com/beauty-blog), at *sallypotter.com*, submitted on January 30, 2009, accessed April 9, 2009.
[7] Dave Itzkoff, *Berlin Film Festival Announces Lineup* (http://www.nytimes.com/2008/12/13/arts/13arts-BERLINFILMFE_BRF.html?ref=arts), The New York Times, published December 12, 2008.
[8] *Berlin* (http://www.sallypotter.com/berlin) at *sallypotter.com*, submitted on 11/12/2008, accessed January 4, 2009.
[9] *Competition: Rage* (http://www.berlinale.de/en/archiv/jahresarchive/2009/06_streaming_2009/06_Streaming_2009-PopUp_6865.html), Press Conference and Red Carpet, streaming video at *berlinale.de*, submitted on February 8, 2009, accessed February 20, 2009.
[10] *RAGE ON BABELGUM* (http://www.sallypotter.com/rageonbabelgum), at *sallypotter.com*, submitted on May 15, 2009, accessed October 8, 2009.
[11] Peter Knegt, *Potter's "Rage" Finds Unique Home* (http://www.indiewire.com/article/2009/05/11/potters_rage_finds_unique_home/), *indiewire.com*, submitted May 11, 2009, accessed June 23, 2009
[12] Jeremy Kay, *Rage to receive multi-territory online and mobile release* (http://www.screendaily.com/5000990.article), *screendaily.com*, submitted May 12, 2009, accessed June 23, 2009
[13] *Coming to Babelgum on September 21st* (http://www.babelgum.com/rage), accessed September 21, 2009.
[14] *The Box* (http://www.sallypotter.com/node/1192), submitted September 22, 2009, accessed October 4, 2009.

External links

- Official website (http://ragethemovie.com/)
- *Rage* (http://www.imdb.com/title/tt1234550/) at the Internet Movie Database
- *Sally Potter* (http://movies.nytimes.com/person/106934/Sally-Potter) at New York Times, accessed November 4, 2008.
- *Sally Potter* (http://www.sallypotter.com/) Official website
- *Gallery Rage* (http://www.sallypotter.com/gallery), sallypotter.com, accessed February 26, 2009.
- *POLL: Which Actor Makes the Best Lady?* (http://www.people.com/people/article/0,,20256889,00.html), People, originally posted February 4, 2009, accessed April 9, 2009.
- Kevin Maher, *Sally Potter explains why her new film will go direct to our mobile phones* (http://entertainment.timesonline.co.uk/tol/arts_and_entertainment/film/article6838430.ece), timesonline.co.uk, September 19, 2009.
- Melissa Silverstein, *Interview with Sally Potter, Director of Rage* (http://www.huffingtonpost.com/melissa-silverstein/interview-with-sally-pott_b_303006.html), huffingtonpost.com, September 29, 2009.

Quantum of Solace (film)

Quantum of Solace	
 Theatrical release poster	
James Bond	Daniel Craig
Also starring	Olga Kurylenko Mathieu Amalric Gemma Arterton Judi Dench Jeffrey Wright Giancarlo Giannini
Directed by	Marc Forster
Produced by	Michael G. Wilson Barbara Broccoli
Novel/Story by	Ian Fleming (leadcharacter) Michael G. Wilson (plot)
Screenplay by	Joshua Zetumer (uncredited) Paul Haggis Neal Purvis Robert Wade
Cinematography	Roberto Schaefer
Music by	David Arnold
Main theme	"Another Way to Die"
Composer	Jack White
Performer	Alicia Keys Jack White
Editing by	Matt Chesse Rick Pearson
Studio	EON Productions
Distributed by	Metro-Goldwyn-Mayer Columbia Pictures

Release date(s)	31 October 2008 (United Kingdom) 14 November 2008 (United States)
Running time	106 minutes
Country	United Kingdom United States
Budget	US$200 million[1]
Worldwide gross	US$586,090,727[2]
Preceded by	*Casino Royale*
Followed by	*Bond 23*

Quantum of Solace is the 22nd James Bond film, produced by EON Productions and is the direct sequel to the 2006 film *Casino Royale*. Directed by Marc Forster, it features Daniel Craig's second performance as James Bond. In the film, Bond battles wealthy businessman Dominic Greene (Mathieu Amalric), a member of the Quantum organization posing as an environmentalist who intends to stage a coup d'état in Bolivia to seize control of the nation's water supply. (In fact, the story is remarkably similar to a real-life event in which Bechtel was the major player.) Bond seeks revenge for the death of his lover, Vesper Lynd (Eva Green), and is assisted by Camille Montes (Olga Kurylenko), who is also seeking revenge.

Producer Michael G. Wilson developed the film's plot while *Casino Royale* was being shot. Neal Purvis, Robert Wade, Paul Haggis, and Joshua Zetumer contributed to the script. The title was chosen from a 1960 short story in Ian Fleming's *For Your Eyes Only*, though the film does not contain any elements of the original story. Location filming took place in Mexico, Panama, Chile, Italy, Austria, and Wales while interior sets were built and filmed at Pinewood Studios. Forster aimed to make a modern film that also featured classic cinema motifs: a vintage Douglas DC-3 was used for a dogfight sequence, and Dennis Gassner's set designs are reminiscent of Ken Adam's work on several early Bond films. Taking a course away from the usual Bond villains, Forster rejected any grotesque appearance for the character Dominic Greene to emphasize the hidden and secret nature of the film's contemporary villains.

The film premiered at the Odeon Leicester Square on 29 October 2008, gathering mixed reviews which mainly praised Craig's gritty performance and the film's action sequences while feeling that *Quantum of Solace* was not as impressive as the predecessor *Casino Royale*. It is also the second highest grossing James Bond film, without adjusting for inflation, making $586,090,727 worldwide, while becoming one of the highest grossing Bond films in the United States.

Plot

James Bond (Daniel Craig) is driving from Lake Como to Siena, Italy with the captured Mr. White (Jesper Christensen). After evading pursuers, Bond and M (Judi Dench) interrogate White regarding his organization, Quantum. M's bodyguard, Mitchell, a double agent, attacks M, enabling White to escape; Bond chases Mitchell across Siena and kills him.

Bond and M travel search Mitchell's flat and discover he had a contact in Haiti. Bond heads to Haiti to investigate Mitchell's contact, Edmund Slate, and learns that Slate was sent to kill Camille Montes (Olga Kurylenko) at the behest of her lover, Dominic Greene (Mathieu Amalric), the chairman of an ecological organization called Greene Planet. While observing her meeting with Greene, Bond learns that Greene is helping the Bolivian general Medrano (Joaquin Cosio)—who murdered Camille's family—overthrow his government in exchange for a seemingly barren piece of desert.

After rescuing Camille from Medrano, Bond follows Greene to a performance of *Tosca* in Austria; en route, CIA agent Gregg Beam (David Harbour) strikes a non-interference deal with Greene to maintain access to Bolivian oil, overruling the objections of Felix Leiter (Jeffrey Wright). Bond infiltrates Quantum's meeting at the opera, and a gunfight ensues in the adjoining restaurant. A Special Branch bodyguard of Quantum member Guy Haines, an advisor to the British Prime Minister, is killed, and M, assuming Bond is the killer, has his passports and credit cards revoked. Bond convinces his old ally René Mathis (Giancarlo Giannini) to accompany him to La Paz. They are greeted by Strawberry Fields (Gemma Arterton), an MI6 field operative from the British Consulate, who demands that Bond return to the UK on the next available flight; nonetheless, Bond soon seduces her before they attend a party Greene holds that night.

At the party, Bond rescues Camille again from Greene. Leaving, Bond and Camille are pulled over by Bolivian police working for Medrano; they had earlier attacked Mathis and put him in the trunk of Bond's car to frame him, and in the ensuing struggle Mathis is killed. Bond and Camille survey Quantum's intended land acquisition in a Douglas DC-3 plane, but are shot down by an Aermacchi SF.260 fighter and a Bell UH-1 Iroquois helicopter. They parachute out of the burning plane into a sinkhole. In the cave, Bond and Camille discover Quantum is not after oil but is damming Bolivia's supply of fresh water, normally flowing in subterranean rivers, to create a monopoly. Back in La Paz, Bond meets M and learns that Quantum murdered Fields by drowning her naked in crude oil. M orders Bond arrested for disobeying orders but he defies her and escapes.

Bond meets Leiter, who discloses Greene and Medrano will meet at an eco-hotel in the Bolivian desert to finalize the coup; warned by Leiter, he evades American special forces attempting to kill him. At the hotel, Greene and Medrano negotiate their terms. Greene then finally reveals his true plans. By gaining control of the majority of Bolivia's water supply, Greene badgers Medrano into accepting a new contract that makes Greene Planet Bolivia's sole water utility company at significantly higher rates. Bond infiltrates the hotel and executes the chief of police for betraying Mathis, and then confronts Greene. The hotel is destroyed during the battle, but Camille kills Medrano, and Bond captures Greene. After interrogating him about Quantum, Bond leaves Greene stranded in the middle of the desert with only a can of motor oil. Bond and Camille kiss before they part.

Bond goes to Kazan, Russia, where he confronts Vesper Lynd's former lover, Yusef Kabira (Simon Kassianides), who is with Corrine (Stana Katic), a Canadian agent. Yusef is a member of Quantum who seduces women with valuable connections, such as Vesper. In an act of restraint, Bond decides not to kill Yusef and allows MI6 to arrest him. Outside, M tells Bond that Greene was found in the middle of the desert dead, with motor oil in his stomach, but Bond denies knowing anything. M also reveals that Felix has been promoted and has taken Beam's place. She reinstates Bond as an agent; he tells M that he never left. As he leaves, he drops the necklace Yusef had given Vesper in the snow.

Cast

- Daniel Craig as James Bond. Craig's physical training for his reprise of the role placed extra effort into running and boxing, to spare him the injuries he sustained on his stunts in the first film.[3] Craig felt he was fitter, being less bulky than in the first film.[4] He also practiced speedboating and stunt driving. Craig felt *Casino Royale* was [physically] "a walk in the park" compared to *Quantum of Solace*,[5] and required a different performance from him because *Quantum of Solace* is a revenge film, not a love story like *Casino Royale*.[4] While filming in Pinewood, he suffered a gash when kicked in his face,[6] which required eight stitches, and a fingertip was sliced off. He laughed these off, noting they did not delay filming, and joked his finger wound would enable him to have a criminal career (though it had grown back when he made this comment).[4] He also had minor plastic surgery on his face.[7] The actor advised Paul Haggis on the script and helped choose Marc Forster as the director.[8]
- Olga Kurylenko as Camille Montes, a Russian-Bolivian agent with her own vendetta regarding Greene and Medrano. Forster chose her because out of the 400 women who auditioned, she seemed the least nervous.[9] When she read the script, she was glad she had no love scene with Craig because it would have distracted viewers from her performance.[10] Kurylenko spent three weeks training to fight with weapons, and she learned a form of indoor skydiving known as body flying.[11] Kurylenko dislikes stunts,[12] but overcame her fears because she

found Craig helpful.[13] She was given a DVD box set of the films since the Bond franchise was not easily available to watch where she grew up in Ukraine.[11] Kurylenko found Michelle Yeoh in *Tomorrow Never Dies* inspiring "because she did the fight scenes by herself."[9] The producers had intended to cast a South American actress in the role.[14] Kurylenko trained with a dialect coach to perform with a Spanish accent,[15] which was easy as "I have a good ear, so I can imitate people," and because her accent was not made heavy.[12] When reflecting on her experience as a Bond girl, she stated she was most proud of overcoming her fears in performing stunts.[16]

- Mathieu Amalric as Dominic Greene, Main villain. A leading member of Quantum posing as a businessman working in reforestation and charity funding for environmental science. Amalric acknowledged taking the role was an easy decision because, "It's impossible to say to your kids that 'I could have been in a Bond film but I refused.'"[11] Amalric wanted to wear make-up for the role, but Forster explained that he wanted Greene not to look grotesque, but to symbolise the hidden evils in society.[6] Amalric modelled his performance on "the smile of Tony Blair [and] the craziness of Sarkozy," the latter of whom he called "the worst villain we [the French] have ever had [...] he walks around thinking he's in a Bond film."[17] He later claimed this was not criticism of either politician, but rather an example of how a politician relies on performance instead of a genuine policy to win power. "Sarkozy, is just a better actor than [his presidential opponent] Ségolène Royal – that's all," he explained.[18] Amalric and Forster reconceived the character, who was supposed to have a "special skill" in the script, to someone who uses pure animal instinct when fighting Bond in the climax.[19] Bruno Ganz was also considered for the part,[14] but Forster decided Amalric gave a pitiful quality.[19]
- Gemma Arterton as MI6 Agent Strawberry Fields, who works at the British consulate in Bolivia. Fields, who is merely an office worker as described by M, takes herself seriously and tries to over-power Bond when the pair meet. She later was seduced by Bond and infiltrates Greene's fund raiser party with him and ended up paying the ultimate price. Forster found Arterton a witty actress and selected her from a reported 1,500 candidates. One of the casting directors asked her to audition for the role, having seen her portray Rosaline in *Love's Labour's Lost* at the Globe Theatre.[20] Arterton said Fields was "not so frolicsome" as other Bond girls, but is instead "fresh and young, not [...] a femme fatale."[21] Arterton described Fields as a homage to the 1960s Bond girls, comparing her red wig to Diana Rigg, who played Tracy Bond in *On Her Majesty's Secret Service*. Rigg, alongside Honor Blackman, is one of her favourite Bond girls.[20] Arterton had to film her character's death scene first day on the set. Although she found the experience unpleasant, she believes the scene will be an iconic part of the film.[22] The character's first name, which is a reference to the Beatles song Strawberry Fields Forever, is never actually uttered on screen; when Bond asks her for her name, she replies, "Just Fields."
- Giancarlo Giannini as René Mathis, Bond's ally who was mistakenly believed to be a traitor in *Casino Royale*. Having been acquitted, he chooses to aid Bond again and watches as Bond is under the strict authority of Fields.
- Jeffrey Wright as Felix Leiter, Bond's ally at the CIA. This marked the first time the same actor played Leiter twice in a row. Only David Hedison had previously played the character twice, in *Live and Let Die* (1973) and *Licence to Kill* (1989), but these performances were not consecutive.[11] Early script drafts gave Leiter a larger role, but his screentime was restricted by on-set rewrites.[23]
- Judi Dench as M. Forster felt Dench was underused in the previous films and wanted to make her part bigger, having her interact with Bond more because she is "the only woman Bond doesn't see in a sexual context," which Forster finds interesting.[24]
- Anatole Taubman as Elvis, Greene's second-in-command. His name was chosen by Paul Haggis,[12] while Taubman chose the bowl cut.[25] Amalric and Taubman improvised a backstory for Elvis: he is Dominic's cousin and once lived on the streets before being inducted into Quantum. He called Elvis "a bit of a goofball. He thinks he's all that but he's not really. [...] He's not a comic guy. He definitely takes himself very serious, but maybe by his taking himself too serious he may become friendly."[26]
- David Harbour as Gregg Beam, the CIA Section Chief for South America and a contact of Felix Leiter.

- Joaquín Cosío as General Medrano, the exiled general whom Greene is helping to get back into power, in return for support of his organisation. He is responsible for the murder of Camille's entire family when she was a young girl.
- Jesper Christensen as Mr. White, whom Bond captured after he stole the money won at *Casino Royale* in Montenegro.
- Rory Kinnear as Bill Tanner, M's aide.
- Tim Pigott-Smith as the British Secretary of State for Foreign and Commonwealth Affairs.
- Neil Jackson as Edmund Slate, a henchman who fights Bond in Haiti.
- Simon Kassianides as Yusef, who has a confrontation with Bond in Kazan towards the end of the film.
- Stana Katic as Corrine Veneau, a Canadian agent.
- Glenn Foster as Craig Mitchell, M's bodyguard and a double agent.
- Oona Castilla Chaplin as 'damsel in distress' - girl saved by Kurylenko in one of last sequences.

Directors Guillermo del Toro and Alfonso Cuarón are friends of Marc Forster and while filming he asked them to cameo, providing voices in the Spanish language. Cuarón appears as a Bolivian helicopter pilot, while del Toro provides several other voices.[27]

Production

Development

> "If you remember in *Chinatown*, if you control the water you control the whole development of the country. I think it's true. Right now it appears to be oil, but there's a lot of other resources that we don't think about too much but are all essential, and they're very limited and every country needs it. Because every country knows that raising the standard of living (and populations are getting bigger) is the way we're all going."
>
> —–Michael G. Wilson on the plot.[23]

In July 2006, as *Casino Royale* entered post-production, EON Productions announced that the next film would be based on an original idea by producer Michael G. Wilson.[28] It was decided beforehand the film would be a direct sequel, to exploit Bond's emotions following Vesper's death in the previous film.[29] Just as *Casino Royale*'s theme was terrorism, the sequel focuses on environmentalism.[18] The film was confirmed for a 2 May 2008 release date, with Craig reprising the lead role.[30] Roger Michell, who directed Craig in *Enduring Love* and *The Mother*, was in negotiations to direct, but opted out because there was no script.[31] Sony Entertainment vice-chairman Jeff Blake admitted a production schedule of eighteen months was a very short window, and the release date was pushed back to late 2008.[32] Neal Purvis and Robert Wade completed their draft of the script by April 2007,[33] and Paul Haggis – who polished the *Casino Royale* script – began his rewrite the next month.[34]

In June 2007, Marc Forster was confirmed as director.[35] He was surprised that he was approached for the job, stating he was not a big Bond film fan through the years, and that he would not have accepted the project had he not seen *Casino Royale* prior to making his decision: he felt Bond had been humanised in that film, arguing since traveling the world had become less exotic since the series' advent, it made sense to focus more on Bond as a character. Born in Germany and raised in Switzerland, Forster was the first Bond director not to come from the British Commonwealth of Nations, although he noted Bond's mother is Swiss, making him somewhat appropriate to handle the British icon.[36] The director collaborated strongly with Barbara Broccoli and Michael G. Wilson, noting they only blocked two very expensive ideas he had.[14] The director found *Casino Royale*'s 144 minute running time too long, and wanted his follow-up to be "tight and fast [...] like a bullet."[37]

> "Because Bond plays it real, I thought the political circumstances should be real too, even though Bond shouldn't be a political film. I thought the more political I make it, the more real it feels, not just with Bolivia and what's happening in Haiti, but with all these corporations like Shell and Chevron saying they're green because it's so fashionable to be green. During the Cold War, everything was very clear, the good guys and the

bad guys. Today there's much overlapping of good and bad. It isn't as morally distinct, because we all have both elements in us."

—Marc Forster on the political landscape of the film.[38]

Haggis, Forster and Wilson rewrote the story from scratch.[39] Haggis said he completed his script two hours before the 2007–2008 Writers Guild of America strike officially began.[36] Forster noted a running theme in his films were emotionally repressed protagonists, and the theme of the picture would be Bond learning to trust after feeling betrayed by Vesper.[40] Forster said he created the Camille character as a strong female counterpart to Bond rather than a casual love interest: she openly shows emotions similar to those which Bond experiences but is unable to express.[41] Haggis located his draft's climax in the Swiss Alps,[42] but Forster wanted the action sequences to be based around the four classical elements of earth, water, air and fire.[43] The decision to homage *Goldfinger* in Fields's death came about as Forster wanted to show oil had replaced gold as the most precious material.[38] The producers rejected Haggis's idea that Vesper Lynd had a child, because "Bond was an orphan [...] Once he finds the kid, Bond can't just leave the kid."[44]

Michael G. Wilson decided on the film's title *Quantum of Solace* only "a few days" before its announcement on 24 January 2008.[21] It was the name of a short story in Ian Fleming's anthology *For Your Eyes Only* (1960).[45] The film is related to the title in one of its thematic elements: "...when the 'Quantum of Solace' drops to zero, humanity and consideration of one human for another is gone."[46] Daniel Craig admitted, "I was unsure at first. Bond is looking for his quantum of solace and that's what he wants, he wants his closure. Ian Fleming says that if you don't have a quantum of solace in your relationship then the relationship is over. It's that spark of niceness in a relationship that if you don't have you might as well give up."[11] He said that "Bond doesn't have that because his girlfriend [Vesper Lynd] has been killed,"[45] and therefore, "[Bond is] looking for revenge [...] to make himself happy with the world again."[21] Afterwards, Quantum was made the name of the organisation introduced in *Casino Royale*.[47] Craig noted the letter Q itself looks rather odd.[4] Near the end of the film, the Camille Montes character and Bond have a discussion about their individual quests to avenge the deaths of their loved ones. Montes asks Bond to "let me know what it feels like" when he succeeds, the implication of the title being that it will be a small amount of solace compared to his despair. Bond's lack of emotion when he does exact revenge shows this to be the case.

During filming, after the strike ended, Forster read a spec script by Joshua Zetumer, which he liked, and hired him to reshape scenes for the later parts of the shoot, which the director was still unsatisfied with.[39] Forster had the actors rehearse their scenes, as he liked to film scenes continually.[18] Zetumer rewrote dialogue depending on the actors' ideas each day.[18]

Filming

Quantum of Solace was shot in six countries,[1] Second unit filming began in Italy at the Palio di Siena horse race on 16 August 2007:[48] though at this point Forster was unsure how it would fit into the film.[43] Some scenes were filmed also in Maratea and Craco, two little and characteristics towns in Basilicata.[49] Other places used for location shooting were Madrid in August 2007;[50] Baja California, Mexico in early 2008, for shots of the aerial battle;[51] [52] Malcesine, Limone sul Garda and Tremosine in Italy during March,[53] and at Talamone during the end of April.[54] The main unit began on 3 January 2008,[14] at Pinewood Studios. The 007 Stage was used for the fight in the art gallery,[11] and an MI6 safehouse hidden within the city's cisterns,[55] while other stages housed Bond's Bolivian hotel suite,[56] and the MI6 headquarters.[55] Interior and exterior airport scenes were filmed at Farnborough Airfield and the snowy closing scenes were filmed at the Bruneval Barracks in Aldershot.[57]

Shooting in Panama City began on 7 February 2008 at Howard Air Force Base. The country doubled for Haiti and Bolivia, with the National Institute of Culture of Panama standing in for a hotel in the latter country. A sequence requiring several hundred extras was also shot at nearby Colón.[58] Shooting in Panama was also carried out at Fort Sherman, a former US military base on the Colón coast. Forster was disappointed he could only shoot the boat chase in that harbour, as he had a more spectacular vision for the scene.[59] Officials in the country worked with the locals to "minimise inconvenience" for the cast and crew, and in return hoped the city's exposure in the film would increase tourism.[60] The crew was going to move to Cusco, Peru for ten days of filming on 2 March,[58] but the location was cancelled for budget reasons.[1] Twelve days of filming in Chile began on 24 March at Antofagasta. There was shooting in Cobija, the Paranal Observatory, and other locations in the Atacama Desert.[61] Forster chose the desert and the observatory's ESO Hotel to represent Bond's rigid emotions, and being on the verge of committing a vengeful act as he confronts Greene in the film's climax.[47] [62]

Marine shooting being carried out at Fort Sherman

Marc Forster chose the Atacama Desert to represent Bond's vengefulness in the climax

While filming in Sierra Gorda, Chile, the local mayor, Carlos Lopez, staged a protest because he was angry at the filmmakers' portrayal of the Antofagasta region as part of Bolivia, as it had been invaded and occupied by the Chilean army in 1883. He was arrested, detained briefly, and put on trial two days later. EON dismissed his claim that they needed his permission to film in the area.[63] [64] Michael G. Wilson also explained Bolivia was appropriate to the plot, because of the country's history of water problems,[62] and was surprised the two countries disliked each other a century after the War of the Pacific.[65] In a poll by Chilean daily newspaper *La Segunda*, 75% of its readers disagreed with Lopez's actions, due to the negative image they felt it presented of Chile, and the controversy's potential to put off productions looking to film in the country in the future.[66]

From 4–12 April, the main unit shot on Sienese rooftops.[54] Shooting on the real rooftops turned out to be less expensive than building them at Pinewood.[1] The next four weeks were scheduled for filming the car chase at Lake Garda and Carrara.[54] On 19 April, an Aston Martin employee driving a DBS to the set crashed into the lake. He survived, and was fined £400 for reckless driving.[67] Another accident occurred on 21 April, and two days later, two stuntmen were seriously injured, with one, Greek stuntman Aris Comninos, having to be put in intensive care. Filming of the scenes was temporarily halted so that Italian police could investigate the causes of the accidents.[68] Stunt co-ordinator Gary Powell said the accidents were a testament to the realism of the action.[42] Rumours of a "curse" spread among tabloid media, something which deeply offended Craig, who disliked that they compared Comninos' accident to something like his minor finger injury later on the shoot (also part of the "curse"). Comninos recovered safely from his injury.[4]

Preparations for the performance of *Tosca* at Bregenzer Festspiele

Filming took place at the floating opera stage at Bregenz, Austria from 28 April–9 May 2008. The sequence, where Bond stalks the villains during a performance of *Tosca*, required 1500 extras.[69] The production used a large model of an eye, which Forster felt fitted in the Bond style, and the opera itself has parallels to the film.[70] A short driving sequence was filmed at the nearby Feldkirch, Vorarlberg.[71] The crew returned to Italy from 13–17 May to shoot a (planned) car crash at the marble quarry in Carrara,[72] and a recreation of the Palio di Siena at the Piazza del Campo in Siena. 1000 extras were hired for a scene where Bond emerges from the *Fonte Gaia*. Originally, he would have emerged from the city's cisterns at Siena Cathedral, but this was thought disrespectful.[54] By June, the crew returned to Pinewood for four weeks,[70] where new sets (including the interior of the hotel in the climax) were built.[39] [56] The wrap party was held on 21 June.[73]

Design

Production designer Peter Lamont, a crew member on eighteen previous Bond films, retired after *Casino Royale*.[74] Forster hired Dennis Gassner in his stead, having admired his work on *The Truman Show* and the films of the Coen brothers.[40] Craig said the film would have "a touch of Ken Adam,"[75] while Michael G. Wilson also called Gassner's designs "a postmodern look at modernism."[56] Forster said he felt the early Bond films' design "were ahead of their time,"[40] and enjoyed the clashing of an older style with his own because it created a unique look unto itself.[76] Gassner wanted his sets to emphasise Craig's "great angular, textured face and wonderful blue eyes," and totally redesigned the MI6 headquarters because he felt Judi Dench "was a bit tired in the last film, so I thought, let's bring her into a new world."[77]

Louise Frogley replaced Lindy Hemming as costume designer, though Hemming remained as supervisor. Hemming hired Brioni for Bond's suits since her tenure on the series began with 1995's *GoldenEye*, but Lindsay Pugh, another supervisor, explained their suits were "too relaxed." Tom Ford was hired to tailor "sharper" suits for Craig. Pugh said the costumes aimed towards the 1960s feel, especially for Bond and Fields. Prada provided the dresses for both Bond girls. Jasper Conran designed Camille's ginger bandeau, bronze skirt and gold fish necklace,[78] while Chrome Hearts designed gothic jewellery for Amalric's character, which the actor liked enough to keep after filming.[79] Sophie Harley, who created Vesper Lynd's earrings and Algerian loveknot necklace in *Casino Royale*, was called upon to create another version of the necklace.[80]

The film returns to the traditional gun barrel opening shot, which was altered into part of the story for *Casino Royale* where it was moved to the end of the title sequence. In this film the gun barrel sequence was moved to the end of the movie, which Wilson explained was done for a surprise,[81] and to signify the conclusion of the story begun in the previous film. The opening credits sequence was created by MK12; Having worked on Forster's *Stranger than Fiction* and *The Kite Runner*, MK12 spontaneously began developing the sequence early on in production, and had a good idea of its appearance which meant it did not have to be redone when the title singer was changed. MK12 selected various twilight colours to represent Bond's mood and focused on a dot motif based on the gunbarrel shot. MK12 also worked on scenes with graphical user interface, including the electronic table MI6 use,[82] and the Port-au-Prince, Haiti title cards.[83]

Effects

Aston Martin DBS V12 on display at the 2008 San Diego Comic-Con International

Quantum of Solace was the last in Ford Motor's three-film deal that began with 2002's *Die Another Day*. Although Ford sold over 90% of the Aston Martin company in 2007, the Aston Martin DBS V12 returned for the film's car chase around Lake Garda;[84] Dan Bradley was hired as second unit director because of his work on the second and third *Bourne* films, so the film would continue the gritty action style begun in *Casino Royale*.[85] He had intended to use Ford GTs for the opening chase,[86] but it was replaced by the Alfa Romeo 159.[87] After location filming in Italy, further close-ups of Craig, the cars and the truck were shot at Pinewood against a bluescreen.[88] Originally three Alfa Romeos were in the sequence: but Forster felt the scene was running too long and re-edited the scene so it only looked like two Romeos were chasing Bond.[89] Six Aston Martins were destroyed during filming, and one of them was purchased by a fan.[4]

Fourteen cameras were used to film the Palio di Siena, footage which was later edited into the main sequence. Aerial shots using helicopters were banned, and the crew were also forbidden from showing any violence "involving either people or animals."[48] To shoot the foot chase in Siena in April 2008 four camera cranes were built in the town, and a cable camera was also used.[53] Framestore worked on the Siena chase, duplicating the 1000 extras during principal photography to match shots of the 40,000 strong audience at the real Palio, removing wires that held Craig and the stuntmen in the rooftop segment of the chase, and digital expansion of the floor and skylight in the art gallery Bond and Mitchell fall into.[88] The art gallery fight was intended to be simple, but during filming Craig's stunt double accidentally fell from the construction scaffolding. Forster preferred the idea of Bond hanging from ropes reaching for his gun to kill Mitchell, rather than having both men run out of the building to continue their chase as specified in the script, and the number of effects shots increased.[88]

To film the aerial dogfight, a "Snakehead" camera was built and placed on the nose and tail of a Piper Aerostar 700. SolidWorks, who provided the software used to design the camera, stated "pilots for the first time can fly as aggressively as they dare without sacrificing the drama of the shot." The camera could turn 360 degrees and was shaped like a periscope.[90] The crew also mounted SpaceCams on helicopters, and placed cameras with 1600 mm lenses underground, to cover the action.[51] Forster wanted to film the planefight as a homage to Alfred Hitchcock's *North by Northwest*, and chose planes like the Douglas DC-3 to suit that.[76] [91]

The free-fall scene involved its own set of challenges, Craig disliked the idea of "being hung by wires and blown by a large fan in front of a green screen" but actual sky diving coverage has serious drawbacks. It's not only difficult, dangerous and time-consuming, but nearly always results in problematic head-replacements for close-ups. Stunt co-ordinator Gary Powell and VFX Designer Kevin Tod Haug, presented the idea of filming the scene in a large vertical wind tunnel in Bedford in order to do this sequence as practically as possible. While a great solution for the actors' performances the technique presented enormous VFX challenges: relighting shots captured in a tall white tube to match the sky over the Bolivian desert, and the impossibility of filming medium to wide shots of the actors. An array of eight Dalsa Origin cameras (supported by 7 HD cameras and a 35mm hand-held camera, all running in sync) was used to create a virtual camera with which to shoot the actors floating in the simulator. Ged Wright and his team at Double Negative[89] developed a method to use the data from these cameras that allowed these real performances to be placed in a synthetic environment as seen by a synthetic camera. During the shooting in the wind tunnel Craig and Kurylenko wore wind-resistant contact lenses that enabled them to open their eyes as they fell. For safety and comfort, they only shot for thirty seconds at a time.[92] Forster wished he had more time to work on the free-fall scene.[88]

The Moving Picture Company created the climactic hotel sequence. The fire effects were supervised by Chris Corbould, and post-production MPC had to enhance the sequence by making the smoke look closer to the actors, so it would look more dangerous.[88] A full-scale replica of the building's exterior was used for the exploding part Bond and Camille escape from. The boat chase was another scene that required very little CGI. Machine FX worked on replacing a few shots of visible stuntmen with a digital version of Craig's head,[89] and recreated the boats Bond jumps over on his motorcycle to make it look more dangerous.[88] Crowd creation was done for the *Tosca* scene by Machine FX, to make the performance look like it had sold out.[89] Forster edited the opera scene to resemble *The Man Who Knew Too Much*.[59] In total, there are 900+ visual effects shots in *Quantum of Solace*.[88]

Music

David Arnold, who composed the scores for the previous four Bond films, returned for *Quantum of Solace*. He said that Forster likes to work very closely with his composers and that, in comparison to the accelerated schedule he was tied to on *Casino Royale*, the intention was to spend a long time scoring the film to "really work it out." He also said he would be "taking a different approach" with the score.[93] Arnold composed the music based on impressions from reading the script, and Forster edited those into the film.[94] As with *Casino Royale*, Arnold kept use of the James Bond Theme to a minimum.[43] Arnold collaborated with Kieran Hebden for "Crawl, End Crawl," a remix of the score played during the end credits.[95]

Jack White of The White Stripes and Alicia Keys collaborated on "Another Way to Die," the first Bond music duet.[96] [97] They had wanted to work together for two years beforehand.[98] The song was recorded in Nashville, Tennessee; White played the drums while Keys performed on the piano.[99] The Memphis Horns also contributed to the track.[98] White's favourite Bond theme is John Barry's instrumental piece for *On Her Majesty's Secret Service*, and he watched various opening credit sequences from the series for inspiration while mixing the track.[99] Mark Ronson and Amy Winehouse had recorded a demo track for the film,[100] but Ronson explained Winehouse's well-publicised legal issues in the preceding weeks made her "not ready to record any music" at that time.[101]

Release

The film premiered at the Odeon Leicester Square on 29 October 2008. Princes William and Harry of Wales attended, and proceeds from the screening were donated to the charities Help for Heroes and the Royal British Legion.[102] The film was originally scheduled to be released in the UK and North America on 7 November; however, EON pushed forward the British date to 31 October during filming,[103] while the American date was pushed back in August to 14 November, after *Harry Potter and the Half-Blood Prince* had been moved to 2009, thereby allowing the distributors to market the film over the Fall blockbuster Thanksgiving holiday weekend.[104] In Australia, the film was moved a week to 19 November, after 20th Century Fox chose to release *Australia* on *Quantum of Solace*'s original date of 26 November.[105]

Marketing

Returning product placement partners from *Casino Royale* included Ford, Heineken Pilsener, Smirnoff, Omega SA, Virgin Atlantic Airways and Sony Ericsson.[106] A reported £50 million was earned in product placement, which tops the Bond film's record of £44 million for *Die Another Day*.[107] The 2009 Ford Ka is driven by Camille in the film.[108] Avon created a fragrance called Bond Girl 007 with Gemma Arterton as the "face" of the product.[109] Coca-Cola became a promotional partner, rebranding Coke Zero as "Coke Zero Zero 7." A tie-in advert featured the orchestral element of "Another Way to Die."[110] In the film, Coca-Cola was briefly seen being served at Dominic Greene's party. Sony held a competition, "Mission for a Million," enabling registered players to use their products to complete certain tasks. Each completed "mission" gives consumers a chance to win $1 million and a trip to a top secret location.[111]

Merchandise

Corgi International Limited made 5-inch action figures and gadgets (such as a voice-activated briefcase), as well as their traditional die-cast toy vehicles.[112] [113] They also created 7-inch figures of characters from the previous films.[114] Scalextric released four racing sets to coincide with the film.[115] Activision released their first James Bond game, also titled *Quantum of Solace*, which is based on both *Casino Royale* and *Quantum of Solace*. It is the first Bond game to feature Craig's likeness and the first seventh generation console game in the series. Swatch designed a series of wrist watches, each of them inspired by a Bond villain.[116]

The cover of *Cigar Aficionado*'s special *Quantum of Solace* James Bond edition written by David Giammarco.

Though there was no novelisation despite its original storyline, Penguin Books published a compilation of Fleming's short stories entitled *Quantum of Solace: The Complete James Bond Short Stories*, with a UK release date of 29 May 2008[117] and a North American release date of 26 August 2008.[118] The book combines the contents of Fleming's two short story collections, *For Your Eyes Only*—including the original "Quantum of Solace" short story—and *Octopussy and The Living Daylights*.

The November/December 2008 issue of Cigar Aficionado was a special James Bond edition written by David Giammarco, noted author of For Your Eyes Only: Behind the Scenes of the James Bond Films, and featured an extensive 20-page feature on the making of *Quantum of Solace* from his exclusive interviews on location with Daniel Craig, Gemma Arterton, Olga Kurylenko, Mathieu Amalric, director Marc Forster, and producers Barbara Broccoli and Michael G. Wilson. This tribute issue of the upscale magazine also featured Giammarco's in-depth profile of 007 author Ian Fleming and the 46-year history of the James Bond films. The *Cigar Aficionado* James Bond special edition became the magazine's biggest-selling issue around the world.

Reception

Box office

Upon its opening in the UK, the film grossed £4.9 million ($8 million), breaking the record for the largest Friday opening (31 October 2008) in the UK.[119] The film then broke the UK opening weekend record, taking £15.5 million ($25 million) in its first weekend, surpassing the previous record of £14.9 million held by *Harry Potter and the Goblet of Fire*. It earned a further £14.2 million in France and Sweden – where it opened on the same day –. The weekend gross of the equivalent of $US10.6 million in France was a record for the series, surpassing what *Casino Royale* made in five days by 16%. The $US2.7 million gross in Sweden was the fourth-highest opening for a film there.[120] [121]

The following week, the film was playing in sixty countries. It grossed the equivalent of $US39.3 million in the UK, $US16.5 million in France and $US7.7 million in Germany on 7 November 2008.[122] The film broke records in Switzerland, Finland, United Arab Emirates, Nigeria, Romania and Slovenia. Its Chinese and Indian openings were the second largest ever for foreign-language films.[123]

The film grossed $27 million on its opening day in 3,451 theatres in Canada and the United States, where it was the #1 film for the weekend, with $US67.5 million and $US19,568 average per theatre.[124] It was the highest-grossing opening weekend Bond film in the US,[125] and tied with *The Incredibles* for the biggest November opening outside of the *Harry Potter* series. The film earned a B- from CinemaScore's audience surveys.[126] From the 31 October British opening through to the November 14 US opening weekend, the film had grossed a total $US319,128,882 worldwide. As of 10 February 2010, it has grossed the equivalent of $US417,722,300 in countries other than Canada and the U.S.A., where it grossed $US168,368,427, to give a total of $US586,090,727.[2]

Critical response

Reviews for *Quantum of Solace* have been mixed. Of the 241 reviews listed on Rotten Tomatoes, 63% are positive, with an average rating of 6.1/10. However, only 36% of selected notable reviewers gave it a positive write-up, with an average rating of 5.6/10.[127] Metacritic calculated a score of 58 out of 100 from 38 reviews, indicating a "mixed or average" response.[128] Critics generally preferred *Casino Royale*, but continued to praise Craig's depiction of Bond, and agree that the film is still an enjoyable addition to the series. The action sequences and pacing were praised, but criticism grew over the serious and gritty feel that the film carried over.[129]

Roger Moore, the third actor to play Bond in the films, continued to feel Craig was a "damn good Bond but the film as a whole, there was a bit too much flash cutting [and] it was just like a commercial of the action. There didn't seem to be any geography and you were wondering what the hell was going on."[130]

Kim Newman of *Empire* gave it 4/5, remarking it was not "bigger and better than *Casino Royale*, [which is] perhaps a smart move in that there's still a sense at the finish that Bond's mission has barely begun." However, he expressed nostalgia for the more humorous Bond films.[131] *The Sunday Times* review noted that "[f]ollowing *Casino Royale* was never going to be easy, but the director Marc Forster has brought the brand's successful relaunch crashing back to earth — with a yawn"; the screenplay "is at times incomprehensible" and the casting "is a mess." The review concludes that "Bond has been stripped of his iconic status. He no longer represents anything particularly British, or even modern. In place of glamour, we get a spurious grit; instead of style, we get product placement; in place of fantasy, we get a redundant and silly realism."[132]

The Guardian gave a more positive review, rating it as 3/5 stars, and was particularly fond of Craig's performance, saying he "made the part his own, every inch the coolly ruthless agent-killer, nursing a broken heart and coldly suppressed rage" and calling the film "a crash-bang Bond, high on action, low on quips, long on location glamour, short on product placement"; it concludes "*Quantum of Solace* isn't as good as *Casino Royale*: the smart elegance of Craig's Bond debut has been toned down in favour of conventional action. But the man himself powers this movie; he carries the film: it's an indefinably difficult task for an actor. Craig measures up."[133]

Screen Daily says "Notices will focus - rightly - on Craig's magnetism as the steely, sexy, murderous MI6 agent, but two other factors weigh in and freshen up proceedings: Forster's new technical team, led by cinematographer Roberto Schaefer and production designer Dennis Gassner. And the ongoing shift of M, as played by Judi Dench, to front and centre: the Bond girls fade into insignificance as she becomes his moral counterpoint and theirs is the only real relationship on screen." The review continues, "Bond is, as has been previously noted, practically the Martin Scorsese of the BAFTAs: 22 films later, with grosses probably close to the GDP of one of the small nations it depicts, it's still waiting for that Alexander Korda award. The best *Casino Royale* could achieve was a gong for sound. Will this be the year that changes its fortunes?"[134]

Roger Ebert of *The Chicago Sun-Times*, who praised the previous film, disliked *Quantum of Solace*. He wrote that the plot was mediocre, characters weak and that Bond lacked his usual personality, despite his praise for Craig's interpretation of the role. Throughout his review, he emphasised that "James Bond is not an action hero," and also criticised the lack of a fantastical villainous lair and the Bond girls' names not being double entendres.[135] Some writers criticised the choice of *Quantum of Solace* as a title. "Yes, it's a bad title," wrote Marni Weisz, the editor of *Famous*, a Canadian film publication distributed in movie theatres in that country, in an editorial entitled "At least it's not *Octopussy*."[136]

Awards

The film was nominated for Best Original Score, Best Original Song, Visual Effects, Film and Sound Editing at the 2008 Satellite Awards, winning Best Song.[137] It was nominated for Best Action Movie at the 2009 Critics' Choice Awards,[138] and at the Empire Awards, which is voted for by the public, it was shortlisted for Best Actor, Best Actress, Best Newcomer, Best Thriller and Best Soundtrack.[139] It was nominated for the Saturn Award for Best Action/Adventure/Thriller Film, while Kurylenko and Dench were both nominated for the Best Supporting Actress award.[140] An editorial by *The Times* also listed the film's pre-titles sequence as the tenth greatest car chase in film history.[141]

Home Media

Quantum of Solace was released on DVD and Blu-ray by 20th Century Fox Home Entertainment in Australia, the UK and North America from 18 to 24 March 2009. At the DVD sales chart the film opened at #3, grossing $21,894,957 from 1.21m DVD units sold.[142] As of November 1, 2009 2,643,250 DVD units have been sold, generating $44,110,750 in sales revenue.[142] These figures do not include Blu-ray sales or DVD rentals. They released the DVD in a standard one disc set and a deluxe two disc special edition. There are no audio commentaries or deleted scenes on these editions.[143]

Like *Casino Royale*, no book adaptation of the movie was released despite having no relations with the short story except for its title. Instead, Penguin Books released *Quantum of Solace: The Complete James Bond Short Stories* which is a compilation of both *Octopussy and The Living Daylights* and *For Your Eyes Only*, both written by Ian Fleming.

Sequel

Michael G.Wilson and Barbara Broccoli stated that they were happy to start work on the next James Bond film in September 2009 without giving a title. Daniel Craig was signed to star in Bond 23 for release in late 2011. The story was originally set to follow Bond continueing to try and discover the truth about Quantum and get his revenge on them for killing Vesper Lynd. Wilson stated that the film would be set in the Middle East inspired from Sebastian Faulk's 2008 Bond novel Devil May Care. In March 2010, however, it was announced that plans to make Bond 23 were scrapped as the producers could not think of a suitable plot for the film and struggled to find a director when Quantum of Solace director Marc Forster stated that he would not return to direct Bond 23 as he wanted to work on his next film. In August 2010, Wilson and Broccoli decided to wipe clean the original script and write a new one which will not follow on directly from Casino Royale and Quantum of Solace. Sam Mendes has said that he hopes to direct the new Bond 23 and Judi Dench has already been confirmed to reprise her role as M while Jeffrey Wright will not return as Felix Leiter. Filming is likely to begin in December 2010 with a slated release for November 2012.

See also

- Differences between James Bond novels and films

References

Notes

[1] Randee Dawn (2008-11-11). "'Quantum' is Marc Forster's 007 art film" (http://www.hollywoodreporter.com/hr/content_display/film/news/e3ie9098baec9eb95cd02a01aebbd96a968). *The Hollywood Reporter*. . Retrieved 2008-11-13.

[2] "Quantum of Solace (2008)" (http://www.boxofficemojo.com/movies/?id=jamesbond22.htm). Box Office Mojo. . Retrieved 2009-04-06.

[3] Martyn Palmer (2007-11-24). "The man with the golden touch" (http://entertainment.timesonline.co.uk/tol/arts_and_entertainment/film/article2900516.ece?token=null&offset=0). *The Times* (London). . Retrieved 2007-11-25.

[4] John Naughton (November 2008). "Spy Harder". *GQ*: pp. 278–335.

[5] "Newswrap" (http://www.007.com/) (Flash video). Official site. . Retrieved 2008-03-01.

[6] Benjamin Svetkey (2008-10-30). "Bond is back!" (http://www.ew.com/ew/article/0,,20237005,00.html). *Entertainment Weekly*. . Retrieved 2008-11-01.

[7] "Bond actor admits plastic surgery" (http://news.bbc.co.uk/1/hi/entertainment/7660808.stm). *BBC News Online*.2008-10-09. . Retrieved 2008-10-12.

[8] Jennifer Vineyard (2007-12-06). "Daniel Craig Says He's Feeling The 'Pressure' Of James Bond Follow-Up" (http://www.mtv.com/movies/news/articles/1575858/20071205/story.jhtml). *MTV*. . Retrieved 2007-12-07.

[9] Matt Mueller. "On the Set of 'Quantum Of Solace': Olga Kurylenko: The Bond Girl" (http://www.premiere.com/Feature/On-the-Set-of-Quantum-Of-Solace/On-the-Set-of-Quantum-Of-Solace2). *Premiere*. . Retrieved 2009-01-14.

[10] Tim Masters (2008-10-31). "Talking Shop: Olga Kurylenko" (http://news.bbc.co.uk/1/hi/entertainment/7695332.stm).*BBC News Online*. . Retrieved 2008-10-31.

[11] Mark Brown (2008-01-24). "Everything changes but Bond" (http://www.guardian.co.uk/film/2008/jan/24/features).*The Guardian* (London). . Retrieved 2008-01-24.

[12] Liane Bonin. "Bond Rumor Report" (http://movies.aol.com/movie-photo-bts/quantum-of-solace).*Moviefone*. . Retrieved 2008-04-11.

[13] "Chile Soundbites videos" (http://sony.epk.tv/campaign/quantum-of-solace). Sony Electronic Press Kit. . Retrieved 2008-04-11.

[14] "Bond 22 Pre-Production Diary (22)" (http://www.mi6.co.uk/sections/articles/bond_22_preprod_diary22.php3?t=&s=articles). *MI6.co.uk*. 2007-12-30. . Retrieved 2007-12-31.

[15] Chris Tilly (2008-01-31). "Olga Kurylenko Q&A" (http://uk.movies.ign.com/articles/848/848813p1.html). *IGN*. . Retrieved 2008-01-31.

[16] David Giammarco. "From Ukraine, with love" (http://www.theherald.co.uk/features/features/display.var.2446992.0.From_Ukraine_with_love.php). *The Herald*. . Retrieved 2008-09-18.

[17] "Mathieu Amalric to model Bond Villain on Tony Blair" (http://www.thelondonpaper.com/cs/Satellite/london/news/article/1157150397402?packedargs=aid=1157150397402&suffix=ArticleController). *thelondonpaper*. 2008-01-24. . Retrieved 2008-01-31.

[18] Karl Rozemeyer (2008-03-18). "Mathieu Amalric on Being the 'Bond 22' Villain" (http://www.premiere.com/features/4455/mathieu-amalric-on-being-the-bond-22-villain.html). *Premiere*. . Retrieved 2008-03-19.

[19] Williams, Murphy (2008-10-02). "Quantum of Solace: Mathieu Amalric on playing James Bond's nemesis" (http://www.telegraph.co.uk/arts/main.jhtml?xml=/arts/2008/10/23/sm_mathieuamalric.xml). *The Daily Telegraph* (London). . Retrieved 2008-10-23.

[20] Chris Tilly (2008-01-30). "Gemma Arteron Q&A" (http://uk.movies.ign.com/articles/848/848237p1.html). *IGN*. . Retrieved 2008-01-30.

[21] "New Bond film title is confirmed" (http://news.bbc.co.uk/1/hi/entertainment/7206997.stm). *BBC News Online*.2008-01-24. . Retrieved 2008-01-24.

[22] "Gemma Arterton is Fields...Agent Fields" (http://commanderbond.net/article/5822). *CommanderBond.net*. 2008-11-18. . Retrieved 2009-05-02.

[23] "The Secrets of Quantum of Solace" (http://uk.movies.ign.com/articles/864/864542p1.html). *IGN*. 2008-04-05. . Retrieved 2008-04-05.

[24] "Fostering change" (http://www.star-ecentral.com/news/story.asp?file=/2008/10/11/movies/2202154&sec=movies).*The Star*. 2008-10-11. . Retrieved 2008-10-13.

[25] "Anatole Taubman On Elvis" (http://mi6.co.uk/sections/articles/bond_22_qos_capsule_elvis.php3?t=qos&s=qos&id=02075). *MI6.co.uk*. 2008-11-07. . Retrieved 2008-11-09.

[26] "Elvis Rocks Bond's World" (http://uk.movies.ign.com/articles/874/874700p1.html). *IGN*.2008-05-16. . Retrieved 2008-05-16.

[27] "Del Toro, Cuaron do voices in new Bond film" (http://ap.google.com/article/ALeqM5hU3ob2X-IVqYjDCrXtxIbZUi8ZkAD9405TFO0). Associated Press. 2008-10-23. . Retrieved 2008-10-23.

[28] Tatiana Siegel and Borys Kit (2006-07-17). "Roger Michell in Talks for Bond 22" (http://www.hollywoodreporter.com/hr/search/article_display.jsp?vnu_content_id=1002840141). *The Hollywood Reporter*. . Retrieved 2006-07-17.

[29] Liane Bonin. "10 Questions With: Daniel Craig" (http://www.moviefone.com/insidemovies/2008/04/14/daniel-craig-interview-for-quantum-of-solace/). *Moviefone*. . Retrieved 2008-04-11.

[30] Columbia Pictures (2006-07-20). "22nd James Bond Coming May 2, 2008!" (http://www.superherohype.com/news/jamesbondnews.php?id=4521). *Superhero Hype!*. . Retrieved 2007-08-06.

[31] "They call him Director No" (http://entertainment.timesonline.co.uk/tol/arts_and_entertainment/stage/theatre/article1877785.ece). *The Times* (London). 2007-07-04. . Retrieved 2008-01-27.

[32] "Bond 22 Targeting November 7, 2008" (http://www.comingsoon.net/news/movienews.php?id=16308). *Superhero Hype!*. 2006-09-01. . Retrieved 2006-09-01.

[33] Michael Fleming (2007-04-11). "'Barbarella' back in action" (http://www.variety.com/article/VR1117962920.html?categoryid=13&cs=1). *Variety*. . Retrieved 2007-08-06.

[34] "Paul Haggis on board to work on Bond 22 script, but turns down directing role" (http://www.mi6.co.uk/news/index.php?itemid=5040&catid=106). *MI6.co.uk*. 2007-05-23. . Retrieved 2007-05-23.

[35] "Forster back in action with 'Bond 22'" (http://www.hollywoodreporter.com/hr/search/article_display.jsp?vnu_content_id=1003600629). *The Hollywood Reporter*. 2007-06-20. . Retrieved 2007-06-19.

[36] Terrence Rafferty (2007-12-09). "A License to Pursue the Inner Bond" (http://www.nytimes.com/2007/12/09/movies/09raff.html?_r=2&ref=movies&oref=slogin&oref=slogin). *The New York Times*. . Retrieved 2007-12-09.

[37] Alistair Harkness (2008-10-30). "A Quantum leap" (http://thescotsman.scotsman.com/features/A-Quantum-leap.4643021.jp). *The Scotsman.* . Retrieved 2008-10-30.
[38] Ciaran Carty (2008-11-02). "'I felt there was pain in Bond'" (http://www.tribune.ie/arts/films/article/2008/nov/02/i-felt-there-was-pain-in-bond/). *Sunday Tribune.* . Retrieved 2008-11-02.
[39] "A James Bond Set Visit and Seven Exclusive Quantum of Solace Images!" (http://uk.rottentomatoes.com/m/quantum_of_solace/news/1719930/a_james_bond_set_visit_and_seven_exclusive_quantum_of_solace_images). *Rotten Tomatoes.*2008-04-04. . Retrieved 2008-04-05.
[40] "Marc Forster on directing 007" (http://mi6.co.uk/sections/articles/bond_22_qos_capsule_forster.php3?t=qos&s=qos&id=02080). *MI6.co.uk.* 2008-11-11. . Retrieved 2008-11-13.
[41] Jim Vejvoda (2008-09-22). "007 Responds to IGN Readers" (http://uk.movies.ign.com/articles/911/911930p1.htm).*IGN.* . Retrieved 2008-09-22.
[42] Ian Nathan (October 2008). "Quantum's Leap". *Empire*: pp. 82 – 90.
[43] Anne Thompson (2008-10-23). "'Solace' offers thinking person's 007" (http://www.variety.com/article/VR1117994573.html?categoryid=2508&cs=1). *Variety.* . Retrieved 2008-11-01.
[44] Logan Hill (2008-11-03). "How James Bond Nearly Became a Father" (http://nymag.com/daily/entertainment/2008/11/how_james_bond_nearly_became_a.html). *New York.* . Retrieved 2008-11-03.
[45] "Daniel: the title is meant to confuse". *Press and Journal.* 2008-01-24.
[46] See, Wikipedia,*For Your Eyes Only*http://en.wikipedia.org/wiki/For_Your_Eyes_Only_%28short_story_collection%29 (as of March 9, 2010, 01:50 GMT)
[47] "Seeking Solace on the Bond set" (http://www.usatoday.com/life/flash.htm?gid=459). *USA Today.*2008-04-03. . Retrieved 2008-04-04.
[48] Richard Owen (2007-08-13). "Bond has activists on his tail over new film's 'brutal' horse race finale" (http://entertainment.timesonline.co.uk/tol/arts_and_entertainment/film/article2246486.ece). *The Times* (London). . Retrieved 2007-08-13.
[49] www.imdb.com (2008-11-11). "Filming locations for Quantum of Solace" (http://www.imdb.com/title/tt0830515/locations). . Retrieved 2009-06-02.
[50] "Bond 22 filming takes place in Madrid, Spain during last week of August" (http://www.mi6.co.uk/news/index.php?itemid=5327). *MI6.co.uk.* 2007-08-31. . Retrieved 2008-03-25.
[51] "Newswrap #2 video" (http://www.reelzchannel.com/movie/233698/quantum-of-solace?clipid=32934). *ReelzChannel.*2008-03-20. . Retrieved 2008-03-20.
[52] David Allen (2008-02-28). "A bond with Chino" (http://www.dailybulletin.com/ci_8399719). Los Angeles Newspaper Group. . Retrieved 2008-03-02.
[53] "Production Diary (16)" (http://www.mi6.co.uk/sections/articles/bond_22_prod_diary16.php3?t=qos&s=qos).*MI6.co.uk.* 2008-03-17. . Retrieved 2008-03-20.
[54] "Production Diary (19)" (http://www.mi6.co.uk/sections/articles/bond_22_prod_diary19.php3?t=&s=). *MI6.co.uk.*2008-03-27. . Retrieved 2008-03-28.
[55] Tim Marsters (2008-01-25). "Behind the scenes on the Bond set" (http://news.bbc.co.uk/1/hi/entertainment/7208410.stm). *BBC News Online.* . Retrieved 2008-01-25.
[56] "Quantum of Solace - Production Diary (7)" (http://www.mi6.co.uk/sections/articles/bond_22_prod_diary07.php3?t=&s=). *MI6.co.uk.* 2008-01-26. . Retrieved 2008-01-26.
[57] Rebecca Connop Price (2008-10-30). "Barracks and airport provide location for Bond film" (http://www.gethampshire.co.uk/news/s/2038353_barracks_and_airport_provide_location_for_bond_film). *Get Hampshire.* . Retrieved 2008-11-18.
[58] "Production Diary (11)" (http://www.mi6.co.uk/sections/articles/bond_22_prod_diary11.php3?t=qos&s=qos).*MI6.co.uk.* 2008-02-09. . Retrieved 2008-02-09.
[59] Edward Douglas (2008-11-10). "Marc Forster Finds His Quantum of Solace" (http://www.comingsoon.net/news/movienews.php?id=50314). *ComingSoon.net.* . Retrieved 2008-11-10.
[60] "Production Diary (9)" (http://www.mi6.co.uk/sections/articles/bond_22_prod_diary09.php3?t=qos&s=qos).*MI6.co.uk.* 2008-02-02. . Retrieved 2008-02-08.
[61] "Production Diary (17)" (http://www.mi6.co.uk/sections/articles/bond_22_prod_diary17.php3?t=qos&s=qos).*MI6.co.uk.* 2008-03-19. . Retrieved 2008-03-20.
[62] Anthony Breznican (2008-04-04). "James Bond series takes a 'Quantum' leap" (http://www.usatoday.com/life/movies/news/2008-04-03-bond-quantum_N.htm). *USA Today.* . Retrieved 2008-04-04.
[63] Simon Gardner (2008-04-02). "James Bond has new nemesis: irate Chilean mayor" (http://uk.reuters.com/article/topNews/idUKN0237294620080402). Reuters. . Retrieved 2008-09-13.
[64] "'Mayor' protests on Chile 007 set" (http://news.bbc.co.uk/1/hi/entertainment/7326582.stm). *BBC News Online.*2008-04-02. . Retrieved 2008-04-03.
[65] "Production Diary (22)" (http://www.mi6.co.uk/sections/articles/bond_22_prod_diary22.php3?t=qos&s=qos).*MI6.co.uk.* 2008-04-07. . Retrieved 2008-04-10.
[66] "¿Apoya Ud. las protestas del alcalde de Sierra Gorda por la filmación de James Bond en su comuna?" (http://www.lasegunda.com/edicionOnline/interaccion/encuestas/resultado.asp?idencuesta=2512&idclasificacion=3&fg=) (in Spanish). *La Segunda.* 2008-03-02. . Retrieved 2008-04-02.
[67] Nick Pisa (2008-04-22). "Driver of James Bond's Aston Martin cheated death in dramatic crash". *The Daily Telegraph.*

[68] Paul Bompard (2008-04-24). [ghttp://entertainment.timesonline.co.uk/tol/arts_and_entertainment/film/article3810782.ece "James Bond production halted amid fears of a curse"]. *The Times* (London). ghttp://entertainment.timesonline.co.uk/tol/arts_and_entertainment/film/article3810782.ece. Retrieved 2008-04-24.
[69] "Production Diary (10)" (http://www.mi6.co.uk/sections/articles/bond_22_prod_diary10.php3?t=qos&s=qos).*MI6.co.uk*. 2008-02-08. . Retrieved 2008-02-09.
[70] "Solace on the Lake" (http://movies.msn.com/movies/hitlist/05-13-08). *MSN*. 2008-05-08. . Retrieved 2008-05-16.
[71] "Production Diary (1)" (http://www.mi6.co.uk/sections/articles/bond_22_prod_diary01.php3?t=&s=articles).*MI6.co.uk*. 2008-01-03. . Retrieved 2008-01-08.
[72] "Production Diary (32)" (http://www.mi6.co.uk/sections/articles/bond_22_prod_diary32.php3?t=qos&s=qos).*MI6.co.uk*. 2008-05-16. . Retrieved 2008-05-16.
[73] "`Quantum of Solace` wrap party held on Saturday night, David Arnold confirms" (http://www.mi6.co.uk/news/index.php?itemid=6394). *MI6.co.uk*. 2008-06-22. . Retrieved 2008-06-22.
[74] "Peter Lamont bows out from Bond 22, Dennis Gassner to be Production Designer" (http://www.mi6.co.uk/news/index.php?itemid=5206). *MI6.co.uk*. 2007-07-23. . Retrieved 2007-07-23.
[75] Olly Richards (2008-01-24). "Daniel Craig Talks Quantum of Solace" (http://www.empireonline.com/news/story.asp?NID=21855). *Empire*. . Retrieved 2008-01-24.
[76] "Capone talks with James Bond himself, Daniel Craig, and Quantum of Solace director Marc Forster in London!!!" (http://www.aintitcool.com/node/38427). *Ain't It Cool News*. 2008-09-21. . Retrieved 2008-09-22.
[77] "James Bond: licence to redesign" (http://blog.macleans.ca/2008/11/17/james-bond-licence-to-redesign/). *Maclean's*.2008-11-17. . Retrieved 2008-11-18.
[78] "Jasper Conran Spring Summer 2008 Collection" (http://www.jasperconran.com/collections/womenswear/archive/james-bond,116,ART.html). Jasperconran.com. . Retrieved 2010-09-12.
[79] Jessica Fellowes (2008-10-22). "James Bond week: 007 and his girls are back with a crisp new look" (http://www.telegraph.co.uk/fashion/main.jhtml?xml=/fashion/2008/10/22/efbond322.xml). *The Daily Telegraph* (London). . Retrieved 2008-10-25.
[80] Jessica Fellowes (2008-10-22). "Necklace with a starring role" (http://www.telegraph.co.uk/fashion/main.jhtml?xml=/fashion/2008/10/22/efbond222.xml). *The Daily Telegraph* (London). . Retrieved 2008-10-25.
[81] Mark Caro (2008-11-09). "James Bond: 15 facts to know now" (http://www.chicagotribune.com/features/arts/chi-bond-1109-covernov09,0,4869399.story). *Chicago Tribune*. . Retrieved 2008-11-08.
[82] Bill Desowitz (2009-01-16). "MK12 Has a Blast with Quantum Main Titles" (http://vfxworld.com/index.php?atype=articles&id=3881). *VFXWorld*. . Retrieved 2009-01-26.
[83] Yves Peters (2008-12-19). "MK12 Create Custom Type for Quantum of Solace Title Sequence" (http://fontfeed.com/archives/mk12-quantum-of-solace-title-sequence/). *The Font Feed* (FontShop). . Retrieved 2008-12-22.
[84] "Aston Martin DBS to star in new James Bond film" (http://www.astonmartin.com/thecompany/news?a=14d34f22-1324-4ca5-acbb-764f80c7d7f2). *Aston Martin*. 2007. . Retrieved 2007-12-11.
[85] Borys Kit (2007-09-04). "Bradley tapped to aid Bond stunts" (http://www.hollywoodreporter.com/hr/content_display/film/news/e3i61cdc71247ef46a7ec4bddbba9463397). *The Hollywood Reporter*. . Retrieved 2008-01-10.
[86] "Dan Bradley interview" (http://www.bournestuntsimulator.com/danbradley/). *Bourne Stunt Simulator*. . Retrieved 2008-01-16.
[87] Moore, Malcolm (2008-04-28). "James Bond filming suspended after third accident leaves stuntman in coma" (http://www.telegraph.co.uk/news/worldnews/1902288/James-Bond-filming-suspended-after-third-accident-leaves-stuntman-in-coma.html).*The Daily Telegraph* (London). . Retrieved 2008-04-28.
[88] Bill Desowitz (2008-12-03). "A Quantum of VFX for James Bond" (http://vfxworld.com/?atype=articles&id=3844&page=1#). *VFX World*. . Retrieved 2008-12-04.
[89] Bill Dawes (2008-11-16). "Back into Bondage" (http://www.fxguide.com/article508.html). *fxguide*. . Retrieved 2008-11-22.
[90] Chris Reidy (2008-05-12). ""Snakehead" films James Bond dogfight footage" (http://www.boston.com/business/ticker/2008/05/_the_concord_of.html). *The Boston Globe*. . Retrieved 2008-05-12.
[91] "For Your Eyes Only: RT in Austria with James Bond" (http://uk.rottentomatoes.com/m/quantum_of_solace/news/1727255/2/for_your_eyes_only_rt_in_austria_with_james_bond). *Rotten Tomatoes*. 2008-05-09. . Retrieved 2008-05-16.
[92] "Your Quantum of Solace Questions Answered!" (http://movieblog.ugo.com/index.php/movieblog/more/your_quantum_of_solace_questions_answered/). *UGO Networks*. 2008-09-21. . Retrieved 2008-09-22.
[93] Tommy Pearson, David Arnold. (November year 2007 title=Interview with David Arnold) (mp3). [Audio interview]. http://www.stageandscreenonline.com/_Media/DavidArnoldPart3.mp3. Retrieved 2008-04-25.
[94] Mark Beaumont (2008-10-18). "The Midas touch of David Arnold and his influence on Bond" (http://entertainment.timesonline.co.uk/tol/arts_and_entertainment/music/article4948366.ece). *The Times* (London). . Retrieved 2008-10-18.
[95] "`Crawl, End Crawl` track from `Quantum of Solace` now on iTunes" (http://www.mi6.co.uk/news/index.php?itemid=7146&t=mi6&s=news). *MI6.co.uk*. 2008-12-09. . Retrieved 2008-12-09.
[96] "Alicia Keys, Jack White Team For Bond Theme" (http://www.billboard.com/bbcom/news/article_display.jsp?vnu_content_id=1003832786). Billboard. 2008-07-29. . Retrieved 2008-07-29.
[97] "Quantum of Solace - News - Alicia Keys, Jack White Team For "Quantum of Solace" Theme Song (Press Release)" (http://www.007.com/download/ThemeSong_QOS_PressRelease.pdf) (PDF). Columbia Pictures. 2008-07-29. . Retrieved 2008-08-02.

[98] "Jack White Talks Bond" (http://uk.music.ign.com/articles/901/901612p1.html). *IGN*. 2008-08-21. . Retrieved 2008-08-21.
[99] Brian Hiatt (2008-10-02). "Jack White and Alicia Keys: Bond's New Duo" (http://www.rollingstone.com/news/story/23064110/jack_white_and_alicia_keys_bonds_new_duo). *Rolling Stone*. . Retrieved 2008-09-16.
[100] "Winehouse working on 'Bond theme'" (http://news.bbc.co.uk/1/hi/entertainment/7371949.stm). *BBC News Online*.2008-04-28. . Retrieved 2008-04-28.
[101] "Troubled Winehouse 'not ready' for Bond theme" (http://web.archive.org/web/20080506020030/http://www.cnn.com/2008/SHOWBIZ/Music/05/03/winehouse.bond.ap/index.html). CNN/AP. 2008-05-03. Archived from the original (http://www.cnn.com/2008/SHOWBIZ/Music/05/03/winehouse.bond.ap/index.html) on May 6, 2008. . Retrieved 2008-05-03.
[102] ""Quantum of Solace" World Premiere Announced" (http://www.mi6.co.uk/sections/articles/bond_22_premiere_announced.php3?t=qos&s=qos&id=01974). *MI6.co.uk*. 2008-08-05. . Retrieved 2008-08-06.
[103] Olly Richards (2008-03-19). "Quantum of Solace Gets Earlier Release" (http://www.empireonline.com/news/story.asp?NID=22223). *Empire*. . Retrieved 2008-03-19.
[104] Columbia Pictures (2008-08-21). "Quantum of Solace Moved Back a Week" (http://www.comingsoon.net/news/movienews.php?id=48142). *ComingSoon.net*. . Retrieved 2008-08-21.
[105] Garry Maddox (2008-09-06). "Bond blinks first in battle of blockbusters" (http://www.smh.com.au/news/film/bond-blinks-first-in-battle-of-the-blockbusters/2008/09/05/1220121520755.html). *Sydney Morning Herald*. . Retrieved 2008-09-06.
[106] Marc Graser (2008-08-14). "Brands line up for Bond sequel" (http://www.variety.com/article/VR1117990584.html?categoryid=13&cs=1). *Variety*. . Retrieved 2008-08-15.
[107] Steve McGinty (2008-10-27). "Does this mean Bond's past his sell-by date?" (http://thescotsman.scotsman.com/features/Does-this-mean-Bond39s-past.4630875.jp). *The Scotsman*. . Retrieved 2008-11-15.
[108] " Bond girl Olga Kurylenko introduces Ford Ka at Paris Motor Show (video) (http://www.mi6.co.uk/news/index.php?itemid=6802&catid=106&t=mi6&s=news)," *MI6.co.uk* (2008-03-10). Retrieved on 2008-11-08.
[109] "Avon to introduce Bond Girl 007 fragrance with Gemma Arterton" (http://www.mi6.co.uk/news/index.php?itemid=6273). *MI6.co.uk*. 2008-05-23. . Retrieved 2008-08-12.
[110] Mark Sweney (2008-09-11). ""Coca-Cola launches ad featuring Jack White's Quantum of Solace music"" (http://www.guardian.co.uk/media/video/2008/sep/11/advertising.jamesbond). *The Guardian* (London). . Retrieved 2008-09-18.
[111] "Mission for a Million" (http://www.sonymissionmillion.com/). Sony. . Retrieved 2008-10-04.
[112] "New 007 Toys & Gadgets 2008" (http://www.mi6.co.uk/sections/articles/collecting_corgi_2008_toyfair3.php3).*MI6.co.uk*. 2008-02-13. . Retrieved 2008-02-27.
[113] "New Corgi Cars 2008" (http://www.mi6.co.uk/sections/articles/collecting_corgi_2008_toyfair2.php3). *MI6.co.uk*.2008-02-03. . Retrieved 2008-02-27.
[114] "New Corgi Action Figures" (http://www.mi6.co.uk/sections/articles/collecting_corgi_2008_toyfair1.php3).*MI6.co.uk*. 2008-02-24. . Retrieved 2008-02-27.
[115] "Scalextric 007 Racing Sets Unveiled" (http://www.mi6.co.uk/sections/articles/collecting_scalextric_2008_toyfair.php3?t=&s=). *MI6.co.uk*. 2008-02-24. . Retrieved 2008-02-27.
[116] "Swatch Launch 007 Villains Watches" (http://www.mi6.co.uk/sections/articles/collecting_swatch_2008_launch.php3?t=&s=&id=02007). *MI6.co.uk*. 2008-09-09. . Retrieved 2008-11-14.
[117] Amazon.co.uk listing (http://www.amazon.co.uk/dp/0141189622).Retrieved 28 June 2008.
[118] Amazon.com listing (http://www.amazon.com/dp/0143114581), accessed 24 May 2008
[119] Archie Thomas (2008-11-01). "'Solace' makes quantum leap in U.K." (http://www.variety.com/article/VR1117995122.html?categoryid=13&cs=1). *Variety*. . Retrieved 2008-11-01.
[120] "Bond film smashes weekend records" (http://news.bbc.co.uk/1/hi/entertainment/7705631.stm). *BBC News Online*.2008-11-03. . Retrieved 2008-11-03.
[121] Dave McNary (2008-11-02). "James Bond finds overseas 'Solace'" (http://www.variety.com/article/VR1117995151.html?categoryid=13&cs=1). *Variety*. . Retrieved 2008-11-03.
[122] Pamela McClintock (2008-11-08). "'Quantum' leap in overseas box office" (http://www.variety.com/article/VR1117995539.html?categoryid=13&cs=1). *Variety*. . Retrieved 2008-11-09.
[123] Dave McNary (2008-11-09). "'Quantum' rules foreign box office" (http://www.variety.com/article/VR1117995548.html?categoryid=13&cs=1). *Variety*. . Retrieved 2008-11-10.
[124] "Weekend Box Office Results from 11/14 - 11/16" (http://www.boxofficemojo.com/weekend/chart/?view=&yr=2008&wknd=46&p=.htm). Box Office Mojo. . Retrieved 2008-11-14.
[125] "James Bond Movies" (http://www.boxofficemojo.com/franchises/chart/?id=jamesbond.htm). Box Office Mojo. . Retrieved 2008-11-14.
[126] Joshua Rich (2008-11-16). "'Quantum of Solace' Stirs up a Win" (http://www.ew.com/ew/article/0,,20240780,00.html). *Entertainment Weekly*. . Retrieved 2008-11-17.
[127] "*Quantum of Solace*" (http://www.rottentomatoes.com/m/quantum_of_solace/). *Rotten Tomatoes*.. Retrieved 2008-10-25.
[128] "Quantum of Solace" (http://www.metacritic.com/film/titles/quantumofsolace). *Metacritic*. . Retrieved 2008-11-15.
[129] Tom Butler (2008-10-31). "UK Tomatometer Preview: Quantum Of Solace - Is the New Bond Shaken or Stirred?" (http://uk.rottentomatoes.com/m/quantum_of_solace/news/1777726/

uk_tomatometer_preview_quantum_of_solace_is_the_new_bond_shaken_or_stirred). *Rotten Tomatoes*. . Retrieved 2008-11-01.

[130] "Sir Roger Moore weighs in on `Quantum of Solace`" (http://www.mi6.co.uk/news/index.php?itemid=7432&t=mi6&s=news). *MI6.co.uk*. 2009-03-16. . Retrieved 2009-03-17.

[131] Kim Newman. "*Quantum of Solace* (12A)" (http://www.empireonline.com/reviews/reviewcomplete.asp?FID=134523). *Empire Online*. . Retrieved 2008-10-22.

[132] Cosmo Landesman (2008-10-26). "Quantum of Solace - The Sunday Times review" (http://entertainment.timesonline.co.uk/tol/arts_and_entertainment/film/film_reviews/article5001623.ece). *The Sunday Times* (London). . Retrieved 2008-10-28.

[133] Peter Bradshaw (2008-10-18). "Quantum of Solace" (http://www.guardian.co.uk/film/2008/oct/18/jamesbond1). *The Guardian* (London). . Retrieved 2008-10-28.

[134] "Quantum of Solace" (http://www.screendaily.com/ScreenDailyArticle.aspx?intStoryID=41477). *Screen Daily*. 2008-10-20. . Retrieved 2008-11-01.

[135] Review (http://rogerebert.suntimes.com/apps/pbcs.dll/article?AID=/20081111/REVIEWS/811129989) by Roger Ebert, November 12, 2008

[136] Marni Weisz, "At least it's not Octopussy," *Famous*, October 2008, p. 6

[137] "2008 13th Annual SATELLITE Awards" (http://www.pressacademy.com/satawards/awards2008.shtml).International Press Academy. . Retrieved 2008-12-15.

[138] Dade Hayes (2008-12-09). "Critics Choice favors 'Milk,' 'Button'" (http://www.variety.com/article/VR1117997072.html?categoryId=13&cs=1). *Variety*. . Retrieved 2008-12-09.

[139] "Empire Awards nominate `Quantum of Solace` five times, vote now online" (http://www.mi6.co.uk/news/index.php?itemid=7396&t=mi6&s=news). *MI6.co.uk*. 2009-03-02. . Retrieved 2009-03-03.

[140] "Nominations for the 35th Annual Saturn Awards" (http://www.saturnawards.org/nominations.html).Academy of Science Fiction, Fantasy & Horror Films. . Retrieved 2009-03-17.

[141] Michael Moran (2008-11-20). "The 20 greatest car chases in movie history" (http://entertainment.timesonline.co.uk/tol/arts_and_entertainment/film/article5199765.ece?token=null&offset=0&page=1). *The Times* (London). . Retrieved 2008-12-03.

[142] "Quantum of Solace - DVD Sales" (http://www.the-numbers.com/movies/2008/JB22-DVD.php). The Numbers. . Retrieved 2009-11-01.

[143] "Quantum of Solace Hits DVD & Blu-ray in March" (http://www.comingsoon.net/news/movienews.php?id=51899).*ComingSoon.net*. 2009-01-13. . Retrieved 2009-01-13.

Bibliography

- *Bond on Set: Filming Quantum of Solace*, Greg Williams, DK ADULT (October 20, 2008), ISBN 0-7566-4120-9

External links

- Official website (http://www.007.com)
  - Official blog (http://007.com/blog/)
- *Quantum of Solace (film)* (http://www.imdb.com/title/tt0830515/) at the Internet Movie Database
- *Quantum of Solace (film)* (http://www.allmovie.com/work/356351) at Allmovie
- *Quantum of Solace (film)* (http://www.rottentomatoes.com/m/quantum_of_solace/) at Rotten Tomatoes
- *Quantum of Solace (film)* (http://www.boxofficemojo.com/movies/?id=jamesbond22.htm) at Box Office Mojo

Go Inside to Greet the Light

Go Inside to Greet the Light is a film sponsored by Quaker Outreach in Yorkshire and the Yorkshire Sculpture Park. Narrated by Judi Dench, this film gives a flavour of the spiritual experience of Quaker meetings for worship in James Turrell's Deershelter Skyspace. Its world premiere was on 29 September 2007.

Notes on a Scandal (film)

Notes on a Scandal

Promotional movie poster

Directed by	Richard Eyre
Produced by	Robert Fox Scott Rudin
Written by	Zoë Heller (novel) Patrick Marber (screenplay)
Starring	Judi Dench Cate Blanchett Bill Nighy
Music by	Philip Glass
Cinematography	Chris Menges
Editing by	John Bloom Antonia Van Drimmelen
Distributed by	Fox Searchlight Pictures
Release date(s)	25 December 2006
Running time	92 minutes
Country	United Kingdom
Language	English
Budget	£15,000,000 (production)
Gross revenue	$49,752,391 (worldwide)

Notes on a Scandal is a 2006 psychological drama film, adapted from the 2003 novel of the same name by Zoë Heller. The screenplay was written by Patrick Marber and the film was directed by Richard Eyre. Many parts of the film were shot in Islington Arts and Media School. The soundtrack was composed by Philip Glass.

It was nominated for four Academy Awards — Best Actress, Best Supporting Actress, Best Adapted Screenplay, and Best Original Score.

Plot

Barbara Covett (Judi Dench) teaches history at a comprehensive school in London. A lonely old spinster, Barbara's only "intimate relationship" is with herself by means of a diary. When a new, younger teacher Sheba Hart (Cate Blanchett) starts at the school, Barbara feels drawn to her and believes that she "may be the one." Barbara discovers that Sheba is having an affair with a student, Steven Connolly (Andrew Simpson), and confronts her. When Sheba asks her to not tell the school administration until Christmas so that she can be with her family, Barbara explains she has no intention of telling, as long as she ends the relationship. However, Sheba does not end the affair with Steven, causing Barbara to taunt her emotionally and draw her down, leading her to end the affair with Steven. In months passing, Barbara's grasp on Sheba slowly starts to take hold, with Barbara manipulating and emotionally blackmailing her, causing her attentions to be divided between her family and Barbara.

When Barbara's cat dies and Sheba's loyalties are easily divided, Sheba's husband Richard shouts in anger that her friend is being an evident pain and that his wife is being twisted by Barbara. With Barbara being left alone and angry, she seeks revenge by revealing Sheba's affair to a fellow teacher who comes to her asking her if Sheba is interested in him. The fellow teacher spreads the "playground rumour" to Steven's mother. Mrs Connolly then comes to Sheba's home and hits Sheba. Afterwards Sheba and her husband Richard bitterly argue. In Barbara's voiceover, she reveals she is glad that they are arguing, knowing that Sheba will come to her for comfort, which had been Barbara's plan to start with. The next day the media, as well as the school administration, are alerted, and Sheba's affair and her life are turned upside down by the collapse of her marriage, the destroyed relationship with her children, and the loss of her job. Barbara is fired from the school after denying to the headmaster that she knew of the relationship; he confronts her with a copy of a restraining order taken out against Barbara by another fellow teacher whom she had previously befriended.

Sheba ends up moving into Barbara's house, believing that the affair became known because Steven confessed it to his mother, but Sheba soon finds Barbara's diary and learns that it was Barbara who leaked the story of the affair, on account of the rather sexual attraction Barbara seems to have for her. When Barbara returns from a shopping round, she is confronted by a furious Sheba, who strikes her in anger. Barbara says she has done her a favour by getting her out of a hopeless marriage. The two of them continue to shout and fight with one another, and Sheba claims that Barbara never really liked her, but in fact manipulated her for her own personal needs. Sheba runs outside with Barbara's journal, to streams of reporters and photographers. She shouts at them in a deluded fashion, but becomes hemmed in by a crush of reporters and photographers, at which point Barbara rescues her. Sheba's emotions spent, she quietly tells Barbara that she had initiated the friendship because she had liked her (Barbara) and they could have been friends. Barbara says she needs more than a friend, implying but not saying that she needs someone who is a close companion and lover.[1] Sheba leaves Barbara, placing the journal on the table. Sheba returns to her family home. Richard answers the door. Sheba faces her husband with the silent questions "Can you forgive me? Can I come in?".[2] Richard silently considers, and then allows her to enter.

Sheba is sentenced to 10 months, and the last scene is Barbara meeting another younger woman who is reading a newspaper reporting the Sheba Hart affair. Barbara says she used to know Sheba, but then says she didn't know her well. Barbara quickly introduces herself, and the other woman introduces herself as Annabelle. The pair continue to talk. Barbara mentions about attending a classical concert, but then saying that she would much like a friendly companion to join her, which is implied to be Annabelle.

Cast

Actor	Role
Judi Dench	Barbara Covett
Cate Blanchett	Bathsheba "Sheba" / "Bash" Hart
Tom Georgeson	Ted Mawson
Michael Maloney	Sandy Pabblem
Joanna Scanlan	Sue Hodge
Shaun Parkes	Bill Rumer
Emma Williams	Linda
Andrew Simpson	Steven Connolly
Phil Davis	Brian Bangs
Bill Nighy	Richard Hart
Juno Temple	Polly Hart
Max Lewis	Ben Hart

Differences from the novel

- The novel is narrated from the perspective of Barbara, who is shown to be an imperfect narrator, while the film presents a more objective depiction of events. In the novel, Barbara depicts the other characters in a strongly cynical light, and takes care to justify herself as blameless. The film depicts Barbara more critically, and the other characters in a more favourable light.
- The ending in the film differs. Sheba returns to her family and, eventually, a prison sentence while Barbara is left alone and, it would seem, befriends someone else. The ending in the novel is much more open-ended — Barbara and Sheba stay together and Sheba is, it would appear, emotionally dependent on Barbara. It is not revealed whether or not Sheba is imprisoned, and Annabelle (Barbara's supposed new friend) isn't featured in the novel.
- In the film, Barbara is frequently seen writing in her diary. In the novel, there is no diary. The novel is epistolary and takes the form of a manuscript, written by Barbara, recording the entire events.
- In the film, Sheba is portrayed as a caring woman, despite her indiscretions, whereas in the novel she is a lot less likeable and notably more selfish. For instance, in the film, she is reluctant to accompany Barbara to the vet (to put down her terminally ill cat) because her son is in a school play. In the novel, it is so she can meet up with Steven.
- In the film, Barbara discovers the affair between Sheba and Steven on the night of a school play. In the book, it is on Bonfire Night, and Sheba actually confesses the affair to Barbara.
- The film clearly albeit discreetly reveals Barbara's wish for physical intimacy with Sheba. The references to this desire in the novel are more opaque and uncertain.
- In the book, Barbara mentions having some nieces and nephews, with whom she has a warm, if distant, relationship and mentions visiting them from time to time. They do not appear in the film.
- The film focuses primarily on the relationship between Barbara and Sheba. The novel's broader focus includes the supporting characters, such as Barbara's sister and Sheba's family, as well as the other teachers at St. George's School.

Filming

The film was shot on location in the Parliament Hill, Gospel Oak and Camden Town areas of north-west London

Soundtrack

The original score for the movie was composed by Philip Glass. The film features a song by Toots & The Maytals.

Reception

Critical reaction

The film opened to generally positive reviews, receiving a *Rotten Tomatoes* certified fresh rating of 87 percent.[3] *The Guardian* called the film a "delectable adaptation" with "tremendous acting from Judi Dench and Cate Blanchett, with many blue-chip supporting contributions and a "screenwriting masterclass from Patrick Marber".[4] *The Times* praised the film, saying: "Notes on a Scandal, is screenwriting at its vicious best... Richard Eyre directs the film like a chamber play. He leans on Philip Glass's ever-present and insistent music like a crutch. But his natural gift for framing scenes is terrifically assured. A potent and evil pleasure."[5]

American publications also gave the film acclaim, with the *Los Angeles Times* describing the film as "Sexy, aspirational and post-politically correct, Notes on a Scandal could turn out to be the Fatal Attraction of the noughties."[6] *The Washington Post* noted the "dark brilliance" and that it "offers what is possibly the only intelligent account of such a disaster ever constructed, with a point of view that is somewhat gimlet-eyed and offered with absolutely no sentimentality whatsoever." The reviewer also identified the film as a "study in the anthropology of British liberal-left middle-class life."[7] *Chicago Sun-Times* film critic Roger Ebert heaped praise on the film and the acting performances "Perhaps the most impressive acting duo in any film of 2006. Dench and Blanchett are magnificent. 'Notes on a Scandal' is whip-smart, sharp and grown up."[8]

Commercial

The film was also a commercial success. It grossed $49,752,391 worldwide,[9] exceeding its £15 million budget.[10]

Awards and nominations

79th Academy Awards nominees:

- Nominated: Best Actress — Judi Dench
- Nominated: Best Supporting Actress — Cate Blanchett
- Nominated: Best Adapted Screenplay — Patrick Marber
- Nominated: Best Original Score — Philip Glass

BAFTA Awards

- Nominated: Best British Film
- Nominated: Best Actress — Judi Dench
- Nominated: Best Adapted Screenplay — Patrick Marber

British Independent Film Awards

- Nominated: Best British Independent Film
- Won: Best Performance by an Actress in a British Independent Film — Judi Dench
- Nominated: Best Performance by a Supporting Actor or Actress in a British Independent Film — Cate Blanchett
- Won: Best Screenplay — Patrick Marber

Broadcast Film Critics Association Awards

- Nominated: Best Actress — Judi Dench
- Nominated: Best Picture
- Nominated: Best Supporting Actress — Cate Blanchett

Chicago Film Critics Association Awards

- Nominated: Best Actress — Judi Dench
- Nominated: Best Supporting Actress — Cate Blanchett
- Nominated: Best Adapted Screenplay — Patrick Marber
- Nominated: Best Original Score

Dallas-Fort Worth Film Critics Association Awards

- Won: Best Supporting Actress — Cate Blanchett

Evening Standard British Film Awards

- Won: Best Actress — Judi Dench

Florida Film Critics Circle Awards

- Won: Best Supporting Actress — Cate Blanchett

Golden Globe Awards

- Nominated: Best Actress in a Motion Picture, Drama — Judi Dench
- Nominated: Best Supporting Actress — Cate Blanchett
- Nominated: Best Screenplay — Patrick Marber

London Film Critics Circle Awards

- Nominated: Actress of the Year — Judi Dench
- Nominated: British Actress of the Year — Judi Dench
- Nominated: British Supporting Actor of the Year — Bill Nighy

Oklahoma Film Critics Circle Awards

- Won: Best Supporting Actress — Cate Blanchett

Online Film Critics Awards

- Nominated: Best Actress — Judi Dench
- Nominated: Best Supporting Actress — Cate Blanchett
- Nominated: Best Original Score — Phillip Glass

Phoenix Film Critics Society Awards

- Won: Best Supporting Actress — Cate Blanchett

Screen Actors Guild Awards

- Nominated: Best Actress — Judi Dench
- Nominated: Best Supporting Actress — Cate Blanchett

Toronto Film Critics Association Awards

- Won: Best Supporting Actress — Cate Blanchett

References

[1] Notes on a Scandal 1:20:34

[2] Notes on a Scandal 1:22:32

[3] "Notes on a Scandal (2006)" (http://uk.rottentomatoes.com/m/notes_on_a_scandal/). *Rotten Tomatoes*. . Retrieved 2009-02-28.

[4] Bradshaw, Peter (2007-02-02). "Notes on a Scandal" (http://www.guardian.co.uk/film/2007/feb/02/drama.periodandhistorical). *The Guardian* (London). . Retrieved 2009-08-22.

[5] Christopher, James (01-02-2007). "Notes on a Scandal" (http://entertainment.timesonline.co.uk/tol/arts_and_entertainment/film/film_reviews/article1311586.ece). *The Times* (London). . Retrieved 2009-08-22.

[6] "Notes on a Scandal (2006)" (http://uk.rottentomatoes.com/m/notes_on_a_scandal/?critic=creamcrop). *Rotten Tomatoes*. . Retrieved 2009-08-22.

[7] Hunter, Stephen (2006-12-27). "'Scandal': A Lesson Not Soon Forgotten" (http://www.washingtonpost.com/wp-dyn/content/article/2006/12/26/AR2006122601009.html). *The Washington Post*. . Retrieved 2009-08-22.

[8] "Critics: Who Doesn't Love a Good Scandal?" (http://content.foxsearchlight.com/blogonascandal/node/589). *Fox Searchlight*. . Retrieved 2009-08-22.

[9] "NOTES ON A SCANDAL (2007)" (http://www.boxofficemojo.com/movies/?id=notesonascandal.htm). *Box Office Mojo*. . Retrieved 07-06-2009.

[10] Gritten, David (2007-01-26). "How to make a scandalously good movie" (http://www.telegraph.co.uk/culture/film/3662746/How-to-make-a-scandalously-good-movie.html).*The Telegraph* (London). . Retrieved 2009-08-22.

External links

- *Notes on a Scandal* (http://www.imdb.com/title/tt0465551/) at the Internet Movie Database
- *Notes on a Scandal* (http://www.rottentomatoes.com/m/notes_on_a_scandal/) at Rotten Tomatoes
- *Notes on a Scandal* (http://www.allmovie.com/work/326925) at Allmovie

Casino Royale (2006 film)

Casino Royale	
 Theatrical release poster	
James Bond	Daniel Craig
Also starring	• Eva Green • Mads Mikkelsen • Judi Dench • Jeffrey Wright
Directed by	Martin Campbell
Produced by	• Michael G. Wilson • Barbara Broccoli
Novel/Story by	Ian Fleming
Screenplay by	• Neal Purvis • Robert Wade • Paul Haggis
Cinematography	Phil Meheux
Music by	David Arnold
Main theme	"You Know My Name"
Composer	• David Arnold • Chris Cornell
Performer	Chris Cornell
Editing by	Stuart Baird
Studio	Pinewood Studios BarrandovStudios
Distributed by	• Columbia Pictures • Metro-Goldwyn-Mayer
Release date(s)	November 17, 2006
Running time	144 minutes

Country	• United States • United Kingdom • Denmark • Czech Republic
Budget	$150 million
Worldwide gross	$594,239,066[1]
Preceded by	*Die Another Day*
Followed by	*Quantum of Solace*

Casino Royale (2006) is the 21st film in the James Bond film series and the first to star Daniel Craig as MI6 agent James Bond. It was directed by Martin Campbell and written by Neal Purvis, Robert Wade, and Paul Haggis. *Casino Royale* is set at the beginning of Bond's career as Agent 007, just as he is earning his licence to kill. After preventing a terrorist attack at Miami International Airport, Bond falls for Vesper Lynd, the treasury agent assigned to provide the money he needs to foil Le Chiffre's plans by beating him in a high-stakes poker game. The story arc continues in the following Bond film, *Quantum of Solace* (2008).

The film is a reboot, establishing a new timeline and narrative framework not meant to precede or succeed any previous Bond film.[2] This allowed the film to show a less experienced and more vulnerable Bond.[3] Casting the film involved a widespread search for a new actor to portray James Bond, and significant controversy around Craig when he was selected to succeed Pierce Brosnan in October 2005. Location filming took place in the Bahamas, Italy, and the United Kingdom with interior sets built at Pinewood Studios. *Casino Royale* was produced by EON Productions for Metro-Goldwyn-Mayer and Columbia Pictures, making it the first official Bond film to be co-produced by the latter studio. It is the third screen adaptation of Ian Fleming's 1953 novel of the same name, which was previously produced as a 1954 television episode and a 1967 satirical film.

Casino Royale premiered at the Odeon Leicester Square on November 14, 2006. It received largely positive critical response, with reviewers highlighting Craig's performance and the reinvention of the character of Bond. It earned over $594 million worldwide, making it the highest-grossing James Bond film to date.

Plot

In the opening sequence, James Bond is on a mission that, if successful, will qualify him for double-0 status. He goes to Prague and kills an MI6 section chief, Dryden, who has leaked classified information, and his ally, Fisher. Elsewhere, Mr. White serves as a middleman introducing a banker, Le Chiffre, to a guerrilla group seeking a safe haven for its funds. Le Chiffre assures them that there is "no risk in the portfolio", but his investments actually involve considerable risk: he short-sells stock in successful companies and then engineers terrorist attacks to sink their share prices.

In his first mission as Agent 007, Bond goes to Madagascar in pursuit of an international bomb-maker named Mollaka. After a free running chase to the Nambutu embassy, Bond kills his target and blows up a part of the building in order to escape. He obtains Mollaka's mobile phone and discovers that it has received calls from Alex Dimitrios, an associate of Le Chiffre in the Bahamas. Bond travels there and seduces Dimitros' wife, Solange. While answering a phone call, Solange reveals that her husband is flying to Miami. Bond leaves to pursue him. In Miami, 007 kills Dimitrios and then follows Le Chiffre's henchman, Carlos, to the Miami Airport. There, Bond foils Le Chiffre's plan to destroy the prototype *Skyfleet* airliner and thus leaves the banker with a major loss.

Now under pressure to recoup his clients' money, Le Chiffre sets up a high-stakes Texas hold 'em tournament at the Casino Royale in Montenegro. Hoping that a defeat would force Le Chiffre to aid the British government in exchange for protection from his creditors, MI6 enters Bond into the tournament. He meets up with Mathis, his ally in Montenegro, and Vesper Lynd, a Treasury agent, who is assigned to look after his handling of the $10 million buy-in. After the tournament is underway for some time, Bond loses his initial stake. Vesper says that it would be a waste of money to continue to stake Bond and refuses to give him the $5 million he needs for a re-buy so he can continue playing.

Distraught over his failure, Bond resolves to assassinate Le Chiffre. Before he can, CIA agent Felix Leiter, who is also playing in the tournament, intervenes and offers to stake Bond in exchange for custody of Le Chiffre. Back in the game, Bond begins to amass chips. Le Chiffre and his associates attempt to kill Bond by poisoning his drink, but he survives and wins the tournament. Soon afterward, Le Chiffre abducts Vesper and uses her to lure Bond into a near-fatal car chase, which results in his capture as well. Le Chiffre tortures Bond's genitals for the access code to the game's winnings. When it becomes clear that Bond will not give in, Le Chiffre advances to castrate him, but Mr. White enters and kills Le Chiffre and his associates for their failure. Bond and Vesper are left alive.

Bond awakens in a hospital on Lake Como and orders Mathis, whom Le Chiffre identified as a double agent, arrested. Bond admits his love for Vesper and vows to quit the service before it strips him of his humanity. Accordingly, he posts his resignation to M and goes on a romantic holiday in Venice with Vesper. However, Bond soon learns that his poker winnings were never deposited in the Treasury's account. Realizing that Vesper has stolen them, he pursues her and members of the organization she is working for into a building under renovation. After killing the enemy guards outside and inside the building, Bond finds Vesper imprisoned in an elevator. Apologizing to him tearfully, she locks the inside door and the elevator plunges underwater. Bond attempts to rescue her, but she drowns before he can reach her. Mr. White, watching from a balcony, walks away with the money.

Bond, feeling betrayed, learns from M that Vesper had a French-Algerian boyfriend who was kidnapped by the organization behind Le Chiffre and Mr. White and that she agreed to deliver the money only if they would consent to leave Bond alive. He then discovers White's name and number in Vesper's mobile phone. White, arriving at a palatial estate near Lake Como, receives a phone call. As soon as he answers, he is shot in the leg. As he painfully crawls towards the villa, Bond appears, gun in hand, and responds, "The name's Bond. James Bond."

Cast

- Daniel Craig as James Bond: A British agent who, after being assigned 00-status, is sent on a mission to arrest a bomb maker in Madagascar, where he stumbles upon Le Chiffre's terrorist cell and is then sent to defeat him in a high-stakes poker game at Casino Royale.
- Eva Green as Vesper Lynd: An agent for HM Treasury assigned to supervise Bond and finance his poker table exploits.
- Mads Mikkelsen as Le Chiffre: Main villain. A banker who services many of the world's terrorists. He is a mathematical genius and chess expert, and uses these skills when playing poker.
- Judi Dench as M: The strict head of MI6. Though she feels she has promoted Bond too soon and expresses abhorrence of his rash actions, she acts as an important maternal figure in his life. Dench was the only cast member carried through from the Brosnan films.
- Jeffrey Wright as Felix Leiter: A quiet CIA operative participating in the poker tournament while assisting Bond. This is the first official Bond film in which Leiter is played by a black actor. (The only other black actor to portray Felix Leiter was Bernie Casey in *Never Say Never Again*, which was not produced by EON.)
- Giancarlo Giannini as René Mathis: Bond's contact in Montenegro.
- Simon Abkarian as Alex Dimitrios: Another contractor in the international terrorist underworld and associate of Le Chiffre, based in the Bahamas.
- Caterina Murino as Solange Dimitrios: Dimitrios's wife, whom Bond seduces. She is killed by Le Chiffre for unintentionally revealing one of his plans to Bond.
- Ivana Miličević as Valenka: Le Chiffre's girlfriend.
- Isaach De Bankolé as Steven Obanno: A feared leader of the Lord's Resistance Army, introduced to Le Chiffre by Mr. White to account his finances.
- Jesper Christensen as Mr. White: A mysterious liaison for an unnamed terrorist organisation.

- Sébastien Foucan as Mollaka: A bombmaker pursued by Bond through a construction site in Madagascar.
- Tobias Menzies as Villiers: M's young secretary at MI6 Headquarters.
- Ludger Pistor as Mendel: A Swiss banker responsible for all monetary transactions during and after the poker tournament.
- Claudio Santamaria as Carlos: A terrorist employed by Le Chiffre to blow up an aircraft.
- Clemens Schick as Kratt: Le Chiffre's bald bodyguard who often accompanies his boss wherever he travels
- Joseph Millson as Carter: An MI6 agent who accompanies Bond in Madagascar.
- Immanuel-Roger Abraham as Williams: An MI6 agent who debriefs Bond in London.
- Daud Shah as Fisher: Dryden's underground contact whom he is paying to find out and sell the secrets of MI6 and M sends 007 to kill him. He is killed from a shot by 007 to his head after feigning his drowning death after a long fight in a men's washroom in Pakistan.

Casino Royale includes a cameo by British entrepreneur Richard Branson (seen being frisked at Miami airport). The cameo was cut out of the in-flight versions shown on all airlines' in-flight entertainment systems, as was a shot of the Virgin Atlantic aircraft Branson supplied.[4]

Production

EON Productions gained the rights for *Casino Royale* in 1999 after Sony Pictures Entertainment exchanged them for MGM's rights to *Spider-Man*.[5] In March 2004, Neal Purvis and Robert Wade began writing a screenplay for Pierce Brosnan as Bond, aiming to bring back an Ian Fleming flavor.[6] Paul Haggis' main contribution was to rewrite the climax of the film. He explained, "the draft that was there was very faithful to the book and there was a confession, so in the original draft the character confessed and killed herself. She then sent Bond to chase after the villains; Bond chased the villains into the house. I don't know why but I thought that Vesper had to be in the sinking house and Bond has to want to kill her and then try and save her."[7]

Director Quentin Tarantino expressed interest in directing an adaptation of the *Casino Royale* novel,[8] though this was only a personal interest, and he did not follow this up with EON. Tarantino also expressed interest *Casino Royale* after *Pulp Fiction*. He claims to have worked behind the scenes with the Fleming family, and believed this was the reason why filmmakers finally went ahead with *Casino Royale*.[9] In February 2005, Martin Campbell was announced as the film's director.[10] Later in 2005, Sony led a consortium that purchased MGM, allowing Sony to gain distribution rights starting with the film.[11]

EON admitted that they had relied too heavily on CGI effects in the more recent films, particularly *Die Another Day*, and were keen to accomplish the stunts in *Casino Royale* "the old fashioned way".[12] In keeping with this drive for more realism, screenwriters Purvis, Wade, and Haggis wanted the script to follow as closely as possible to the original 1953 novel, keeping Fleming's darker storyline and characterisation of Bond.[13]

Casino Royale became the first Bond film to take its title from a Fleming novel or short story since 1987's *The Living Daylights*. It is also the first Bond film since then not to be adapted as a novelisation. Instead, a film tie-in edition of Fleming's original novel was published.[14]

Casting

Pierce Brosnan had originally signed a deal for four films when he was cast in the role of James Bond. This was fulfilled with the production of *Die Another Day* in 2002. However, at this stage Brosnan was approaching his 50th birthday, and speculation began that the producers were seeking to replace him with a younger actor.[15] Brosnan officially announced he was stepping down in February 2005. At one point producer Michael G. Wilson claimed there was a list of over 200 names being considered for his replacement.[16] According to Martin Campbell, Henry Cavill was the only actor in serious contention for the role. But being only 22 years old at the time, he was considered too young.[17] Sam Worthington was also considered.[18]

In May 2005, Daniel Craig announced that MGM and producers Michael G. Wilson and Barbara Broccoli had assured him that he would get the role of Bond, and Matthew Vaughn told reporters that MGM offered him the opportunity to direct, but EON Productions at that point had not approached either of them.[19] A year beforehand, Craig rejected the offer as he felt the series had descended into formula: only when he read the script did he become interested. Craig read all of Fleming's novels to prepare for the part, and cited Mossad and British Secret Service agents who served as advisors on the set of *Munich* as inspiring because, "Bond has just come out of the service and he's a killer. [...] You can see it in their eyes, you know immediately: oh, hello, he's a killer. There's a look. These guys walk into a room and very subtly they check the perimeters for an exit. That's the sort of thing I wanted."[20]

On 14 October 2005, EON Productions, Sony Pictures Entertainment, and MGM announced at a press conference in London that Craig would be the sixth actor to portray James Bond.[21] A tuxedo-clad Craig arrived via a Royal Navy speedboat.[22] Significant controversy followed the decision, as it was doubted if the producers had made the right choice. Throughout the entire production period Internet campaigns such as danielcraigisnotbond.com expressed their dissatisfaction and threatened to boycott the film in protest.[23] Craig, unlike previous actors, was not considered by the protesters to fit the tall, dark, handsome and charismatic image of Bond to which viewers had been accustomed.[24] *The Daily Mirror* ran a front page news story critical of Craig, with the headline, *The Name's Bland- James Bland.*[25]

The next important casting was that of the lead Bond girl, Vesper Lynd. Casting director Debbie McWilliams acknowledged that Hollywood actresses Angelina Jolie and Charlize Theron were "strongly considered" for the role and that Belgian actress Cécile de France had also auditioned, but her English accent "wasn't up to scratch."[26] Audrey Tautou was also considered, but not chosen because of her role in *The Da Vinci Code* that was released in May 2006.[27] It was announced on February 16, 2006 that Eva Green would play the part.[28]

Filming

Principal photography for *Casino Royale* commenced on 30 January 2006 and concluded on 21 July 2006. The film was primarily shot at Barrandov Studios in Prague, with additional location shooting in the Bahamas, Italy, and the United Kingdom. The shoot concluded at Pinewood Studios.[29]

Craig in Venice during filming.

Initially, Michael G. Wilson confirmed that *Casino Royale* would either be filmed or take place in Prague and South Africa. However, EON Productions encountered problems in securing film locations in South Africa.[30] After no other locations became available, the producers had to reconsider their options. In September 2005, Martin Campbell and director of photography Phil Meheux were scouting Paradise Island in the Bahamas as a possible location for the film.[31] On 6 October 2005, Martin Campbell confirmed that *Casino Royale* would film in the Bahamas and "maybe Italy". In addition to the extensive location filming, studio work including choreography and stunt coordination practice was performed at the Barrandov Studios in Prague and at Pinewood Studios where the film used several stages as well as the paddock tank and the historic 007 Stage. Further shooting in the UK was scheduled for Dunsfold Aerodrome in Surrey, the cricket pavilion at Eton College (although that particular scene was cut from the completed movie) and the Millbrook Vehicle Proving Ground in Bedfordshire.[24]

After Prague, the production moved to the Bahamas. Several locations around New Providence were used for filming during February and March, particularly on Paradise Island. Footage set in Mbale, Uganda was filmed at Black Park, Country Park in Buckinghamshire on 4 July 2006. Additional scenes took place at Albany House, an estate owned by golfers Ernie Els and Tiger Woods.[32] The crew returned to the Czech Republic in April, and continued there, filming in Prague, Planá and Loket, before completing in the town of Karlovy Vary in May. A famous Czech spa, Karlovy Vary, in German known as the Karlsbad, was used as the exterior of the Casino Royale, with the Grandhotel Pupp serving as "Hotel Splendide".[33] The main Italian location was Venice, where the majority of the film's ending is set. Other scenes in the later half of the film were shot in late May and early June at the Villa del Balbianello on the shores of Lake Como.[34] Further exterior shooting for the movie took place at properties such as the Villa la Gaeta, near the lakeside town of Menaggio.[24]

A recreation of the Body Worlds exhibit provided a setting for one scene in the film. Among the Body Worlds plastinates featured in that scene were the *Poker Playing Trio* [35] (which plays a key role in one scene) and *Rearing Horse and Rider* [36]. The exhibition's developer and promoter, German anatomist Gunther von Hagens, also has a cameo appearance in the film,[35] although only his trademark hat is actually visible on screen.

On 30 July 2006, a fire broke out at the 007 Stage. The damage was significant, but had no effect on the release of *Casino Royale* as the incident occurred one week after filming had been completed, and the sets were in the process of being dismantled.[36] On 11 August 2006, Pinewood Studios confirmed that no attempt would be made to salvage the remains of the stage,[37] instead it would be rebuilt from scratch.[38]

Effects

In designing the credit sequence for the film, graphic designer Daniel Kleinman was inspired by the cover of the 1953 British first edition of *Casino Royale*, which featured Ian Fleming's original design of a playing card bordered by eight red hearts dripping with blood. Kleinman said, "The hearts not only represent cards but the tribulations of Bond's love story. So I took that as inspiration to use playing card graphics in different ways in the titles," like a club representing a puff of gun smoke, and slashed arteries spurting thousands of tiny hearts.[39] In creating the shadow images of the sequence, Kleinman digitised the footage of Craig and the film's stuntmen on the Inferno visual effects system, at Framestore CFC in London; the actors' silhouettes were incorporated into more than 20 digitally animated scenes depicting intricate and innovative card patterns. Kleinman decided not to use the female silhouettes commonly seen throughout the Bond title sequences, considering that the women did not fit with both the film's spirit and the storyline following Bond falling in love.[40]

For the rest of the film, Special Effects and Miniature Effects Supervisor Chris Corbould returned to a more realistic style of film making and significantly reduced digital effects. According to Corbould, "CGI is a great tool and can be very useful, but I will fight to the tooth and nail to do something for real. It's the best way to go".[29] Three scenes involving primarily physical effects in the film were the chase at a building site in Madagascar, the Miami Airport chase sequence, and the sinking Venetian house, with sets located on the Grand Canal and in Pinewood Studios.[29]

First on the schedule were the scenes on the Madagascar building site, shot in the Bahamas on the site of a derelict hotel which Michael G. Wilson had become acquainted with in 1977 during the filming of *The Spy Who Loved Me*.[29] In the scene, Bond drives a digger toward the building, slamming into the concrete plinth on which Mollaka is running. The stunt team built a model and put forward several ways in which the digger could conceivably take out the concrete, including taking out the pillar underneath. A section of the concrete wall was removed to fit the digger, and reinforced with steel.[29]

The sequence at Miami International Airport was partly shot at the Dunsfold Aerodrome in Surrey, with some footage from the Prague and Miami airports.[29] In filming the scene in which the engine thrust of the moving aircraft blows the police car high into the air, second unit directors Ian Lowe, Terry Madden, and Alex Witt used a crane with a strong lead cable attached to the rear bumper of the vehicle to move it up and backwards at the moment of full extension away from the plane.[29]

The Skyfleet S570 aircraft in the film was an ex-British Airways 747-200B G-BDXJ which had its engines removed and was modified for its appearance in the film. The modified aircraft had the outboard engines replaced by external fuel tanks, while the inboard engines were replaced by a mockup pair of engines on each inboard pylon. The cockpit profile was altered to make the 747 look like a prototype of an advanced airliner.[41] The plane used can be seen on the BBC Motoring programme *Top Gear* on the Test Track.

The sinking of the Venetian house at the climax of the film featured the largest rig ever built for a Bond film.[29] For the scene involving Bond following Vesper into the house undergoing renovation supported by inflatable balloons, a tank was constructed at the 007 stage at Pinewood, consisting of a Venetian piazza and the interior of the three-story dilapidated house. The rig, weighing some 90 tons, incorporated electronics with hydraulic valves which were closely controlled by computer because of the dynamic movement within the system on its two axes. The same computer system also controlled the exterior model which the effects team built to one-third scale to film the building eventually collapsing into the Venetian canal. The model elevator within the rig could be immersed in 19 feet (5.8 m) of water, and used banks of compressors to strictly regulate movement.[29]

The scene involving the car crash was devised using an Aston Martin DB9 that was especially modified to look like Bond's Aston Martin DBS V12 and reinforced to withstand the impact. Due to the low centre of gravity of the vehicle, an 18-inch (450 mm) ramp had to be implemented on the road tarmac at Millbrook Proving Grounds and stunt driver Adam Kirley had to use an air cannon located behind the driver's seat to propel the car into a roll at the precise moment of impact. At a speed exceeding 70 mph (113 km/h), the car rotated seven times while being filmed, and was confirmed by the Guinness Book of Records on 5 November 2006 as a new world record.[29]

Music

The soundtrack of *Casino Royale*, released by Sony Classical on 14 November 2006 featured music composed by veteran composer David Arnold, his fourth soundtrack for the Bond film series, while Nicholas Dodd orchestrated and conducted the score. Producers Michael G. Wilson and Barbara Broccoli announced on 26 July 2006 that Chris Cornell, who was the lead singer for Audioslave and Soundgarden, composed and performed the title song "You Know My Name".[42] The song's main notes are played throughout the film as a substitute for the James Bond theme, to represent Bond's immaturity. The classic theme only plays during the end credits to signal the end of his character arc.[43]

Release

Casino Royale premiered at the Odeon Leicester Square, the Odeon West End and the Empire simultaneously in London on 14 November 2006. It marked the 60th Royal Film Performance and benefited the Cinema & Television Benevolent Fund (CTBF), whose patron, Queen Elizabeth II, was in attendance at with the Duke of Edinburgh. It is the third James Bond premiere that the Queen attended following *You Only Live Twice* and *Die Another Day*.[44] Along with the cast and crew, numerous celebrities and 5,000 paying guests were also in attendance with half the proceeds benefiting the CTBF.[45]

Only two days following the premiere, pirated copies appeared for sale in London. "The rapid appearance of this film on the streets shows the sophistication and organisation behind film piracy in the UK," said Kieron Sharp, from the Federation Against Copyright Theft.[46] Pirated copies of the DVD were selling for less than £1.57. Craig himself was offered such a DVD while walking anonymously through the streets of Beijing wearing a hat and glasses in order to avoid being identified.[47]

In January 2007, *Casino Royale* became the first Bond film ever to be shown in mainland Chinese cinemas. The Chinese version was edited before release, with the reference to the Cold War re-dubbed and new dialogue added during the poker scene explaining the process of Texas Hold'em, as the game is less familiar in China (this addition is reminiscent of dialogue that was added to the 1954 American TV adaptation in order to explain the rules of baccarat, the game featured in the original book). *Casino Royale* earned approximately $11.7 million in China since its opening on 30 January on 468 screens,[48] including a record opening weekend collection for a non-Chinese film, with $1.5 million.[49]

After critics dubbed *Die Another Day* "Buy Another Day" because of around twenty product placement deals, EON limited their promotions for *Casino Royale*. Partners included Ford Motors, Heineken Pilsener (which Eva Green starred in adverts for), Smirnoff, Omega SA, Virgin Atlantic Airways and Sony Ericsson.[50]

Box office

The film achieved GB£2 million of ticket sales in the UK on its first day of release. Weekend opening total in the UK was GB£13,400,000. The film also opened in the Republic of Ireland with over €1,100,000 in the first 2 weeks. Altogether the film took about €4,200,000 in Ireland. From 16 November to 19 November 2006, the film took in over $40,000,000.[51]

Opening day estimates in the United States and Canada showed *Casino Royale* on top with $14,750,000, while opening weekend estimates showed it in second place with $40,600,000,[52] as well as earning another $42,000,000 internationally. Although *Happy Feet* won the overall weekend box office contest, the significance of such a comparison in earnings is problematic, as *Happy Feet* has little more than half the running time of *Casino Royale*, and therefore had significantly more screenings per day, which translates into more potential gross. A better indication of the film's relative performances is that *Casino Royale*, per theatre, outperformed *Happy Feet*, which was released in 370 more theatres. According to Box Office Mojo, *Casino Royale* took in, on average, $11,890 per theatre, while *Happy Feet* grossed $10,918 per theatre.[1] [53]

Casino Royale opened at the first position in 27 countries, with a weekend gross of $43,407,886 worldwide.[1] As of 10 February 2010, it has grossed over $594 million worldwide,[54] breaking both the domestic and international box office records of *Die Another Day*. The film held the opening weekend record in India, taking in over $3,386,987, which was the highest for a foreign language film at the time.[55] [56] In Russia, the film made over $4.5 million, the eighth largest opening for a non-Russian film.[57]

Accounting for inflation, *Casino Royale* is currently the fifth most successful of all James Bond films, behind *Thunderball*, *Goldfinger*, *You Only Live Twice*, and *The Spy Who Loved Me*. It achieved the highest inflation-adjusted gross for a James Bond film since 1977.

Home media

Casino Royale was simultaneously released on DVD, UMD, and Blu-ray Disc on 16 March 2007.[58] In the UK, *Casino Royale* was released on 16 March 2007 on DVD and Blu-ray Disc.[59] The DVD and Blu-ray Disc releases broke sales records: the region 1 Blu-ray Disc edition became the highest selling high-definition title to date, selling more than 100,000 copies since its release.[60] The region 2 DVD edition achieved the record of fastest selling title for its first-week release. The UK DVD has continued to sell well, with 1,622,852 copies sold since March 19.[61] A copy of the Blu-ray Disc edition of *Casino Royale* was given out to the first 500,000 PAL PlayStation 3 owners who signed up to the PlayStation Network.[62] The DVD release includes the official music video for the film, and three documentaries detailing how Daniel Craig was chosen for the role of Bond, the filming, and an expanded version of the *Bond Girls Are Forever* documentary incorporating new interviews with *Casino Royale* cast members.

A two-disc edition of *Casino Royale* on DVD was released in the United Kingdom on 31 October 2008, coinciding with the theatrical release of *Quantum of Solace* (the following week in the United States). As well as features present from the 2007 release, the collector's edition contains an audio commentary, deleted scenes, featurettes and a storyboard-to-film comparison.[63] A two-disc Blu-Ray version also followed in late 2008, featuring additional supplementary materials, enhanced interactivity through BD-Live, and the previous version's 5.1 PCM soundtrack was replaced with a similar 5.1 Dolby TrueHD soundtrack.

Reception

Reviews

Critics gave the film a positive response, in particular Craig's performance and credibility. During production this had been subject to debate by the media and the public, as Craig did not appear to fit Ian Fleming's original portrait of the character as tall, dark, and suave. *The Daily Telegraph* compared the quality of Craig's characterization of Bond to Sean Connery's and praised the script as smartly written, noting how the film departed from the series' conventions. *The Times* compared the more assertive portrayal by Craig to Timothy Dalton, and praised the action as edgy,[64] with another reviewer citing in particular the action sequence involving the cranes in Madagascar.[65] Critics Paul Arendt of BBC Films,[66] Kim Newman of *Empire*[67] and Todd McCarthy of *Variety*[68] all described Craig as the first actor to truly embody Ian Fleming's James Bond from the original novel: ironic, brutal, and cold.

The film was similarly well received in North America. MSNBC gave the movie a perfect 5 star rating.[69] The film was described as taking James Bond "back to his roots", similar to *From Russia with Love*,[70] where the focus was on character and plot rather than the high-tech gadgets and visual effects that were strongly criticised in *Die Another Day*.[68] *Rotten Tomatoes* gave the movie an aggregate rating of 94%, the highest rating for a wide-release of the year. It is the fourth-highest rating for a Bond film on the site behind *Goldfinger* which received a 96%, *From Russia with Love* which received a 96%,[71] [72] and *Dr. No*, with a 98% score.[73] Metacritic gave the movie a Metascore of 81, signifying "Universal Acclaim."[74] *Entertainment Weekly* named the film as the fifth best of the series,[75] and chose Vesper Lynd as the fourth best Bond girl in the series.[76] Some newspaper columnists and critics were impressed enough by Craig's performance to consider him a viable candidate for an Academy Award nomination.[77] [78] [79] Roger Ebert gave the film a four out of four star rating, the first for any of the James Bond films he reviewed. Ebert wrote that "Craig makes a superb Bond", "who gives the sense of a hard man, wounded by life and his job, who nevertheless cares about people and right and wrong", and that the film "has the answers to all my complaints about the 45-year-old James Bond series", specifically "why nobody in a Bond movie ever seems to have any real emotions."[80]

Vicky Allan of the *Sunday Herald* noted Bond himself, and not his love interests, was sexually objectified in this film. A moment where he rises from the sea is reminiscent of Ursula Andress in *Dr. No*; he feels "skewered" by Vesper Lynd's criticism of him; "and though it would be almost unthinkable now have a female character in a mainstream film stripped naked and threatened with genital mutilation, that is exactly what happens to Bond in [the film]." So although the film backed off from past criticism of Bond girls being sex objects, "the once invincible James Bond becomes just another joint at the meat market".[81] This sentiment is shared by the University of Leicester's James Chapman, author of *License to Thrill*, who also notes Craig's Bond is "not yet the polished article"; he felt his incarnation of Bond is close to Fleming's because he is "humourless", but is also different because "Fleming's Bond did not enjoy killing; Craig's Bond seems almost to relish it."[82]

Roger Moore wrote, "Daniel Craig impressed me so greatly in his debut outing, *Casino Royale*, by introducing a more gritty, unrefined edge to the character that I thought Sean might just have to move over. Craig's interpretation was like nothing we'd seen on screen before; Jimmy Bond was earning his stripes and making mistakes. It was intriguing to see him being castigated by M, just like a naughty schoolboy would be by his headmaster. The script showed him as a vulnerable, troubled and flawed character. Quite the opposite to my Bond! Craig was, and is, very much the Bond Ian Fleming had described in the books – a ruthless killing machine. It was a Bond that the public wanted." So impressed was Moore that he chose to buy the DVD.[83] Raymond Benson, the author of nine Bond novels, called *Casino Royale* "a perfect Bond film."[84]

However, the film met with mixed reactions from other critics. Rob Gonsalves of eFilmCritic.com gave the film a positive review, but commented, "When you strip the 007 films down for action and 'realism,' you lose the soul of those old beloved Bond movies — they might as well be Jason Bourne movies."[85] John Beifuss of The Commercial Appeal, said "Who wants to see Bond learn a lesson about ego, as if he were Greg Brady in his 'Johnny Bravo' phase?"[86] Anthony Lane of the New Yorker criticised the more imperfect and self-aware depiction of the character, saying, "Even James Bond, in other words, wants to be 007." [87]

Though American radio personality Michael Medved gave the film three stars out of four, describing it as "intriguing, audacious and very original... more believable and less cartoonish, than previous 007 extravaganzas," he commented that the "sometimes sluggish pacing will frustrate some Bond fanatics."[88] Similarly, a reviewer for *The Sun* praised the film for its darkness and Craig's performance, but felt that "like the novel, it suffers from a lack of sharpness in the plot" and believed that it required additional editing, particularly the finale.[89] Commentators such as Emanuel Levy concurred, feeling the ending was too long, and that the film's terrorist villains lacked depth, although he praised Craig and gave the film a B+ overall.[90] Other reviewers responded negatively, including Tim Adams of *The Observer* who felt the film came off uncomfortably in an attempt to make the series grittier.[91]

The opening shot of Craig sporting swimming trunks topped the sexiest male celebrity poll of *The Sun*,[92] and in 2009 Del Monte Foods launched an ice lolly moulded to resemble Craig emerging from the sea.[93] In 2008, *Entertainment Weekly* named it the 19th best film of the past quarter-century.[94]

Top Ten Lists

The film appeared on many critics' top ten lists of the best films of 2006.[95]

- 1st - Owen Gleiberman, *Entertainment Weekly*
- 3rd - *Empire*
- 3rd - Marc Moha, *The Oregonian*
- 3rd - Stephanie Zacharek, *Salon.com*
- 3rd - William Arnold, *Seattle Post-Intelligencer*
- 7th - Jack Mathews, *New York Daily News*
- 8th - *James Berardinelli*, ReelViews
- 8th - Desson Thomson, *Washington Post*
- 8th - Michael Phillips, *Chicago Tribune*
- 9th - Stephen Hunter, *Washington Post*
- 10th - Michael Wilmington, *Chicago Tribune*
- 10th - Mike Russell, *The Oregonian*

Awards

At the 2006 British Academy of Film and Television Arts Awards, *Casino Royale* won the Film Award for Best Sound (Chris Munro, Eddy Joseph, Mike Prestwood Smith, Martin Cantwell, Mark Taylor), and the Orange Rising Star Award, which was won by Eva Green.[96] The film was nominated for eight BAFTA awards, including the Alexander Korda Award for Best British Film of the Year; Best Screenplay (Neal Purvis, Robert Wade, Paul Haggis); the Anthony Asquith Award for Best Film Music (David Arnold); Best Cinematography (Phil Meheux); Best Editing (Stuart Baird); Best Production Design (Peter Lamont, Simon Wakefield); Best Achievement in Special Visual Effects (Steve Begg, Chris Corbould, John Paul Docherty, Ditch Doy); and Best Actor (Daniel Craig). This made Craig the first actor ever to receive a BAFTA nomination for a performance as James Bond.[97] He also received the Evening Standard British Film Award for Best Actor.[98]

Casino Royale won the Excellence in Production Design Award from the Art Directors Guild,[99] and singer Chris Cornell's "You Know My Name" won the International Press Academy Satellite Award for Best Original Song.[100] The film was nominated for five Saturn Awards— Best Action/Adventure/Thriller Film, Best Actor (Daniel Craig), Best Supporting Actress (Eva Green), Best Writing (Purvis, Wade and Haggis) and Best Music (David Arnold).[101] The 2006 Golden Tomato Awards named *Casino Royale* the Wide Release Film of the Year.[102] *Casino Royale* was also nominated for, and has won, many other international awards for its screenplay,[103] film editing,[104] visual effects,[105] and production design.[106] At the 2007 Saturn Awards, the film was declared to be the Best

Action/Adventure/Thriller film of 2006.[107] Several members of the crew were also recipients of 2007 Taurus World Stunt Awards, including Gary Powell for Best Stunt Coordination and Ben Cooke, Kai Martin, Marvin Stewart-Campbell, and Adam Kirley for Best High Work.[108]

Broadcast television versions

The film made its major network premiere on ABC on August 29, 2010. Scenes such as the torture scene were trimmed for obvious reasons. Scenes where Bond and Vesper make love in the hospital room and when Solange was riding her horse along the Jamaican beach were cut.

See also

- Differences between James Bond novels and films

References

[1] "Casino Royale (2006)" (http://www.boxofficemojo.com/movies/?id=jamesbond21.htm). *Box Office Mojo*. . Retrieved 2006-11-21.

[2] "IGN: Interview: Campbell on Casino Royale" (http://movies.ign.com/articles/659/659741p1.html).*IGN.com*. IGN Entertainment, Inc. 19 October 2005. . Retrieved 2007-03-22.

[3] "New James Bond Proves Worthy of Double-0 Status" (http://www.space.com/entertainment/061116_bond_review.html). *Space.com*. 21 October 2006. . Retrieved 2007-06-16.

[4] "BA cuts Branson from Bond movie" (http://news.bbc.co.uk/1/hi/entertainment/6579839.stm). *BBC News Online*. 21 April 2007. . Retrieved 2008-10-23.

[5] Sterngold, James (30 March 1999). "Sony Pictures, in an accord with MGM, drops its plan to produce new James Bond movies" (http://select.nytimes.com/gst/abstract.html?res=F30814FC35540C738FDDAA0894D1494D81&n=Top/News/Business/SmallBusiness/Marketing and Advertising). *The New York Times*. . Retrieved 2007-06-20.

[6] "Purvis & Wade Talk Bond & Jinx" (http://www.mi6.co.uk/sections/articles/event_purvis_wade_talk.php3?t=bond21&s=bond21). *MI6.co.uk*. 9 March 2004. . Retrieved 2007-03-10.

[7] Lawson, Mark (4 December 2007). "Paul Haggis" (http://www.guardian.co.uk/film/2007/dec/04/guardianinterviewsatbfisouthbank1). *guardian.co.uk* (London). . Retrieved 2007-12-07.

[8] "Kill Bill director aims for Bond" (http://news.bbc.co.uk/1/hi/entertainment/film/3718975.stm). *BBC News Online*. 16 May 2004. . Retrieved 2007-03-05.

[9] Heath, Chris (June 2007). "Quentin Tarantino Interview". *GQ*.

[10] EON Productions (3 February 2005). "James Bond 21 Is Casino Royale" (http://www.mi6.co.uk/sections/articles/bond_21_announced.php3). *MI6.co.uk*. . Retrieved 2007-03-10.

[11] Sony Corporation (23 September 2004). "Consortium Led by Sony Corporation of America, Providence Equity Partners, Texas Pacific Group, Comcast Corporation and DLJ Merchant Banking Partners Enters into Definitive Agreement to Acquire Metro-Goldwyn-Mayer" (http://www.sony.com/SCA/press/040924.shtml).Press release. . Retrieved 2007-04-29.

[12] Alberge, Dayla (14 March 2006). "Fake stunts banished as new Bond keeps it real" (http://www.thetimes.co.uk/tto/arts/film/article2433165.ece). *The Times* (London). . Retrieved 2006-11-21.

[13] Silberg, Jon (December 2006). "High Stakes for 007" (http://web.archive.org/web/20070402131840/http://www.ascmag.com/magazine_dynamic/December2006/CasinoRoyale/page1.php). *American Cinematographer*. Archived from the original (http://www.ascmag.com/magazine_dynamic/December2006/CasinoRoyale/page1.php)on April 2, 2007. . Retrieved 2007-04-17.

[14] "Casino Royale (movie tie-in) (James Bond OO7) (Paperback)" (http://www.amazon.com/gp/product/0143037668). Amazon.com. 31 October 2006. . Retrieved 2007-06-20.

[15] "Is Brosnan too old to be 007?" (http://www.dailymail.co.uk/tvshowbiz/article-207653/Is-Brosnan-old-007.html). *Daily Mail* (London). 9 February 2004. . Retrieved 2008-08-05.

[16] "Michael G. Wilson said 200 actors had been considered" (http://news.bbc.co.uk/1/hi/entertainment/film/4337224.stm). BBC.co.uk. November 14 2006. . Retrieved 2007-04-04.

[17] Chavez, Kellvin. "Exclusive interview with Martin Campbell on Zorro and Bond" (http://web.archive.org/web/20070418142549/http://www.latinoreview.com/films_2005/sonypictures/zorro2/mc-interview.html). *Latino Review*. Archived from the original (http://www.latinoreview.com/films_2005/sonypictures/zorro2/mc-interview.html) on 2007-04-18. . Retrieved 2007-03-23.

[18] Fleming, Michael (5 November 2008). "Casting begins for *War, Titans*" (http://www.variety.com/article/VR1117995318.html?categoryid=13&cs=1). *Variety*. . Retrieved 2008-11-08.

[19] "Craig, Vaughn on Bond" (http://filmforce.ign.com/articles/609/609721p1.html). *IGN*. 3 May 2005. . Retrieved 2006-08-10.

[20] Grant, Richard (11 October 2008). "Daniel Craig: Quantum of Solace" (http://www.telegraph.co.uk/arts/main.jhtml?xml=/arts/2008/10/11/sm_danielcraig111.xml). *The Daily Telegraph* (London). . Retrieved 2008-10-11.

[21] "Daniel Craig confirmed as 006th screen Bond" (http://www.guardian.co.uk/uk/2005/oct/14/film.filmnews).*guardian.co.uk* (London). 2005-10-14. . Retrieved 2007-05-15.

[22] "Film of the arrival" (http://shatterhand007.com/MadRoyale/MADROYALEDanielCraig007.wmv). . Retrieved 2010-09-12.

[23] "Anti-Craig Bond Fans Call for 'Casino Royale' Boycott" (http://web.archive.org/web/20070319164649/http://www.moono.com/news/news01533.html). *Moono*. February 23, 2006. Archived from the original (http://www.moono.com/news/news01533.html) on March 19, 2007. . Retrieved 2007-04-03.

[24] La Monica, Paul R. (6 November 2006). "Blond, James Blond" (http://money.cnn.com/2006/11/08/commentary/mediabiz/index.htm). *CNN*. . Retrieved 2007-04-02.

[25] "The Name's Bland.. James Bland" (http://www.mirror.co.uk/news/tm_objectid=16251427&method=full&siteid=94762&headline=the-name-s-bland---james-bland-name_page.html). *Daily Mirror*. 15 October 2005. . Retrieved 2006-12-27.

[26] "Casino Royale Bond girl candidates" (http://www.mi6.co.uk/sections/articles/bond_21_girl_casting_rumours.php3?t=bond21&s=bond21). *MI6.co.uk*. 7 July 2006. . Retrieved 2006-11-21.

[27] "The New Bond Girls!" (http://www.superherohype.com/news/jamesbondnews.php?id=4470). *Superhero Hype!*. 7 July 2006. . Retrieved 2006-03-04.

[28] "New Bond Girl Will Be "Very Much an Equal to Bond"" (http://us.imdb.com/news/sb/2006-02-17#film5). *Internet Movie Database*. . Retrieved 2007-03-23.

[29] *James Bond: For Real*. [DVD]. Special Treats Productions. 2006.

[30] Cox, John (8 August 2005). "Eon facing South African detour" (http://commanderbond.net/2877/eon-facing-south-african-detour.html). *CommanderBond.net*. . Retrieved 2006-11-21.

[31] Cox, John (13 September 2005). "Bond bound for Bahamas" (http://commanderbond.net/2922/bond-bound-for-bahamas.html). *CommanderBond.net*. . Retrieved 2006-11-21.

[32] "James Bond takes over Ernie and Tiger's pad" (http://web.archive.org/web/20060618111857/http://www.ernieels.com/search.aspx?i_MediaEntryID=506). Ernie Els Official Website. 12 June 2006. Archived from the original (http://www.ernieels.com/search.aspx?i_MediaEntryID=506) on 2006-06-18. . Retrieved 2006-11-21.

[33] "On set report from Casino Royale getaway chase sequence" (http://www.mi6.co.uk/news/index.php?itemid=3701&catid=2). *MI6.co.uk*. 23 May 2006. . Retrieved 2006-11-21.

[34] "OO7 Nel Bel Paese" (http://web.archive.org/web/20071011102258/qn.quotidiano.net/archivio_art.php?art=http://qn.quotidiano.net/2006/02/27/pages/artl5405032.html). *Il Giorno*. 25 February 2006. Archived from the original (http://qn1.quotidiano.net/chan/musica:5405032:/2006/02/27:) on September 29, 2007. . Retrieved 2007-06-20.

[35] Devin Zydel. "Casino Royale's Cold War Symbols, Featuring Body Worlds" (http://commanderbond.net/article/3742). *Commanderbond.net*. . Retrieved 2010-08-09.

[36] "Fire wrecks James Bond film stage" (http://news.bbc.co.uk/2/hi/uk_news/5228794.stm). *BBC News Online*. 30 July 2006. . Retrieved 2006-11-21.

[37] "007 stage destroyed by fire" (http://www.mi6.co.uk/sections/articles/event_pinewood_fire.php3?t=bond21&s=bond21). *MI6.co.uk*. 30 July 2006. . Retrieved 2006-11-21.

[38] "Pinewood receives planning permission to rebuild 007 stage, bigger than ever next year" (http://www.mi6.co.uk/news/index.php?itemid=4114&catid=4). *MI6.co.uk*. 21 September 2006. . Retrieved 2006-11-21.

[39] "Credits design" (http://www.mi6.co.uk/news/index.php?itemid=4511). *MI6.co.uk*. 6 December 2006. . Retrieved 2007-04-03.

[40] "Design / Casino Royale's Title Sequence" (http://www.framestore.com/#/Design/CasinoRoyale,TitleSequence).Framestore. . Retrieved 2010-01-29.

[41] "Boeing 747 in Casino Royale" (http://www.aerospaceweb.org/question/planes/q0297.shtml). .

[42] Columbia TriStar Motion Picture Group (26 July 2006). "Chris Cornell Has Written and Will Perform the Main Title Song for Casino Royale" (http://www.prnewswire.com/cgi-bin/stories.pl?ACCT=104&STORY=/www/story/07-26-2006/0004404210&EDATE=). Press release. . Retrieved 2006-07-26.

[43] Bregt De Lange and Mario Schuurmans. "Interview with David Arnold at the World Soundtrack Awards 2007" (http://www.maintitles.net/features/interview-david-arnold-wsa-2007). *maintitles.net*. . Retrieved 2008-03-16.

[44] "Daniel Craig makes his 007 debut at premiere of Casino Royale" (http://www.dailymail.co.uk/pages/live/articles/showbiz/showbiznews.html?in_article_id=416461&in_page_id=1773&ico=Homepage&icl=TabModule&icc=picbox&ct=5). *Daily Mail* (London). 18 November 2006. . Retrieved 2006-11-21.

[45] "Stars out for Bond royal premiere" (http://news.bbc.co.uk/1/hi/entertainment/6146090.stm). *BBC News Online*. 14 November 2006. . Retrieved 2006-11-21.

[46] "Studio claims 007 box office coup" (http://news.bbc.co.uk/2/hi/entertainment/6157066.stm). *BBC News Online*. 17 November 2006. . Retrieved 2007-02-28.

[47] "The name's Qi, Ling Ling Qi" (http://www.metro.co.uk/fame/article.html?in_article_id=35129&in_page_id=7).*Metro*. 29 January 2007. . Retrieved 2007-01-30.

[48] "Casino Royale (2006) - International Box Office" (http://boxofficemojo.com/movies/?page=intl&id=jamesbond21.htm). *Box Office Mojo*. . Retrieved 2007-03-29.

[49] Dave McNary (31 January 2007). "China shows 007 the love" (http://www.variety.com/article/VR1117958463.html?categoryid=13&cs=1&query=casino+royale). *Variety*. . Retrieved 2007-03-20.

[50] Graser, Marc (14 August 2008). "Brands line up for Bond sequel" (http://www.variety.com/article/VR1117990584.html?categoryid=13&cs=1). *Variety*. . Retrieved 2008-08-15.

[51] "Box Office History for James Bond Movies" (http://the-numbers.com/movies/series/JamesBond.php). *The Numbers*. . Retrieved 2007-11-08.

[52] "Casino Royale grosses $40.6 million" (http://www.superherohype.com/news/jamesbondnews.php?id=4922).*Superhero Hype!*. 19 November 2006. . Retrieved 2006-11-19.

[53] "Happy Feet (2006)" (http://www.boxofficemojo.com/movies/?id=happyfeet.htm). *Box Office Mojo*.. Retrieved 2006-11-21.

[54] Mohr, Ian (28 December 2006). "*Dreamgirls* banking on expansion" (http://www.variety.com/article/VR1117956403.html?categoryid=13&cs=1). *Variety*. . Retrieved 2006-12-30.

[55] "*Spider-Man 3* breaks all records!" (http://sify.com/movies/tamil/fullstory.php?id=14446385). Sify. 9 May 2007. . Retrieved 2007-05-27.

[56] "Bond breaks records" (http://www.thehindubusinessline.com/2006/12/23/stories/2006122301350500.htm). *Business Line*. 23 December 2006. . Retrieved 2007-05-06.

[57] "Russia - CIS Box Office November 16 – 19, 2006" (http://www.boxofficemojo.com/intl/cis/?yr=2006&wk=46&p=.htm). *Box Office Mojo*. 19 November 2006. . Retrieved 2007-06-20.

[58] "Casino Royale (2-Disc Widescreen Edition)" (http://www.amazon.com/Casino-Royale-Two-Disc-Widescreen-Daniel/dp/B000MNP2KI). Amazon.com. . Retrieved 2007-06-20.

[59] "Casino Royale and more from Sony!" (http://web.archive.org/web/20061216010557/http://www.dvdtimes.co.uk/content.php?contentid=63473). DVD Times. Archived from the original (http://www.dvdtimes.co.uk/content.php?contentid=63473) on December 16, 2006. . Retrieved 2006-12-09.

[60] "Casino Royale Blu-ray Reaches Unit Milestone" (http://movies.netscape.com/story/2007/03/28/casino-royale-blu-ray-reaches-unit-milestone). *Netscape*. 28 March 2007. . Retrieved 2007-06-20.

[61] "Bond Breaks Records" (http://www.empireonline.com/news/story.asp?NID=20554). *Empire Online*. 29 March 2007. . Retrieved 2007-03-29.

[62] "Casino Royale Blu-ray for PS3 early adopters" (http://www.eurogamer.net/article.php?article_id=72870).Eurogamer. 12 February 2007. . Retrieved 2007-07-05.

[63] "Casino Royale Collectors Edition DVD Preview" (http://www.mi6.co.uk/sections/articles/dvd_cr_collectors_edition_preview.php3?t=&s=&id=01966).*MI6.co.uk*. 29 July 2008. . Retrieved 2008-07-29.

[64] ""Brilliant" Bond seduces critics" (http://news.bbc.co.uk/1/hi/entertainment/6116286.stm?ls). *BBC News Online*. 4 November 2006. . Retrieved 2006-11-21.

[65] Wavell, Stuart (5 November 2006). "Potato Head shoots way to 007 triumph" (http://www.thesundaytimes.co.uk/sto/news/uk_news/article167203.ece). *The Sunday Times* (London). . Retrieved 2006-11-21.

[66] Arendt, Paul. "Casino Royale (2006)" (http://www.bbc.co.uk/films/2006/11/06/casino_royale_2006_review.shtml).*bbc.co.uk*. . Retrieved 2006-11-21.

[67] Newman, Kim. "Casino Royale" (http://www.empireonline.com/reviews/reviewcomplete.asp?FID=10199). *Empire Online*. . Retrieved 2006-11-21.

[68] McCarthy, Todd (2006-11-09). "Casino Royale" (http://www.variety.com/VE1117932077.html).*Variety*. . Retrieved 2006-11-21.

[69] Hartl, John. ""Casino Royale" is Prime Bond" (http://movies.msn.com/news/article.aspx?news=241821). *msnbc.com*. . Retrieved 2006-11-17.

[70] Honeycutt, Kirk (10 October 2006). "Casino Royale" (http://www.hollywoodreporter.com/hr/film/reviews/article_display.jsp?&rid=8223). *The Hollywood Reporter*. . Retrieved 2007-03-21.

[71] "The Spy Who Loved Me" (http://www.rottentomatoes.com/m/spy_who_loved_me/). *Rotten Tomatoes*.. Retrieved 2007-03-20.

[72] "From Russia With Love" (http://www.rottentomatoes.com/m/from_russia_with_love/). *Rotten Tomatoes*. . Retrieved 2007-03-20.

[73] "Dr. No" (http://www.rottentomatoes.com/m/dr_no/). *Rotten Tomatoes*. . Retrieved 2007-03-20.

[74] "Casino Royale at Metacritic" (http://www.metacritic.com/film/titles/casinoroyale?q=Casino Royale). *Metacritic*. . Retrieved 2007-08-19.

[75] Svetkey, Benjamin; Joshua Rich (24 November 2006). "Ranking the Bond Films" (http://www.ew.com/ew/article/0,,1560072_18,00.html). *Entertainment Weekly*. . Retrieved 2008-03-04.

[76] Rich, Joshua (30 March 2007). "The 10 Best Bond Girls" (http://www.ew.com/ew/article/0,,1557446_8,00.html).*Entertainment Weekly*. . Retrieved 2007-03-30.

[77] Caro, Mark (21 December 2006). "Bond, Oscar Bond" (http://www.webcitation.org/5rrTJ3Xcd). *Chicago Tribune*. Archived from the original (http://featuresblogs.chicagotribune.com/entertainment_popmachine/2006/12/bond_oscar_bond.html) on August 9, 2010. . Retrieved 2008-05-13.

[78] Boedecker, Hal (28 December 2006). "Hey Oscar, have you met James Bond?" (http://blogs.orlandosentinel.com/entertainment_tv_tvblog/2006/12/looking_ahead_t.html). *Orlando Sentinel*. . Retrieved 2008-05-13.

[79] Hammond, Pete (7 December 2006). "THE SEASON: As critics ramp up, dark horses are at the gate" (http://www.hollywoodwiretap.com/?module=news&action=story&id=9137). Hollywood Wiretap. . Retrieved 2008-05-13.

[80] Ebert, Roger (17 September 2007). "*Casino Royale* review" (http://rogerebert.suntimes.com/apps/pbcs.dll/article?AID=/20070816/REVIEWS/708160301/1023).*Chicago Sun-Times*. . Retrieved 2008-07-03.

[81] Allan, Vicky (27 October 2008). "For your eyes only?" (http://www.sundayherald.com/arts/arts/display.var.2463325.0.0.php). Sunday Herald. . Retrieved 2008-10-27.

[82] "Daniel Craig's Bond "relishes killing", professor claims" (http://www.inthenews.co.uk/printerfriendly.aspx?itemid=1246720). In the news. 28 October 2008. . Retrieved 2008-10-28.

[83] Moore, Roger (4 October 2008). "Bye bye to Ian Fleming's James Bond?" (http://www.webcitation.org/5rrWp8oPN). *The Times* (London). Archived from the original (http://entertainment.timesonline.co.uk/tol/arts_and_entertainment/film/london_film_festival/article4866756.ece) on 2010-08-09. . Retrieved 2008-10-05.

[84] "JAMES BOND AUTHOR RAYMOND BENSON REVIEWS THE ULTIMATE - Cinema Retro - Celebrating Films of the 1960s & 1970s" (http://www.cinemaretro.com/index.php?/archives/20-JAMES-BOND-AUTHOR-RAYMOND-BENSON-REVIEWS-THE-ULTIMATE.html). Cinema Retro. . Retrieved 2010-09-12.

[85] Rob Gonsalves (November 20, 2006). "Casino Royale (2006)" (http://efilmcritic.com/review.php?movie=15275&reviewer=416). *eFilmCritic.com*. .

[86] "Rotten Reviews for Casino Royale-RT.com" (http://www.rottentomatoes.com/m/casino_royale/?critic=columns&sortby=rotten&name_order=asc&view=#contentReviews). *Rottentomatoes.com*. .

[87] Anthony Lane (November 20, 2006). "Of human bondage" (http://www.newyorker.com/archive/2006/11/20/061120crci_cinema?currentPage=2#ixzz0upUk9q3P). *The New Yorker*. . Retrieved 2010-08-09.

[88] Medved, Michael. "Casino Royale" (http://townhall.com/TalkRadio/Show.aspx?RadioShowID=4&ContentGuid=43306526-93fb-41b5-80aa-44ec67611670). Townhall.com. . Retrieved 2010-09-02.

[89] "The best Bond since Connery" (http://www.thesun.co.uk/article/0,,2-2006480716,00.html). *The Sun*. 20 October 2006. . Retrieved 2006-11-21.

[90] Levy, Emanuel. "Casino Royale B+" (http://www.emanuellevy.com/article.php?articleID=3668). Emanuel Levy. . Retrieved 2006-11-21.

[91] Adams, Tim (5 November 2006). "You might be shaken, but this Bond won't leave you stirred" (http://observer.guardian.co.uk/uk_news/story/0,,1939830,00.html). *The Observer* (London). . Retrieved 2006-11-21.

[92] "Daniel Craig voted sexiest man" (http://www.thesun.co.uk/sol/homepage/news/article74969.ece). *The Sun*. 1 June 2009. .

[93] "Daniel Craig in 007 Lolly" (http://www.telegraph.co.uk/news/newstopics/celebritynews/5416143/Daniel-Craig-in-007-lolly.html). London: Daily Telegraph. 1 June 2009. . Retrieved 2010-04-14.

[94] "Casino Royale, Daniel Craig" (http://www.ew.com/ew/gallery/0,,20207076_20207079_20207442_6,00.html).Entertainment Weekly. 2008. .

[95] "Metacritic: 2006 Film Critic Top Ten Lists" (http://web.archive.org/web/20080209171331/http://www.metacritic.com/film/awards/2006/toptens.shtml). *Metacritic*. Archived from the original (http://www.metacritic.com/film/awards/2006/toptens.shtml)on February 9, 2008. . Retrieved 2008-02-25.

[96] "Awards Database - The BAFTA site" (http://www.bafta.org/awards-database.html?year=2006&category=Film&award=Orange+Rising+Star+Award). British Academy of Film and Television Arts. February 2007. . Retrieved 2010-08-09.

[97] "Awards Database - The BAFTA site" (http://www.bafta.org/awards-database.html?year=2006&category=Film&award=false). British Academy of Film and Television Arts. January 2007. . Retrieved 2010-08-09.

[98] "Craig named best actor at Brit film nods" (http://web.archive.org/web/20070930221221/http://www.hollywoodreporter.com/hr/content_display/international/news/e3i942a6313d5bbee0094106779c885314f). The Hollywood Reporter. 5 February 2007. Archived from the original (http://www.hollywoodreporter.com/hr/content_display/international/news/e3i942a6313d5bbee0094106779c885314f)on 2007-09-30. . Retrieved 2007-03-20.

[99] "ADG Awards 2006" (http://www.altfg.com/awards/2006/art-directors-guild.htm). Alternative Film Guide. . Retrieved 2007-04-30.

[100] "Satellite Awards - 2006" (http://www.altfg.com/awards/2006/satellite-awards.htm). Alternative Film Guide. . Retrieved 2007-04-30.

[101] "Casino Royale receives five Saturn Award nominations" (http://www.mi6.co.uk/news/index.php?itemid=4761). *MI6*. . Retrieved 2010-08-09.

[102] "Golden Tomato Awards. *Casino Royale* and *The Queen* take top honors in awards for well-reviewed films" (http://web.archive.org/web/20070205132336/http://www.newsday.com/entertainment/movies/ny-ettomatoaward0110,0,1075435.story).*Newsday*. 10 January 2007. Archived from the original (http://www.newsday.com/entertainment/movies/ny-ettomatoaward0110,0,1075435.story) on 2007-02-05. . Retrieved 2007-04-03.

[103] "Mystery Writers of America Announces 2007 Edgar Award Nominees" (http://www.prnewswire.com/cgi-bin/stories.pl?ACCT=104&STORY=/www/story/01-19-2007/0004509088&EDATE=). *Mystery Writers of America*. PR Newswire Association LLC.. 19 January 2007. . Retrieved 2007-03-20.

[104] Crabtree, Sheigh (12 January 2007). "10 make cut for ACE noms" (http://www.hollywoodreporter.com/hr/search/article_display.jsp?vnu_content_id=1003531899). *The Hollywood Reporter*. . Retrieved 2007-03-20.

[105] Visual Effects Society (11 February 2007). "Visual Effects Society 5th Annual VES Awards Announced" (http://web.archive.org/web/20070302213721/http://www.vesawards.com/5thvesannounced.pdf) (PDF). Press release. Archived from the original (http://www.vesawards.com/5thvesannounced.pdf) on 2007-03-02. . Retrieved 2007-04-03.

[106] Thompson, Anne; Carl DiOrio (18 February 2007). "*Casino*, *Curse*, top ADG Awards" (http://www.hollywoodreporter.com/hr/content_display/awards_festivals/news/e3i00c30daf8fb3b8f130ce2fd34b5f81bf?imw=Y). *The Hollywood Reporter*. . Retrieved 2007-04-03.

[107] Cohen, David S. (10 May 2007). "*Superman* tops Saturns" (http://www.variety.com/awardcentral_article/VR1117964717.html?nav=news&categoryid=1983&cs=1). *Variety*. . Retrieved 2007-05-11.

[108] "The 2007 Taurus World Stunt Awards Ended With A Bang On Sunday Night" (http://www.taurusworldstuntawards.com/index.php?id=88&tx_ttnews[tt_news]=11&tx_ttnews[backPid]=87&cHash=88da1adeaa). Taurus Worlds Stunt Awards. 21 May 2007. . Retrieved 2008-01-23.

External links

- Official website (http://www.sonypictures.com/movies/casinoroyale/site)
- *Casino Royale* (http://www.imdb.com/title/tt0381061/) at the Internet Movie Database
- *Casino Royale* (http://www.allmovie.com/work/292159) at Allmovie
- *Casino Royale* (http://www.rottentomatoes.com/m/casino_royale/) at Rotten Tomatoes
- *Casino Royale* (http://www.boxofficemojo.com/movies/?id=jamesbond21.htm) at Box Office Mojo
- *Casino Royale* Blu-ray Disc Review (http://www.hd-report.com/2007/03/13/blu-ray-disc-review-casino-royal/) at HD Report

The Magic Roundabout (film)

The Magic Roundabout *(Doogal in North America)*	

Directed by	Dave Borthwick Jean Duval Frank Passingham
Produced by	Claude Gorsky Laurent Rodon Pascal Rodon
Written by	Paul Bassett Raolf Sanoussi Stephane Sanoussi Butch Hartman (US)
Narrated by	Judi Dench
Starring	Kylie Minogue Joanna Lumley Robbie Williams Jim Broadbent Bill Nighy Ian McKellen Tom Baker Ray Winstone Lee Evans (UK) Kylie Minogue Whoopi Goldberg Daniel Tay William H. Macy Jimmy Fallon Ian McKellen Jon Stewart Bill Hader Chevy Chase Kevin Smith (US)
Distributed by	The Weinstein Company (North America) Pathé (Europe) 20th Century Fox (UK DVD) Alliance Films (Canada) Universal Studios Home Entertainment (Canadian DVD)

Release date(s)	Europe: February 11, 2005 North America: February 24, 2006
Running time	85 minutes (Europe) 78 minutes (North America)
Country	France United Kingdom United States
Language	English French
Budget	$20,000,000
Gross revenue	$26,691,243

The Magic Roundabout, (released in France as *Pollux, le manège enchanté* and a North American version as *Doogal*), is a film based on the television series of the same name. The film was released on February 11, 2005 in the United Kingdom and France, and on February 24, 2006 in North America. The plot concerns a dog named Dougal (Doogal in North America) who has to save his best friend, Florence, as well as the whole world, from being frozen by an evil spring named ZeeBad. The film was received positively in the United Kingdom, but was largely panned in the United States.

Plot

The film begins with a shaggy, candy-loving dog named Dougal trying to get sweets from a candy cart. He goes so far as to place a tack in the road to pop its tire, thinking to be rewarded for watching the cart. After convincing the driver to leave, Dougal is trying to decide which candy he will request when he accidentally starts the cart up again and causes it to collide with the titular magic roundabout at the center of the village. A blue jack-in-the-box-like creature emerges from the top and flies away, snatching a decorative Foot Guard figurine from the roundabout before leaving. The roundabout freezes over, trapping repairman Mr. Rusty, Dougal's young owner Florence, and two other children named Basil and Coral within an icy cell.

The villagers are horrified by this development, therefore call upon the resident wizard, Zebedee, also a jack-in-the-box-like creature, for help. He explains that the roundabout acted as a mystical prison for the evil ice wizard Zeebad. With it broken Zeebad is free to work his magic on the world again (it is implied he started the first ice age). The only way to return Zeebad to his prison is to place three magic diamonds in the roundabout, or watch the world slowly freeze over again. Zebedee sends Dougal, Brian the cynical snail, Ermintrude the opera-singing cow, Dylan the hippie rabbit, and the magic Train to accomplish this mission. Zeebad animates the Foot Guard figurine, Sergeant Sam, and enlists him to find the enchanted diamonds first, for with them Zeebad can freeze the sun itself. Meanwhile, Zebedee's fellowship makes camp in the icy mountains near Zeebad's old lair. Dougal wanders off during the night and is captured by Zeebad. Ermintrude breaks him out of his prison; after a short chase, Zebedee shows up to battle his evil counterpart. Zeebad gains the upper hand and overpowers Zebedee, freezing him and collapsing the cliff on which he stands.

Mourning their dispatcher as dead, Dougal and his friends embark to recover the diamonds. This task takes them to a lava-bordered volcano, an ancient temple filled with booby-traps and evil skeleton guards (at which point Dylan reveals an exceptional knowledge of several types of martial arts), and a final showdown with Zeebad, where it is revealed that Sergeant Sam had contained the third diamond in his chest. Zeebad obtains all three diamonds during the course of the film, and attempts to freeze the Sun. Ermintrude, Brian, Dylan, and finally Dougal intervene to stop him; when they have done so, Zeebad is imprisoned in the carousel again and Zebedee is restored to his friends. The ice surrounding the carousel melts, freeing the people trapped therein; of them, Florence is comatose and must be revived by a desperate Dougal. A moose, whose color had been changed from brown to blue by Zeebad in the earlier scenes of the film, is restored to his true color by Zebedee. Dougal, who vowed to give up sugar when it seemed all was lost, forgets his former pledge completely, but now realizes the true value of his friends and the good qualities of selflessness, courage, and humility.

Main characters and talents

Animals

- Dougal/Doogal: sugar-loving Skye Terrier.
- Dylan: guitar-playing hippie and very skilled martial artist rabbit
- Brian: bashful snail in love with Ermintrude
- Ermintrude: opera-singing cow
- The Moose: cautious interloper encountered up north, who periodically breaks wind in U.S. version. Turned blue by Zeebad; later helps Brian and Ermintrude find Dougal. Restored to natural color by Zebedee. He only speaks in the US dub.

Humans

- Florence: girl/orphan who, when in danger, has faith in *Dougal.*
- Basil and Coral: Florence's friends
- Mr. Rusty the repairman: appears similar to the Mad Hatter of Alice in Wonderland.

Magical toy-beings

- Zebedee: a good magician, uses warmth and love magic. Is essentially a jack-in-the-box, like Zeebad.
- Zeebad Carpenter: evil ice sorcerer, uses cold magic. Like Zebedee, channels magic through his moustache.
- Soldier Sam: Zeebad's slave, who holds one of the magic diamonds.
- The Train: Not to be confused with Thomas the Tank Engine (although the latter is mentioned); always comes in the nick of time, though is slow, according to Ermintrude.

Voice cast

Character	United Kingdom	United States
Dougal (Doogal)	Robbie Williams	Daniel Tay
Dylan	Bill Nighy	Jimmy Fallon
Zeebad	Tom Baker	Jon Stewart
Ermintrude	Joanna Lumley	Whoopi Goldberg
Brian	Jim Broadbent	William H. Macy
Train	Lee Evans	Chevy Chase
Narrator	Judi Dench	Judi Dench
Florence	Kylie Minogue	Kylie Minogue
Zebedee	Ian McKellen	Ian McKellen
Moose	Michael Angelis	Kevin Smith
Soldier Sam	Ray Winstone	Bill Hader
Coral	Daniella Loftus	Heidi Brook Myers

Reception

British reception

The Magic Roundabout gained generally favourable reviews from critics in Britain, for retaining its charm from the original television series and its superb animation. While some critics questioned the update for today's children and its subtle drug references, the reviews were mostly positive. The public also supported the film, and while some were disappointed on the nostalgia factor, their praise earned this film a total gross of £5.8 million at the box office, as of April 2005.

American reception

In 2006, the film was released in the US as "Doogal". As of March 16, 2006, it grossed a total of $7.2 million in the United States, which is considered exceptionally low by CGI animated film standards (the average domestic gross for a computer animated film is $134,571,721). In the North American version of the film, where audiences are unfamiliar with the series, the majority of original British voices have been replaced by celebrities more familiar to the American public, such as Jon Stewart and Chevy Chase. Only two original voices remained - those of Kylie Minogue and Ian McKellen. The US version also featured narration by Judi Dench and a new storyline made to accommodate multiple pop culture references and flatulence jokes (neither of which were present in the original release). Americans panned the movie. Rotten Tomatoes ranked the film 83rd in the 100 worst reviewed films of the 2000s, with a rating of 6%,[1] and an F rating from *Entertainment Weekly* magazine. After being advertised for a short time, its distribution ceased, but is widely carried in United States retail outlets such as Safeway as a children's DVD in retail stores and rental shops. The original French/British version of the film is available in the US under the title *Sprung! The Magic Roundabout* and occasionally airs on American TV networks.

Soundtrack

- Magic by Pilot is used, its 3rd use in a movie soundtrack after Disney's *Herbie Fully Loaded* and Happy Gilmore
- Mr. Blue Sky, by the Electric Light Orchestra from their album *Out Of The Blue* is a classic 70s tune that is key to the ending of the movie. Buyers should know it is not included on the US soundtrack.
- "Sugar, Sugar" by The Archies, number one single of 1969 is used only during the closing credits and album.

1. Main Titles - Mark Thomas
2. The Magic Roundabout - Kylie Minogue – VOCAL
3. Meet Doogal - James Venable
4. Magic – Pilot - VOCAL
5. You Really Got Me - Bill Nighy & Catherine Bott - VOCAL
6. Doogal the Mechanic - James Venable
7. Zeebad Escapes - Mark Thomas
8. Sam Marches - John M. Davis
9. The Magic Roundabout - Andrea Remanda and Goldust – VOCAL
10. Meet Zeebad - James Venable
11. Setting Up Camp - Mark Thomas
12. Spinning - Andrea Remanda and Goldust - VOCAL
13. Duel Of The Springs 2 - Mark Thomas
14. Simply Wonderful - Andrea Remanda and Goldust - VOCAL
15. The What-a-Snails Waltz - Mark Thomas
16. Zeebad Threatens - James Venable
17. Train's Back - Mark Thomas
18. Lost In The Cold - Mark Thomas

19. See The City - Mark Thomas
20. The Frozen City - Mark Thomas
21. Frozen Florence - John M. Davis
22. The End Of Zeebad - Mark Thomas
23. Florence Awakes - Mark Thomas
24. Sugar, Sugar - The Archies - VOCAL
25. I Love To Boogie - T.Rex - VOCAL
26. Lean Mean Machine - Andrea Remanda and Goldust - VOCAL
27. Believe Yourself - Andrea Remanda and Goldust - VOCAL (Used during the scene with Dylan fighting the skeleton guards in the UK version)
28. Bust This Joint - Andrea Remanda and Goldust - VOCAL

See also

- List of animated feature films
- List of films considered the worst

References

[1] http://www.rottentomatoes.com/m/1156283-doogal/

External links

- "Magic Roundabout" Official Website (http://magicroundabout.com)
- *Doogal* official website (http://www.doogalmovie.com)
- *The Magic Roundabout* (http://www.imdb.com/title/tt0339334/) at the Internet Movie Database
- *Doogal* (http://www.imdb.com/title/tt0763304/) at the Internet Movie Database

Mrs Henderson Presents

Mrs Henderson Presents

Film poster

Directed by	Stephen Frears
Produced by	Norma Heyman Bob Hoskins
Written by	Martin Sherman
Starring	Judi Dench Bob Hoskins Kelly Reilly Will Young Christopher Guest
Music by	George Fenton
Cinematography	Andrew Dunn
Editing by	Lucia Zucchetti
Studio	BBC Films Pathé Pictures Future Films
Distributed by	Pathé The Weinstein Company
Release date(s)	25 November 2005
Running time	103 minutes
Country	United Kingdom
Language	English

Mrs Henderson Presents is a 2005 British comedy film directed by Stephen Frears. It stars Judi Dench, Bob Hoskins, Kelly Reilly, and Will Young in his acting debut.

Plot

The film is based on the true story of the Windmill Theatre in London. Eccentric 70-year-old widow Mrs Laura Henderson purchases it as a post-widowhood hobby, and appoints autocratic manager Vivian Van Damm. In 1937 they start a continuous variety review called 'Revudeville', but after other theatres in London copy this innovation, they begin to lose money. Mrs Henderson suggests they add female nudity similar to the Moulin Rouge in Paris. This is unprecedented in the United Kingdom. The Lord Chamberlain reluctantly allows this under the condition that the nude performers do not move so it can be considered art.

Because the theatre's auditorium is below street level it is relatively safe during the bombing of London, and performances continue. The performers bravely go on with the show even during frightening bombing raids, to the extent of the posed nude girls resuming their poses after ducking as the whole theatre is shaken and the scene flats all round them sway, following a bomb landing close by. Eventually, the authorities want the theatre to close because of the danger of crowds gathering in the street outside the theatre. However, Mrs Henderson successfully argues that for soldiers going to die in the war this is their last chance, and for many of the young soldiers their only chance, to see female nudity.

Maureen, one of the cast, becomes involved at Mrs Henderson's instigation with a young soldier, one of the audience regulars. Maureen becomes pregnant, is very upset about how it will affect her life, and hands in her notice. However, before the issue can be resolved, she is killed by a bomb while leaving the theatre.

Other scenes depict life in the theatre during the period. Mrs Henderson and Mr Van Damm frequently clash and squabble, but also show great appreciation of each other. The film's closing credits explain that on her death in 1944 Mrs Henderson bequeaths the theatre to Mr Van Damm.

Cast

- Judi Dench as Laura Henderson
- Bob Hoskins as Vivian Van Damm
- Will Young as Bertie
- Christopher Guest as Lord Cromer
- Kelly Reilly as Maureen
- Thelma Barlow as Lady Conway
- Anna Brewster as Doris
- Rosalind Halstead as Frances
- Sarah Solemani as Vera
- Natalia Tena as Peggy
- Sir Thomas Allen as Eric Woodburn
- Richard Syms as Ambrose

Reception

The film received mostly positive reviews. According to Rotten Tomatoes 65% of the critics gave the film a positive review out of 133 reviews. The website *Future Movies* regarded "very funny, sweet and charming". Roger Ebert reacted fairly positively to the film, saying ""Mrs. Henderson Presents" is not great cinema, and neither was the Windmill great theater, but they both put on a good show.".

Awards

The film won four minor awards and was nominated for 26, among them four BAFTA Awards, two Oscars, three Golden Globe Awards and eight British Independent Film Awards.[1]

Music

For details, see Mrs. Henderson Presents (soundtrack).

References

[1] IMDb awards page for Mrs Henderson Presents (http://www.imdb.com/title/tt0413015/awards)

External links

- *Mrs Henderson Presents* (http://www.imdb.com/title/tt0413015/) at the Internet Movie Database
- Official site (http://www.mrshendersonpresentsmovie.co.uk/)
- BBC page (http://www.bbc.co.uk/bbcfilms/releases/mrshendersonpresents.shtml)
- MrsHendersonPresents.com - Unofficial site (http://www.mrshendersonpresents.com)

Pride & Prejudice (2005 film)

Pride and Prejudice	

Directed by	Joe Wright
Produced by	Tim Bevan Eric Fellner Paul Webster
Written by	Deborah Moggach Jane Austen (novel)
Starring	Keira Knightley Matthew Macfadyen Brenda Blethyn Donald Sutherland Tom Hollander Rosamund Pike Jena Malone Judi Dench
Music by	Dario Marianelli (Piano performed by Jean-Yves Thibaudet)
Cinematography	Roman Osin
Editing by	Paul Tothill
Studio	StudioCanal Working Title Films
Distributed by	Focus Features
Release date(s)	11 September 2005 (TIFF) 16 September 2005 (United Kingdom) 18 January 2006 (France)
Running time	129 minutes
Country	France United Kingdom
Language	English
Budget	$28 million

Gross revenue	$121,147,947

Pride & Prejudice is a 2005 film based on the Jane Austen novel of the same name. This second major motion-picture adaption of the novel was produced by Working Title Films, directed by Joe Wright and based on a screenplay by Deborah Moggach. It was released on September 16, 2005 in the UK and on November 11, 2005 in the US. (A previous film version was released in 1940.)

Plot

The story takes place at the turn of the 19th century in rural England. The Bennet family, consisting of Mr. and Mrs. Bennet and their five daughters - Jane, Elizabeth, Mary, Catherine, and Lydia - live in comparative financial independence as gentry on a working farm, Longbourn. As Longbourn is destined to be inherited by Mr. Bennet's cousin, Mr. Collins, Mrs. Bennet is anxious to marry off her five daughters before Mr. Bennet dies. However, Elizabeth, the heroine, is convinced that she should never marry unless she feels compelled to do so by true love.

Mr. Bingley, a wealthy bachelor who has recently moved into Netherfield, a large house in the neighborhood, is introduced to local society at an assembly ball, along with his haughty sister, Caroline, and reserved friend, Mr. Darcy, who "owns half of Derbyshire." Bingley is enchanted with the gentle and beautiful Jane, while Elizabeth takes an instant dislike to Darcy after he coldly rebuffs her attempts at conversation and she overhears him describe her as "not handsome enough to tempt me." When Jane becomes sick on a visit to Netherfield, Elizabeth goes to stay with her, and verbally spars with Caroline and Darcy.

Later the Bennets are visited by Mr. Collins, a pompous minister who talks of nothing but his patroness, Lady Catherine de Bourgh. Meanwhile, the handsome and charming Lieutenant Wickham of the newly-arrived militia captures the girls' attention; he slanders Darcy, telling Elizabeth that Darcy cheated him of his inheritance. At a ball at Netherfield, Elizabeth, startled by his abrupt appearance and request, accepts a dance with Mr. Darcy, but vows to her best friend Charlotte Lucas that she has "sworn to loathe him for all eternity." During the dance, she makes her disgust with him clear with biting sarcasm, and Darcy responds in kind. Their complete absorption with each other causes the other guests to "disappear" for a time, until the music stops.

The next day, at Longbourn, Mr. Collins proposes to Elizabeth, much to her chagrin; she refuses him, which causes hysterics in her mother, but she has the support of her father. When Bingley unexpectedly returns to London, Elizabeth dispatches Jane to their aunt and uncle in London, the Gardiners, in hopes of re-establishing contact between Jane and Bingley. Then Elizabeth is appalled to learn that Charlotte will marry Mr. Collins, not because she loves him but entirely to gain financial security.

Months later, Elizabeth visits the Collinses at Rosings, the manor estate of the overbearing Lady Catherine; they are invited to dine at the grand house and there meet Darcy and Colonel Fitzwilliam, Lady Catherine's nephews. Here Darcy pursues a greater interest in Elizabeth, especially when she replies to Lady Catherine's jabs with spirited wit. The next day, Colonel Fitzwilliam lets slip to Elizabeth that Darcy separated Bingley from Jane. Distraught, she flees out into the rain; Darcy chooses that moment to track her down and to propose marriage — and thus follows the infamous "train-wreck" marriage proposal. He claims that he loves her "most ardently," despite her "lower rank." Elizabeth refuses him, citing his treatment of Jane and Bingley, and of Wickham, and they argue fiercely. The scene provides a close-up of their faces, their minds intense with anger and indecision. Darcy leaves angry and heartbroken. He finds her later only to give her a letter, which explains that he misjudged Jane's affection for Bingley. The letter also exposes Wickham as a gambler who secretly but unsuccessfully courted Darcy's 15-year-old sister, Georgiana, to obtain her £30,000 inheritance.

Elizabeth does not tell Jane what she has learned. Later, the Gardiners take Elizabeth on a trip to the Peak District and visit Darcy's estate, Pemberley. Elizabeth is stunned by its wealth and beauty and hears nothing but good things about Darcy from his housekeeper. Then she accidentally runs into Darcy, who invites her and the Gardiners to meet his sister. His manners have softened considerably, and Georgiana takes an instant liking to Elizabeth. When

Elizabeth learns that her immature and flirtatious youngest sister Lydia, who was sent on holiday unsupervised, has run away with Wickham, she tearfully blurts out the news to Darcy before returning home. Her family assumes their ruin for having a disgraced daughter, but they are soon relieved to hear that Mr. Gardiner has discovered the pair in London, and that they will be married. Lydia later reveals to Elizabeth that it was Mr. Darcy who found them and who paid for the marriage.

When Bingley and Darcy return to Netherfield, Jane accepts Bingley's proposal of marriage. The same evening, Lady Catherine pays Elizabeth a surprise visit and insists that Elizabeth renounce Darcy, as he is supposedly going to marry her own daughter, Anne. Elizabeth refuses, and unable to sleep, she goes walking on the moors at dawn. There, she meets Darcy, who has also been unable to sleep after hearing of his aunt's behavior. He admits his continued love, and Elizabeth accepts his second proposal. Mr. Bennet gives his consent after Elizabeth assures him of her love for Darcy. In the U.S. version of the film, an additional last scene shows a newly-married Elizabeth and Darcy outside of their Pemberley estate showing affection for each other.

Cast

- Keira Knightley as Elizabeth Bennet
- Matthew Macfadyen as Mr. Darcy
- Talulah Riley as Mary Bennet
- Rosamund Pike as Jane Bennet
- Jena Malone as Lydia Bennet
- Carey Mulligan as Catherine "Kitty" Bennet
- Donald Sutherland as Mr. Bennet
- Brenda Blethyn as Mrs. Bennet
- Claudie Blakley as Charlotte Lucas
- Simon Woods as Mr. Charles Bingley
- Kelly Reilly as Caroline Bingley
- Rupert Friend as Mr. George Wickham
- Tom Hollander as Mr. William Collins
- Judi Dench as Lady Catherine de Bourgh
- Rosamund Stephen as Anne de Bourgh
- Cornelius Booth as Colonel Fitzwilliam
- Penelope Wilton as Mrs. Gardiner
- Peter Wight as Mr. Gardiner
- Meg Wynn Owen as Mrs. Reynolds
- Tamzin Merchant as Georgiana Darcy
- Sinead Matthews as Betsy

Co-producer Paul Webster found the casting of Darcy difficult because of the character's iconic status and because "Colin Firth cast a very long shadow" as the Darcy from the 1995 television adaptation.[1]

Production

Adaptation of the novel

Most works of literature undergo significant cuts when adapted for film; in this production, the story was compressed into 2 hours and 9 minutes of screen time. Some of the most notable changes from the original book include:

- Heavy time compression of several major sequences, including Elizabeth's visit to Rosings Park and Hunsford Parsonage, Elizabeth's visit to Pemberley, and Lydia's elopement and its subsequent crisis.
- The elimination of several supporting characters, including Louisa Hurst, Mr. Hurst, Lady and Maria Lucas, Mr. and Mrs. Phillips, the Gardiners' children, Mrs. Annesley (Georgiana Darcy's governess), several of Lydia's friends (including Colonel and Mrs. Forster), and various military officers and townspeople.
- The elimination of several sections in which characters reflect or converse on events that have recently occurred - for example, Elizabeth's chapter-long change of mind after reading Darcy's letter.

The filmmakers changed several scenes to more romantic locales than the ones in the book. For instance, in the film, Darcy first proposes outdoors in a rainstorm near a beautiful lake; in the book, this scene takes place inside a parsonage. In the film, his second proposal occurs on the misty moors as dawn breaks; in the book, he and Elizabeth are walking down a country lane in broad daylight.

The North American release version included a final scene (not in the novel) of the married Darcys enjoying a romantic evening at Pemberley. This ending did not test well with British audiences, so it was cut for UK and international release. The British version ends with Mr. Bennet's blessing upon Elizabeth and Mr. Darcy's union, thus circumventing the last chapter in the novel, which summarizes the lives of the Darcys and the other main characters over the next several years.

Filming

It was filmed entirely on location within England[2] in the summer of 2004 and used several stately homes, including Chatsworth House in Derbyshire and Wilton House in Salisbury (as Pemberley), Groombridge Place in Kent (as Longbourn), Basildon Park in Berkshire (as Netherfield Park) and Burghley House in Cambridgeshire (as Rosings - the adjacent town of Stamford served as Meryton). The Temple of Apollo and Palladian Bridge of Stourhead also appeared (as set in the Gardens of Rosings).

Reaction

Critical reception

London bus with *Pride & Prejudice* ad

The 2005 film was only the second faithful film version after "the famed, but oddly flawed, black-and-white 1940 adaptation, starring Greer Garson and Laurence Olivier,"[3] and until 2005, *The Times* considered the 1995 television adaptation starring Jennifer Ehle and Colin Firth "so dominant, so universally adored, [that] it has lingered in the public consciousness as a cinematic standard."[3] Comparing six major adaptations of *Pride and Prejudice* in 2005, the *Daily Mirror* gave the only top marks of 9/10 to the 1995 serial and the 2005 film, leaving the other adaptations behind with six and fewer points.[4] The 2005 film is rated 85% fresh by Rotten Tomatoes.[5] Metacritic reported *Pride & Prejudice* had an average score of 82 out of 100, based on 37 reviews, and classified the film as a universal acclaim.[6]

Some critics noted the 2005 film's time constraints do not capture the depth and complexity of the television serials[7] and called the film "obviously [not as] daring or revisionist" as the 1995 TV serial.[8] Joan Klingel Ray, president of the Jane Austen Society of North America, preferred the young age of Knightley and Macfadyen, saying that Jennifer Ehle had formerly been "a little too 'heavy' for the role,"[9] while Peter Bradshaw of *The Guardian*, while heavily praising Keira Knightley for having given an outstanding performance as Lizzy Bennet "which lifts the whole movie," considered the casting of the 2005 leads "arguably a little more callow than Firth and Ehle." He does add that "Only a snob, a curmudgeon, or someone with necrophiliac loyalty to the 1995 BBC version with Colin Firth and Jennifer Ehle could fail to enjoy her performance."[8] Critics were divided about Matthew Macfadyen's portrayal of Darcy, expressing pleasant surprise,[9] dislike for his lack of gradual emotional shift as in the novel,[9] and praise for his matching the insecure and sensitive personality of the book character better than Firth.[7]

Box office

The movie took the number one spot in the UK its first week, earning £2.5 million ($4.5 million) while playing on 400 screens. It stayed on the top spot for two more weeks, earning a total of over £14 million at the UK box office at that time and was featured on 1,335 screens at its widest domestic release.

The film debuted with an opening weekend of US$2.9 million on 215 screens. Two weeks later, this was increased to 1,299 screens, and box office returns increased to $7.2 million. The film has grossed over $121,147,947 worldwide at the cinema box office.[10]

Awards and accolades

Pride & Prejudice garnered a number of nominations in the 2005/2006 film awards season, most notably four nominations in the Academy Awards: Best Actress in a Leading Role for Keira Knightley, Achievement in Art Direction, Achievement in Costume Design for Jacqueline Durran, and Achievement in Music Written for Motion Pictures (Original Score) for Dario Marianelli's score. It was nominated for five BAFTAs and won the BAFTA Carl Foreman Award for Most Promising Newcomer (for Joe Wright, director).[11]

Awards Ceremony	Award Category	Subject	Result
Academy Awards	Academy Award for Best Actress	Keira Knightley	Nominated
	Academy Award for Best Original Score	Dario Marianelli	Nominated
	Academy Award for Best Art Direction	-	Nominated
	Academy Award for Best Costume Design	Jacqueline Durran	Nominated
Golden Globes	Golden Globe for Best Film - Musical or Comedy	-	Nominated
	Golden Globe for Best Actress - Musical or Comedy	Keira Knightley	Nominated
British Academy Film Awards	BAFTA for Best Film - British	-	Nominated
	BAFTA Award for Best Actress in a Supporting Role	Brenda Blethyn	Nominated
	BAFTA Award for Most Promising Newcomer	Joe Wright	Won
	BAFTA Award for Best Adapted Screenplay	Deborah Moggach	Nominated
	BAFTA Award for Best Costume Design	Jacqueline Durran	Nominated
	BAFTA Award for Best Makeup & Hair	-	Nominated

DVD release

The standard DVD was released for home use on February 28, 2006 in widescreen and fullframe.[12]

The deluxe edition includes both widescreen and fullframe, the original soundtrack CD, collectible book, collectible booklet, and 9-dual layer.[13]

References

[1] Alberge, Dalya (June 11, 2004). "Hunt for Darcy nets star of TV spy drama" (http://www.timesonline.co.uk/tol/news/uk/article443894.ece). *The Times*. . Retrieved 2008-06-02.
[2] Pride & Prejudice filming locations - UK Onscreen (http://www.ukonscreen.com/ijefcfb-Pride-and-Prejudice-(2005).html)
[3] Briscoe, Joanna (July 31, 2005). "A costume drama with muddy hems" (http://entertainment.timesonline.co.uk/tol/arts_and_entertainment/film/article549627.ece). *The Times*. . Retrieved 2008-06-02.
[4] Edwards, David (September 9, 2005). *Pride and Passion. Daily Mirror*
[5] Movie Reviews, Pictures - Rotten Tomatoes (http://www.rottentomatoes.com/m/pride_and_prejudice/)
[6] "Pride & Prejudice (2005 film): Reviews" (http://www.metacritic.com/film/titles/prideandprejudice?q=pride and prejudice). Metacritic. . Retrieved 2008-02-21.
[7] Holden, Stephen (November 11, 2005). "Pride & Prejudice (2005) – Marrying Off Those Bennet Sisters Again, but This Time Elizabeth Is a Looker" (http://movies.nytimes.com/2005/11/11/movies/11prid.html). *The New York Times*. . Retrieved 2008-06-02.
[8] Bradshaw, Peter (September 16, 2005). "Pride & Prejudice" (http://film.guardian.co.uk/News_Story/Critic_Review/Guardian_review/0,,1570740,00.html). *The Guardian*. . Retrieved 2008-06-02.
[9] Hastings, Chris (August 8, 2005). "Colin Firth was born to play Mr Darcy. So can anyone else shine in the lead role?" (http://www.telegraph.co.uk/news/uknews/1497098/Colin-Firth-was-born-to-play-Mr-Darcy.-So-can-anyone-else-shine-in-the-lead-role.html).*The Daily Telegraph*. . Retrieved 2008-06-03.
[10] http://www.boxofficemojo.com/movies/?id=prideandprejudice05.htm
[11] Pride & Prejudice (2005) - Awards (http://www.imdb.com/title/tt0414387/awards)
[12] http://prideandprejudicemovie.net/splash.html
[13] http://www.walmart.com/catalog/product.do?product_id=7732204

External links

- Official website (http://prideandprejudicemovie.net/)
- *Pride & Prejudice* (http://www.imdb.com/title/tt0414387/) at the Internet Movie Database
- *Pride & Prejudice* (http://www.allmovie.com/work/309976) at Allmovie
- *Pride & Prejudice* (http://www.boxofficemojo.com/movies/?id=prideandprejudice05.htm) at Box Office Mojo
- *Pride & Prejudice* (http://www.rottentomatoes.com/m/1153077-1153077-pride_and_prejudice/) at Rotten Tomatoes
- *Pride & Prejudice* Companion Book (http://www.workingtitlefilms.com/featurePhoto.php?featureID=57)
- *Pride & Prejudice* Production Notes (http://www.bahcecikdevekusu.com/movies/2005/pride.htm)

Ladies in Lavender

Ladies in Lavender	
 Original poster	
Directed by	Charles Dance
Produced by	Nicolas Brown, Elizabeth Karlsen
Written by	Charles Dance based on a story by William J. Locke
Starring	Judi Dench Maggie Smith Daniel Brühl Natascha McElhone
Music by	Nigel Hess
Distributed by	Lakeshore International
Release date(s)	12 November 2004 (UK) 29 April 2005 (US)
Running time	103 minutes
Language	English
Gross revenue	$20,439,793 (USD)

Ladies in Lavender is a 2004 British drama film written and directed by Charles Dance, who based his screenplay on a short story by William J. Locke.

Plot

Set in picturesque coastal Cornwall, in a tight-knit fishing village in the 1930s, *Ladies in Lavender* stars Judi Dench and Maggie Smith playing the leading roles of sisters Ursula (Dench) and Janet Widdington (Smith). Andrea is played by Daniel Brühl. A gifted young Polish violinist from Krakow, Andrea is bound for America when he is swept overboard by a storm. When the Widdington sisters discover the handsome stranger on the beach below their house, they nurse him back to health. However, the presence of the musically talented young man disrupts the peaceful lives of Ursula and Janet and the community in which they live.

Production

William Locke's original story was published in 1916. The title is a play on words of the phrase *Lace in Lavender* and refers to the custom of sprinkling dried lavender among clothing packed in storage to keep it smelling fresh and keeping moths away. In both Poland and Germany, Andrea is a feminine name with the respective masculine counterparts Andrzej and Andreas. At the end of Locke's original story, the sisters never hear from Andrea after he departs for London.

The film marked the directorial debut of actor Charles Dance. Longtime friends Maggie Smith and Judi Dench were appearing together in a play in London's West End when Dance first approached them about the project. They immediately accepted his offer without even reading the script. The film is the first English language role for German actor Daniel Brühl.

Exteriors were filmed in Cadgwith, Helston, St. Ives and Prussia Cove in Cornwall. Interiors were filmed at the Pinewood Studios in Buckinghamshire. The violin music played by Andrea, including compositions by Felix Mendelssohn, Niccolò Paganini, Jules Massenet, Claude Debussy, Pablo de Sarasate and Johann Sebastian Bach, is performed by Joshua Bell.

Principal cast

- Judi Dench as Ursula Widdington
- Maggie Smith as Janet Widdington
- Daniel Brühl as Andrea Marowski
- Natascha McElhone as Olga Danilof
- Miriam Margolyes as Dorcas
- David Warner as Dr. Mead

Soundtrack

Ladies in Lavender (Original Motion Picture Soundtrack)	
Soundtrack by Nigel Hess	
Released	8 November 2004
Genre	Classical
Length	55:34
Label	Sony Classical Records

The film's original music was written by Nigel Hess and performed by Joshua Bell and the Royal Philharmonic Orchestra. Hess received a Classical BRIT Awards nomination for Best Soundtrack Composer.[1]

1. "Ladies in Lavender" (Joshua Bell) – 4:06
2. "Olga" (Joshua Bell) – 3:31
3. "Teaching Andrea" (Joshua Bell) – 2:53
4. "Fantasy for Violin and Orchestra" (Joshua Bell) – 3:40
5. "Méditation from Thaïs" (Joshua Bell) – 5:01
6. "Our Secret" (Joshua Bell) – 2:01
7. "On the Beach" (Royal Philharmonic Orchestra) – 2:33
8. "Introduction and Tarantella, Op. 43" (Joshua Bell) – 5:16
9. "The Letter" (Joshua Bell) – 2:25
10. "Polish Dance - Zabawa Weselna" (Joshua Bell) – 2:41

11. "Stirrings" (Joshua Bell) – 1:50
12. "Potatoes" (Joshua Bell) – 1:49
13. "The Girl With Flaxen Hair" (Joshua Bell) – 2:33
14. "A Broken Heart" (Joshua Bell) – 3:33
15. "Two Sisters" (Royal Philharmonic Orchestra) – 2:22
16. "The Carnival of Venice" (Joshua Bell) – 9:20

Reception

Ladies in Lavender grossed £2,604,852 (UKP) in the UK and $6,759,422 (USD) in the US (on limited release). Its total worldwide gross was $20,439,793 (USD).[2] It received its New York premiere at the 4th Annual Tribeca Film Festival.[3] Prior to its release in the UK, the film was shown at the Taormina Film Festival and the Toronto Film Festival. It was released as *Les Dames de Cornouailles* in France, *Der Duft von Lavendel* in Germany, *Lavendelflickorna* in Sweden, and *Parfum de lavande* in French-speaking Canada. Both Judi Dench and Maggie Smith were nominated for Best European Actress at the European Film Awards. Dench was nominated for the ALFS Award for British Actress of the Year by the London Film Critics Circle. The film was positively received by the critics.

In his review in the *New York Times*, Stephen Holden said, "[Dench and Smith] sink into their roles as comfortably as house cats burrowing into a down quilt on a windswept, rainy night . . . This amiably far-fetched film . . . heralds the return of the Comfy Movie (increasingly rare nowadays), the cinematic equivalent of a visit from a cherished but increasingly dithery maiden aunt. In this fading, sentimental genre peopled with grandes dames (usually English) making "grande" pronouncements, the world revolves around tea, gardening and misty watercolor memories." [4]

Roger Ebert of the *Chicago Sun-Times* called the film "perfectly sweet and civilized . . . It's a pleasure to watch Smith and Dench together; their acting is so natural it could be breathing." [5]

In *The Guardian*, Peter Bradshaw observed that "despite a bit of shortbread-sugary emotion and an ending that fizzles out disappointingly, there's some nice period detail and decent lines in Charles Dance's directing debut," [6] while Philip French of *The Observer* commented on the "beautiful setting, a succession of implausible incidents, and characteristically excellent work from Smith (all suppression and stoicism) and Dench (exuding unfulfilled yearning)." [7]

Peter Keough of the *Boston Phoenix* said, "This exercise in scenery and music is as innocuous as a nosegay." [8]

In the *Chicago Tribune*, Robert K. Elder awarded the film two out of a possible four stars and added, "[it] exemplifies that kind of polite, underdramatic *Masterpiece Theatre* staging that can either provide a surgical examination of English society or bore the pants off you. *Ladies in Lavender* does a bit of both . . . director Dance's momentum fades soon after Andrea's ankle mends, and we're left with a vague back story involving Andrea's intent to emigrate to America, though the mystery of how he ended up in Cornwall is never revisited nor revealed. [He] becomes sort of a blank character, a personality on whom we can impose our own curiosity and emotions . . . as compelling and original as this theme is, it's not enough to keep our attention, no matter how lovely the ladies in lavender are." [9]

References

[1] Terfel leads Classical Brits nods (http://news.bbc.co.uk/2/hi/entertainment/4461601.stm)
[2] Ladies in Lavender (2005) (http://www.boxofficemojo.com/movies/?id=ladiesinlavender.htm)
[3] http://www.tribecafilm.com/filmguide/archive/Ladies_in_Lavender.html
[4] *New York Times* review (http://movies.nytimes.com/2005/04/29/movies/29ladi.html?_r=1&oref=slogin)
[5] *Chicago Sun-Times* review (http://rogerebert.suntimes.com/apps/pbcs.dll/article?AID=/20050512/REVIEWS/50503003/1023)
[6] *The Guardian* review (http://film.guardian.co.uk/News_Story/Critic_Review/Guardian_review/0,,1348661,00.html)
[7] *The Observer* review (http://film.guardian.co.uk/News_Story/Critic_Review/Observer_review/0,,1350600,00.html)
[8] *Boston Phoenix* review (http://www.bostonphoenix.com/boston/movies/trailers/documents/04715308.asp)
[9] *Chicago Tribune* review (http://chicago.metromix.com/movies/review/movie-review-ladies-in/159570/content)

External links

- *Ladies in Lavender* (http://www.imdb.com/title/tt0377084/) at the Internet Movie Database
- Interview with Charles Dance (http://www.dvdtown.com/news/on-ladies-in-lavender/2701)
- Charles Dance's *Ladies in Lavender* diary (http://www.charlesdance.co.uk/lavender_blues.html)
- *Ladies in Lavender* at the Tribeca Film Festival Website (http://www.tribecafilm.com/filmguide/archive/Ladies_in_Lavender.html)
- *Ladies in Lavender* at Variety.com (http://www.variety.com/profiles/Film/main/167881/Ladies in Lavender.html?dataSet=1)
- *Ladies in Lavender* at the British Film Catalogue (http://www.britfilms.com/britishfilms/catalogue/browse/?id=D9CDE6321b5e71AFC9SrH3ED7F8F)

The Chronicles of Riddick

The Chronicles of Riddick

Theatrical release one-sheet

Directed by	David Twohy
Produced by	Scott Kroopf Vin Diesel
Written by	David Twohy
Starring	Vin Diesel Judi Dench Thandie Newton Karl Urban Nick Chinlund Colm Feore Alexa Davalos
Music by	Graeme Revell
Cinematography	Hugh Johnson
Editing by	Director's Cut: Tracy Adams Martin Hunter Dennis Virkler
Studio	Radar Pictures
Distributed by	Universal Pictures
Release date(s)	June 11, 2004
Running time	Theatrical Cut: 119 minutes Director's Cut: 135 minutes
Country	United States
Language	English
Budget	$105 million

Gross revenue	$115,766,649
Preceded by	*The Chronicles of Riddick: Dark Fury*

The Chronicles of Riddick is a 2004 American science fiction film. It follows the adventures of Richard B. Riddick, as he attempts to elude capture after the events depicted in the 2000 film *Pitch Black,* and details his meeting with Jack and Imam, his escape from the prison planet Crematoria, and his battle with the Necromonger fleet. It was directed by David Twohy, also the director of *Pitch Black*, and stars Vin Diesel (also co-producer), Karl Urban and Judi Dench, with Thandie Newton and Colm Feore. The critical and commercial response was mixed.

After the release of the film, *The Chronicles of Riddick* became the brand name of the series.

Plot

The film opens with a narrative, explaining the motives of the Necromongers, a race of conquerors traveling across space toward the Underverse, a dark mirror of the normal universe where death has no meaning. Their leader, the Lord Marshal (Colm Feore), commands his troops to overrun worlds and convert their inhabitants into Necromongers; those who oppose conversion are killed.

The story begins on the icy world of the planet *U.V.6* where Richard B. Riddick (Vin Diesel) is evading bounty hunter Toombs (Nick Chinlund) and his crew. Toombs is trying to collect the 1.5 million bounty placed on Riddick's head. Riddick kills or disables all but Toombs and leaves the planet with their ship, setting a course for the planet *Helion Prime*, from which the bounty originated. In the Director's Cut, Riddick is plagued by visions from a character named Shirah (Kristin Lehman) during the flight, who tells Riddick he is the last of a warrior-race called the Furyans.

When Riddick lands on Helion Prime, he confronts Imam (Keith David) in the city of New Mecca, believing he is responsible for the bounty. Imam explains that he only gave information on Riddick's location to the one who placed the bounty. Imam also tells Riddick that Jack, the other survivor from *Pitch Black*, went looking for him five years earlier, missing his brother-like influence. She became a criminal and was sent to prison on the planet Crematoria. He introduces Aereon (Judi Dench), an envoy of the Elementals, who arranged for Riddick to be brought to Helion. She explains he is part of a prophecy that states a lone Furyan will one day challenge an unstoppable evil and bring balance back to the universe, and says the Necromongers are the ones the prophecy foretells.

Following this revelation, the Necromonger army attacks Helion Prime, wiping out the planet's defenses in one night. Imam is killed in the attack while protecting his family. An enraged Riddick heads to the city forum, where the Helion Prime leaders are gathered before the Necromongers and the Lord Marshal. He challenges and dispatches Imam's killer easily. Suspicious of his abilities, the Lord Marshal has Riddick taken into his fortress to confirm his identity. Placed before the psychic Quasi-Deads, who claim Riddick is a Furyan, the Lord Marshal orders his death. Riddick escapes, only to run into Toombs again. Toombs has hired a new crew. Riddick allows himself to be captured so he can be transported to Crematoria, a dead world where daytime surface temperatures scorch the face of the planet.

Riddick is reunited with Jack (Alexa Davalos), who now goes by the name of Kyra. She blames him for leaving her and Imam in New Mecca, but eventually they reconcile. Back on Helion Prime, the Lord Marshal commands Necromonger Commander Vaako (Karl Urban) to find Riddick and have him killed, so Vaako sets out with a small group of Necromongers and a Purifier (Linus Roache) to bring him down. Vaako is curious as to why the Lord Marshal is so afraid of Riddick. With encouragement from his rabidly ambitious wife, Dame Vaako (Thandie Newton), the two learn, before he achieved his current title, the Lord Marshal destroyed the Furyans' homeworld of Furya and its citizens. This occurred after a seer foretold that a male Furyan would cause his downfall. They deduce Riddick is the one in the prophecy.

When Toombs and his crew argue over Riddick's bounty with the prison warden and his guards, the warden reveals he has pictures of the incoming Necromongers, who have picked up the trail left behind by Toombs's ship. A gunfight erupts, with the staff emerging victorious. The warden and guards depart, running through man-made tunnels towards the ship hangar, locking the rest of prison down to prevent the inmates from escaping. Riddick, Kyra, and some of the inmates decide to reach the hanger first by traveling on the surface, surviving by keeping pace with the temperate zone created between the scorching heat and freezing cold of Crematoria's daily cycles. They reach the hangar, but Vaako and his contingent of soldiers have arrived on the planet, hastily taking out the warden and his guards. Riddick and company are forced to fight the Necromongers.

Amidst the numerous casualties, Vaako narrowly defeats Riddick. In the Director's Cut, Riddick suddenly manifests a powerful energy burst which knocks out both himself and most of the Necromongers. Vaako leaves Riddick for dead as the rising sun burns Crematoria's surface. Vaako and the surviving Necromongers make their escape, taking Kyra, who believes Riddick has perished. Riddick nearly burns to death, but is suddenly saved by the Purifier. He states the Lord Marshal has offered to spare Riddick's life in exchange for assurance that Riddick will not attempt to kill him; however, the Purifier goes on to say Vaako will likely claim Riddick's death, in fear of failure, leaving the Lord Marshal vulnerable. Before walking into the sunlight and his death, the Purifier reveals himself to also be a Furyan.

Vaako returns to the Legion Vast, where the Lord Marshal promotes him. Riddick flies Toombs's ship back to Helion Prime, intending to rescue Kyra. Not quite convinced of Riddick's death, the Lord Marshal orders the "Final Protocol", which will ultimately destroy all life on Helion Prime. Dame Vaako spots Riddick, who has infiltrated the mother ship. She suggests to her husband that he be allowed to fight the Lord Marshal, hopefully injuring him and allowing Vaako to deal the final blow so he may assume power, based on the Necromonger philosophy, "you keep what you kill." Riddick makes his way to the throne room, where he comes face to face with the Lord Marshal, who reveals Kyra has converted to their faith. After lamenting to himself that the Necromonger has killed everyone he loved, Riddick does battle with the Lord Marshal, whose unique powers prove too great for Riddick to handle.

Before the Lord Marshal can deliver the final blow, Kyra stabs him in the back, but he backhands her into a spike on a column, mortally wounding her. Vaako, sensing an opportunity to vanquish his superior and claim leadership, strikes out at the Lord Marshal, who narrowly escapes the blow. Riddick, however, has positioned himself where the Lord Marshall has retreated to, and stabs the Lord Marshal in the head, killing him.

Riddick turns to the mortally wounded Kyra, and she dies in his arms after telling Riddick that she was "always" with him. As he collapses with grief on the Necromonger throne, the Legion Vast kneel before him, and Riddick remains silent while Aereon ruminates on the irony of the situation. In the Director's Cut, the film abruptly ends with Riddick repeating the Necromonger adage "you keep what you kill," realizing he is the new leader of their empire. In the theatrical cut, the Necromonger fleet abruptly departs, sparing Helion Prime. The epilogue of the novel adaptation goes even further with Riddick ordering the Necromonger fleet to the Threshold, gateway to the Underverse.

Lord Marshal

Lord Marshal is the title of the ruler of the Necromongers, The One Rank that cannot be superseded. It is the task of the Lord Marshal to wage a crusade against humanity and bring all converts to the Underverse. On his armor are the faces of the previous rulers. The first act of an new Lord Marshal is a pilgrimage to the Underverse. From a world they named Asylum six would write the darkest chapters in the galaxy:

Covu"The Transcended" , the first Lord Marshal. Covu discovered the Underverse, began the order "Necroism" and ordered the Necropolis built.

Oltovm, the 2nd Lord Marshal and builder of the Necropolis created the great Necromonger armada.

Naphemil "The Navigator" , the third Lord Marshal, father of the Necro Philosophy, ordered the Necropolis unearthed and entombed in a large Basilica ship.

Baylock "The Trutal", the fourth Lord Marshal and last to be born to Necroism would not live to see his visage eventually grace the Conquest Icons left in the Necromonger's wake on so many murdered worlds.

Kryll, the fifth Lord Marshal brought about the Quasi-Dead, fragile yet powerful beings whose use to the Necros evolves even today.

Zhylaw "The Last" , The sixth Lord Marshal and the most powerful, adopted the Necromongers darkest philosophy, for those races unwilling to convert, their penance shall be infanticide.

Riddick, The seventh Lord Marshal, and a Furyan survivor, believed to bring massive change to the Necromonger world. These changes have yet to be seen, however.

Powers and Abilities

Since Covu "The Transcended" discovered the gate to the Underverse, called "The Threshold", each successive Lord Marshal has made a pilgrimage to the Underverse. His trip to the Underverse grants him a plethora of inhuman powers. All the Lord Marshals are extremely long lived.

Zhylaw The Last discovered a great ancient artifact on Helion Prime, within the secrets of the Threshold were written, after studying and destroying the artifact so that nobody could ever find it, He would use it in his great crusade. With this knowledge he could use more of the Soulpower than any other Lord Marshal making him the most powerful Lord Marshal in history.

He has enhanced strength lift (press) over 10 tons, enhanced stamina, and enhanced durability to easily outmatch that of a Furyan. He also has the ability to detach his soul from his body, granting him super speed, by means of his soul moving to a different place and his body following it. This acts to give him speed in short bursts (or long term use for long distance travel), and allows him to go anywhere his soul can get to, regardless of whether his body (under normal conditions) could or not (e.g., on top a statue to the right of his throne). He's able to fly with this ability.

He can also use his soul for extrasensory purposes (when Vaako tried to sneak up on Zhylaw, he turned his soul to look at Vaako without ever turning his body). He also has the ability to grab a person's soul out of their body, killing them but he's unable to absorb the souls to become more powerful, since the Soulpower recharges he doesn't need to. This so called Soulpower he gained during his trip to the Underverse grants him also healing powers, which he can use to regenerate and to protect himself against harm. With the Soulpower he can also live outside the vacuum of space and under water (even under high pressure). This Soulpower is probably giving him all of these mentioned powers. This explains perhaps that when Covu stepped through the Threshold his family rose again from the dead.

The Soulpower can be seen as some kind of energy source, and those who are worthy and able to wield it, are able to use it. Thanks to the Soulpower the Lord Marshal doesn't need to drink or eat. Not all are able to use this power, since all converted (Necromongers) have a little of the soulpower but dont have any of the powers the Lord Marshal has.

That is what the name quasi-dead means, they only have a fracture of the power the Lord Marshal has. Only the Lord Marshal is capable of controlling the Ascension Protocol.

The Lord Marshal is able to control his voice inhumanly, as shown when he shouted for Vaako not to question his orders. One of the major powers but not shown in the movie is that he can shoot energy blasts from his hands (all energized by his Soulpower), and when he charges the blast will become more powerful to a certain extent. He may also possess some sort of telepathy to maintain his subjects' loyalty without question; this is doubtful, however, since neither Vaako nor his wife were truly loyal to Zhylaw.

"Leading them, The Lord Marshal, He alone has made a pilgrimage to the gates of the Underverse and returned a different being, Stronger, Stranger, Half Alive and Half Something Else" ~ Air Elemental Aereon.

The Purifier's commentary on Lord Marshals is as follows: "There have been six Lord Marshals since the beginning--since Khovu the Transcended walked across the threshold and beheld his lifeless family reborn into the UnderVerse. And since that first journey, each successive Lord Marshal has made his own journey to the threshold. And from it, each has gained greater power. They are the half-dead. And ascendence to the rank of Lord Marshal comes to pass in many ways. But it is most often a violent transition. And this is why all Necromongers know that you keep what you kill."

Cast

Actor	Role
Vin Diesel	Richard B. Riddick
Colm Feore	Lord Marshal
Thandie Newton	Dame Vaako
Judi Dench	Aereon
Karl Urban	Vaako
Alexa Davalos	Jack/Kyra
Linus Roache	Purifier
Yorick van Wageningen	The Guv
Nick Chinlund	Toombs
Keith David	Imam
Christina Cox	Eve Logan

Reception

The Chronicles of Riddick received poor reviews from film critics, receiving a 30% Fresh rating with an average score of 4.7/10 on aggregate review site Rotten Tomatoes.[1] and an average 38/100 score on MetaCritic[2] Domestically the film was a box office disappointment ($57 million), though its total global box office take was $115 million. Vin Diesel's performance in the film earned him a Golden Raspberry Award nomination for Worst Actor.

The film spun off books, animation and video games. The Xbox game *The Chronicles of Riddick: Escape from Butcher Bay*, later ported to the PC, released simultaneously with the film was well received[3] as was the animated short film *The Chronicles of Riddick: Dark Fury* by *Æon Flux* director Peter Chung. The Unrated Director's Cut DVD (featuring scenes which were cut in order to obtain a PG-13 rating) was released on November 16, 2004 and sold 1.5 million copies on the first day alone. On April 7, 2009, a remake of the video game was included with the release of *The Chronicles of Riddick: Assault on Dark Athena*.

Sequels

In a March 8, 2006, article on Comingsoon.net, it was reported that Vin Diesel claimed that a sequel to *The Chronicles of Riddick* was in the works.[4] According to him, he had already written a storyline that covered a trilogy which began with the Chronicles of Riddick. Another article on Comingsoon.net, written on March 11, 2005, reports that Vin Diesel states that Chronicles 2 was to deal with The Underverse, while Chronicles 3 was to conclude the series with a return to Furya.[5]

An article dated November 10, 2007, on countingdown.com, further indicates that a sequel may be in works - "We're talking about it". David Twohy indicates however that it "probably won't be a Universal movie and probably will be an independent movie" seeing a much smaller budget.[6]

Two more sequels have been confirmed for production, and David Twohy is now writing the scripts.[7] Diesel told MTV News that in spite of the poor reception, the time between the sequels is only about getting it right, not about trying to find support.

"Everyone knows I love the Riddick character and I'm always working on it," Diesel asserted. "It just takes five years to make another one because David Twohy and I are so precise about it."[8]

On March 20, 2009, Vin Diesel commented on a sequel in an interview on *Friday Night with Jonathan Ross*, stating that David Twohy has nearly finished scripts, and is planning to start production on the third film in early 2010.[9]

On November 30, 2009 Vin Diesel left an update on his Facebook page effectively announcing that pre-production work is underway on the Chronicles of Riddick sequel.[10]

On February 9, 2010, Vin Diesel confirmed in an update on his Facebook page that one of the locations used in the upcoming sequel would be the White Desert in Farafra, Egypt. He mentioned the terrain features, unique to the area, would lend to the off-planet atmosphere of the film.[11]

References

[1] "The Chronicles of Riddick on Rotten Tomatoes" (http://www.rottentomatoes.com/m/chronicles_of_riddick/). . Retrieved 2008-12-17

[2] "The Chronicles of Riddick on MetaCritic" (http://www.metacritic.com/video/titles/chroniclesofriddick?q=chronicles of riddick). . Retrieved 2007-07-23

[3] "The Chronicles of Riddick: Escape From Butcher Bay - Developer's Cut" (http://www.gamespot.com/pc/action/chroniclesofriddick/index.html?tag=result;title;0). Gamespot.com. . Retrieved 2010-07-09.

[4] "ComingSoon.net" (http://www.comingsoon.net/news/movienews.php?id=13540).ComingSoon.net. . Retrieved 2010-07-09.

[5] "ComingSoon.net" (http://www.comingsoon.net/news/topnews.php?id=8722). ComingSoon.net. . Retrieved 2010-07-09.

[6] "David Twohy Gives "Chronicles of Riddick 2" Update!" (http://countingdown.com/movies/3531221/news?item_id=4003970). Countingdown.com. 2007-11-19. . Retrieved 2010-07-09.

[7] "Diesel talks more sequels" (http://www.filmwad.com/two-more-riddick-sequels-en-route-says-vin-6800-p.html). Filmwad.com. 2008-08-28. . Retrieved 2010-07-09.

[8] "Two More Riddick Sequels En Route Says Vin" (http://www.filmwad.com/two-more-riddick-sequels-en-route-says-vin-6800-p.html). Filmwad.com. 2008-08-28. . Retrieved 2010-07-09.

[9] Submitted by Rottenjesus on Wed, 12/02/2009 - 8:59pm.. "Riddick Getting Set to Return for Round 3!" (http://www.dreadcentral.com/news/34787/riddick-getting-set-return-round-3). Dreadcentral.com. . Retrieved 2010-07-09.

[10] Parfitt, Orlando (2009-12-03). "Riddick 3 Moves Ahead - Movies News at IGN" (http://movies.ign.com/articles/105/1051560p1.html). Movies.ign.com. . Retrieved 2010-07-09.

[11] "New Concept Art from Third Riddick Film" (http://www.dreadcentral.com/news/36867/new-concept-art-third-riddick-film). Dreadcentral.com. . Retrieved 2010-07-09.

External links

- Official website (http://www.thechroniclesofriddick.com)
- *The Chronicles of Riddick* (http://www.imdb.com/title/tt0296572/) at the Internet Movie Database
- *The Chronicles of Riddick* (http://www.allmovie.com/work/286673) at Allmovie
- *The Chronicles of Riddick* (http://tcmdb.com/title/title.jsp?stid=452705) at the TCM Movie Database
- *The Chronicles of Riddick* (http://www.rottentomatoes.com/m/chronicles_of_riddick/) at Rotten Tomatoes
- *The Chronicles of Riddick* (http://www.boxofficemojo.com/movies/?id=chroniclesofriddick.htm) at Box Office Mojo
- Vin Diesel interview for *The Chronicles Of Riddick* (http://www.moviehole.net/news/20040607_3747.html)

Home on the Range (film)

Home on the Range	

Directed by	Will Finn John Sanford
Produced by	Alice Dewey
Written by	Will Finn John Sanford
Starring	Roseanne Barr Judi Dench Cuba Gooding, Jr. Randy Quaid Jennifer Tilly Steve Buscemi
Music by	Alan Menken Glenn Slater
Editing by	Mark A. Hester H. Lee Peterson
Studio	Walt Disney Feature Animation
Distributed by	Walt Disney Pictures Buena Vista Distribution
Release date(s)	April 2, 2004
Running time	76 minutes
Country	United States
Language	English
Budget	$110,000,000
Gross revenue	$103,951,461

Home on the Range is a 2004 American animated musical feature film produced by Walt Disney Feature Animation and released by Walt Disney Pictures on April 2, 2004, and was named after the popular country song "Home on the Range". The 45th feature in the Walt Disney Animated Classics, it was the last traditionally animated Disney film until 2009's *The Princess and the Frog*, and the last Disney animated film to be released on VHS.

Set in the old west, the plot centers on a mismatched trio of dairy cows – brash, adventurous Maggie, prim, proper Mrs. Calloway and ditzy, happy-go-lucky Grace (voiced by Roseanne Barr, Judi Dench and Jennifer Tilly respectively) – who must capture an infamous cattle rustler, for his bounty, in order to save their idyllic farm from foreclosure. (As Grace puts it, "Who better to catch a cattle thief...than a cow?") Aiding them in their quest is Lucky Jack, a feisty, peg-legged rabbit, but a selfish horse named Buck (Cuba Gooding Jr.), eagerly working in the service of Rico, a famous bounty hunter, seeks the glory for himself.

The film stars the voices of Roseanne Barr, Judi Dench, Jennifer Tilly, Steve Buscemi, G.W. Bailey, Cuba Gooding, Jr. and Randy Quaid.

Plot

Grace, Mrs Calloway and Maggie (from left to right)

Maggie is the only cow left on the Dixon Ranch after Alamida Slim (a cattle rustler capable of stealing 500 in a single night) stole all the rest of Dixon's cattle. Mr. Dixon sells Maggie to Pearl, a kind and elderly woman that runs a small farm called Patch of Heaven.

The local Sheriff arrives to tell Pearl that her bank is cracking down on debtors. Pearl has three days to pay the bank $750, or her farm will be sold to the highest bidder. Hearing this, Maggie convinces the other cows on the farm (Grace, a happy-go-lucky character, and Mrs. Calloway, who has had leadership gone to her head) to go to town to attempt winning prize money at a fair.

While the cows are in town, a bounty hunter named Rico (who Buck, the Sheriff's horse, idolizes) drops a criminal off and collects the reward. Stating he needs a replacement horse to go after Alamida Slim while his own horse rests, he takes Buck. When Maggie find out that the reward for capturing Slim is of exactly $750, she convinces the other cows to try and capture him to save Patch of Heaven.

That night, they hide among a large heard of steers, when Alamida Slim appears. Before any of them can do anything, Slim beings a yodeling song which sends all the cattle (except Grace, who is tone deaf) into a trance that causes them to dance madly and follow Slim anywhere. Grace is able to bring Maggie and Mrs. Calloway back to their senses just before Slim closes the path behind him with a rockslide to stop Rico and his men from chasing him.

As Rico discusses with his men what his next move will be, Buck starts talking with Maggie, Grace, and Mrs. Calloway as old friends and miming actions. This causes Rico to believe Buck is frightened by cows, and sends Buck back to the Sheriff. Buck escapes, determined to capture Slim for himself to prove his worth. Maggie, Grace, and Mrs. Calloway are left behind, but they meet a peg-legged rabbit named Lucky Jack, who leads them to the Slim's hideout mine.

At the mine, Slim reveals that he has been stealing all cattle from his former patrons. When his former patrons can't support their land anymore, he buys the land when it is auctioned off, under the guise of the respectable-looking Mr. O'delay, using the very money he gets from selling the cattle he stole.

After arriving to Slim's hideout, the cows capture Slim. They run off with Slim's accomplices and buyer in pursuit on a steam train. Rico arrives. When the chase stops, Rico is revealed to work for Slim.

Slim dons his O'delay costume and leaves the cows stranded in the middle of the desert with the train, while he goes to attend the auction. However, the cows arrive using the train to the farm and expose Slim. Slim is arrested by the police, and Patch of Heaven is saved by the reward money.

Production

Prior to the film's release, Disney stated that it would be their last film in their animated features canon to use traditional animation. Although Disney animated films have featured some computer-generated effects for many years, Disney announced plans to move entirely to CGI animation after *Home on the Range,* beginning with 2005's *Chicken Little*, and laid off most of its animation department. However, after the company's acquisition of Pixar in early 2006, new leaders John Lasseter and Ed Catmull decided to revive traditional animation, and announced the upcoming 2D animation film, *The Princess and the Frog*. Still, Home on the Range is the final feature in the canon to use the CAPS system which was first fully used in *The Rescuers Down Under*. The film began pre-production after the release of *Pocahontas* in 1995. In August 2000, the film was announced as *Sweating Bullets* and scheduled for a fall 2003 release. The title was changed to *Home on the Range* in April, 2002. This film was originally slated to have been released in November 2003, but story and production problems forced Disney to swap release dates with *Brother Bear* (originally slated for spring 2004) in December 2002. The studio also broke from its own tradition of releasing major films at either Thanksgiving or summer vacation (to maximize the family audience), releasing it on April 2.

Cast

Actor	Role
Roseanne Barr	Maggie
Judi Dench	Mrs. Calloway
Jennifer Tilly	Grace
Cuba Gooding, Jr.	Buck
Randy Quaid	Alameda Slim
Charles Dennis	Rico
Charles Haid	Lucky Jack
Carole Cook	Pearl Gesner
Joe Flaherty	Jeb the Goat
Steve Buscemi	Wesley
Richard Riehle	Sam the Sheriff
Lance LeGault	Junior the Buffalo
G.W. Bailey	Rusty
Patrick Warburton	Patrick
Estelle Harris	Audrey the Chicken
Sam J. Levine	Willie Brothers (speaking)
Ann Richards	Annie

Crew

Crew Position	
Written and Directed by	Will Finn John Sanford
Produced by	Alice Dewey
Songs by	Alan Menken Glenn Slater
Original Score by	Alan Menken
Associate Producer	David J. Steinberg
Art Director	David Cutler
Film Editor	H. Lee Peterson
Artistic Supervisors	Jean Christophe-Poulain (Layout supervisor) Christy Maltese (Background supervisor) Marshall Toomey (Clean-up supervisor) Marlon West (Effects supervisor)
Supervising Animators	Chris Buck (Maggie) Duncan Marjoribanks (Mrs. Caloway) Mark Henn (Grace/Wesley/Rusty) Michael Surrey (Buck) Dale Baer (Alameda Slim/Junior) Russ Edmonds (Rico/Willies/Horses) Sandro Lucio Cleuzo (Sheriff/Jeb) Bruce W. Smith and Mark Henn (Pearl) James Lopez (Farm Animals) Shawn Keller (Lucky Jack)
Based on a Story by Character Design Artistic Coordinator Production Manager	Will Finn John Sanford Michael LaBash Sam Levine Mark Kennedy Robert Lence Joseph C. Mosier Dennis M. Blakely Tamara Boutcher

Reception

Rotten Tomatoes reported that 55% of critics gave positive reviews based on 118 reviews. According to Metacritic, the film's average rating was 50%, based on 30 reviews. Users gave the film a 4.2/10 approval rating based on 12 votes.

The film had a budget of about $110 million, making a U.S. box office gross of $50,026,353, and a worldwide gross of $76,482,461.[1]

A Dairy Tale

A Dairy Tale is a 3-minute spinoff released in 2004. Mrs. Caloway tries to tell the story of the Three Little Pigs but is interrupted by Maggie, Grace, Buck, Jeb, Ollie and Audery, who tell the story in their own ways. The characters are featured in super deformed and 'storybook' style.

Soundtrack

Home on the Range: An Original Walt Disney Records Soundtrack	

Soundtrack by Various Artists	
Released	March 30, 2004
Label	Walt Disney Records
Producer	Alan Menken Glenn Slater
Professional reviews	
• Allmusic link [2]	

Home on the Range: An Original Walt Disney Records Soundtrack is the soundtrack to Disney's 2004 animated feature *Home on the Range*. It contains music written by Alan Menken and Glenn Slater, and vocal songs performed by k.d. lang, Randy Quaid, Bonnie Raitt, Tim McGraw, and The Beu Sisters along with the film's score composed by Alan Menken. The album was released on March 30, 2004 by Walt Disney Records.

1. (You Ain't) Home On The Range - Chorus
2. Little Patch of Heaven - k.d. lang
3. Yodel-Adle-Eedle-Idle-Oo - Randy Quaid and Chorus
4. Will The Sun Ever Shine Again - Bonnie Raitt
5. (You Ain't) Home On The Range - Echo Mine Reprise - Chorus
6. Wherever The Trail May Lead - Tim McGraw
7. Anytime You Need A Friend - The Beu Sisters
8. Cows In Town/Saloon Song (Score)
9. On The Farm (Score)
10. Bad News (Score)
11. Storm And The Aftermath (Score)
12. Cows To The Rescue (Score)
13. Buck (Score)
14. My Farm Is Saved/Little Patch of Heaven(Reprise) (Score)
15. Anytime You Need a Friend - Alan Menken

References

[1] Home on the Range - Box Office Data, Movie News, Cast Information - The Numbers (http://www.the-numbers.com/movies/2004/HMRNG.php)

External links

- Official website (http://disney.go.com/disneyvideos/animatedfilms/homeontherange)
- *Home on the Range* (http://www.bcdb.com/cartoons/23327-Home_On_The_Range) at the Big Cartoon DataBase
- *Home on the Range* (http://www.imdb.com/title/tt0299172/) at the Internet Movie Database
- *Home on the Range* (http://www.allmovie.com/work/290407) at Allmovie
- *Home on the Range* (http://www.ultimatedisney.com/homeontherange.html) at UltimateDisney.com
- *Home on the Range* (http://www.rottentomatoes.com/m/home_on_the_range/) at Rotten Tomatoes
- *Home on the Range* (http://www.metacritic.com/film/titles/homeontherange) at Metacritic
- *Home on the Range* (http://www.boxofficemojo.com/movies/?id=homeontherange.htm) at Box Office Mojo

Angelina Ballerina

Angelina Ballerina is a fictional mouse, created by author Katharine Holabird and illustrator Helen Craig, who is featured in a popular series of children's books. The first book in the series was published in 1983, and since then, there has been over 20 books in the series.

In 2002, an animated TV series of 39 fifteen minute episodes based on the books was produced by HIT Entertainment in the United Kingdom. The series featured actress Finty Williams as the voice of Angelina, and her mother Judi Dench as Miss Lilly. The series aired on PBS in the United States, where it was presented by Connecticut Public Television; and can currently be seen on Nick Jr. in the UK and PBS Kids Sprout in the US.

A computer-animated revival, *Angelina Ballerina: The Next Steps*, premiered on PBS stations in September 2009. Consisting of 80 stories, it is directed by Davis Doi and animated at SD Entertainment.[1] WNET, after purchasing CPTV's production unit, is the producer of the program. English National Ballet took a live version of Angelina Ballerina called *Angelina's Star Performance* on tour in autumn 2007. It is a fairly short ballet aimed at children.

Angelina Ballerina appears on the single cover sleeve of Peter Kay's The Official BBC Children in Need Medley, and makes a cameo on the music video.

In 2010 HIT Entertainment announces partnership with Vital Theatre Company to bring "Angelina Ballerina, The Musical" to the stage beginning October 2010.

Angelina Ballerina opens in NYC, October 2, 2010, starring Whitney Autumn Meyer [2] as Angelina. The show runs through January 2, 2011.

- Angelina Mouseling is a little mouse who loves to dance and dreams of becoming a famous ballerina. Voiced by Finty Williams. She often wears a pink leotard, pink tutu, pink hair ribbon, and pink ballet slippers.
- William Longtail is one of two boys (the other is Angelina's cousin Henry) in Miss Lilly's ballet class. He is in love with Angelina. Voiced by Keith Wickham.
- Alice Nimbletoes is Angelina's best friend, who is very skilled at gymnastics. She likes Sammy, and is usually happy. She's very clever. Voiced by Jo Wyatt. She often wears a green leotard, tutu, hair ribbon, and ballet slippers. She loves her food, which is cheese pie. She also appears on 'Angelina Ballerina: The Next Steps'.
- Miss Lilly is Angelina's ballet teacher. She grew up in Dachovia, a far-away land. Voiced by Judi Dench. She is sometimes mentioned in 'Angelina Ballerina: The Next Steps', and a picture of her is seen at Angelina's new school.

- Penelope and Priscilla Pinkpaws are twin sisters who tease and belittle nearly everyone, sometimes including each other. They are particularly jealous of Angelina for her dancing ability. They also have a new baby brother. Voiced by Jonell Elliott and Jo Wyatt. Priscilla wears blue leotards, tutus, and pointe shoes but wears a purple hair ribbon, and Penelope wears a purple leotard, tutu, and ballet slippers, but wears a blue hair ribbon.
- Sammy Watts is an older mouse in Angelina's school, who often causes trouble for William and Angelina particularly but has a heart of gold. Voiced by Jo Wyatt.
- Mr. Maurice Mouseling is Angelina's father and the proprietor of the *Mouseland Gazette*. Voiced by Keith Wickham.
- Mrs. Matilda Mouseling is Angelina's mother. Voiced by Jonell Elliott.
- Polly Mouseling is the second child and daughter of Mr. and Mrs. Mouseling, little sister of Angelina, and second cousin of Henry. Polly is 4 years old and can speak in 'Angelina Ballerina: The Next Steps'.
- Grandma and Grandpa are Angelina's grandparents. Voiced by Keith Wickham and Adrienne Posta. They are sometimes mentioned in 'Angelina Ballerina: The Next Steps'.
- Uncle Louis is Mr. Mouseling's brother, Angelina's uncle and Henry's father. Voiced by Rob Rackstraw.
- Henry is Angelina's little cousin. Voiced by Jo Wyatt.
- Mrs Hodgepodge is Angelina's next-door neighbour. She always seems grumpy and is viewed with fear by most of the Chipping Cheddar mouselings, but occasionally she helps the mouselings often when they least expect it. Voiced by Mellissa Greenspann (Season 1). Usually, Finty Williams (Season 2, until the first series was cancelled).
- Doctor Tuttle is the doctor in the town of Chipping Cheddar. Voiced by Keith Wickham.
- Mr. Operatski is an old friend of Miss Lilly's. Angelina is convinced wrongly, as it turns out that he hates mouselings. He has a moustache and a medium-pitched Russian accent. Voied by Derek Jacobi.
- Queen Seraphina is a childhood friend of Miss Lilly's, who is now the Queen of Mouseland. She might had been inspired by the late Princess Diana.
- Princess Valentine is the daughter of Queen Seraphina.
- Anya is a mouseling who comes to Chipping Cheddar as part of a migrant family working through the harvest season. She is teased by the Pinkpaws twins, and befriended by Angelina. She later joins Miss Lilly's ballet class.

Books in the series

Book Title	Year Written
Angelina Ballerina	1983
Angelina and the Princess	1984
Angelina's Christmas	1985
Angelina at the Fair	1985
Angelina on Stage	1986
Angelina and Alice	1987
Angelina's Birthday	1989
Angelina's Baby Sister	1991
Angelina's Ice Skates	1993
Angelina's Halloween	2000
Angelina and the Butterfly	2001
Angelina's Ballet Class	2001
Angelina and Henry	2002

Angelina Loves	2002
Angelina and the Rag Doll	2002
Angelina Ballerina's Invitation to the Ballet	2003
Angelina, Star of the Show	2004
Angelina's Silver Locket	2004
Angelina at the Palace	2005
Angelina at the Royal Wedding	2010

References

[1] Bloom, Julie (3 September 2009). "Ballet Masters Put a Mouse on Her Toes" (http://www.nytimes.com/2009/09/04/arts/dance/04angelina.html?_r=1&scp=1&sq=Angelina Ballerina&st=cse). *The New York Times*: p. C1. . Retrieved 2009-09-10.

External links

- Official *Angelina Ballerina* website (http://www.hitentertainment.com/angelinaballerina/)
- Official *Angelina Ballerina, The Musical* website (http://www.angelinaballerinathemusical.com/)
- Angelina Ballerina on Nick Jr. UK (http://www.nickjr.co.uk/shows/angelina/index.aspx)
- Angelina Ballerina on Sprout (http://www.sproutonline.com/sprout/characters/?preset=angelina)
- *Angelina Ballerina* opening theme song (:23 min) (http://angelina-ballerina.littletoons.com/)
- English National Ballet performs *Angelina's Star Performance* (http://www.ballet.org.uk/angelina)
- *Angelina Ballerina, The Musical* presented by Vital Theatre Company (http://www.vitaltheatre.org/angelinaballerinathemusical.php)

Die Another Day

<table>
<tr><th colspan="2">Die Another Day</th></tr>
<tr><td colspan="2">
Theatrical release poster</td></tr>
<tr><td>James Bond</td><td>Pierce Brosnan</td></tr>
<tr><td>Also starring</td><td>Halle Berry
Toby Stephens
Rick Yune
Rosamund Pike
John Cleese
Judi Dench Will
Yun Lee
Michael Madsen
Rachel Grant</td></tr>
<tr><td>Directed by</td><td>Lee Tamahori</td></tr>
<tr><td>Produced by</td><td>Michael G. Wilson
Barbara Broccoli</td></tr>
<tr><td>Novel/Story by</td><td>Neal Purvis
Robert Wade</td></tr>
<tr><td>Screenplay by</td><td>Neal Purvis
Robert Wade</td></tr>
<tr><td>Cinematography</td><td>David Tattersall</td></tr>
<tr><td>Music by</td><td>David Arnold</td></tr>
<tr><td>Main theme</td><td>Die Another Day</td></tr>
<tr><td>Composer</td><td>Madonna
Mirwais Ahmadzaï</td></tr>
<tr><td>Performer</td><td>Madonna</td></tr>
<tr><td>Editing by</td><td>Christian Wagner</td></tr>
<tr><td>Distributed by</td><td>Metro-Goldwyn-Mayer
20th Century Fox</td></tr>
<tr><td>Release date(s)</td><td>November 20, 2002</td></tr>
</table>

Running time	133 minutes
Country	United Kingdom United States
Budget	$140 million
Worldwide gross	$431,971,116[1]
Preceded by	*The World Is Not Enough*
Followed by	*Casino Royale*

Die Another Day (2002) is the twentieth spy film in the James Bond series, and the fourth and last film to star Pierce Brosnan as the fictional MI6 agent James Bond; it is also the last Bond film of the original timeline with the series being rebooted with *Casino Royale*. In the pre-title sequence, Bond leads a mission to North Korea, during which he is found out and, after seemingly killing a rogue North Korean colonel, he is captured and imprisoned. More than a year later, Bond is released as part of a prisoner exchange, and, surmising that someone within the British government betrayed him, he follows a trail of clues in an effort to earn redemption by finding his betrayer and learning the intentions of Gustav Graves, who in typical Bond fashion, is not all that he seems.

Die Another Day, produced by Michael G. Wilson and Barbara Broccoli, and directed by Lee Tamahori, marks the franchise's 40th anniversary. The series began in 1962 with Sean Connery starring as Bond in U.K.'s *Dr. No*. *Die Another Day* includes references to each of the preceding films and also alludes to several *Bond* novels.

The 2002 film received mixed reviews—some critics praised Lee Tamahori's work on the film, while others claimed the plot was damaged by excessive use of CGI. Thus lauded by some and despite criticism, it was the highest-grossing James Bond film to that date.

Plot

James Bond infiltrates a North Korean military base belonging to Colonel Tan-Sun Moon, and poses as an arms dealer trading African conflict diamonds for weaponry. Bond attempts to assassinate Moon, but has his true identity revealed by Zao, Moon's assistant, during the transaction when someone transmits Bond's top-secret MI6 personnel file to Zao. A hovercraft chase results in the disfiguring of Zao's face and the apparent death of Colonel Moon after Bond runs him off a cliff. Bond is captured and imprisoned by the Colonel's father, General Moon, and subsequently tortured.

After fourteen months of captivity, Bond is traded at the Korean border for Zao in a prisoner exchange. Bond is informed by M that his 00 status has been suspended. His freedom was a result of the Americans and MI6 believing he was releasing sensitive information to North Korea under torture and they wanted to get him back under their control before he was able let out any more information. Bond, knowing that he never revealed any information, instead surmises that someone within MI6 betrayed him, first by revealing his identity to Moon and Zao, and then by revealing the identities of deep-cover operatives who were subsequently assassinated.

Nonetheless, M explains he is to be transported to the Falkland Islands where he will be detained indefinitely until he is considered no longer a threat. By intentionally stopping his heart rate through meditation, Bond escapes his recovery room in a British destroyer off the shore of Hong Kong and learns through a Chinese Intelligence contact that Zao is in Havana, Cuba. While in Havana, Bond meets NSA agent Giacinta 'Jinx' Johnson, although at the time neither are aware of the other's profession.

Bond and Jinx meet in Cuba.

Bond follows Zao and Jinx to a gene therapy clinic where patients can have their appearances altered through DNA restructuring. Jinx is posing as a client to find information on Zao, but Bond finds him first. Zao escapes Bond and Jinx, but leaves evidence of several conflict diamonds bearing the laser signature of British tycoon Sir Gustav Graves. Bond later encounters Graves at a London fencing club along with his assistant Miranda Frost, also an undercover MI6 agent. Bond is invited to Iceland for a scientific demonstration after showing Graves one of his diamonds.

At the demonstration in Iceland, Graves unveils a new orbital mirror satellite (dubbed "Icarus") the ostensible purpose of which is to harness solar energy and focus it to areas of earth to provide day and year-round sunshine for crop development. Jinx, who is at the ceremony now posing as a journalist, infiltrates the command center of the Iceland mansion and locates Zao, who is using the same gene therapy equipment found in Cuba. She is shocked unconscious and has her hands and feet strapped down. She is tortured using a laser. Bond's rescue attempt sees the death of Mr. Kil. After seeing Zao, Bond realizes that Colonel Moon survived their original encounter and is using the technology to assume the identity and appearance of Gustav Graves.

Bond confronts Graves, but Frost arrives to reveal herself as the traitor and the one who exposed Bond in North Korea. Frost has also tampered with Bond's gun when they slept together the night before. Bond escapes onto the ice and is pursued by the solar beam of the Icarus satellite, controlled by Moon. Bond returns to the facility to rescue Jinx, where he is discovered and chased by Zao. Zao dies after Bond tricks him into crashing his car into a flooded portion of the facility and causing a chandelier to fall on him. Bond then revives a drowned Jinx in the hot water pool in Graves' biodome.

Bond and Jinx pursue Graves and Frost to the Korean peninsula and stow away on Graves' cargo plane. Graves reveals his true identity to his father, General Moon, and the purpose of the Icarus satellite. He plans to cut a path through the Korean Demilitarized Zone with concentrated sunlight, allowing North Korean troops to invade South Korea and reunite the countries through force. General Moon disapproves of the plan, and is murdered by his son.

From left: Gustav Graves, Miranda Frost, Verity, James Bond.

Bond engages Graves in a fist fight to stop the attack while Jinx attempts to regain control of the plane although Frost finds and subsequently engages Jinx in a sword fight. During the simultaneous fights the plane passes through the Icarus beam and is severely damaged. Jinx kills Frost, and Bond is able to pull a ripcord from Graves' attached parachute (which draws him closer to the door) and then electrocute him, which sends him flying out the plane, only to be ingested by the engine. Bond and Jinx escape the disintegrating plane via a helicopter in the cargo hold along with a stash of Graves' diamonds. They take shelter and use the diamonds as part of sexual play, but state that they will return them eventually.

Cast

- Pierce Brosnan as James Bond 007, an MI6 agent who is betrayed during a mission and subsequently dismissed under accusations that he leaked information to North Korea. Once reinstated with MI6, he tracks down Zao and uncovers a plot to reunite North and South Korea using military force.
- Halle Berry as Giacinta 'Jinx' Johnson, an NSA agent who collaborates with Bond to track Zao and find his connection to the mysterious Gustav Graves. Berry described her character, Jinx, as "more modern" than her counterparts from previous films, "fashion-forward", and "the next step in the evolution of women in the *Bond* movies."[2] According to an ITV news poll, Jinx was voted the fourth toughest on-screen girl of all time.[3]
- Toby Stephens as Gustav Graves, Main antagonist. A British entrepreneur, though actually is Colonel Moon, who changed his appearance with the assistance of gene therapy technology and creates a satellite that uses diamonds to bring sunshine to the world at night. His real aim, however, is to assist North Korea's conquest of South Korea by destroying a mine field along the DMZ and taking out nuclear warheads fired by North Korea's enemies.
- Rick Yune as Zao, a North Korean who helps Graves implement his plans. Yune described Zao as one of the most "extreme" looking Bond villains; Yune's makeup—which included the implantation of real diamonds—required three hours a day to make.[4]
- Rosamund Pike as Miranda Frost, a double agent who initially poses as Bond's ally but later reveals herself to be an affiliate of Graves. Of filming her scenes with Brosnan, Pike said "We had pretty fantastic sex." But movie producers decided much of the footage was "too hot" and the sex scenes were trimmed.[5]
- Judi Dench as M, the strict head of MI6 who revokes Bond's licence to kill when he is released from prison, but later re-enlists him to help foil Graves' scheme.
- Will Yun Lee as Colonel Moon, a rogue North Korean army colonel who, though Bond thinks him dead after their first encounter, is found to be alive, and has altered his appearance to take on the identity of British tycoon Gustav Graves.
- Kenneth Tsang as General Moon, Colonel Moon's father. He is a strong advocate of North Korea's peaceful reunion with the South. He opposes his son's plan for reunification through violent conquest and is killed by his son for what the ex-colonel perceives as a lack of vision.
- John Cleese as Q, MI6's "quartermaster" who supplies Bond with multi-purpose vehicles and gadgets which prove useful in the latter's mission. Having previously played the role of Q's protege "R" in *The World Is Not Enough*, Cleese takes over the role of Q following Desmond Llewelyn's death. He pointedly refers to his predecessor when discussing some of his own work.
- Ho Yi as Hotel manager Mr. Chang, who also happens to be a Chinese special agent
- Rachel Grant as Peaceful Fountains of Desire, a Chinese agent working for Mr Chang, undercover as a masseuse.
- Emilio Echevarría as Raoul, the manager of a Havana cigar factory, and a British sleeper. He helps Bond find Zao in Cuba.
- Samantha Bond as Miss Moneypenny, M's secretary.
- Lawrence Makoare as Mr. Kil, one of Gustav Graves' henchmen.
- David Decio as Mr. Kil's PA, Mr. Kil's personal assistant.
- Michael Madsen as Damian Falco, a high-ranking official in the NSA. In a 2002 interview Madsen remarked that "It's not a big role, but it's somewhat pivotal in that it introduces a new recurring character."[6] A recurring character that has yet to recur, Madsen did not appear in either of the two following films.
- Madonna as Verity, Bond's fencing instructor.

Production

Filming

The opening sequence was shot with surfers at Peahi, or Jaws, off of the North coast of Maui in December 2001.

Principal photography of *Die Another Day* began on 11 January 2002 at Pinewood studios.[7] The film was shot primarily in the United Kingdom, Iceland, and Cádiz, Spain. Other locations included Pinewood Studios' historic 007 Stage, and scenes shot in Maui, Hawaii, in December 2001. Laird Hamilton and other professional surfers were hired to perform in the pre-title surfing scene, which was shot near Cádiz and Newquay, Cornwall. Scenes inside Graves' diamond mine were also filmed in Cornwall, at the Eden Project. The scenes involving the Cuban locations Havana and the fictional Isla Los Organos were filmed at La Caleta, Spain.[8]

The scenes featuring Berry in a bikini were shot in Cádiz; the location was reportedly cold and windy, and footage has been released of Berry wrapped in thick towels between takes to avoid catching a chill.[9] Berry was injured during filming when debris from a smoke grenade flew into her eye. The debris was removed in a 30-minute operation.[10]

In London, the Reform Club was used to shoot several places in the film, including the lobby at the Blades Club, MI6 Headquarters, Buckingham Palace, Green Park, and Westminster. Svalbard, Norway and Jökulsárlón, Iceland were used for the car chase on the ice with additional scenes filmed at Jostedalsbreen National Park, Norway and RAF Little Rissington, Gloucestershire.[8]

Jökulsárlón, Iceland.

The scene where Bond surfs the wave that Icarus created when Graves was trying to kill Bond was shot on the blue screen. The waves and all of the glaciers in the scene were digitally produced.

The hangar interior of the "US Air Base in South Korea", shown crowded with Chinook helicopters, was filmed at RAF Odiham in Hampshire, UK, as were the helicopter interior shots during the Switchblade sequence although this took place entirely on the ground with the sky background being added post-shooting using blue screen techniques. Although in the plot the base is American, in reality all the aircraft and personnel in the shot are British. In the film, a Switchblade (one-man glider shaped like a fighter jet) is used by Bond and Jinx to enter North Korea undetected. The Switchblade was based on a workable model called "PHASST" (Programmable High Altitude Single Soldier Transport). Kinetic Aerospace Inc.'s lead designer, Jack McCornack was impressed by director Lee Tamahori's way of conducting the Switchblade scene and said, "It's brief, but realistic. The good guys get in unobserved, thanks to a fast cruise, good glide performance, and minimal radar signature. It's a wonderful promotion for the PHASST."[11] Also, Graves' plane was a 20-foot-wide (6.1 m) model that was controlled by a computer. When the plane flew through the Icarus beam, engineers cut the plane away piece by piece so that it looked like it was burning and falling apart.

The sex scene between Bond and Jinx—the first time onscreen in the series in which Bond is depicted actually having sex as opposed to a post-coital scenario—had to be trimmed for the American market. An early cut of *Die Another Day* featured a brief moment—seven seconds in length—in which Jinx is heard moaning strongly. The MPAA ordered that the scene be trimmed so that *Die Another Day* could get the expected PG-13 rating. The scene was cut as requested, earning the film a PG-13 rating for "action violence and sexuality."[12]

Music

The soundtrack was composed by David Arnold and released on Warner Bros. Records.[13] He again made use of electronic rhythm elements in his score, and included two of the new themes created for *The World is not Enough*. The first, originally used as Renard's theme, is heard during the mammoth "Antonov" cue on the recording, and is written for piano. The second new theme, used in the "Christmas in Turkey" track of *The World Is not Enough*, is reused in the "Going Down Together" track.

The title song for *Die Another Day* was written and sung by Madonna, who also had a cameo in the film as a fencing instructor. This is the first *Bond* theme to directly depict the film's plot since *Dr. No*; all of the other previous *Bond* titles are stand-alone set pieces. The concept of the title sequence is to represent Bond trying to survive 14 months of torture at the hands of the North Koreans. Critics' opinions of the song were sharply divided—it was nominated for a Golden Globe for Best Original Song and the 2004 Grammy Award for Best Dance Recording,[14] but also for a Golden Raspberry Award for Worst Original Song of 2002. In a MORI poll for the Channel 4 programme *"James Bond's Greatest Hits"*, the song was voted 9th out of 22, and also came in as an "overwhelming number one" favorite among those under the age of 24.[15]

References to other films

Zao's Jaguar XKR used in *Die Another Day*, seen at a James Bond convention.

To acknowledge that *Die Another Day* marked the 40th anniversary of the James Bond film series and was the 20th entry in the official series, references to every one of the preceding nineteen films were incorporated.[16] The smuggling of diamonds and the use of a satellite with a powerful laser, and the villain surviving the pre-title sequence and returning with a new identity were the themes lifted from *Diamonds Are Forever*. So is Gustav Graves' comment that "diamonds are for everyone" and the clear, ovate, cross-hatched floor in his office, which was last seen in Willard Whyte's penthouse lair. The Venice fight scene in *Moonraker* wherein display cases and other valuable artifacts are destroyed, was also remade as the fencing match. The exterior of Graves' command center is a tropical forest, also akin to *Moonraker*. The revocation of Bond's licence to kill and his loss of double-0 status traced its origin to *Licence to Kill*. Graves' starting a man-made ice mountain avalanche to kill Bond is from *On Her Majesty's Secret Service*; the uniforms worn by the guards at Graves' ice palace also resemble the ones worn by Blofeld's men at Piz Gloria in that film. There are several gadgets that appear in Q's laboratory, such as the shoe blade and trick attaché case that appeared in *From Russia with Love*, the jet-pack and the underwater rebreather from *Thunderball*, the 'Snooper' device from *A View to a Kill*, and the Acro-jet and the alligator submarine from *Octopussy*. Also, the scene in the Hong Kong hotel room where Bond catches Chang trying to film him making love is a reference to Grant and Klebb filming the same scene in *From Russia with Love*. Like Honey Rider in *Dr. No*, Jinx is first seen rising out of the sea, wearing a bikini, knife, and belt. The gunbarrel sound from *Dr. No* can be heard in the background as Bond climbs up the side of a dock after escaping a hospital ship. Jinx is strapped to a table and threatened with a laser in a reference to *Goldfinger*. The Union Jack parachute that Graves uses echoes Bond's parachute in *The Spy Who Loved Me*. Bond going through a room filled with mirrors while chasing Zao in the gene clinic, and M meeting Bond inside a wrecked ship are both from *The Man With The Golden Gun*. Bond eating some grapes after a kill inside the clinic is similar to a scene in the health clinic in *Thunderball*. Q's line from *Goldfinger*, "I never joke about my work," is also reprised. The Aston Martin car chase on the ice and the climax inside a cargo jet plane are reminiscent of similar sequences in *The Living Daylights*, while a shot-by-shot reference to the ending of *Goldfinger* (someone shoots a bullet through a plane window, causing cabin depressurisation and eventually Graves' death through the open window) is used. The ice chase takes place on the same glacial lagoon location (Jökulsárlón) used in the pre-credits sequence of *A View to a Kill*.

In addition to the film-specific references, Bond's new watch is described as "your twentieth" and the film also refers to the creation of the name "James Bond". When 007 picks up the book *Birds of the West Indies*, it is a nod to the author of the book, James Bond, whose name Ian Fleming used. The film also mentions land and water speed racer Donald Campbell; post-Fleming Bond author John Pearson wrote a book about him entitled *Bluebird and the Dead Lake*. *Die Another Day* is the first film since 1989's *Licence to Kill* to include notable elements from the James Bond novels. In particular, the name of the North Korean villain Colonel Tan-Sun Moon, traces its origins to that of Kingsley Amis' novel *Colonel Sun*. A number of elements from Fleming's original novel *Moonraker* are also included; in both of these, a villain adopts a new identity of a British millionaire and creates a desirable space-device but actually intends to use it for destructive purposes. In addition, the club called Blades, a fencing club in the film, was featured as a card club in *Moonraker*.[17] According to actress Rosamund Pike in her DVD commentary track for the film, her character Miranda Frost was originally named Gala Brand, which was the name of a character in the *Moonraker* novel, but this was changed before filming began.[18]

Marketing tie-ins

MGM and Eon Productions granted Mattel the license to sell a line of Barbie dolls based around the franchise. Mattel announced that the Bond Barbies will be at her "stylish best", clad in evening dress and red shawl. Lindy Hemming created the dress, which is slashed to the thigh to reveal a telephone strapped to Barbie's leg. The doll was sold in a gift set, with Barbie's boyfriend Ken posing as Bond in a tuxedo designed by the Italian fashion house Brioni.[19]

Revlon also collaborated with the makers of *Die Another Day* to create a cosmetics line based round the character Jinx. The limited edition 007 Colour Collection was launched on 7 November 2002 to coincide with the film's release. The product names were loaded with puns and innuendo, with shades and textures ranging from the "warm" to "cool and frosted".[20]

Carrera, a slot car manufacturer, sold a 1:43 scale slot car set based on the film which included an Aston Martin Vanquish and a Jaguar XKR as well as track. Corgi, a British toy car manufacturer, released 1:30 scale replicas of the Vanquish and Jaguar XKR.

Release and reception

Die Another Day was released on 20 November 2002 in both the United States and London. The Queen and Prince Philip were guests of honour at the world première, which was the second to be attended by the Queen after *You Only Live Twice*.[21] The Royal Albert Hall had a make-over for the screening and had been transformed into an ice palace. Proceeds from the première, about £500,000, were donated to the Cinema and Television Benevolent Fund of which the Queen is patron.[22] On the first day, ticket sales reached £1.2 million.[23] *Die Another Day* was the highest grossing James Bond film until the release of *Casino Royale*. It earned $432 million worldwide, becoming the sixth highest grossing film of 2002.

Die Another Day became a controversial subject in eastern Asia. The North Korean government disliked the portrayal of their state as brutal and war-hungry. The South Koreans boycotted 145 theatres where it was released on 31 December 2002, as they were offended by a scene where an American officer issues orders to the South Korean army in the defence of their homeland, and by a lovemaking scene near a statue of the Buddha. The Jogye Buddhist Order issued a statement that the film was "disrespectful to our religion and does not reflect our values and ethics".

The Washington Post reported growing resentment in the nation towards the United States. An official of the South Korean Ministry of Culture and Tourism said that *Die Another Day* was "the wrong film at the wrong time."[24]

The amount of product placement in the film was a point of criticism, specifically from various news outlets such as the BBC, *Time* and Reuters who all used the pun "Buy Another Day". Reportedly 20 companies, paying $70 million, had their products featured in the film, a record at the time,[25] although *USA Today* reported that number to be as high as $100 million.[26] By choice, the number of companies involved in product placement dwindled to only eight for the next Bond film *Casino Royale* in 2006.[26]

Rotten Tomatoes listed *Die Another Day* with a 59% rating.[27] *Metacritic* gave the film a 56 out of 100 rating, representing "Mixed or average reviews."[28] Michael Dequina of *Film Threat* praised the film as the best of the series to star Pierce Brosnan and "the most satisfying installment of the franchise in recent memory."[28] Larry Carroll of *CountingDown.com* praised Lee Tamahori for having "magnificently balanced the film so that it keeps true to the Bond legend, makes reference to the classic films that preceded it, but also injects a new zest to it all."[29] *Entertainment Weekly* magazine also gave a positive reaction, saying that Tamahori, "a true filmmaker", has re-established the series' pop sensuality.[30] Dana Stevens of *The New York Times* called the film the best of the James Bond series since *The Spy Who Loved Me.*[28] Kyle Bell of Movie Freaks 365 stated in his review that the "first half of Die Another Day is classic Bond", but that "Things start to go downhill when the ice palace gets introduced."[31] According to a ITV news poll Jinx was voted the fourth toughest girl on screen of all time.[3]

However, *Die Another Day* was strongly criticized for relying too much on gadgets and special effects, with the plot being neglected. James Berardinelli of *Reelviews.net* said, "This is a train wreck of an action film — a stupefying attempt by the filmmakers to force-feed James Bond into the mindless *xXx* mold and throw 40 years of cinematic history down the toilet in favor of bright flashes and loud bangs."[32] Gary Brown of the *Houston Community Newspapers* also described the weak point of the film as "the seemingly non-stop action sequences and loud explosions that appear to take center stage while the Bond character is almost relegated to second string."[33] Roger Moore remarked, "I thought it just went too far — and that's from me, the first Bond in space! Invisible cars and dodgy CGI footage? Please!"[34]

Novelization

The novelization to *Die Another Day* was written by the then-current official James Bond writer, Raymond Benson, based on the screenplay by Neal Purvis and Robert Wade. Fan reaction to it was above average.[35] Months after its publication, Benson retired as the official James Bond novelist. A new series featuring the secret agent's adventures as a teenager, by Charlie Higson was launched in 2005. As a result, the novel *Die Another Day*, as it was published after Benson's final original 007 novel, *The Man with the Red Tattoo*, was the final literary work featuring Bond as originally conceived by Ian Fleming until the publication of another novel in 2008 to mark the 100th anniversary of Fleming's birth, *Devil May Care* by Sebastian Faulks.[36]

References

[1] "Die Another Day (2002)" (http://www.boxofficemojo.com/movies/?id=dieanotherday.htm). Box Office Mojo. . Retrieved 2007-09-19.

[2] "Halle's big year". *Ebony*. November 2002. "Of her character, Berry said: She's the next step in the evolution of women in the Bond movies. She's more modern and not the classic villain. She also said that Jinx is fashionable. She's fashion-forward, very sexy and takes fashion risks, and I love her for that."

[3] "Halle Berry's "Jinx" named fourth toughest female screen icon" (http://www.mi6.co.uk/news/index.php?itemid=1276&catid=1). . Retrieved 2009-06-17.

[4] Larry Carroll (21 November 2002). "Interview: Rick Yune" (http://www.countingdown.com/features/?feature_id=265168). Counting Down. . Retrieved 2008-09-09.

[5] "Bond Sex Scenes Too Hot" (http://news.sky.com/skynews/article/0,,30500-12167415,00.html). 12 November 2002. . Retrieved 2009-06-17.

[6] "James Bond - 20: Interview" (http://www.webwombat.com.au/entertainment/movies/bond20_int.htm). . Retrieved 2009-06-17.

[7] Davies, Hugh (2002-01-12). "Brosnan meets the two-faced Bond villain" (http://www.telegraph.co.uk/news/main.jhtml?xml=/news/2002/01/12/nbond12.xml). London: Telegraph. . Retrieved 2009-06-17.
[8] "Die Another Day filming locations" (http://www.movie-locations.com/movies/d/dieanother.html).. Retrieved 2007-09-20.
[9] *Die Another Day*. [DVD]. 2002.
[10] Hugh Davies (10 Aril 2002). "Halle Berry hurt in blast during Bond film scene" (http://www.telegraph.co.uk/news/main.jhtml?xml=/news/2002/04/10/wberry10.xml). London: Telegraph. . Retrieved 2009-16-17.
[11] "Bond Flies PHASST" (http://www.kineticaerospace.com/). Kinetic Aerospace Inc. (news release). . Retrieved 2006-11-18.
[12] "*Die Another Day* (Alternate versions)" (http://www.imdb.com/title/tt0246460/alternateversions). Internet Movie Database. . Retrieved 2009-06-17.
[13] "Die Another Day at Soundtracknet" (http://www.soundtrack.net/albums/database/?id=3150). . Retrieved 2007-09-20.
[14] "Die Another Day at CD Universe" (http://www.cduniverse.com/search/xx/music/pid/5310300/a/Die+Another+Day.htm). . Retrieved 2007-09-20.
[15] Geoffrey Palmer (Narrator). (2006). *James Bond's Greatest Hits*. [Television]. UK: North One Television.
[16] "Episode No. 4". *Main Hoon Bond*. Star Gold. No. 4, season 1. 25 minutes in.
[17] "Episode No. 1". *Main Hoon Bond*. Star Gold. No. 1, season 1. 25 minutes in.
[18] *Die Another Day*. [DVD]. 2003.
[19] "New Bond girl is a real doll" (http://www.telegraph.co.uk/news/main.jhtml?xml=/news/2002/10/18/nbond18.xml).*The Daily Telegraph* (London). . Retrieved 2009-06-17.
[20] "Discover your inner Bond girl with bullet-shaped mascaras and 007 blushes" (http://www.telegraph.co.uk/fashion/main.jhtml?xml=/fashion/2002/09/03/efjenni03.xml). *The Daily Telegraph* (London). . Retrieved 2009-06-17.
[21] "Daniel Craig makes his 007 debut at premiere of Casino Royale" (http://www.dailymail.co.uk/pages/live/articles/showbiz/showbiznews.html?in_article_id=416461&in_page_id=1773&ico=Homepage&icl=TabModule&icc=picbox&ct=5). *Daily Mail* (London). 2006-11-18. . Retrieved 2007-09-19.
[22] "STARS COME OUT TO SUPPORT THE CINEMA & TELEVISION BENEVOLENT FUND'S 60TH ROYAL FILM PERFORMANCE" (http://web.archive.org/web/20070815074942/http://www.ctbf.co.uk/events/events_q4.html). Archived from the original (http://www.ctbf.co.uk/events/events_q4.html) on August 15, 2007. . Retrieved 2009-06-17.
[23] "Die Another Day explodes at the box office" (http://news.bbc.co.uk/cbbcnews/hi/tv_film/newsid_2505000/2505093.stm). *BBC News*. 2002-11-22. . Retrieved 2007-09-21.
[24] "Both sides of the DMZ irked by James Bond" (http://web.archive.org/web/20061116151009/http://www.nwasianweekly.com/archive/commentary04.htm). Northwest Asian Weekly. Archived from the original (http://www.nwasianweekly.com/archive/commentary04.htm) on November 16, 2006. . Retrieved 2006-11-18.
[25] "New Bond film "a giant advert"" (http://news.bbc.co.uk/2/hi/business/2488151.stm). BBC News. 2002-11-18. . Retrieved 2006-03-23.
[26] Howard, Theresa (2006-07-24). "Bond reunites with Smirnoff" (http://www.usatoday.com/money/advertising/2006-07-23-bond-usat_x.htm). USA Today. . Retrieved 2006-07-24.
[27] "Die Another Day at Rotten Tomatoes" (http://www.rottentomatoes.com/m/die_another_day/). . Retrieved 2007-09-19.
[28] "Die Another Day at Metacritic" (http://www.metacritic.com/video/titles/dieanotherday?q=Die Another Day). . Retrieved 2007-09-19.
[29] "Review: Die Another Day" (http://countingdown.com/features?feature_id=2651677). . Retrieved 2007-09-19.
[30] "Die another Day at EW.com" (http://www.ew.com/ew/article/0,,392638~1~0~dieanotherday,00.html). . Retrieved 2007-09-19.
[31] "Die Another Day Review" (http://moviefreaks365.com/review.php?artid=63). . Retrieved 2009-04-02.
[32] "Review: Die Another Day" (http://www.reelviews.net/movies/d/die_another.html). . Retrieved 2007-09-21.
[33] "Not a good *Day* at the office for James Bond" (http://web.archive.org/web/20071012141108/http://ppl.nhmccd.edu/~garyb/reviews/dieanotherday.html). Archived from the original (http://ppl.nhmccd.edu/~garyb/reviews/dieanotherday.html) on October 12, 2007. . Retrieved 2007-09-21.
[34] Roger Moore (4 October 2008). "Bye bye to Ian Fleming's James Bond?" (http://entertainment.timesonline.co.uk/tol/arts_and_entertainment/film/london_film_festival/article4866756.ece). *The Times* (London). . Retrieved 2008-10-05.
[35] "Novelised *Die Another Day*" (http://commanderbond.net/article/1717). *Commanderbond.net*. 11 November 2002. . Retrieved 2007-09-22.
[36] "Faulks pens new James Bond novel" (http://news.bbc.co.uk/1/hi/entertainment/6289186.stm). *BBC News*. 11 July 2007. . Retrieved 2007-09-22.

External links

- *Die Another Day* (http://www.imdb.com/title/tt0246460/) at the Internet Movie Database
- *Die Another Day* (http://www.allmovie.com/work/267158) at Allmovie
- *Die Another Day* (http://www.rottentomatoes.com/m/die_another_day/) at Rotten Tomatoes
- *Die Another Day* (http://www.boxofficemojo.com/movies/?id=dieanotherday.htm) at Box Office Mojo
- The New York Times Review (http://movies2.nytimes.com/gst/movies/movie.html?v_id=267158)
- Locations site (http://www.movie-locations.com/movies/d/dieanother.html)

The Importance of Being Earnest (2002 film)

The Importance of Being Earnest	
 Theatrical release poster	
Directed by	Oliver Parker
Produced by	David Brown Uri Fruchtmann Barnaby Thompson
Written by	Julian Fellowes
Starring	Colin Firth Rupert Everett Reese Witherspoon Judi Dench Frances O'Connor
Music by	Charlie Mole
Distributed by	Miramax Films
Release date(s)	17 May 2002
Running time	97 min.
Country	United Kingdom
Language	English

The Importance of Being Earnest is a 2002 film directed by Oliver Parker, based on Oscar Wilde's classic comedy of manners play *The Importance of Being Earnest*. The original music score is composed by Charlie Mole. The movie grossed about $8.3 million.[1]

Cast

- Rupert Everett - Algernon Moncrieff
- Colin Firth - Jack Worthing/Ernest
- Frances O'Connor - Gwendolen Fairfax
- Reese Witherspoon - Cecily Cardew
- Judi Dench - Lady Bracknell
- Tom Wilkinson - Dr Chasuble
- Anna Massey - Miss Prism
- Edward Fox - Lane
- Patrick Godfrey - Merriman

Plot

The plot revolves around two men in Victorian England, John (Jack) Worthing and Algernon (Algy) Moncrieff. Whenever Jack travels to London from his Hertfordshire estate he says he is going to see his (fictitious) wayward brother Ernest. Once in London he keeps his privacy by calling himself Ernest. This tactic is especially important as his beloved, Gwendolen, declares that she could only love a man named Ernest. Her cousin, Algy, is the one person who knows Jack's secret and one day he travels down to the estate, announcing himself to Jack's attractive ward Cecily as the infamous Ernest. Cecily is enamoured with him and his name, and upon Jack's return home and Gwendolen's unexpected arrival it becomes clear there are both too many and too few Ernests earnestly courting.

Production notes

- Actress Finty Williams, who plays Lady Bracknell as a young dancer, is the daughter of Dame Judi Dench, who plays the older Lady Bracknell.
- The scenes where Rupert Everett slaps Colin Firth on his rear end and where Everett kisses Firth's cheek were ad libbed. Director Oliver Parker thought Firth's stunned reaction was so humorous he decided to leave it in.
- The business with 'Earnest's' bill at the Savoy, and with the money collectors coming to Jack's country home, are taken from material Wilde cut from the play prior to its publication.
- Though cut from the revised version, the gardener Molton can be seen in the background of many scenes.
- The producers of the film paid £50,000 to use West Wycombe Park as Jack's home in the country.

Reception

Roger Ebert of the *Chicago Sun-Times* awarded the film three out of four stars, saying the actors were well cast, and performed well.[2]

Awards and nominations

The film won the 2003 Italian National Syndicate of Film Journalists's Silver Ribbon award for Best Costume Design, the movie's costumes being designed by Maurizio Millenotti.

Reese Witherspoon was nominated for a Teen Choice Award (Choice Actress - Comedy) for her performance as Cecily.

References

[1] Films of 2002, by total gross (http://www.the-movie-times.com/thrsdir/moviesofyear.mv?moviesof2002+ByTGross2)
[2] Ebert, Roger The Importance of Being Earnest review (http://rogerebert.suntimes.com/apps/pbcs.dll/article?AID=/20020524/REVIEWS/205240303/1023)24 May 2002

External links

- *The Importance of Being Earnest* (http://www.imdb.com/title/tt0278500/) at the Internet Movie Database
- *The Importance of Being Earnest* (http://www.allmovie.com/work/261812) at Allmovie
- *The Importance of Being Earnest* (http://www.rottentomatoes.com/m/importance_of_being_earnest/) at Rotten Tomatoes
- Where Did They Film that? (http://www.wheredidtheyfilmthat.co.uk/location.php?loc_id=130) *The Importance of Being Earnest*
- Official Site (http://www.miramax.com/theimportanceofbeingearnest/index.html)

The Shipping News (film)

The Shipping News	

Directed by	Lasse Hallström
Produced by	Rob Cowan Leslie Holleran Irwin J. Winkler
Written by	E. Annie Proulx (novel), Robert Nelson Jacobs (screenplay)
Starring	Kevin Spacey Julianne Moore Judi Dench Cate Blanchett
Music by	Christopher Young
Cinematography	Oliver Stapleton
Editing by	Andrew Mondshein
Distributed by	Miramax Films
Release date(s)	18 December 2001 (premiere)
Running time	111 minutes
Language	English
Budget	$35,000,000
Gross revenue	$24,405,825 (worldwide)

The Shipping News is a 2001 drama film directed by Lasse Hallström, based on the Pulitzer Prize winning novel by E. Annie Proulx.

It stars Kevin Spacey as the protagonist Quoyle, Judi Dench as Agnis Hamm and Julianne Moore as Wavey Prowse. It also stars Pete Postlethwaite, Scott Glenn, Rhys Ifans, Cate Blanchett, Jason Behr, and Gordon Pinsent.

Overview

The film makes a multitude of changes from the book, notably: Quoyle had two daughters in the novel, but only one in the film; in the film he does not begin working as a reporter until after arriving in Newfoundland; and a number of characters, such as the younger Buggit family, were deleted or merged.

It climaxes with a storm which destroys the Quoyle's ancestral family home and almost drowns the *Gammy Bird's* editor Jack Buggit, caught in the rope of a lobster pot while fishing. Though thought dead, at Buggit's wake it is found that the man was actually in a state of shock resulting from hypothermia, regaining consciousness in front of a large crowd of mourners, central to the theme of rebirth in the optimistic ending of the story.

Reception

Some critics felt that three significant themes were not fully realised in the movie: Quoyle learning that love could be comfortable rather than painful, Quoyle growing from being a bumbling incompetent to being a competent manager, and his daughter Bunny learning about death (while overcoming her fears and learning to be more secure in the process).

The film drew some criticism within Canada for what some saw as stereotyped portrayals of Newfoundlanders, although a number of themes from the book, such as the allegations of incest reported in the newspaper, were toned down significantly in the screenplay.

Cast

- Kevin Spacey - Quoyle
- Julianne Moore - Wavey Prowse
- Judi Dench - Agnis Hamm
- Cate Blanchett - Petal
- Pete Postlethwaite - Tert Card
- Scott Glenn - Jack Buggit
- Rhys Ifans - Beaufield Nutbeem
- Gordon Pinsent - Billy Pretty
- Jason Behr - Dennis Buggit
- Larry Pine - Bayonet Melville
- Jeanetta Arnette - Silver Melville
- Katherine Moennig - Grace Moosup
- Lauren Gainer - Bunny Quoyle
- Alyssa Gainer - Bunny Quoyle
- Kaitlyn Gainer - Bunny Quoyle

Quoyle Point and Killick-Claw

Quoyle Point is a fictional point of land on the Newfoundland coast bearing the family name of the protagonist in both the book and the movie. The actual town used for "Killick-Claw" in the movie was New Bonaventure in the Trinity Bight area of Newfoundland. This area is home to approximately 2,000 Newfoundlanders, most of whom are descendants of 18th-century settlers from England's West Country, the Channel Islands and Southeast Ireland.

In the movie, Quoyle Point is a remote, spectacular site with a cove and dramatic cliffs. There is a desolate, weathered green house on the point, the old family home of the Quoyles. At some time in the past, the house had been dragged across the sea-ice from a neighboring island and cabled to the ground at the four corners to protect it from being blown away.

The film crew pre-built the green house on a stage in Halifax, Nova Scotia, disassembled it, transported it via ferry to Newfoundland, and then reassembled it piece-by-piece on 'Quoyle Point,' using snowmobiles so as not to disturb the natural location. All traces of it were removed at the end of filming.

Awards

Won

- Florida Film Critics:
  1. Best Supporting Actress (Cate Blanchett)
- National Board of Review:
  1. Best Supporting Actress (Cate Blanchett)

Nominated

- Art Directors Guild (ADG):
  1. Excellence in Production Design Award Feature Film - Contemporary Film
- BAFTA Awards:
  1. Best Actor (Kevin Spacey)
  2. Best Supporting Actress (Judi Dench)
- Berlin International Film Festival:
  1. Golden Berlin Bear (Lasse Hallström)
- Broadcast Film Critics:
  1. Best Composer (Christopher Young)
  2. Best Picture
- Golden Globe Awards:
  1. Best Actor - Motion Picture Drama (Kevin Spacey)
  2. Best Original Score (Christopher Young)
- Screen Actors Guild (SAG):
  1. Outstanding Performance by a Female Actor in a Supporting Role (Judi Dench)
- USC Scripter Award:
  1. USC Scripter Award (Robert Nelson Jacobs and E. Annie Proulx)
- Young Artist Awards:
  1. Best Ensemble in a Feature Film

External links

- *The Shipping News* [1] at the Internet Movie Database
- *The Shipping News* [2] at Allmovie

Iris (2001 film)

Iris	
 *Iris* film poster	
Directed by	Richard Eyre
Produced by	Robert Fox Scott Rudin
Written by	John Bayley (novel) Richard Eyre Charles Wood (screenplay)
Starring	Kate Winslet Judi Dench Jim Broadbent Hugh Bonneville
Music by	James Horner
Cinematography	Roger Pratt
Editing by	Martin Walsh
Distributed by	Miramax Films
Release date(s)	December 14, 2001
Running time	92 minutes
Country	United Kingdom United States
Language	English
Budget	$5,500,000 *(estimated)*
Gross revenue	$16,153,953 *(worldwide)*

Iris is a 2001 biographical film that tells the story of Irish novelist Iris Murdoch and her relationship with John Bayley. The film contrasts the start of their relationship, when Murdoch (played by Kate Winslet) was an outgoing, dominant individual as compared to her timid and scholarly partner Bayley (played by Hugh Bonneville), and their later life, when Murdoch (now played by Judi Dench) was suffering from Alzheimer's disease and tended to by a frustrated Bayley (played by Jim Broadbent) in their North Oxford home in Charlbury Road.

The film, which was directed by Richard Eyre, is based on Bayley's memoir *Elegy for Iris.* The beach scenes were filmed at Southwold in Suffolk, one of Murdoch's favourite haunts.

Broadbent received the Academy Award for Best Supporting Actor for his role. Dench and Winslet were both nominated, for Best Actress and Best Supporting Actress respectively.

Plot

When the young Iris Murdoch meets fellow student John Bayley at the University of Oxford, he is a naive virgin easily flummoxed by her libertine spirit, arch personality, and obvious artistic talent. Decades later, little has changed and the couple keeps house, with John doting on his more famous wife. When Iris begins experiencing forgetfulness and dementia, however, the ever-doltish but devoted John struggles with hopelessness and frustration to become her caretaker, as his wife's mind deteriorates from the ravages of Alzheimer's disease.

Cast

- Judi Dench as Iris Murdoch
- Kate Winslet as Young Iris Murdoch
- Jim Broadbent as John Bayley
- Hugh Bonneville as Young John Bayley
- Penelope Wilton as Janet Stone
- Juliet Aubrey as Young Janet Stone
- Timothy West as Maurice
- Samuel West as Young Maurice
- Kris Marshall as Dr Gudgeon

Awards and nominations

Academy Awards record
1. Best Supporting Actor
BAFTA Awards record
1. Best Actress in a Leading Role
Golden Globe Awards record
1. Best Supporting Actor

- Academy Awards
  - Best Actress in a Leading Role: Judi Dench
  - Best Actor in a Supporting Role: Jim Broadbent - WON
  - Best Actress in a Supporting Role: Kate Winslet
- BAFTA Awards
  - Best British Film
  - Best Performance by an Actor in a Leading Role: Jim Broadbent
  - Best Performance by an Actress in a Leading Role: Judi Dench - WON
  - Best Performance by an Actor in a Supporting Role: Hugh Bonneville
  - Best Performance by an Actress in a Supporting Role: Kate Winslet
  - Best Screenplay - Adapted
- Broadcast Film Critics Association

  - Best Supporting Actor - Jim Broadbent
- Golden Globe Awards
  - Best Performance by an Actress in a Motion Picture - Drama: Judi Dench
  - Best Supporting Actor - Motion Picture - Jim Broadbent: WON
  - Best Supporting Actress - Motion Picture: Kate Winslet
- Los Angeles Film Critics Association
  - Best Supporting Actor: Jim Broadbent (also for Moulin Rouge!) - WON
  - Best Supporting Actress: Kate Winslet - WON
- Satellite Awards
  - Best Performance by an Actress in a Motion Picture, Drama: Judi Dench
  - Best Performance by an Actor in a Supporting Role, Drama: Jim Broadbent
  - Best Performance by an Actress in a Supporting Role, Drama: Kate Winslet
- Screen Actors Guild Awards
  - Outstanding Performance by a Female Actor in a Leading Role: Judi Dench
  - Outstanding Performance by a Male Actor in a Supporting Role: Jim Broadbent

References

External links

- *Iris* (http://www.imdb.com/title/tt0280778/) at the Internet Movie Database
- *Iris* (http://www.rottentomatoes.com/m/1111227-iris/) at Rotten Tomatoes
- *Iris* at Literary Fiction, BellaOnline (http://www.bellaonline.com/articles/art51719.asp)

Chocolat (2000 film)

Chocolat	
 Theatrical release poster	
Directed by	Lasse Hallström
Produced by	Harvey Weinstein Bob Weinstein
Written by	Joanne Harris (novel) Robert Nelson Jacobs
Starring	Juliette Binoche Judi Dench Alfred Molina Lena Olin Johnny Depp
Music by	Rachel Portman
Cinematography	Roger Pratt
Editing by	Andrew Mondshein
Distributed by	Miramax Films
Release date(s)	December 15, 2000 (limited) January 19, 2001
Running time	121 minutes
Country	United Kingdom United States
Language	English French
Budget	$25 million
Gross revenue	$152,699,946

Chocolat (French pronunciation: [ʃɔkɔla]) is a 2000 British/American romance film based on the novel of the same name by Joanne Harris, and was directed by Lasse Hallström. Adapted by screenwriter Robert Nelson Jacobs, *Chocolat* tells the story of a young mother, played by Juliette Binoche, who arrives at the fictional, repressed French village of Lansquenet-sous-Tannes with her six-year-old daughter and opens *La Chocolaterie Maya*, a small chocolaterie. Her chocolate quickly begins to change the lives of the townspeople.

The film was shot in the village of Flavigny-sur-Ozerain in Burgundy, France, and on the Rue De L'ancienne Poste in Beynac-et-Cazenac on the Dordogne River in Dordogne, France. The river scenes were filmed at Fonthill Lake at Fonthill Bishop in Wiltshire, England and interior scenes at Shepperton Studios, Surrey, England.

The film was nominated for 5 Academy Awards, 8 BAFTAs, and 4 Golden Globes. It won a Screen Actors Guild Award.

Plot

Vianne Rocher (Juliette Binoche) like her ancestors, drifts across France. In the winter of 1959, she travels to a tranquil French village, where she and her daughter, Anouk (Victoire Thivisol), open a small chocolaterie. The store imbues both wonder and angst within the classical villagers as it opens during the forty days of Lent.

Soon, Vianne's allure and confections enliven a married couple's aphrodisia, encourage an elderly man's secret love, bring rapport with a willful diabetic, and comfort an awkward woman who longs to leave her drunk and abusive husband. Nevertheless, the devout village mayor, Comte Paul de Reynaud (Alfred Molina), sees Vianne as an immoral provocateur and quietly contests against her. The battle peaks when a band of river gypsies camp on the village outskirts and Vianne finds a strong, mutual sexual attraction with the Manush Romani (Gypsy) Roux (Johnny Depp).

Cast

- Juliette Binoche as Vianne Rocher
- Johnny Depp as Roux
- Judi Dench as Armande Voizin
- Alfred Molina as Comte de Reynaud
- Leslie Caron as Madame Audel
- Victoire Thivisol as Anouk
- Carrie-Anne Moss as Caroline Clairmont
- Antonio Gil Martinez as Jean-Marc Drou
- Helene Cardona as Francoise Drou
- Hugh O'Conor as Pere Henri
- Harrison Pratt as Dedou Drou
- Gaelan Connell as Didi Drou
- Lena Olin as Josephine Muscat
- Elisabeth Commelin as Yvette Marceau
- Peter Stormare as Serge Muscat
- Ron Cook as Alphonse Marceau
- Aurélien Parent-Koenig as Luc Clairmont
- John Wood as Guillaume Blerot

Reception

The film grossed some US$152,699,946 worldwide, on a production budget of US$25 million.[1]

The film was nominated for many awards, including 5 Academy Awards including Best Picture. Among significant awards won for work on this picture were the Art Directors Guild award, 2001, for Excellence in Production Design, the Bogey Award given by the German journal "Blickpunkt: Film", based on audience numbers in a certain time, the Audience Award, 2001, of the European Film Awards, for Juliette Binoche, and the Screen Actors Guild award 2001, to Judi Dench for Outstanding Performance by a Female Actor in a Supporting Role. The film also attracted numerous BAFTA nominations and Rachel Portman's score was nominated for a Grammy Award.

Awards

Won

- Art Directors Guild (ADG):
  - Excellence in Production Design Award Feature Film - Contemporary Films
- European Film Awards:
  - Best Actress (Juliette Binoche)
- Palm Springs International Film Festival:
  - Audience Award (Lasse Hallström)
- San Diego Film Critics:
  - Best Screenplay - Adapted (Robert Nelson Jacobs)
- Screen Actors Guild (SAG):
  - Best Supporting Actress (Judi Dench)

Nominated

- Academy Awards:
  - Best Actress (Juliette Binoche)
  - Best Picture
  - Best Original Music (Rachel Portman)
  - Best Screenplay - Adapted (Robert Nelson Jacobs)
  - Best Supporting Actress (Judi Dench)
- BAFTA Awards:
  - Best Actress (Juliette Binoche)
  - Best Cinematography (Roger Pratt)
  - Best Costume Design (Renee Ehrlich Kalfus)
  - Best Makeup & Hair (Naomi Donne)
  - Best Production Design (David Gropman)
  - Best Screenplay - Adapted (Robert Nelson Jacobs)
  - Best Supporting Actress (Judi Dench)
  - Best Supporting Actress (Lena Olin)
- Golden Globe Awards:
  - Best Actress - Motion Picture Musical or Comedy (Juliette Binoche)
  - Best Original Score (Rachel Portman)
  - Best Picture - Musical or Comedy
  - Best Supporting Actress - Motion Picture (Judi Dench)
- Satellite Awards:
  - Best Supporting Actress - Drama (Judi Dench)

- Screen Actors Guild (SAG):
  - Best Actress (Juliette Binoche)
  - Best Cast - Motion Picture
- USC Scripter Award:
  - USC Scripter Award [Joanne Harris (author) and Robert Nelson Jacobs (screenwriter)]
- World Soundtrack Awards:
  - Soundtrack Composer of the Year (Rachel Portman)
- Writers Guild of America (WGA):
  - Best Screenplay - Adapted (Robert Nelson Jacobs)

References

[1] Chocolat (2000) box revenue summary (http://boxofficemojo.com/movies/?id=chocolat.htm), Box Office Mojo, accessed 2 December, 2007

External links

- *Chocolat* (http://www.imdb.com/title/tt0241303/) at the Internet Movie Database
- *Chocolat* (http://www.boxofficemojo.com/movies/?id=chocolat.htm) at Box Office Mojo
- *Chocolat* (http://www.rottentomatoes.com/m/1103080-chocolat/) at Rotten Tomatoes

The Last of the Blonde Bombshells

The Last of the Blonde Bombshells	

Directed by	Gillies MacKinnon
Produced by	Su Armstrong
Written by	Alan Plater
Starring	Judi Dench Ian Holm
Music by	John Keane
Cinematography	Richard Greatrex
Editing by	Pia Di Ciaula
Release date(s)	August 26, 2000 3 September 2000
Running time	84 minutes
Country	United Kingdom/United States
Language	English

The Last of the Blonde Bombshells is a 2000 British/American television movie directed by Gillies MacKinnon. The script by Alan Plater focuses on the efforts of a recently widowed woman to reunite the members of the World War II-era swing band with which she played saxophone.

The film was a joint project of BBC Films and HBO. It premiered in the US on August 26 and in the UK on September 3.

Plot synopsis

After her husband's death, Elizabeth decides to return to her musical roots and begins busking with young guitarist Paul in a plaza overlooking a London ice rink, much to the dismay of her daughter Patricia and son Edward. One day she is spotted by Patrick, who attempted to avoid enlistment during World War II by dressing as a woman and playing drums with the Blonde Bombshells, a supposedly all-female band with which Elizabeth performed when she was only fifteen years old.

The two reminisce, prompting them to begin searching for other band members for a reunion concert at a school dance organized by Elizabeth's granddaughter Joanna. At first they have little success - one has died, another is suffering from dementia, a third is serving time - but eventually they locate piano player Betty working in a seaside saloon, singer Gwen performing in a nightclub, trombonist Annie dedicated to the Salvation Army, and trumpeter Dinah, an alcoholic living in a secluded manor in Scotland.

Early rehearsals prove to be disastrous, but encouraged by Joanna and determined to shine in the limelight one more time, the group steadily improves. On the night of the dance, they are joined by double bass player Madeleine, who had left the band to join the French Resistance and finally was tracked down by Joanna. Embraced by the younger generation, they relive their former glory.

The present-day story is interspersed with flashbacks to the band in its wartime heyday that capture the music and atmosphere of the period.

Principal cast

- Judi Dench ..... Elizabeth
- Ian Holm ..... Patrick
- Joan Sims ..... Betty
- Olympia Dukakis ..... Dinah
- Cleo Laine ..... Gwen
- Leslie Caron ..... Madeleine
- Billie Whitelaw ..... Evelyn
- June Whitfield ..... Annie
- Valentine Pelka ....Leslie
- Millie Findlay ..... Joanna
- Felicity Dean ..... Patricia
- Nicholas Palliser ..... Edward
- Dom Chapman ..... Paul

Critical reception

Steven Oxman of *Variety* observed that "despite delightful performances from a star-studded cast, the film's thoroughly predictable storyline and low-key charm are ultimately more a sedative than a tonic." He added, "Alan Plater's screenplay is pretty thin ... and director Gillies Mackinnon can't manage to make the finish as feel-good as it needs to be ... The soundtrack's nice, Richard Greatrex's cinematography is nice and the acting is quite nice. But taken together, these niceties wind up as members of the bland." [1]

Awards and nominations

- British Academy Television Award for Best Actress (Judi Dench, winner)
- Golden Globe Award for Best Performance by an Actress In A Mini-series or Motion Picture Made for Television (Judi Dench, winner)
- Emmy Award for Outstanding Lead Actress - Miniseries or a Movie (Judi Dench, nominee)
- Emmy Award for Outstanding Supporting Actor - Miniseries or a Movie (Ian Holm, nominee)
- Emmy Award for Outstanding Casting - Miniseries, Movie, or a Special (nominee)
- Emmy Award for Outstanding Costumes for a Miniseries, Movie or a Special (nominee)
- Emmy Award for Outstanding Hairstyling for a Miniseries, Movie or a Special (nominee)
- Screen Actors Guild Award for Outstanding Performance by a Female Actor in a Miniseries or Television Movie (Judi Dench, nominee)

- American Comedy Award for Funniest Female Performer in a TV Special (Judi Dench, nominee)

References

[1] *Variety* review (http://www.variety.com/review/VE1117787878.html?categoryid=32&cs=1&p=0)

External links

- *The Last of the Blonde Bombshells* (http://www.imdb.com/title/tt0220608/) at the Internet Movie Database

Into the Arms of Strangers: Stories of the Kindertransport

Into the Arms of Strangers	

Directed by	Mark Jonathan Harris
Produced by	Deborah Oppenheimer
Written by	Harris
Starring	Judi Dench (narrator)
Music by	Lee Holdridge
Distributed by	Warner Bros.
Release date(s)	September 7, 2000 (United States) November 24, 2000 (United Kingdom)
Running time	122 minutes
Country	United Kingdom United States
Language	English

Into the Arms of Strangers: Stories of the Kindertransport is a 2000 documentary film directed by Mark Jonathan Harris and narrated by Judi Dench. It tells the story of the kindertransport, an underground railroad that saved the lives of over 10,000 Jewish children. The movie uses archival footage and interviews to recount the stories of children sent to live in England, after fleeing from Nazi Germany.

Interviewed subjects

The documentary relies heavily on filmed interviews in which the children of the kindertransport (now grown men and women in their 60s and 70s) recall their feelings and experiences of the kindertransport. These interview subjects include:[1]

- Lorraine Allard, *kind*
- Lory Cahn, *kind*
- Mariam Cohen, foster mother of Kurt Fuchel
- Hedy Epstein, *kind*
- Kurt Fuchel, *kind*
- Alexander Gordon, *kind*
- Franzi Groszmann, mother of Lore Segal
- Eva Hayman, *kind*
- Jack Hellman, *kind*
- Bertha Leverton, *kind*
- Ursula Rosenfeld, *kind*
- Inge Sadan, *kind* (Bertha Leverton's sister)
- Lore Segal, *kind*
- Robert Sugar, *kind*
- Nicholas Winton, rescuer
- Norbert Woolheim, rescuer

Alexander Gordon was also one of the refugees on HMT Dunera, one of the most notorious events of British maritime history.

Reactions

An overwhelming majority of American film critics responded positively to *Into the Arms of Strangers* writing that it both intellectually and emotionally captures this chapter of history.[2] The film went on to win the prestigious Academy Award for Best Documentary Feature.[2] The film had an extremely limited theatrical release (18 theaters at its widest) and grossed $382,807 domestically.[4]

See also

- List of Holocaust films
- 1930s
- anti-Semitism

References

[1] (http://www2.warnerbros.com/intothearmsofstrangers/)

[2] "NY Times: Into the Arms of Strangers: Stories of the Kindertransport" (http://movies.nytimes.com/movie/207046/Into-the-Arms-of-Strangers-Stories-of-the-Kindertransport/details). *NY Times*. . Retrieved 2008-11-22.

External links

- *Into the Arms of Strangers: Stories of the Kindertransport* (http://www.imdb.com/title/tt0248912/) at the Internet Movie Database
- *Into the Arms of Strangers* (http://www.allmovie.com/work/207046) at Allmovie
- Into the Arms of Strangers official website (http://www2.warnerbros.com/intothearmsofstrangers/)
- Into the Arms of Strangers: Stories of the Kindertransport at Rotten Tomatoes.com (http://www.rottentomatoes.com/m/into_the_arms_of_strangers_stories_of_the_kindertransport/)
- Into the Arms of Strangers (2000) at Box Office Mojo (http://www.boxofficemojo.com/movies/?id=intothearmsofstrangers.htm)

The World Is Not Enough

The World Is Not Enough	
 *The World Is Not Enough* film poster	
James Bond	Pierce Brosnan
Also starring	Sophie Marceau Robert Carlyle Denise Richards
Directed by	Michael Apted
Produced by	Michael G. Wilson Barbara Broccoli
Novel/Story by	Neal Purvis & Robert Wade
Screenplay by	Neal Purvis & Robert Wade and Bruce Feirstein
Cinematography	Adrian Biddle, BSC
Music by	David Arnold
Main theme	The World Is Not Enough
Composer	David Arnold Don Black (lyricist)
Performer	Garbage
Editing by	Jim Clark
Distributed by	Metro-Goldwyn-Mayer
Release date(s)	19 November 1999
Running time	128 min.
Country	United Kingdom United States
Budget	$135,000,000
Worldwide gross	$361,832,400

Preceded by	*Tomorrow Never Dies*
Followed by	*Die Another Day*

The World Is Not Enough (1999) is the nineteenth spy film in the James Bond film series, and the third to star Pierce Brosnan as the fictional MI6 agent James Bond. The film was directed by Michael Apted, with the original story and screenplay written by Neal Purvis, Robert Wade and Bruce Feirstein.[1] It was produced by Michael G. Wilson and Barbara Broccoli.

The film's plot revolves around the assassination of billionaire Sir Robert King by the terrorist Renard and Bond's subsequent assignment to protect King's daughter, Elektra, who had previously been held for ransom by Renard. During his assignment, Bond unravels a scheme to increase petroleum prices by triggering a nuclear meltdown in the waters of Istanbul.

Despite the film's mixed critical reception, it earned $361,832,400 worldwide.

Title

The title *The World Is Not Enough* is an English translation of the Latin phrase *Orbis non sufficit*, which in real life was the motto of Sir Thomas Bond. In the novel *On Her Majesty's Secret Service* and its film adaptation, this is revealed to be the Bond family motto.

Plot

The pre-title sequence finds Bond (Pierce Brosnan) at a Swiss bank in Bilbao, Spain, retrieving a large sum of money that belongs to Sir Robert King, a British oil tycoon and personal friend of M. While there, Bond decides to find the truth about the death of his partner, 0012, and tries to question the banker; the man is murdered by his assistant Giulietta da Vinci (Maria Grazia Cucinotta) before he can talk. After the killing of another bank assistant, Bond escapes. Upon Bond's arrival with the money in London, Sir Robert (David Calder) is killed by a bomb inside MI6 Headquarters; the recovered money had been rigged to explode, detonated by his lapel pin. Bond immediately hastens to catch the perpetrator — the cigar girl from the Swiss Bank in Bilbao — in a boat on the Thames. The chase ends at the Millennium Dome, where the assassin attempts to escape via hot air balloon. Bond offers her MI6's protection in return for her cooperation; but she refuses and detonates the balloon, killing herself in the process. Bond lets go of the safety line, falling a short distance onto the dome and sustaining a dislocated collarbone as he tumbles down the side.

Bond traces the recovered money to Renard (Robert Carlyle), a KGB agent-turned-terrorist. Following an earlier attempt on his life by MI6, Renard was left with a bullet lodged in his brain; the bullet is gradually killing off Renard's senses, effectively making him immune to pain, although the bullet will eventually kill him. M assigns Bond to protect King's daughter, Elektra (Sophie Marceau); as Renard previously abducted and held Elektra for ransom, MI6 believes that he is targeting her a second time.

Bond flies to Azerbaijan, where Elektra is overseeing the construction of an oil pipeline which will travel through the Caucasus, from the Caspian Sea to Turkey. During a tour of the pipeline's proposed route in the mountains, Bond and Elektra are attacked by a hit squad in armed, paraglider-equipped snowmobiles.

After fending off the hit squad, Bond visits a casino owned by his acquaintance, Valentin Zukovsky (Robbie Coltrane), to acquire information about Elektra's attackers; he discovers that Elektra's head of security, Davidov (Ulrich Thomsen), is secretly in league with Renard. After spending a night with Elektra, then stowing away in Davidov's car to a nearby airstrip, Bond kills him and boards a plane bound for a Russian ICBM base in Kazakhstan. There, Bond poses as Russian nuclear scientist Mikhail Arkov (Jeff Nuttall) to enter the silo and find out why Renard's men are there. He is tailed closely by Dr. Christmas Jones (Denise Richards), an American nuclear physicist who is suspicious of his identity. Inside the silo, Bond watches as Renard removes the GPS locator card and a half quantity of weapons-grade plutonium from a bomb. Before Bond can kill him, Christmas blows his cover and Renard steals the bomb and flees, leaving everyone to die in the booby-trapped missile silo. Bond escapes the exploding silo with Christmas in tow, but not before retrieving the locator card.

Back in Azerbaijan, Bond discloses to M that Elektra may not be as innocent as she seems, and hands her the locator card as proof of the theft. The pair are interrupted by a surprise attack on the pipeline: the pilfered bomb from Kazakhstan is attached to an inspection rig heading toward the pipeline's oil terminal. Bond and Christmas enter the pipeline, ahead of the bomb, on a separate rig. In the process of defusing it, Christmas discovers that half of the plutonium is missing. Bond, realizing they have been duped, instructs her to jump clear of the rig and wait for the explosion of the bomb. In the wake of the explosion, Bond radios in and learns that M has been abducted. Elektra and Renard rendezvous at Maiden's Tower in Istanbul, where he exchanges the remaining half of plutonium. In return, Elektra presents a gift of her own: M, imprisoned in a small cell. Renard sets an alarm clock a few feet from M, promising she will die next day at noon.

That night, Bond accosts Zukovsky at his caviar factory in the Caspian Sea, believing he is working for Elektra. As Bond and Christmas interrogate him, the factory is suddenly assailed by Elektra's helicopters, confirming Bond's suspicion. Zukovsky insists their arrangement was in exchange for a Victor III class submarine, currently being captained by Zukovsky's nephew, Nikolai. If Renard were to insert the stolen plutonium into the submarine's nuclear reactor, the resulting meltdown would level Istanbul, sabotaging the Russians' oil pipeline in the Bosporus. Elektra's pipeline is set to go around the ruins of Istanbul, dramatically increasing the value of her own oil. After poisoning Captain Nikolai and his crew, Renard and his men seize their submarine and begin processing the plutonium. M, still carrying the locator card, snatches the alarm clock and uses its battery to power the card's transmitter, revealing her location to Bond.

No sooner does Bond detect her signal than Zukovsky's underling, Mr. Bullion (Goldie), leaves behind an explosive to kill him. Bond and Christmas emerge unscathed, but are captured by Bullion and several of Elektra's henchmen, who leave Zukovsky for dead. Bond is restrained in an ancient Spanish torture device, the garotte, while Christmas is taken aboard the submarine. An injured Zukovsky storms into the room where Elektra is torturing Bond, demanding to know where his nephew is located. Bond gestures to the table, on which Elektra has placed Nikolai's cap; soon as realizing Nikolai is dead, Zukovsky is fatally shot by Elektra. With his dying breath, Zukovsky uses his cane — a concealed gun — to take a shot at Bond. Seemingly deciding as incapacitated by his wounds he aims for Bond's knee to even his old score but eventually shot at one of Bond's restraints, freeing him. Bond chases after Elektra, pausing momentarily to release M. In the end Bond is lead to shoot Elektra, after she refuses to call off the plan, killing her.

Afterwards, Bond dives after the submarine, and boards it. Bond has a brief battle with Renard's men and, in the confusion, causes the submarine to dive rather than surface. The submarine hits bottom, driving its nose into the sea floor and causing its hull to crack. Bond catches up to Renard, who is busy shoving the tip of a plutonium rod into the reactor. Bond hoists himself up to the pressure release, then reconnects the pressure hose and causes the reactor to backfire, impaling Renard with the rod. Bond and Christmas escape using a torpedo tube, leaving the flooded reactor to detonate safely underwater. That evening, Bond and Christmas enjoy some champagne and intimate time together in Istanbul. M, along with the new Q (John Cleese) and others in the Secret Service, spot the two of them in bed together with a thermal imaging camera. However, Q keeps Bond covered by turning the camera off, allowing Bond and Christmas to continue having sex (says Bond: "I thought Christmas only came once a year!").

Cast

- Pierce Brosnan as James Bond 007: British Secret Agent and protagonist
- Sophie Marceau as Elektra King: The first of the film's two main antagonists. An oil heiress who wants to make her mark on the world by sealing an oil trade route with a nuclear explosion.
- Robert Carlyle as Renard: The second of the film's two main antagonists. A Soviet terrorist, Elektra's kidnapper and her father's killer.
- Denise Richards as Dr. Christmas Jones: a nuclear physicist assisting Bond in his mission.[2] The name follows in the tradition of other Bond girls' names that are double entendres.[3] Richards stated that she liked the role because it was "brainy", "athletic", and had "depth of character, in contrast to Bond girls from previous decades."[4]
- Robbie Coltrane as Valentin Zukovsky: A Russian mafia boss and Baku casino owner who aids Bond in order to rescue his nephew from Renard's captivity.
- Judi Dench as M: The strict head of MI6.
- Desmond Llewelyn as Q: MI6's "quartermaster" who supplies Bond with multi-purpose vehicles and gadgets useful for the latter's mission. In an interview on the DVD release of the film, Llewelyn stated that he had no plans to retire and that he would continue playing Q "as long as the producers want me and the Almighty doesn't." Ironically, this movie marks Llewelyn's final appearance as Q before his death (in a car accident) on 19 December 1999.[5]
- John Cleese as R: Q's assistant and successor. The character is never formally introduced as "R" - This was simply an observation on Bond's part: "If you're Q....does that make him R?"
- Samantha Bond as Miss Moneypenny: M's secretary
- Serena Scott Thomas as Dr. Molly Warmflash: An MI6 physician who gives 007 "A clean bill of health."
- John Seru as Gabor: Elektra King's silent bodyguard who is seen accompanying King wherever she travels.
- Ulrich Thomsen as Sasha Davidov: Elektra King's head of security in Azerbaijan.
- Goldie as Bullion: Valentin Zukovsky's gold-toothed bodyguard.
- Maria Grazia Cucinotta as Giulietta da Vinci (Cigar Girl): An experienced assassin working for Renard.

Production

Joe Dante and then Peter Jackson were offered to direct. Barbara Broccoli had enjoyed Jackson's *Heavenly Creatures*, and a screening of *The Frighteners* was arranged for her. She disliked the latter film, however, and showed no further interest in Jackson. Jackson, a lifelong Bond fan, remarked that EON tended to go for less famous directors and he would certainly not be entitled a chance to direct after *The Lord of the Rings*.[6]

Russian Victor III Class Submarine used in filming.

The pre-title sequence lasts for about 14 minutes, the longest pre-title sequence in the Bond series to date. In the "making of" documentaries on the Ultimate Edition DVD release, director Michael Apted said that the scene was originally much longer than that. Originally, the pre-credits sequence was to have ended with Bond's leap from the window and descend to the ground, finishing as Bond rushes away from the area as police cars approach. Then, after the credits the sequence in MI6 headquarters would have been next, with the boat scenes the next major action sequence. However, the pre-credits scenes were viewed as lacklustre when compared to ones from previous 007 movies, so the credits were pushed back to after the boat sequence and thus the longest pre-titles sequence in the series was born. *The Daily Telegraph* claimed that the British Government prevented some filming in front of the actual MI6 Headquarters at Vauxhall Cross, citing a security risk. However, a Foreign Office spokesperson refuted the claims and expressed displeasure with the article.[7]

Initially the film was to be released in 2000, rumoured to be titled *Bond 2000*. Other rumoured titles included *Death Waits for No Man*, *Fire and Ice*, *Pressure Point* and *Dangerously Yours*.[8] The actual working title followed the format of all previous "official" 007 films, being dubbed simply *Bond 19*.

Filming

The pre-title sequence begins in Bilbao, Spain, featuring the Guggenheim Museum. After the opening scene, the film moves to London, England, showcasing the SIS Building and the Millennium Dome on the Thames. Following the title sequence, Eilean Donan castle in Scotland is used by MI6 as a location headquarters. Other locations include Baku, Azerbaijan, the Azerbaijan Oil Rocks and Istanbul, Turkey, where Maiden's Tower is shown.[9]

Brosnan with the BMW Z8 that is used in the film. The backdrop is intended to be Azerbaijan.

The studio work for the film was shot as usual in Pinewood Studios, including Albert R. Broccoli's 007 Stage. Bilbao, Spain was used briefly for the exterior of Swiss bank and flyover-bridge adjacent to the Guggenheim Museum. In London outdoor footage was shot of the SIS Building and Vauxhall Cross with several weeks filming the boat chase on the River Thames eastwards towards the Millennium Dome, Greenwich.[10] The canal footage of the chase where Bond soaks the parking wardens was filmed at Wapping and the boat stunts in Millwall Dock and under Glengall Bridge were filmed at the Isle of Dogs. Stowe School, Buckinghamshire, was used as the site of the King family estate on banks of Loch Lomond. Filming was then shot in Scotland at the Eilean Donan Castle to depict the exterior of MI6 temporary operations centre at "Castle Thane". The skiing chase sequence in the Caucasus was shot on the slopes of Chamonix, France.[9] Filming of the scene was delayed by an avalanche, but the crew wasted no time by helping the rescue operation.[11]

The Q Boat stunt on the River Thames.

The interior (and single exterior shot) of L'Or Noir casino in Baku, Azerbaijan, was shot at Halton House, the Officer's Mess of RAF Halton, and RAF Northolt was used to depict the airfield runway in Azerbaijan.[9] Zukovsky's quay-side caviar factory was shot entirely at the outdoor water tank at Pinewood.

The exterior of Kazakhstan nuclear facility was shot at the Bardenas Reales, in Navarre, Spain, and the exterior of oil refinery control centre at the Motorola building in Groundwell,[12] Swindon. The exterior of oil pipeline was filmed in Cwm Dyli, Snowdonia, Wales, while the production teams shot the oil pipeline explosion in Hankley Common, Elstead, Surrey. Istanbul, Turkey, was indeed used in the film and Elektra King's Baku villa was actually in the city, also using the famous Maiden's Tower which was used as Renard's hideout in Turkey. The underwater submarine scenes were filmed in The Bahamas.[13]

The BMW Z8 driven by Bond in the film was the final part of a three-movie product placement deal with BMW (which began with the Z3 in *GoldenEye* and continued with the 750iL in *Tomorrow Never Dies*) but, due to filming preceding release of the Z8 by a few months, several working mock-ups and models were manufactured for filming purposes.

Music

The soundtrack to *The World Is Not Enough* is the second *Bond* soundtrack to be composed by David Arnold.[14] Arnold broke tradition by not ending the film with a reprise of the opening theme or, as with the previous three films, a new song. Originally, Arnold intended to use the song "Only Myself to Blame" at the end of the film; however, Apted discarded and the song was replaced by a remix of the "James Bond Theme".[15] "Only Myself to Blame", written by Arnold and Don Black and sung by Scott Walker, is the nineteenth and final track on the album and its melody is Elektra King's theme. The theme is heard in "Casino", "Elektra's Theme" and "I Never Miss".[15] Arnold added two new themes to the final score, both of which are reused in the following film, *Die Another Day*.

The title song, "The World Is Not Enough", was written by David Arnold with Don Black and performed by Garbage. It is the fifth *Bond* theme co-written by Black, preceded by "Thunderball",[16] "Diamonds Are Forever",[17] "The Man with the Golden Gun",[18] and "Tomorrow Never Dies".[19] Garbage also contributed to the music heard during the chase sequence ("Ice Bandits"), which was released as the B-side to their single release of the theme song. IGN chose "The World Is Not Enough" as the ninth-best James Bond theme of all time.[20] The song also appeared in two "best of 1999" polls: #87 in 89X's "Top 89 Songs of 1999"[21] and #100 in Q101's "Top 101 of 1999".[22]

Release and reception

The World Is Not Enough premiered on 19 November 1999 in the USA and on 26 November 1999 in the UK.[23] At that time MGM signed a marketing partnership with MTV, primarily for American youths, who were assumed to have considered Bond as "an old-fashioned secret service agent". As a result MTV broadcast more than 100 hours of Bond-related programmes immediately after the film was released, most being presented by Denise Richards.[24]

The film grossed $361 million worldwide, with $126 million in the United States alone, becoming the highest grossing James Bond film of all time until the release of *Die Another Day*.[25] The opening weekend collections in USA were $35.5 million.[26] The film was also selected for the first round of nominations for the Academy Award for Best Special Effects but failed.[27] The film was nominated for a Best Action/Adventure/Thriller Film Saturn Award, Pierce Brosnan won both the Empire Award and the Blockbuster Entertainment Award as Best Actor, and David Arnold won a BMI Film Music Award for his score. The film became the first in the Bond series to win a Golden Raspberry when Denise Richards was chosen as "Worst Supporting Actress" at the 1999 Razzie Awards.[28]

The film was released on DVD and VHS on 16 May 2000, and sold over 5 million copies.[29] The initial release of the DVD includes the featurette "Secrets of 007", which cuts into "making of" material during the movie; the documentary "The Making of The World Is Not Enough"; two commentary tracks—one by director Michael Apted, and the other by production designer Peter Lamont, second unit director Vic Armstrong, and composer David Arnold; a trailer for the video game, and the Garbage music video.[30] The Ultimate Edition released in 2006 had as additional extras a 2000 documentary named "Bond Cocktail", a featurette on shooting the Q Boat scenes, Pierce Brosnan in a press conference in Hong Kong, deleted scenes, and a tribute to Desmond Llewelyn.[31]

Reception was mixed. *Chicago Sun-Times* critic Roger Ebert said the film was a "splendid comic thriller, exciting and graceful, endlessly inventive", and gave it three-and-a-half stars out of four.[32] On the other hand, Eleanor Ringel Gillespie of the *The Atlanta Journal-Constitution* disliked the film, calling it "dated and confused".[33] Rotten Tomatoes gave *The World Is Not Enough* a 51% "rotten" rating,[34] and Metacritic gave the film a score of 59 out of 100.[35] Negative criticism was drawn at the execution of the plot and action scenes which were considered excessive.[36] Norman Wilner of MSN chose it as the third worst Bond movie, ranking it above *A View to a Kill* and *Licence to Kill*,[37] while IGN chose it as the fifth worst.[38]

Richards was criticised as not being credible in the role of a nuclear scientist.[39] [40] Her outfit comprising a tank top and shorts also met a similar reaction.[41] She was ranked as the worst Bond girl of all time by *Entertainment Weekly* in 2008.[42]

Adaptations

The film was adapted into a trading card series which was released by Inkworks. Bond novelist Raymond Benson wrote his adaptation of *The World Is Not Enough* from the film's screenplay. It was Benson's fourth *Bond* novel and followed the story closely, but with some details changed. For instance, Elektra sings quietly before her death and Bond still carries his Walther PPK instead of the newer P99. The novel also gave the cigar girl/assassin the name Giulietta da Vinci and retained a scene between her and Renard that was cut from the film (this scene was also retained in the card series).

In 2000, the film was adapted by Electronic Arts to create a first-person shooter of the same name for the Nintendo 64 and PlayStation. Incidentally, *The World Is Not Enough* was the last *Bond* title to appear on either console. The Nintendo 64 version was developed by Eurocom and the PlayStation version was developed by Black Ops.[43] Versions of *The World Is Not Enough* for the PC and the PlayStation 2 were planned for release in 2000, but both were cancelled.[44] These versions would have used the id Tech 3 game engine. Although this game marks Pierce Brosnan's fifth appearance in a *Bond* video game, the game includes only his likeness; the character is voiced by someone else.

References

- Simpson, Paul (7 November 2002). *The Rough Guide to James Bond*. London: Rough Guides. ISBN 1-84353-142-9.

[1] Simpson, p 26

[2] Parker, Barry R. (2005). *Death Rays, Jet Packs, Stunts & Supercars: The Fantastic Physics of Film's Most Celebrated Secret Agent*. Baltimore: Johns Hopkins University Press. ISBN 978-080188248-7.

[3] LaSalle, Mick (19 November 1999). "More Than 'Enough'" (http://www.sfgate.com/cgi-bin/article.cgi?f=/c/a/1999/11/19/DD3046.DTL). San Francisco Chronicle. . Retrieved 23 December 2007.

[4] Thomas, Rebecca (19 November 1999). "One girl is not enough" (http://news.bbc.co.uk/2/low/special_report/1999/11/99/shaken_not_stirred/523329.stm). BBC NEWS. . Retrieved 23 December 2007.

[5] "Desmond Llewelyn, Actor In Bond Films, Dies at 85" (http://query.nytimes.com/gst/fullpage.html?res=9F0CEED81130F933A15751C1A96F958260). *New York Times*. 20 December 1999. . Retrieved 28 December 2007.

[6] Brian Sibley (2006). *Peter Jackson: A Film-maker's Journey*. London: Harpercollins. pp. 397–8. ISBN 0-00-717558-2.

[7] "Bond is backed... by the government" (http://film.guardian.co.uk/Column/0,4541,45454,00.html). Guardian Unlimited. 27 April 1999. . Retrieved 29 December 2007.

[8] "TWINE & The Rumoured Titles" (http://commanderbond.net/article/361). 26 June 2001. . Retrieved 1 October 2007.

[9] "Filming locations for The World Is Not Enough (1999)" (http://www.imdb.com/title/tt0143145/locations).Internet Movie Database. . Retrieved 16 January 2008.

[10] "British Waterways' Film Map: Canals and rivers on screen" (http://www.waterscape.com/features-and-articles/films). Waterscape.com. . Retrieved 15 January 2008.

[11] Ian Nathan (October 2008). "Unseen Bond". *Empire*: pp. 105.

[12] "Motorola building" (http://www.swindonweb.com/index.asp?m=8&s=115&ss=462&c=1175).SwindonWeb. . Retrieved 7 December 2009.

[13] *The Making of The World Is Not Enough*. [DVD]. Danjaq. 1999.

[14] ""The World Is Not Enough" OST review" (http://allmusic.com/cg/amg.dll?p=amg&sql=10:jxfixqwkldae). *Allmusic*. . Retrieved 16 January 2008.

[15] "David Arnold official website" (http://web.archive.org/web/20071229032830/http://davidarnold.com/cine_menu_11.asp). Archived from the original (http://davidarnold.com/cine_menu_11.asp) on 29 December 2007. . Retrieved 16 January 2008.

[16] *Thunderball*. [Audio CD]. EMI. 2003-02-25. UPN: 7-2435-80589-2-5.

[17] *Diamonds Are Forever*. [Audio CD]. EMI. 2003-02-11. UPN: 7-2435-41420-2-4.

[18] *The Man With The Golden Gun*. [Audio CD]. EMI. 2003-02-25. UPN: 7-2435-41424-2-0.

[19] *Tomorrow Never Dies*. [Audio CD]. A&M Records. 1997-11-25. UPN: 7-3145-40830-2-7.

[20] Spence D. (17 November 2006). "Top 10 James Bond Theme Songs" (http://music.ign.com/articles/746/746590p1.html). IGN. . Retrieved 4 November 2007.

[21] "89X's "Top 89 Songs of 1999" (http://www.rocklists.com/89x-1999.html). Rocklists.com (http://www.rocklists.com/). . Retrieved 2 March 2007.

[22] "Q101's "Top 101 of 1999" (http://www.rocklists.com/q101-1999.html). Rocklists.com (http://www.rocklists.com/). . Retrieved 2 March 2007.

[23] "Bond 19: More than enough" (http://news.bbc.co.uk/2/hi/special_report/1999/11/99/shaken_not_stirred/524858.stm).BBC NEWS. 19 November 1999. . Retrieved 1 October 2007.
[24] "Selling a super spy" (http://news.bbc.co.uk/2/hi/special_report/1999/11/99/shaken_not_stirred/525210.stm). BBC NEWS. 19 November 1999. . Retrieved 1 October 2007.
[25] "James Bond movies" (http://www.boxofficemojo.com/franchises/chart/?id=jamesbond.htm). *Box Office Mojo*. . Retrieved 29 September 2007.
[26] "The World Is Not Enough" (http://www.boxofficemojo.com/movies/?id=worldisnotenough.htm). *Box Office Mojo*. . Retrieved 29 September 2007.
[27] "TWINE Could Be Up For An Oscar" (http://commanderbond.net/article/10). *Commanderbond.net*. 4 January 2000. . Retrieved 1 October 2007.
[28] "Awards for The World Is Not Enough" (http://www.imdb.com/title/tt0143145/awards). Internet Movie Database. . Retrieved 25 December 2007.
[29] "MGM Celebrates One Year Of Profits" (http://www.imdb.com/news/sb/2000-07-27#film3). *StudioBriefing*, IMDb. 27 July 2000. . Retrieved 25 December 2007.
[30] "The World Is Not Enough DVD review" (http://www.timefordvd.com/SR_TheWorldIsNotEnough.html).TimeForDVD.com. . Retrieved 16 January 2008.
[31] "The World Is Not Enough DVD & Soundtrack" (http://web.archive.org/web/20071121130054/http://jamesbond.ugo.com/movies/twine/index.php?p=dvd). UGO. Archived from the original (http://jamesbond.ugo.com/movies/twine/index.php?p=dvd)on 21 November 2007. . Retrieved 16 January 2008.
[32] Ebert, Roger. "The World is Not Enough" (http://rogerebert.suntimes.com/apps/pbcs.dll/article?AID=/19991119/REVIEWS/911190304/1023). Chicago Sun-Times. . Retrieved 17 December 2007.
[33] Gillespie, Eleanor Ringel. "The World Is Not Enough" (http://64.233.169.104/search?q=cache:faSbJ_OvclIJ:www.accessatlanta.com/movies/content/shared/movies/reviews/W/theworldisnotenough.html+site:https://www.accessatlanta.com/&hl=en&ct=clnk&cd=1&client=firefox-a). The Atlanta Journal-Constitution. . Retrieved 16 January 2008.
[34] "The World Is Not Enough" (http://www.rottentomatoes.com/m/world_is_not_enough/). *Rotten Tomatoes*. . Retrieved 29 September 2007.
[35] "The World Is Not Enough" (http://www.metacritic.com/video/titles/worldisnotenough?q=The World Is Not Enough). *Metacritic*. . Retrieved 26 December 2007.
[36] Matt Venendaal (16 May 2006). "The World Is Not Enough (DVD) review" (http://dvd.ign.com/articles/037/037271p1.html). IGN. . Retrieved 25 December 2007.
[37] Norman Wilner. "Rating the Spy Game" (http://movies.sympatico.msn.ca/features/ArticleNormanWilner.aspx?cp-documentid=436189). MSN. . Retrieved 25 December 2007.
[38] "James Bond's Top 20" (http://movies.ign.com/articles/746/746573p1.html). IGN. 17 November 2006. . Retrieved 25 December 2007.
[39] Lisanti, Tom; Paul, Louis (2002). *Film Fatales: Women in Espionage Films and Television, 1962-1973*. Jefferson, NC: McFarland & Co. ISBN 978-078641194-8
[40] Howe, Desson, 19 November 1999, 'World': Bond without end (http://www.washingtonpost.com/wp-srv/entertainment/movies/reviews/worldisnotenoughhowe.htm), *Washington Post*.
[41] Herincx, Gareth (19 November 1999). "Bond 19: More than enough" (http://news.bbc.co.uk/2/hi/special_report/1999/11/99/shaken_not_stirred/524858.stm). BBC NEWS. .
[42] Rich, Joshua (8 January 2008). "James Bond Babes: Best and Worst" (http://www.ew.com/ew/gallery/0,,20170028_20,00.html). *Entertainment Weekly*. . Retrieved 5 February 2008.
[43] Black Ops had previously adapted *Tomorrow Never Dies* for the PlayStation and would go on to develop *Nightfire* in2002.
[44] "The World Is Not Enough preview (PS2)" (http://ps2.ign.com/articles/134/134285p1.html). IGN. . Retrieved 17 December 2007.

External links

- *The World Is Not Enough* (http://www.imdb.com/title/tt0143145/) at the Internet Movie Database
- *The World Is Not Enough* (http://www.allmovie.com/work/181130) at Allmovie
- *The World Is Not Enough* (http://www.rottentomatoes.com/m/world_is_not_enough/) at Rotten Tomatoes
- *The World Is Not Enough* (http://www.boxofficemojo.com/movies/?id=worldisnotenough.htm) at Box Office Mojo
- MGM's official *The World is Not Enough* website (http://www.mgm.com/view/Movie/231/The-World-Is-Not-Enough/)
- The Digital Bits DVD review (http://www.thedigitalbits.com/reviews/worldisnotenough.html)
- Movie Locations Guide.com - Maps and directions to The World is Not Enough Filming Locations (http://www.movielocationsguide.com/World_Is_Not_Enough,_The/filming_locations)

Tea with Mussolini

Tea with Mussolini

Theatrical release poster

Directed by	Franco Zeffirelli
Produced by	Clive Parsons Riccardo Tozzi Giovannella Zannoni Frederick Muller Marco Chimenz Pippo Pisciotto
Screenplay by	John Mortimer
Story by	Franco Zeffirelli (autobiography)
Starring	Cher Joan Plowright Judi Dench Maggie Smith Lily Tomlin
Music by	Stefano Arnaldi Alessio Vlad
Cinematography	David Watkin
Editing by	Tariq Anwar
Distributed by	G2 Films (Theatrical) Metro-Goldwyn-Mayer (DVD)
Release date(s)	March 26, 1999 (Italy) April 2, 1999 (UK) May 14, 1999 (US)
Running time	117 minutes
Country	United States United Kingdom Italy

Language	English Italian
Budget	$12 million
Gross revenue	$14,401,563

Tea with Mussolini is a 1999 American semi-autobiographical film directed by Franco Zeffirelli, telling the story of young Italian boy Luca's upbringing by a circle of English and American women, before and during World War II.

Plot

The film begins in Florence, Italy in 1935, where a group of cultured expatriate British women — called by the Italians the Scorpioni — meet for tea every afternoon. Young Luca (Charlie Lucas) is the illegitimate son of an Italian businessman (Massimo Ghini) who shows little interest in his son's upbringing; the boy's mother, a dressmaker, has recently died. Mary Wallace (Joan Plowright), who works as the man's secretary, steps in to care for him, turning to her Scorpioni friends – including eccentric would-be artist Arabella (Judi Dench) – for support. Together, they teach Luca many lessons about life and especially the arts. Elsa Morganthal (Cher), a brash rich young American widow whom Scorpioni matron Lady Hester Random (Maggie Smith) barely tolerates, sets up a financial trust for Luca when she learns of the death of his mother, whom she was fond of and to whom Elsa still owed money for her dressmaking services.

One day, when the ladies are in a restaurant for afternoon tea, it is vandalized by Fascists, reflecting the increasingly uncertain position of the expatriate community. Lady Hester, widow of Britain's former ambassador to Italy, retains an admiring faith in Benito Mussolini (Claudio Spadaro), and takes it upon herself to visit him, receiving his insincere assurances of their safety, and proudly recounting her "tea with Mussolini". But the political situation continues to deteriorate, and the Scorpioni find their status and liberties diminishing. Luca's father decides that Italy's future is with Germany rather than the United Kingdom, and sends Luca to an Austrian boarding school.

Five years later, Luca (now played by Baird Wallace) returns to Florence with the intention of using Elsa's trust fund to study art. He finds that most British nationals are fleeing the country anticipating Mussolini's declaration of war on Great Britain, and Mary has moved in with Lady Hester and the other English hold-outs. He arrives at the house just as they (and Hester's ineffectual grandson Wilfred (Paul Chequer) disguised as a young woman for his safety) are being rounded up and put onto a transport truck, which he follows to the nearby city of San Gimignano. Because the US is not at war, Elsa and her American compatriot Georgie Rockwell (Lily Tomlin), an openly lesbian archaeologist, remain free, and Elsa uses Luca to deliver forged orders and funds to have the ladies moved from their distressingly barracks-like quarters to an upper-class hotel. Believing that Mussolini himself issued the orders, Lady Hester is delighted, proudly brandishing the newspaper photo of her tea with Il Duce.

As the war progresses, oppression of Jews starts to grow, and Jewish Elsa – protected somewhat by her citizenship and wealth – provides some Italian Jews with fake passports, further enlisting Luca, who has becoming enamored with her, to deliver them. But Luca becomes jealous when she forms a romantic alliance with Vittorio (Paolo Seganti), a shrewd Italian lawyer.

When the US enters the war, Elsa and Georgie are interned with the English women. Elsa falls for Vittorio's scheme to embezzle her art collection and money, and which would ultimately deliver her to the German Gestapo in a phony escape to Switzerland. Luca was aware of the deception, but didn't tell anyone, out of jealous spite for Elsa. Mary learns of it from Elsa's art dealer (Mino Bellei) and scolds Luca. His attitude changes, and he gives his trust funds to members of the Italian resistance movement, which Wilfred has joined. But Elsa refuses to believe the betrayal, and is convinced only when Lady Hester, informed by Mary and Luca of what Elsa has secretly done for them, repents of her contempt for Elsa and offers her gratitude and help. Surprised by Lady Hester's change of heart, Elsa believes her and consents to an escape plan hatched by Mary, Luca, and Wilfred. Before she departs, Elsa tells Luca how she once helped his young mother choose to go through with her pregnancy, thus allowing him to be there for her.

Years later, as Scottish Allied troops advance toward San Gimignano, Arabella frantically defends her beloved frescoes from demolition by German troops, and is heroically joined in the line of fire by Georgie and the English women, including Lady Hester. They are saved when the Germans receive orders to retreat, leaving the women and the towers untouched. The city rejoices as the Scots arrive, with Luca now serving as their commander's Italian interpreter. The major has orders to evacuate the Scorpioni, but Lady Hester refuses to cooperate, resolved that they will resume their former lives in Italy. Mary is delighted to see that Luca – now in British uniform – has become the "English gentleman" his father once wished him to become after all.

Closing texts explain the mostly-happy fates of the characters, concluding with the remark that Luca went on to become an artist and "helped in making this film" — i.e., as writer and director.

Cast

- Cher - Elsa Morganthal Strauss-Almerson
- Maggie Smith - Lady Hester Random
- Judi Dench - Arabella
- Lily Tomlin - Georgie Rockwell
- Joan Plowright - Mary Wallace
- Baird Wallace - Teenage Luca
- Charlie Lucas - Young Luca
- Michael Williams - British Consul (husband of Judi Dench, his final movie role)

Production

Lady Hester Random is based upon a real resident of Florence whom Zeffirelli knew in his childhood. Zeffirelli mentions her and a couple of other ladies of *the Scorpioni* in his autobiography. He said: "I don't remember if she was called Hester, but I remember this terrible, fantastic woman. She was the dowager of the community. I remember the many outrageous things she did because she could afford to be arrogant and bossy."

Reception

The film opened tenth at the U.S. box office with $1,633,183 for the weekend, eventually grossing a total of $14,401,563, considerably more than its budget. Cher's previous film in a starring role, *Faithful*, earned only $2,104,439 in 1996.

Awards and nominations

Won

- 2000 - BAFTA Awards - Best Performance by an Actress in a Supporting Role; Maggie Smith.
- 2000 - Hollywood Makeup Artist and Hair Stylist Guild Awards - Best Period Hair Styling Feature; Vivian McAteer.
- 2000 - Italian National Syndicate of Film Journalists - Best Costume Design (Migliori Costumi); Anna Anni, Alberto Spiazzi.

Nominations

- 1999 - Golden Trailer Awards - Best Drama.
- 2000 - BAFTA Awards - Best Costume Design; Jenny Beavan, Anna Anni, Alberto Spiazzi. [1]

Footnotes

[1] http://www.imdb.com/title/tt0120857/awards

See also

- *The Scorpioni*
- Gran Caffé Doney

External links

- *Tea with Mussolini* (http://www.imdb.com/title/tt0120857/) at the Internet Movie Database

Shakespeare in Love

Shakespeare in Love	

Directed by	John Madden
Produced by	David Parfitt Donna Gigliotti Harvey Weinstein Edward Zwick Marc Norman
Written by	Marc Norman Tom Stoppard
Starring	Joseph Fiennes Gwyneth Paltrow Colin Firth Ben Affleck Geoffrey Rush Judi Dench Tom Wilkinson Imelda Staunton Rupert Everett Martin Clunes Simon Callow Jill Baker
Music by	Stephen Warbeck
Cinematography	Richard Greatrex
Editing by	David Gamble
Distributed by	Miramax Films (USA) Alliance Atlantis (CAN) Universal Pictures (non-USA/CAN)
Release date(s)	December 3, 1998 (New York City) December 11, 1998 (United States) January 29, 1999 (United Kingdom)
Running time	123 minutes

Country	United States United Kingdom
Language	English
Budget	$25 million
Gross revenue	$289,317,794

Shakespeare in Love is a 1998 romantic comedy film directed by John Madden and written by Marc Norman and playwright Tom Stoppard.

The film purports to portray playwright William Shakespeare's involvement in a love affair at the time that he was writing the play *Romeo and Juliet*; it is largely fictional, although several of the characters are based on real people. In addition, many of the characters, lines, and plot devices are references to Shakespeare's plays.

Shakespeare in Love won seven Academy Awards, including Best Picture, Best Actress (for Gwyneth Paltrow), and Best Supporting Actress (for Judi Dench). It was the first comedy film to win the Best Picture award since *Annie Hall* (1977).

Plot

The film centres around the forbidden love of William Shakespeare (Joseph Fiennes) and Viola de Lesseps (Gwyneth Paltrow), the daughter of a wealthy merchant.

As the film begins, theatre manager Philip Henslowe (Geoffrey Rush) finds himself in debt to loan shark Hugh Fennyman (Tom Wilkinson). Henslowe offers Fennyman a partnership in the upcoming production of Shakespeare's newest comedy — *Romeo and Ethel, the Pirate's Daughter* — promising that it will be a hit. However, after learning that his love was cheating on him with his patron, Shakespeare burns the original play and tries to start anew. This play will later be renamed *Romeo and Juliet* and be reworked into a tragedy (but with some comical undertones with a few characters, like the Nurse). Suffering from writer's block, Will Shakespeare is unable to complete the play, but begins auditions for Romeo. A young man named Thomas Kent is cast in the role after impressing Shakespeare with his performance and his love of Shakespeare's previous work. Unknown to Shakespeare and the rest of the theatre company, Kent is young Viola de Lesseps, who desires to act, but, as women are barred from the stage, she must disguise herself as a young man to fulfill her dream.

After Shakespeare discovers his star's true identity, he and Viola begin a passionate secret affair. There are strong parallels between the pair's romance and the one in *Romeo and Juliet*, including the ballroom scene from Act 2 and the balcony scene immediately following it. The element of forbidden love forms the basis of Shakespeare's inspiration, and many of their conversations later show up as some of the most famous quotes in the play.

Inspired by Viola, Shakespeare begins writing feverishly. His work in progress also benefits from the off-hand advice of playwright and friendly rival Christopher 'Kit' Marlowe (Rupert Everett), whose own murder is cleverly worked into the plot later on. Yet Shakespeare and de Lesseps know that their romance is doomed. Shakespeare is married, albeit long separated from his wife, while Viola's parents have arranged her betrothal to Lord Wessex (Colin Firth), an aristocrat who has agreed to marry the social-climbing merchant's daughter in view of his own mounting debts and lack of cash. When Viola is summoned to the court of Queen Elizabeth I (Judi Dench), Shakespeare dons a woman's disguise to accompany her as her country cousin. At court, Shakespeare goads Wessex into betting fifty pounds that a play cannot capture the nature of true love. If *Romeo and Juliet* is a success, Shakespeare as playwright will win the money. The Queen, who enjoys Shakespeare's plays, agrees to witness the wager. The meeting's true purpose is revealed when Wessex announces his intent to marry Viola.

Edmund Tilney (Simon Callow), the Master of the Revels, the Queen's official in charge of the theatres, learns that there is a woman in the theatre company at the Rose playhouse. He orders the theatre closed for violating morality and the law. Left without a stage or lead actor, it seems that *Romeo and Juliet* must close before it even opens, until

Richard Burbage (Martin Clunes), the owner of a competing theatre, the Curtain, offers his stage to Shakespeare. Shakespeare assumes the lead role of Romeo, with a boy actor playing Juliet. Viola learns the play will be performed on her wedding day. After the ceremony, Viola's loyal nurse (Imelda Staunton) helps her slip away to the theatre. In a final twist, shortly before the play begins, the boy playing Juliet starts experiencing the voice change of puberty. Viola takes the stage to replace him and plays Juliet to Shakespeare's Romeo. Their passionate portrayal of two lovers inspires the entire audience.

Tilney arrives at the theatre with Wessex, who has deduced his new bride's whereabouts. Tilney invokes the Queen's name to arrest all there for indecency. Suddenly, Elizabeth I's voice rings out from the back of the theatre: "Mr. Tilney! Have a care with my name; you will wear it out." The Queen had decided to attend the play in disguise, and says that she will handle this matter herself. Although she recognizes Viola in her disguise as Thomas Kent, the Queen does not unmask Viola, instead declaring that the role of Juliet is being performed by the young man Thomas Kent.

However, even a Queen is powerless to break a lawful marriage. Queen Elizabeth orders "Thomas Kent" to fetch Viola so that she may sail with Wessex to a colonial settlement in Virginia. The queen also states that *Romeo and Juliet* has accurately portrayed true love and so Wessex is forced to pay Shakespeare the fifty pounds, the exact amount Shakespeare requires to buy a share in the Chamberlain's Men. The Queen then directs "Kent" to tell Shakespeare to write something "a little more cheerful next time, for Twelfth Night". Viola and Shakespeare part, resigned to their fates. Her ship sinks; only Viola survives, and lands on a beach. The film closes with her on the beach, with a voice over by Shakespeare discussing his plans to write *Twelfth Night, Or What You Will* and musing of its main character, "For she will be my heroine for all time, and her name will be . . . Viola", a strong young woman castaway who disguises herself as a young man.

Cast

- Joseph Fiennes as William Shakespeare. Daniel Day-Lewis reportedly was asked by Julia Roberts to star as the role, but he declined. Kenneth Branagh was also considered. Fiennes was eventually cast.
- Gwyneth Paltrow as Viola de Lesseps. The original Viola was Julia Roberts in 1991. She withdrew six weeks before filming. Kate Winslet turned down the role to star in *Holy Smoke!*. Paltrow won the Academy Award for Best Actress for her role as Viola.
- Colin Firth as Lord Wessex
- Ben Affleck as Ned Alleyn. Affleck joined to be close to then-girlfriend Paltrow.
- Geoffrey Rush as Philip Henslowe. Rush was nominated for the Academy Award for Best Supporting Actor for his role as Philip, but lost to James Coburn.
- Judi Dench as Queen Elizabeth I. Dench won the Academy Award for Best Supporting Actress for her role as Queen Elizabeth. This is the second-shortest performance to win the Supporting Actress Oscar, with only eight minutes of screen time. The shortest was Beatrice Straight in *Network*, with only five minutes and forty seconds. In the same year, Cate Blanchett was nominated for the Academy Award for Best Actress in the same role in *Elizabeth* but lost to Gwyneth Paltrow [*see* above].
- Tom Wilkinson as Hugh Fennyman
- Antony Sher as Dr. Moth
- Imelda Staunton as Nurse
- Rupert Everett as Christopher 'Kit' Marlowe
- Martin Clunes as Richard Burbage
- Simon Callow as Edmund Tilney
- Jim Carter as Ralph Bashford
- Jill Baker as Lady de Lesseps
- Patrick Barlow as Will Kemp

- Mark Williams as Wabash
- Simon Day as First Boatsman

Production

The original idea for *Shakespeare in Love* came to screenwriter Marc Norman in the late 1980s. He pitched a draft screenplay to director Ed Zwick. The screenplay attracted Julia Roberts who agreed to play Viola. However, Zwick disliked Norman's screenplay and hired the playwright Tom Stoppard to improve it (Stoppard's first major success had been with the Shakespeare-influenced play *Rosencrantz & Guildenstern Are Dead*).[1]

The film went into production in 1991 at Universal Pictures, with Zwick as director, but although sets and costumes were in construction, Shakespeare had not yet been cast, because Julia Roberts insisted that only Daniel Day-Lewis could play the role. Day-Lewis was uninterested, and when Roberts failed to persuade him, she withdrew from the film, six weeks before shooting was due to begin. The production went into turnaround, and Zwick was unable to persuade other studios to take up the screenplay.[2]

Eventually, Zwick interested Miramax in the screenplay, but Miramax was not keen on him as director, and froze him out of the project, choosing John Madden instead. Miramax boss Harvey Weinstein acted as producer, and successfully persuaded Ben Affleck to take a small role as Ned Alleyn.[3]

The film was considerably reworked after the first test screenings. The scene with Shakespeare and Viola in the punt was re-shot, to make it more emotional, and some lines were re-recorded to clarify the reasons why Viola had to marry Wessex. The ending was reshot several times, until Stoppard eventually came up with the idea of Viola suggesting to Shakespeare that their parting could inspire his next play.[4]

References to Shakespeare's work

The main source for much of the action in the film is *Romeo and Juliet.* Will and Viola play out the famous balcony and bedroom scenes; like Juliet, Viola has a witty nurse, and is separated from Will by a gulf of duty (although not the family enmity of the play: the "two households" of *Romeo and Juliet* are supposedly inspired by the two rival playhouses). In addition, the two lovers are equally "star-crossed" — they are not ultimately destined to be together (since Viola is of rich and socially ambitious merchant stock and is promised to marry Lord Wessex, while Shakespeare himself is poor and already married). There is also a Rosaline, with whom Will is in love at the beginning of the film.

Many other plot devices used in the film are common in various Shakespearean comedies and in the works of the other playwrights of the Elizabethan era: the Queen disguised as a commoner, the cross-dressing disguises, mistaken identities, the sword fight, the suspicion of adultery (or, at least, cheating), the appearance of a "ghost" (cf. *Macbeth*), and the "play within a play".

The film also has sequences in which Shakespeare and the other characters utter words that will later appear in his plays:

- On the street, Shakespeare hears a Puritan preaching against the two London stages: "The Rose smells thusly rank, by any name! I say, a plague on both their houses!" Two references in one, both to *Romeo and Juliet*; first, "A rose by any other name would smell as sweet" (Act II, scene ii, lines 1 and 2); second, "a plague on both your houses" (Act III, scene I, line 94).
- Backstage of a performance of *The Two Gentlemen of Verona*, Shakespeare sees William Kempe in full make-up, silently contemplating a skull (a reference to *Hamlet*).
- Shakespeare utters the lines "Doubt thou the stars are fire, / Doubt that the sun doth move" (from *Hamlet*) to Philip Henslowe.
- As Shakespeare's writer's block is introduced, he is seen crumpling balls of paper and throwing them around his room. They land near props which represent scenes in his several plays: a skull (*Hamlet*), and an open chest (*The*

Merchant of Venice).

- Viola, as well as being Paltrow's name in the film, is the lead character in *Twelfth Night* who dresses as a man after the supposed death of her brother.
- At the end of the film, Shakespeare imagines a shipwreck overtaking Viola on her way to America, inspiring the second scene of his next play, *Twelfth Night*, and perhaps also *The Tempest*.
- Shakespeare writes a sonnet to Viola which begins: "Shall I compare thee to a summer's day?" (from Sonnet 18).
- Shakespeare tells Henslowe that he still owes him for "one gentleman of Verona", a reference to *Two Gentlemen of Verona*, part of which we also see being acted before the Queen later in the film.

Christopher Marlowe appears in the film as the master playwright whom the characters within the film consider the greatest English dramatist of that time — this is accurate, yet also humorous, since everyone in the film's audience knows what will eventually happen to Shakespeare. Marlowe gives Shakespeare a plot for his next play, "Romeo and Ethel the Pirate's Daughter" ("Romeo is Italian...always in and out of love...until he meets...Ethel. The daughter of his enemy! His best friend is killed in a duel by Ethel's brother or something. His name is Mercutio.") Marlowe's *Doctor Faustus* is quoted repeatedly: "Was this the face that launched a thousand ships/ And burned the topless towers of Ilium?"

The child John Webster who plays with mice is a reference to the leading figure in the Jacobean generation of playwrights. His plays (*The Duchess of Malfi*, *The White Devil*) are known for their blood and gore, which is why he says that he enjoys *Titus Andronicus*, and why he says of *Romeo and Juliet* when asked by the Queen "I liked it when she stabbed herself."

When the clown Will Kempe (Patrick Barlow) says to Shakespeare that he would like to play in a drama, he is told that "they would laugh at Seneca if you played it," a reference to the Roman tragedian renowned for his sombre and bloody plot lines which were a major influence on the development of English tragedy.

Will is shown signing a paper repeatedly, with many relatively illegible signatures visible. This is a reference to the fact that several versions of Shakespeare's signature exist, and in each one he spelled his name differently.

Controversy

The writers of *Shakespeare in Love* were sued in 1999 by Faye Kellerman, author of the book *The Quality of Mercy*. Kellerman claimed that the story was lifted from her book, a detective novel in which Shakespeare and a cross-dressing Jewish woman attempt to solve a murder. Miramax derided the claim of similarity as "[an] absurd...publicity stunt".[5] [6] After the film's release, certain publications, including *Private Eye*, noted strong similarities between the film and the 1941 novel *No Bed for Bacon*, by Caryl Brahms and S J Simon, which also features Shakespeare falling in love and finding inspiration for his later plays. In a foreword to a subsequent edition of *No Bed for Bacon* (which traded on the association by declaring itself "A Story of Shakespeare and Lady Viola in Love") Ned Sherrin, *Private Eye* insider and former writing partner of Brahms', confirmed that he had lent a copy of the novel to Stoppard after he joined the writing team,[7] but that the basic plot of the film had been independently developed by Marc Norman, who was unaware of the earlier work.

Awards

Awards			
Award	Category	Name	Outcome
Academy Awards	Academy Award for Best Picture		Won
	Academy Award for Best Actress	Gwyneth Paltrow	Won
	Academy Award for Best Supporting Actress	Judi Dench	Won
	Academy Award for Best Art Direction	Martin Childs & Jill Quertier	Won
	Academy Award for Costume Design	Sandy Powell	Won
	Academy Award for Best Original Musical or Comedy Score (retired category)	Stephen Warbeck	Won
	Academy Award for Writing Original Screenplay	Marc Norman & Tom Stoppard	Won
	Academy Award for Directing	John Madden	Nominated
	Academy Award for Best Supporting Actor	Geoffrey Rush	Nominated
	Academy Award for Best Cinematography	Richard Greatrex	Nominated
	Academy Award for Film Editing	David Gamble	Nominated
	Academy Award for Makeup	Lisa Westcott & Veronica Brebner	Nominated

British Academy Film Awards	BAFTA Award for Best Film		Won
	BAFTA Award for Best Actress in a Supporting Role	Judi Dench	Won
	BAFTA Award for Best Actor in a Supporting Role	Geoffrey Rush	Won
	BAFTA Award for Best Editing	David Gamble	Won
	BAFTA Award for Best Direction	John Madden	Nominated
	BAFTA Award for Best Actress in a Leading Role	Gwyneth Paltrow	Nominated
	BAFTA Award for Best Actor in a Leading Role	Joseph Fiennes	Nominated
	BAFTA Award for Best Actor in a Supporting Role	Tom Wilkinson	Nominated
	BAFTA Award for Best Cinematography	Richard Greatrex	Nominated
	BAFTA Award for Best Original Screenplay	Marc Norman & Tom Stoppard	Nominated
	BAFTA Award for Best Makeup & Hair	Lisa Westcott	Nominated
	BAFTA Award for Best Sound	Robin O'Donoghue, Dominic Lester, Peter Glossop, John Downer	Nominated
	Anthony Asquith Award for Film Music	Stephen Warbeck	Nominated
	BAFTA Award for Best Costume Design	Sandy Powell	Nominated
	BAFTA Award for Best Production Design	Martin Childs	Nominated
Directors Guild of America Award	Outstanding Directorial Achievement in Motion Pictures	John Madden	Nominated

Golden Globe Awards	Golden Globe Award for Best Motion Picture - Musical or Comedy		Won
	Golden Globe Award for Best Actress - Motion Picture Musical or Comedy	Gwyneth Paltrow	Won
	Golden Globe Award for Best Screenplay	Marc Norman & Tom Stoppard	Won
	Golden Globe Award for Best Director - Motion Picture	John Madden	Nominated
	Golden Globe Award for Best Supporting Actor - Motion Picture	Geoffrey Rush	Nominated
	Golden Globe Award for Best Supporting Actress - Motion Picture	Judi Dench	Nominated
Screen Actors Guild Awards	Screen Actors Guild Award for Outstanding Performance by a Cast in a Motion Picture		Won
	Screen Actors Guild Award - Best Female Actor	Gwyneth Paltrow	Won
Writers Guild of America Award	Best Original Screenplay	Marc Norman & Tom Stoppard	Won

Cultural influence

- *Shakespeare in Love* has since been used as material in the VCE (Victorian Certificate of Education) in Australia.
- *Shakespeare in Love* was spoofed and homaged, along with *Star Wars*, in the 1999 short film *George Lucas in Love*.

References

[1] Peter Biskind, *Down and Dirty Pictures: Miramax, Sundance and the Rise of Independent Film* (New York: Simon & Schuster, 2004), p.327.

[2] Peter Biskind, *Down and Dirty Pictures: Miramax, Sundance and the Rise of Independent Film* (New York: Simon & Schuster, 2004), p.327.

[3] Peter Biskind, *Down and Dirty Pictures: Miramax, Sundance and the Rise of Independent Film* (New York: Simon & Schuster, 2004), p.328-30.

[4] Peter Biskind, *Down and Dirty Pictures: Miramax, Sundance and the Rise of Independent Film* (New York: Simon & Schuster, 2004), p.330-1.

[5] "Novelist sues Shakespeare makers" (http://news.bbc.co.uk/1/hi/entertainment/the_oscars_1999/301620.stm). BBC News. 1999-03-23. . Retrieved 2008-06-30.

[6] "Writer sues makers of 'Shakespeare in Love'" (http://www.cnn.com/SHOWBIZ/Movies/9903/23/shakespeare.lawsuit/). CNN. 1999-03-23. . Retrieved 2008-06-30.

[7] Diarist (6 February 1999). "Closed government" (http://findarticles.com/p/articles/mi_qa3724/is_199902/ai_n8830211/?tag=content;col1). *The Spectator*. . Retrieved 2009-04-13.

External links

- *Shakespeare in Love* (http://www.imdb.com/title/tt0138097/) at the Internet Movie Database
- *Shakespeare in Love* (http://www.allmovie.com/work/174142) at Allmovie
- *Shakespeare in Love* (http://www.boxofficemojo.com/movies/?id=shakespeareinlove.htm) at Box Office Mojo
- *Shakespeare in Love* (http://www.rottentomatoes.com/m/shakespeare_in_love/) at Rotten Tomatoes

Tomorrow Never Dies

Tomorrow Never Dies	
 Theatrical release poster	
James Bond	Pierce Brosnan
Also starring	Jonathan Pryce Michelle Yeoh Teri Hatcher
Directed by	Roger Spottiswoode
Produced by	Michael G. Wilson Barbara Broccoli
Novel/Story by	Bruce Feirstein
Screenplay by	Bruce Feirstein
Cinematography	Robert Elswit
Music by	David Arnold
Main theme	Tomorrow Never Dies
Composer	Sheryl Crow Mitchell Froom
Performer	Sheryl Crow
Distributed by	Metro-Goldwyn-Mayer
Release date(s)	19 December 1997
Running time	119 min.
Country	United Kingdom
Budget	$110,000,000
Worldwide gross	$333,011,068[1]
Preceded by	*GoldenEye*
Followed by	*The World Is Not Enough*

Tomorrow Never Dies (1997) is the eighteenth spy film in the James Bond series, and the second to star Pierce Brosnan as the fictional MI6 agent James Bond. Bruce Feirstein wrote the screenplay, and it was directed by Roger Spottiswoode. It follows Bond as he tries to stop a media mogul from engineering world events and starting World War III.

The film was produced by Michael G. Wilson and Barbara Broccoli, and was the first James Bond film made after the death of producer Albert R. Broccoli. The movie paid tribute to him in the end credits. *Tomorrow Never Dies* performed well at the box office and earned a Golden Globe nomination despite mixed reviews. While its domestic box office surpassed *GoldenEye*,[2] it was the only Pierce Brosnan Bond film not to open at number one at the box office since it opened the same day as *Titanic*.[3]

Plot

MI6 sends James Bond (Pierce Brosnan) into the field to spy on a terrorist arms bazaar on the Russian border. Via television, MI6 and the British military identify several wanted men, including American "techno-terrorist" Henry Gupta (Ricky Jay), who is buying a GPS encoder made by the American military. Despite M's (Judi Dench) insistence that Agent 007 finish his reconnaissance, the British Admiral Roebuck (Geoffrey Palmer) launches a missile attack on the arms bazaar. Bond then discovers there are two Soviet nuclear torpedoes mounted on an L-39 Albatros, the destruction of which would cause potential local radioactive contamination. With the missile already in flight and unable to be aborted, Bond hijacks the L-39 jet and flies it away from the arms bazaar, defeating a pursuing L-39 and a hostile co-pilot by ejecting the co-pilot into the other aircraft. Despite the missile destroying most of the terrorists and weaponry, Gupta escapes with the encoder.

Media baron Elliot Carver (Jonathan Pryce), head of the Carver Media Group Network (CMGN), begins his plans to use the encoder to provoke war between China and the United Kingdom. As the existing Chinese leadership is not receptive to giving Carver Media Group Network exclusive broadcast rights in their country, Carver wants to use a war to eliminate them in favor of politicians more friendly to his plans. Meaconing the GPS signal using the encoder, Gupta sends the British frigate HMS *Devonshire* off-course in the South China Sea, where Carver's stealth ship and its crew plan to steal a number of its missiles[4] . Carver's henchman, Stamper (Götz Otto), sinks the frigate with a sea drill and shoots down a Chinese J-7 fighter jet sent to investigate the British presence, and then the men aboard the stealth ship kill the Devonshire's survivors with Chinese weaponry. Back in London Admiral Roebuck (thinking the ship had been attacked by the Chinese), deploys the British Fleet to recover the frigate, and possibly retaliate, leaving M only forty-eight hours to investigate its sinking.

M sends Bond to investigate Carver after Carver Media releases news with critical details hours before these have become known, and MI6 noticed a spurious signal from one of his CMGN communications satellites when the frigate was sunk. Bond travels to Hamburg and seduces Carver's wife, Paris (Teri Hatcher), an ex-girlfriend; the information she tells Bond helps him sneak into Carver's newspaper headquarters and steal back the GPS encoder. When Carver learns of it, he orders Paris and Bond killed. Paris is killed by Dr. Kaufman (Vincent Schiavelli), but Bond escapes in his Q division car, a BMW 750i with full remote control. Bond then goes to the South China Sea to investigate the wreck, discovering one of the missiles missing. He and Wai Lin (Michelle Yeoh), a Chinese spy on the same case, are captured by Stamper and taken to the CMGN tower Saigon, but they escape and begin collaborating.

They contact the Royal Navy and the People's Liberation Army Air Force (Red Chinese air force) to explain what is happening, then find and board Carver's stealth ship in Ha Long Bay to prevent him firing the stolen British cruise missile at Beijing. During the battle, Wai Lin is captured. Bond captures Gupta to use as his own hostage, but Carver kills Gupta, claiming he has "outlived his contract". Bond gets them out of it by setting off an explosive, damaging part of the ship and exposing it on radar, enabling the Royal Navy to attack it. While Wai Lin heads to disable the engines, Bond leads a large battle to the stolen missile against the crew, and Stamper. Carver is killed by his own sea drill after trying to kill Bond on his own. As Bond begins to start the process of destroying the warhead, Stamper shows that he has Wai Lin hostage. A fight ensues when he tries to drown her. Bond traps him in the missile firing mechanism and leaves him to die, while saving Wai Lin as the stealth ship is destroyed by the missile. Bond and Wai Lin survive amidst the wreckage as HMS *Bedford* searches for them.

Cast

- Pierce Brosnan as James Bond (007): British Secret Agent and protagonist
- Jonathan Pryce as Elliot Carver: Main antagonist. A media mogul modelled on Robert Maxwell, but analyzed as a satire on Rupert Murdoch.[5] He is completely insane and possibly even psychopathic, with scant regard for any of the lives destroyed or simply taken as a result of his media ambition.
- Michelle Yeoh as Colonel Wai Lin: A skilled Chinese spy and Bond's ally.
- Teri Hatcher as Paris Carver: A former girlfriend of Bond who is now Carver's trophy wife.
- Götz Otto as Mr. Stamper: Carver's henchman, skilled in the art of Chakra torture.
- Ricky Jay as Henry Gupta: An American "Techno-terrorist" in the employ of Carver. Bruce Feirstein said he named this character after a Gupta Bakery, which he went past on the way to the studios.[6]
- Joe Don Baker as Jack Wade: Baker reprised his role of CIA liaison Wade from *GoldenEye*, helping Bond with the GPS encoder and providing a plane to get to the *Devonshire*.
- Vincent Schiavelli as Dr. Kaufman: Kaufman is a professional assassin used by Elliot Carver to kill Paris Carver and Bond, with the intention of making it look like Bond did it.
- Judi Dench as M: Dench reprised her role of M from *GoldenEye*. M often acts as Bond's advocate, justifying his actions to the military.
- Desmond Llewelyn as Q: Llewelyn returned for his penultimate Bond film, supplying Bond with gadgets.
- Samantha Bond as Miss Moneypenny : M's secretary.
- Geoffrey Palmer as Admiral Roebuck : M's contentious military contact.
- Colin Salmon as Charles Robinson
- Julian Fellowes as Defence Secretary : The Defence Minister of the British Government that orders the Admiral to send the British fleet to the China sea, previously played by Geoffrey Keen (Sir Frederick Gray)
- Cecilie Thomsen as Professor Inga Bergstrom
- Mark Spalding as Stealth Boat Captain
- Daphne Deckers as PR Lady
- John Cho as Aide #3

Also, Gerard Butler and Julian Rhind-Tutt appeared as crew of the HMS *Devonshire*

Production

After the success of *GoldenEye* in reviving the Bond series, there was pressure to recreate that success in its follow-up. This pressure came both from MGM, which had recently been sold to billionaire Kirk Kerkorian, who wanted the release to coincide with their public stock offering,[7] and the worldwide audience, with co-producer Michael G. Wilson saying "You realize that there's a huge audience and I guess you don't want to come out with a film that's going to somehow disappoint them."[7] This was the first Bond film to be made after the death of Albert R. Broccoli, who had been involved with the production of them since the series began. The rush to complete it meant the budget reached $110 million.[7] [8]

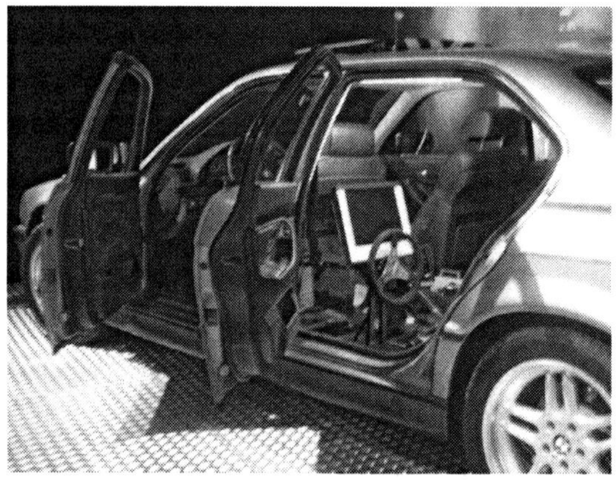

BMW 7 Series car from *Tomorrow Never Dies*, seen at an exhibition at Museum Industriekultur, Nuremberg.

The producers were unable to get Martin Campbell, the director of *GoldenEye*, to return; his agent saying "Martin just didn't want to do two Bond films in a row". Instead, Roger Spottiswoode was chosen in September 1996.[9] The story had its roots in a treatment written by Donald E. Westlake, although what influence it eventually had is unknown.[10] Bruce Feirstein, who had worked on *GoldenEye*, penned the initial script which was then passed to Spottiswoode who reworked it. He gathered seven Hollywood screenwriters in London to brainstorm, eventually choosing Nicholas Meyer to perform rewrites.[9] The script was also worked on by Dan Petrie, Jr. and David Campbell Wilson before Feirstein, who retained the sole writing credit, was brought in for a final polish.[10]

Script

As had been the case previously, with no Ian Fleming novels remaining unadapted, an entirely original story was required. The scriptwriting process was finished very late and after lengthy disputes. Spottiswoode said that MGM had a script in January 1997 revolving round Hong Kong being returned to the Chinese, which happened in July; this couldn't be used for a film opening at the end of the year, so they had to start "almost from scratch at T-minus zero!"[11] Wilson said "we didn't have a script that was ready to shoot on the first day of filming", with Pierce Brosnan saying "we had a script that was not functioning in certain areas."[7] The *Daily Mail* reported on arguments between Spottiswoode and the producers with the former favouring the Petrie version, but the latter reinstating Feirstein to rewrite it two weeks before filming was due to begin. They also said that Jonathan Pryce and Teri Hatcher were unhappy with their new roles, causing further rescripting.[12]

The title was inspired by the Beatles' song "Tomorrow Never Knows".[5] The eventual title came about by accident: one of the potential titles was *Tomorrow Never Lies* (referring to the *Tomorrow* newspaper in the story) and it was faxed to MGM. However, through an error it became *Tomorrow Never Dies*, which MGM liked so much they insisted on using.[11] The title was the first not to have any relation with Fleming.[5]

Casting

Teri Hatcher was three months pregnant at the shooting start, by her then-husband, Jon Tenney; her publicist stated the pregnancy did not affect the production schedule.[13] Hatcher later regretted playing Paris Carver, saying "It's such an artificial kind of character to be playing that you don't get any special satisfaction from it."[14] According to Brosnan, Monica Bellucci screentested for the role but "the fools said no."[15]

The role of Elliot Carver was initially offered to Anthony Hopkins (who also had been offered a role in *GoldenEye*), but he turned it down.[9] [10]

Natasha Henstridge was rumoured as cast in the lead Bond Girl role,[16] but eventually, Yeoh was confirmed in that role. Brosnan was impressed, describing her as a "wonderful actress" who was "serious and committed about her work".[17] She reputedly wanted to perform her own stunts, but was prevented because director Spottiswoode ruled it too dangerous and uninsured.[18] [19]

When Götz Otto was called in for casting, he was given twenty seconds to introduce himself. Saying, "I am big, I am bad, and I am German", he did it in five.[20]

Filming

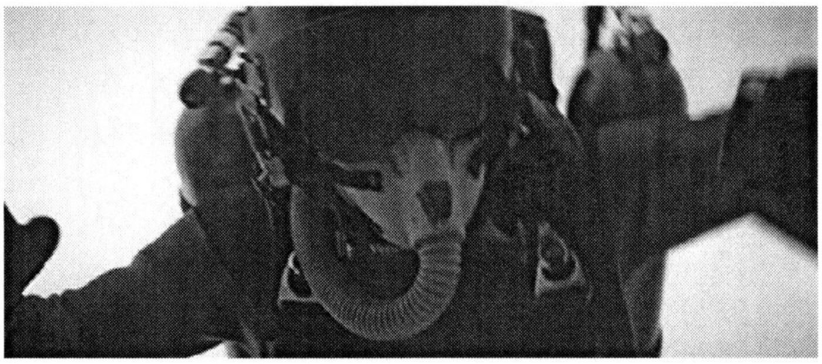

James Bond performing a HALO jump.

Second unit filming began on 18 January 1997 with Vic Armstrong directing; they filmed the pre-credits sequence in the French Pyrenees (using the Aérodrome de Courchevel) and moved on to Portsmouth to film the scenes where the Royal Navy prepares to engage the Chinese.[10] The main unit began filming on 1 April. They were unable to use the Leavesden Film Studios, which they had constructed from an abandoned Rolls-Royce factory for *GoldenEye*, as George Lucas was using it for *Star Wars Episode I: The Phantom Menace*, so instead they constructed sound stages in another derelict industrial site nearby. They also used the 007 Stage at Pinewood Studios.[9]

They planned to film some of the scenes on location in Ho Chi Minh City, Vietnam, and had been granted a visa. This was later rescinded, two months after planning had begun, forcing filming to move to Bangkok, Thailand. Some claim the Chinese government put pressure on Vietnam to do this, because they were unhappy with the story involving corrupt Chinese generals doing the bidding of a media tycoon. However, Bond spokesman Gordon Arnell claimed the Vietnamese were merely unhappy with crew and equipment needed for pyrotechnics, with a Vietnamese official saying it was due to "many complicated reasons".[21]

The car chase sequence took three weeks to film, with Brent Cross car park being used to simulate Hamburg (although the final leap was filmed on location[22]). A stunt involving setting fire to three vehicles produced more smoke than anticipated, causing a member of the public to call the fire brigade.[23] Two locations from previous Bond films were used: Brosnan and Hatcher's love scene was filmed at Stoke Poges golf club, which had been featured in *Goldfinger*, and the bay where they search for Carver's stealth boat is Khow-Ping-Khan island near Phuket, Thailand, previously used for *The Man with the Golden Gun*.[10] [22]

During filming, there were reports of disputes on set. The *Daily Mail* reported that Spottiswoode and Feirstein were no longer on speaking terms and that crew members had threatened to resign, with one saying "All the happiness and teamwork which is the hallmark of Bond has disappeared completely."[12] This was denied by Brosnan who claimed "It was nothing more than good old creative argy-bargy",[7] with Spottiswoode saying "It has all been made up...Nothing important really went wrong."[11] Spottiswoode did not return to direct the next film; he said the producers asked him, but he was too tired.[11] Apparently, Brosnan and Hatcher feuded briefly during filming due to her arriving late onto the set one day. The matter was quickly resolved though and Brosnan apologized to Hatcher after realizing she was pregnant and was late for that reason.[15]

Music

Barbara Broccoli chose David Arnold to score *Tomorrow Never Dies* on a recommendation from prolific James Bond films composer John Barry.[24] Arnold had come to Barry's attention through his successful cover interpretations in *Shaken and Stirred: The David Arnold James Bond Project*, which featured major artists performing the former James Bond title songs in new arrangements. The film's score combined techno music with a recognisably Barry-inspired 'classic Bond' sound–notably Arnold borrowed from Barry's score for *From Russia with Love*. For the music for the indoor car chase sequence, Arnold enlisted the help of the band Propellerheads, who had worked with him before on *Shaken and Stirred*. The soundtrack's reception was good, with Filmtracks describing it as "an excellent tribute to the entire series of Bond score",[25] and Arnold was brought back to score all the subsequent films, four more to date. The theme was chosen through a competitive process. There were around twelve submissions, including songs from Swan Lee, Pulp, Saint Etienne, Marc Almond, Sheryl Crow, and David Arnold.[26] Crow's song was chosen for the main titles while David Arnold's song *Surrender*, performed by k.d. lang, was used for the end titles, its melody cropping up throughout the film.[25] This was the fourth Bond film to have different opening and closing songs. Two different versions of the soundtrack album were released, the first lacking music from the second half of the film, and the second lacking the songs. Pulp's effort was retitled as *Tomorrow Never Lies* and appeared as a b-side on their single "Help The Aged". Moby created a remake of the original James Bond theme to be used for the movie. The original version of the Pulp offering can be heard on the Deluxe Edition of This Is Hardcore as a rough mix.

Release and reception

The film had a World Charity Premiere at The Odeon Leicester Square, on 9 December 1997; this was followed by an after premiere party at Bedford Square, home of original Ian Fleming publisher, Jonathan Cape.[27] The film went on general release in the UK and Iceland on 12 December, and in most other countries during the following week.[28] It opened at #2 in the US, with a weekend gross of $25,143,007 from 2,807 theaters, for an average of $8,957 per theater. It ended up achieving a worldwide gross of over $330 million,[1] although it did not surpass its predecessor *GoldenEye*, which grossed almost $ 20 million more.[29]

The critical reception of the film was mixed, with the film review collection website *Rotten Tomatoes* giving it a 56% "rotten" rating (75% amongst top critics),[30] and similar site Metacritic rating it at 56%.[31] In the *Chicago Sun-Times*, Roger Ebert gave the film three out of four-stars, saying "*Tomorrow Never Dies* gets the job done, sometimes excitingly, often with style" with the villain "slightly more contemporary and plausible than usual", bringing "some subtler-than-usual satire into the film".[32] James Berardinelli described it as "the best Bond film in many years" and said Brosnan "inhabits his character with a suave confidence that is very like Connery's."[33] However, in the *Los Angeles Times*, Kenneth Turan thought a lot of *Tomorrow Never Dies* had a "stodgy, been-there feeling", with little change from previous films,[34] and Charles Taylor wrote for Salon.com that the film was "a flat, impersonal affair".[35]

The title song sung by Sheryl Crow was nominated for a Golden Globe for "Best Original Song - Motion Picture" and a Grammy for "Best Song Written Specifically for a Motion Picture or for Television". The film received four nominations for Saturn Awards, with Brosnan winning "Best Actor". It also won a MPSE Golden Reel Award for "Best Sound Editing - Foreign Feature" and a BMI Film Music Award.[36]

The original UK release received various cuts to scenes of violence and martial arts weaponry, and to reduce the impact of sound effects, in order to receive a more box office friendly 12 certificate. Further cuts were made to the video/DVD release to retain this rating. These edits were restored for the Ultimate Edition DVD release in the UK, which was consequently upgraded to a 15 certificate[37] .

Appearances in other media

1997 British Coronet Books paperback edition.

Tomorrow Never Dies was the first of three Bond films to be adapted into books by then-current Bond novelist, Raymond Benson. Benson's version is expanded from the screenplay including additional scenes with Wai Lin and other supporting characters not in the film. The novel traces Carver's background as that of media mogul Lord Roverman's son. Carver blackmails him into suicide and takes over his business.[38] The novel also attempts to merge Benson's series with the films, particularly continuing a middle of the road approach to John Gardner's continuity. Notably it includes a reference to the film version of *You Only Live Twice* where he states that Bond was lying to Miss Moneypenny when he said he had taken a course in Oriental languages. This was done to counter the scene in *Tomorrow Never Dies* where Bond is unable to read a Chinese keyboard.[39] But this contradicts Benson's previous book *Zero Minus Ten* in which Bond is able to speak fluent Cantonese. *Tomorrow Never Dies* also mentions Felix Leiter, although it states that Felix had worked for Pinkertons Detective Agency which is thus exclusive to the literary series. Subsequent Bond novels by Benson were affected by *Tomorrow Never Dies*, specifically Bond's weapon of choice being changed from the Walther PPK to the Walther P99. Benson said in an interview that he felt *Tomorrow Never Dies* was the best of the three novelizations he wrote."[40]

The film was adapted into a third-person shooter PlayStation video game, *Tomorrow Never Dies*. It was developed by Black Ops and published by Electronic Arts on 16 November 1999. Game Revolution described it as "really just an empty and shallow game",[41] and IGN said it was "mediocre".[42]

The motorbike-scene including Pierce Brosnan and Michelle Yeoh was referenced in the *South Park* episode "Super Fun Time", when Eric Cartman and Butters had to hold hands the whole Episode and rode a coin-operated motorcycle in a fun park. They "performed" the same stunts Brosnan and Yeoh's characters did in *Tomorrow Never Dies*.

Episode EA1303H of the Food Network show, *Good Eats* is a play-on words with this Bond movie, "Tamale Never Dies".

Broadcast television versions

The United Kingdom terrestrial television broadcast by ITV in October 2001 included the "shuriken" and "face stamping" shots that were removed from the UK VHS and DVD releases. Reportedly, in order to tone the violence down for a 12 cinema certificate in the UK, a further 6 seconds of cuts were required to retain this rating for the video version.

References

[1] http://boxofficemojo.com/movies/?id=tomorrowneverdies.htm

[2] James Bond Vs. Himself (http://www.boxofficemojo.com/showdowns/chart/?id=jamesbondvs.htm)

[3] http://boxofficemojo.com/weekend/chart/?yr=1997&wknd=51&p=.htm

[4] Carver's Stealth Ship bears remarkable resemblances to the Zumwalt DDG 1000 manufactured by General Dynamics Bath Iron Works and the Sea Shadow manufactured by Lockheed Martin for the United States Navy.

[5] Bruce Feirstein (2008-01-29). "Bruce Feirstein: The Tao of Bond-Film Naming" (http://www.vanityfair.com/ontheweb/blogs/daily/2008/01/bruce-feirste-2.html). Vanity Fair. . Retrieved 2008-01-31.

[6] Dye, Kerry Douglas (1999-11-15). "His Word is Bond: An Interview With 007 Screenwriter Bruce Feirstein" (http://www.leisuresuit.net/Webzine/articles/bruce_feirstein.shtml). LeisureSuit.net. . Retrieved 2007-01-05.
[7] Ashton, Richard (1997). "Tomorrow Never Dies" (http://www.hmss.com/films/mgw/mgw97.html).hmss.com. . Retrieved 2007-01-06.
[8] "Business Data for Tomorrow Never Dies" (http://www.imdb.com/title/tt0120347/business). IMDb. . Retrieved 2007-01-06.
[9] "Latest Bond Production Shaken, Stirred" (http://www.klast.net/bond/tndnews1.html#variety). Variety. 1996-12-08. . Retrieved 2007-01-05.
[10] "Production Notes - Tomorrow Never Dies" (http://www.mi6.co.uk/sections/movies/tnd_production.php3?t=tnd&s=tnd). mi6.co.uk. . Retrieved 2007-01-05.
[11] Collette, Kevin (2004-04-10). "Yesterday's 'Tomorrow': Spottiswoode Interview" (http://web.archive.org/web/20061115091611/http://www.ianfleming.org/mt_content/000180.html). ianfleming.org. Archived from the original (http://www.ianfleming.org/mt_content/000180.html) on November 15, 2006. . Retrieved 2007-01-05.
[12] Shooter, Anne (1997-05-27). "Bond in the Crossfire" (http://www.klast.net/bond/tndnews1.html#yeoh). Daily Mail. . Retrieved 2007-01-06.
[13] Johns, Elizabeth (1997-05-02). "Teri Hatcher Pregnant" (http://www.eonline.com/news/article/index.jsp?uuid=1d3ea90a-591b-4ae0-8578-2479539b09fd). E!. . Retrieved 2007-01-05.
[14] "Hatcher regrets Bond movie" (http://uk.news.yahoo.com/27112006/364/hatcher-regrets-bond-movie.html). Yahoo! News. 2006-11-27. . Retrieved 2007-01-05.
[15] "Brosnan Bares All For Playboy" (http://commanderbond.net/article/2994). Playboy. 2005-11-05. . Retrieved 2007-01-07.
[16] Ferguson, Amy. "Back In Action" (http://www.tribute.ca/tribute/0901/cover_story.htm). Tribute. . Retrieved 2007-01-05.
[17] Cohen, David (1997-02-11). "Bond girl Yeoh gets licence to thrill 007" (http://www.klast.net/bond/tndnews1.html#yeoh). South China Morning Post. . Retrieved 2007-01-06.
[18] "Bond Leading Lady Won't Do Stunts" (http://www.klast.net/bond/tndnews1.html#yeoh). Associated Press. 1997-05-21. . Retrieved 2007-01-06.
[19] "Much More Than Just A Bond Girl" (http://www.klast.net/bond/tndnews2.html#starburst). South China Morning Post. 1997-05-30. . Retrieved 2007-01-07.
[20] "Promi-Porträt: Götz Otto" (http://www.kwick.de/magazin/promi_portraet_goetz_otto_.9014.html). kwick!. 2007-10-20. . Retrieved 2007-01-06.
[21] "China Resists Western Efforts to Bond" (http://www.klast.net/bond/tndnews1.html#yeoh). New York Daily News. 1997-03-10. . Retrieved 2007-01-06.
[22] "Tomorrow Never Dies filming locations" (http://www.movie-locations.com/movies/t/tomorrownever.html).movielocations.com. . Retrieved 2007-01-07.
[23] Keeling, Judith (1997-06-17). "Bond Goes Down A Bomb In Brent Cross" (http://www.klast.net/bond/tndnews1.html#yeoh). Evening Standard. . Retrieved 2007-01-07.
[24] Macnee, Patrick (Narrator). *The Bond Sound: The Music of 007*. [DVD (Documentary)].
[25] "Review of Original Album" (http://www.filmtracks.com/titles/tomorrow_never.html).*filmtracks.com*. . Retrieved 2007-01-16.
[26] *James Bond's Greatest Hits*. [Television]. UK: North One Television. 2006.
[27] "Tomorrow Never Dies - The Premiere & Press" (http://www.mi6.co.uk/sections/articles/tnd_premiere.php3?t=tnd&s=tnd). mi6.co.uk. 2003-12-12. . Retrieved 2007-01-14.
[28] "Release dates for Tomorrow Never Dies" (http://www.imdb.com/title/tt0120347/releaseinfo). IMDb. . Retrieved 2006-01-14.
[29] "GoldenEye" (http://www.boxofficemojo.com/movies/?page=main&id=goldeneye.htm). Box Office Mojo. . Retrieved 2007-01-14.
[30] "Tomorrow Never Dies (1997)" (http://uk.rottentomatoes.com/m/tomorrow_never_dies/). *rottentomatoes.com*. . Retrieved 2007-01-13.
[31] "Tomorrow Never Dies" (http://www.metacritic.com/video/titles/tomorrowneverdies). *metacritic.com*. . Retrieved 2007-01-13.
[32] Ebert, Roger (1997-12-19). "Tomorrow Never Dies" (http://rogerebert.suntimes.com/apps/pbcs.dll/article?AID=/19971219/REVIEWS/712190304/1023).*Chicago Sun-Times*. . Retrieved 2007-01-13.
[33] Berardinelli, James (1997). "Tomorrow Never Dies" (http://www.reelviews.net/movies/t/tomorrow.html).*www.reelviews.net*. . Retrieved 2006-01-13.
[34] Turan, Kenneth (1997-12-19). "Tomorrow Never Dies" (http://www.calendarlive.com/movies/reviews/cl-movie971230-20,0,306796.story). *Los Angeles Times*. . Retrieved 2007-01-13.
[35] Taylor, Charles (1997-12-19). "Stale Bonding" (http://www.salon.com/ent/movies/1997/12/19tomorrow.html).*Salon.com*. . Retrieved 2007-01-13.
[36] "Awards for Tomorrow Never Dies" (http://www.imdb.com/title/tt0120347/awards). IMDb. . Retrieved 2007-01-14.
[37] http://www.bbfc.co.uk/website/Classified.nsf/c2fb077ba3f9b33980256b4f002da32c/7d12a12ab7c4eff380257177005eef69?OpenDocument
[38] Error on call to Template:Cite interview: Parameter subject (or last) must be specified Retrieved on 2008-02-24.
[39] This scene from the film does not appear in the novelisation.
[40] Benson on Bond - The International Association of Media Tie-In Writers (http://www.iamtw.org/art_bensen.html)
[41] Liu, Johnny (December 1999). "Tomorrow Never Dies" (http://www.gamerevolution.com/oldsite/games/sony/action/tomorrow_never_dies.htm). *Game Revolution*. . Retrieved 2007-01-16.
[42] Perry, Doug (1999-11-19). "Tomorrow Never Dies" (http://uk.psx.ign.com/articles/152/152310p1.html). *IGN*. . Retrieved 2007-01-16.

External links

- Official website (http://www.mgm.com/title_title.do?title_star=TOMNEVER)
- *Tomorrow Never Dies* (http://www.imdb.com/title/tt0120347/) at the Internet Movie Database
- *Tomorrow Never Dies* (http://www.allmovie.com/work/158896) at Allmovie
- *Tomorrow Never Dies* (http://www.rottentomatoes.com/m/tomorrow_never_dies/) at Rotten Tomatoes
- *Tomorrow Never Dies* (http://www.boxofficemojo.com/movies/?id=tomorrowneverdies.htm) at Box Office Mojo

Mrs. Brown

Mrs Brown

Video release poster for the film

Directed by	John Madden
Produced by	Sarah Curtis
Written by	Jeremy Brock
Starring	Judi Dench Billy Connolly Geoffrey Palmer Antony Sher Gerard Butler
Music by	Stephen Warbeck
Cinematography	Richard Greatrex
Editing by	Robin Sales
Distributed by	Buena Vista International (UK) Miramax (USA)
Release date(s)	July 18, 1997 (USA)
Running time	103 minutes
Country	United Kingdom
Language	English

Mrs. Brown (also released and advertised under the title *Her Majesty, Mrs. Brown*) is a 1997 British drama film starring Dame Judi Dench, Billy Connolly, Geoffrey Palmer, Antony Sher and Gerard Butler. It was written by Jeremy Brock and directed by John Madden.

The film was produced by the BBC and Ecosse Films with the intention of being shown on BBC One and on WGBH's *Masterpiece Theatre*. However, it was acquired by Miramax and released to unexpected success, going on to earn more than $13,000,000 worldwide.

The film was screened in the Un Certain Regard section at the 1997 Cannes Film Festival.[1] Dench was nominated for Academy Award for Best Actress, but lost to Helen Hunt from *As Good as It Gets*.

Synopsis

After several screens of text giving some background we see a bust flying over a palace wall and shattering into countless pieces.

This is the story of Queen Victoria (played by Judi Dench) and her relationship with a Scottish servant, John Brown (played by Billy Connolly), and the subsequent uproar it provoked. Brown had been a trusted servant of Victoria's then deceased consort, Prince Albert; Victoria's chief servants thought Brown might help to ease an inconsolable Queen since the prince consort's death in 1861. Hoping to subtly coax the Queen toward resuming public life after years of seclusion, Mr. Brown is summoned to court.

The plan succeeds a little too well for the servants' liking, especially Victoria's chief secretary Sir Henry Ponsonby (played by Geoffrey Palmer) and The Prince of Wales (played by David Westhead) as well as other members of the Royal family; the public, press and politicians soon come to resent Brown's perceived influence over the queen. Brown takes considerable liberties with court protocol, especially by addressing Her Majesty as *"woman"*. He also quickly takes control over the Queen's daily activities, further aggravating the tensions between himself and the royal family and servants.

The moniker *"Mrs. Brown"*, used both at the time and in the film, implied an improper, and perhaps sexual, relationship. The film does not directly address the contemporary suspicions that the Queen and Brown had had a sexual relationship and perhaps had even secretly married (see the article on Brown), though cartoons from the satirical magazine *Punch* are shown as being passed around in Parliament (only one of the cartoons is revealed to the camera, showing an empty throne, with the sceptre lying unhanded across it).

As a result of Victoria's virtual immurement, especially at Balmoral Castle in Scotland, something initially encouraged by Brown, her popularity is failing and there is a growing rise in republican sentiment. Prime Minister Benjamin Disraeli (Antony Sher) has a weakening hold over the House of Commons and a fear of rising anti-monarchical sentiment in the country. He persuades Brown to use his influence with the Queen and persuade her to return to the performance of her public duties, most especially the speech from the throne at the impending opening of Parliament.

Brown is reluctant to do so, rightly fearing that Victoria will take this as a personal betrayal. When Brown urges Victoria to return to London and fulfill her public duties, an argument ensues. Feeling betrayed by Brown, the Queen becomes enraged. She can't believe what she is hearing. When Brown once again refers to her as *"woman"*, she sharply rebukes him. Leaving the room, she turns to Ponsonby and Jenner requesting that they serve her needs, clearly reducing Mr. Brown's contact and influence over her. Their relationship was never to be the same again.

The Queen's eventual acquiescence and her decision to return to public life eventually leads to a revitalization of her popularity and a resurgence in public support of the monarchy.

Brown continues to serve Queen Victoria, until his death in 1883. In his final years, his duties become reduced to head of security. The palace staff has become weary of Brown's dogmatic ways and they mock and rebuke his security efforts as paranoid delusions. Finally, during a public event, a gun wielding assassin appears out of the crowd leaping toward the royal family. An ever vigilant Mr. Brown successfully thwarts the assassination attempt. At dinner the next evening, the Prince of Wales retells the story, bragging to their dinner companions that he had been the one to warn Brown of the assassin. Seeing through her son's bragging, the Queen announces instead that a special medal for bravery, the "Devoted Service Medal," will be minted and awarded to Mr. Brown.

Some years later, Mr. Brown becomes gravely ill with pneumonia after chasing through the woods late at night searching for a possible intruder. Hearing of Brown's illness, the Queen visits Mr. Brown's room and is visibly shaken to see her old friend so ill. Placing a cool damp cloth against Brown's fevered brow, she confesses that she has not been as good a friend as she might have been in recent years. It is clear that her apology is accepted by Brown. The pneumonia proves fatal for Brown and he passes away.

During his years of service, Mr. Brown has kept a diary and upon his passing, Ponsonby and Dr. Jenner discuss its contents stating that it must never be seen by anyone. Holding the diary at his side, Ponsonby walks away and it's implied that the diary will be destroyed or will disappear.

Dr. Jenner also reveals that the Prince of Wales has hurled the Queen's favorite bust of Mr. Brown up and over the *"palace wall"*, referring us back to the film's opening sequence.

The film's closing crawl informs us that: *"John Brown's diary was never found."*

Cast

- Judi Dench - Queen Victoria
- Billy Connolly - John Brown
- Geoffrey Palmer - Henry Ponsonby
- Antony Sher - Prime Minister Benjamin Disraeli
- Gerard Butler - Archie Brown
- David Westhead - Bertie/Prince of Wales
- Bridget McConnell - Lady Ely
- Georgie Glen - Lady Churchill
- Catherine O'Donnell - Lady in waiting
- Sara Stewart - Princess Alexandra
- Finty Williams - Princess Helena
- Claire Nicolson - Princess Louise
- Hattie Ladbury - Princess Alice
- Oliver Kent - Prince Alfred
- Alex Menzies - Prince Arthur
- Simon McKerrell - Prince Leopold
- Jason Morell - Lord Stanley
- Cherith Mellor - Mary Anne Disraeli
- George Hall - Speaker of the House of Commons
- Oliver Ford Davies - Dean of Windsor
- James Vaughan- Sir Charles Dilke

Awards and nominations

Dame Judi Dench

- nominated, Academy Award (US) for Best Actress in a Leading Role
- winner, BAFTA Award for Best Performance by an Actress in a Leading Role
- winner, BAFTA Scotland Award for Best Actress in a Film
- winner, Golden Globe Award for Best Performance by an Actress in a Motion Picture - Drama
- nominated, Screen Actors' Guild (SAG) Award for Outstanding Performance by a Female Actor in a Leading Role

Billy Connolly

- nominated, Screen Actors' Guild (SAG) Award for Outstanding Performance by a Male Actor in a Supporting Role
- nominated, BAFTA Award for Best Performance by an Actor in a Leading Role
- nominated, BAFTA Scotland Award for Best Actor in a Film

Others

- winner, BAFTA Award for Best Costume Design, Deirdre Clancy
- nominated, BAFTA Award for Best Film
- nominated, Alexander Korda Award for Best British Film (also BAFTA)

References

[1] "Festival de Cannes: Mrs. Brown" (http://www.festival-cannes.com/en/archives/ficheFilm/id/4836/year/1997.html). *festival-cannes.com.*. Retrieved 2009-09-27.

External links

- *Mrs. Brown* (http://www.imdb.com/title/tt0119280/) at the Internet Movie Database
- *Mrs. Brown* (http://www.allmovie.com/work/155021) at Allmovie
- Britmovie Website entry (http://www.britmovie.co.uk/genres/drama/filmography/051.html)

See also

Films about Queen Victoria

- The Young Victoria
- Victoria & Albert (TV serial)
- Victoria the Great

Hamlet (1996 film)

Hamlet	
 Film poster for *Hamlet*	
Directed by	Kenneth Branagh
Produced by	David Barron
Written by	William Shakespeare
Starring	Kenneth Branagh Derek Jacobi Julie Christie Richard Briers Michael Maloney Kate Winslet Billy Crystal Gérard Depardieu Robin Williams Charlton Heston Jack Lemmon Rufus Sewell Timothy Spall Reece Dinsdale Brian Blessed Richard Attenborough Nicholas Farrell John Gielgud John Mills Judi Dench Ken Dodd
Music by	Patrick Doyle
Cinematography	Alex Thomson
Editing by	Neil Farrell
Studio	Castle Rock Entertainment
Distributed by	Columbia Pictures
Release date(s)	December 25, 1996

Running time	242 minutes
Country	United Kingdom United States
Language	English
Budget	$18 million
Gross revenue	$4,708,156

Hamlet is a 1996 film version of William Shakespeare's classic play of the same name, adapted and directed by Kenneth Branagh, who also stars in the title role as Prince Hamlet. It co-stars Derek Jacobi as King Claudius, Julie Christie as Queen Gertrude, Kate Winslet as Ophelia, Michael Maloney as Laertes, Richard Briers as Polonius, and Nicholas Farrell as Horatio.

The film is notable as the first unabridged theatrical film version of the play. The complete film runs just over four hours. The longest version of the play prior to the 1996 film was the 1980 BBC television version starring Derek Jacobi, which runs three-and-a-half hours. A shorter edit of the Branagh film, approximately two-and-a-half hours long, was shown in some markets. Although unabridged in dialogue, its setting is slightly modernised with the inclusion of 19th-century architecture, clothing and weaponry. Blenheim Palace is the design for Elsinore Castle, and is used for exterior scenes.[1]

Hamlet also has the distinction of being the last major dramatic film to be filmed entirely in 70 mm film as of 2010.

Cast

The film features a large number of celebrity cameos. The servant Reynaldo, who appears only briefly in a single scene and is often left out of abridged versions of the play, is played by French star Gerard Depardieu, and other appearances by well-known actors include Charlton Heston as the First Player, Robin Williams as the courtier Osric, Richard Attenborough as the English Ambassador, Brian Blessed as the ghost of Hamlet's father, Jack Lemmon as Marcellus, the palace guard, Billy Crystal as the gravedigger, and Rufus Sewell plays Fortinbras. The flashbacks and dream sequences even allow for celebrities appearing in non-speaking roles as characters who are only mentioned in the play: Sir John Gielgud and Dame Judi Dench play Priam and Hecuba (mentioned in the monologue performed by the First Player on his arrival at Elsinore), John Mills plays "Old Norway", uncle of Fortinbras (mentioned by Claudius and Voltemand), and British comedian Ken Dodd plays Yorick.

Some of the celebrity cameos. Top row: Jack Lemmon, Gerard Depardieu, Brian Blessed, John Mills, Charlton Heston. Bottom row: John Gielgud, Judi Dench, Billy Crystal, Robin Williams, Richard Attenborough.

In addition to the film stars, the motion picture also features British theatre stars in tiny roles: for example; Simon Russell Beale plays the second gravedigger, Ray Fearon plays the guard Francisco, Ian McElhinney is Barnardo, and Jeffrey Kissoon plays Fortinbras's captain.

Production

The film's budget was $18 million. *Hamlet* was filmed in Panavision Super 70 by Alex Thomson. As of 2010, it was the last feature film shot entirely in the 70mm film format.[2]

Interpretation

Aspects of the film's staging are based on Adrian Noble's recent Royal Shakespeare Company production of the play, in which Branagh had played the title role.[3]

In a radical departure from previous *Hamlet* films, Branagh set the internal scenes in a vibrantly colourful setting, featuring a throne room dominated by mirrored doors; film scholar Samuel Crowl calls the setting "*film noir* with all the lights on."[4] Branagh chose Victorian era costuming and furnishings, using Blenheim Palace, built in the early 18th century, as Elsinore Castle for the external scenes. Harry Keyishan has suggested that the film is structured as an epic, courting comparison with *Ben Hur*, *The Ten Commandments* and *Doctor Zhivago*.[5] As J. Lawrence Guntner points out, comparisons with the latter film are heightened by the presence of Julie Christie (*Zhivago's* Lara) as Gertrude.[6]

Despite using a full text, Branagh's film is also very visual; it makes frequent use of flashbacks to depict scenes that are either only described but not performed in Shakespeare's text, such as Hamlet's childhood friendship with Yorick, or scenes only implied by the play's text, such as Hamlet's sexual relationship with Kate Winslet's Ophelia. [7] The film also uses very long single takes for numerous scenes.

Branagh's own interpretation of the title role, by his own admission, was considerably less "neurotic" than others; gone completely was the Oedipal fixation so prominently featured in Olivier's 1948 film. However, some critics, such as Leonard Maltin, felt that Branagh's performance was at times too "over-the top" (in the scenes in which Hamlet pretends to be insane, Branagh portrayed the Prince as manic; other members of the court are visibly exasperated by his behavior).

Reception

Hamlet was screened out of competition at the 1997 Cannes Film Festival.[8]

Hamlet received largely positive reviews. It has 94% "fresh" rating at Rotten Tomatoes.[9] Roger Ebert awarded the film four stars, comparing it to Laurence Olivier's lauded 1948 version while Janet Maslin praised both the film and Branagh's performance.[10] [11]

Some critics, notably Stanley Kauffmann, declared the film to be the finest motion picture version of *Hamlet* yet made, and online film critic James Berardinelli has gone so far as to declare the Branagh *Hamlet* the finest Shakespeare film ever made, rating it as the fourth best film of the 90s and one of his top 101 favourite films of all time. Berardinelii writes, "I have seen dozens of versions of this play (either on screen or on stage), and none has ever held me in such a grip of awe." [12] The *New York Review of Books* praised the attention given to Shakespeare's language, "giving the meter of the verse a musician's respect,"[13] ; Branagh himself says his aim is "telling the story with utmost clarity and simplicity."[14] .

The film did have its detractors however, with Lloyd Rose of *The Washington Post* calling it "the film equivalent of a lushly illustrated coffee-table book"[15] and Desson Howe writing of Branagh's performance "...the choices he makes are usually overextended. When it's time to be funny, he skitters over the top. When he's sad or touched, he makes a mechanical, catching noise in his throat."[16]

Hamlet was not a success at the box office, playing on fewer than 100 screens in the U.S. and earning only $5 million in its limited American run.

Awards

Despite lacking commercial appeal, Branagh's *Hamlet* received four Oscar nominations for Best Adapted Screenplay, Best Costume Design, Best Art Direction and Best Original Score. The nomination for Best Adapted Screenplay raised some eyebrows, since Branagh had made little alteration to Shakespeare's text beyond transposing two or three speeches. However, Roger Ebert, in particular, defended the choice,[17] noting, "A screenplay is something more than dialogue ... Screenplays also cover construction, scene choices, character treatments and, in the case of a writer-director like Branagh, the visual strategy."

Award	Category	Recipients and nominees	Outcome
Academy Awards	Best Art Direction	Tim Harvey	Nominated
	Best Costume Design	Alexandra Byrne	Nominated
	Best Original Score	Patrick Doyle	Nominated
	Best Adapted Screenplay	Kenneth Branagh	Nominated
Art Directors Guild	Excellence in Production Design Award	Tim Harvey & Desmond Crowe	Nominated
BAFTA Awards	Best Costume Design	Alexandra Byrne	Nominated
	Best Production Design	Tim Harvey	Nominated
British Society of Cinematographers	Best Cinematography Award	Alex Thomson	Won
	GBCT Operators Award	Martin Kenzie	Won
Broadcast Film Critics Association Awards	Best Picture	-	Nominated
Camerimage	Golden Frog	Alex Thomson	Nominated
Empire Awards	Best British Actress	Kate Winslet	Won
Evening Standard British Film Awards	Special Jury Award	Kenneth Branagh	Won
Nastro d'Argento	Best Dubbing, Male	Massimo Popolizio	Won
Motion Picture Sound Editors	Music Editing	Gerard McCann	Nominated
San Diego Film Critics Society Awards	Best Actor	Kenneth Branagh	Won
Satellite Awards	Best Motion Picture Costume Design	Alex Byrne	Nominated
	Best Supprting Actress - Drama	Kate Winslet	Nominated
	Best Art Direction and Production Design	Tim Harvey	Nominated
	Best Cinematography	Alex Thomson	Nominated
	Best Original Score	Patrick Doyle	Nominated

DVD and Blu-ray releases

A 2-Disc DVD was released in the U.S. and Canada on the 14th of August 2007. It includes a full-length commentary by Branagh and Shakespeare scholar Russell Jackson.[18] A Blu-Ray disc was released on the 17th of August 2010 in the U.S. and Canada, with similar additional features.[19]

References

[1] Alternate versions (http://www.imdb.com/title/tt0116477/alternateversions)
[2] http://www.widescreenmuseum.com/widescreen/splist.htm
[3] Crowl, Samuel "Flamboyant Realist: Kenneth Branagh" in Jackson, Russell *The Cambridge Companion to Shakespeare on Film* (Cambridge University Press, 2000)
[4] Crowl, p.227
[5] Keyishian, p.78
[6] Guntner, pp.122-123.
[7] Keyishian, p.79
[8] "Festival de Cannes: Hamlet" (http://www.festival-cannes.com/en/archives/ficheFilm/id/4801/year/1997.html). *festival-cannes.com*. . Retrieved 2009-09-27.
[9] "Hamlet (1996)" (http://www.rottentomatoes.com/m/1075422-hamlet/). *Rotten Tomatoes*. IGN Entertainment, Inc. . Retrieved 2008-08-09.
[10] "Roger Ebert's Review" (http://rogerebert.suntimes.com/apps/pbcs.dll/article?AID=/19970124/REVIEWS/701240303/1023). *Chicago Sun-Times*. .
[11] "Janet Maslin's Review" (http://www.nytimes.com/library/film/hamlet.html). *The New York Times*. . Retrieved 2010-05-04.
[12] "James Berardinelli's Review" (http://www.reelviews.net/movies/h/hamlet.html). .
[13] O'Brien, Geoffrey *New York Review of Books* 6 February 1997, cited by Samuel Crowl, "Framboyant Realist: Kenneth Branagh" in Jackson, Russell *The Cambridge Companion to Shakespeare on Film* (Cambridge University Press, 2000) p.228
[14] Branagh, Kenneth *Introduction and Notes* to *Much Ado About Nothing: Screenplay* p.ix cited by Crowl, p.228
[15] "'Hamlet': Kenneth Branagh's Inaction Flick" (http://www.washingtonpost.com/wp-srv/style/longterm/movies/review97/hamletrose.htm). *The Washington Post*. 1997-07-22. . Retrieved 2010-05-04.
[16] "Branagh's 'Hamlet': Not to Be" (http://www.washingtonpost.com/wp-srv/style/longterm/movies/review97/hamlethowe.htm). *The Washington Post*. 1997-07-22. . Retrieved 2010-05-04.
[17] "Ebert on Oscar Nomination" (http://rogerebert.suntimes.com/apps/pbcs.dll/article?AID=/19970223/ANSWERMAN/702230303). *Chicago Sun-Times*. .
[18] Kenneth Branagh's Hamlet (http://www.kenbranagh.com/news.htm)
[19] (http://www.wbshop.com/Hamlet-Bluray-Book/1000122740,default,pd.html?cgid=&adid=0810HamEml)

External links

- *Hamlet* (http://www.imdb.com/title/tt0116477/) at the Internet Movie Database
- *Hamlet* (http://www.allmovie.com/work/136644) at Allmovie
- *Hamlet* (http://www.rottentomatoes.com/m/1075422-hamlet/) at Rotten Tomatoes
- 101+ reasons to watch Kenneth Branagh's Hamlet (http://www.ocf.berkeley.edu/~ngoc/101.htm)

GoldenEye

GoldenEye

Promotional poster for *GoldenEye*

James Bond	Pierce Brosnan
Also starring	Sean Bean Izabella Scorupco Famke Janssen Judi Dench
Directed by	Martin Campbell
Produced by	Albert R. Broccoli (*consulting producer, uncredited*) Michael G. Wilson Barbara Broccoli
Novel/Story by	Michael France
Screenplay by	Jeffrey Caine Bruce Feirstein
Cinematography	Phil Meheux
Music by	Éric Serra
Main theme	GoldenEye
Composer	Bono The Edge
Performer	Tina Turner
Editing by	Terry Rawlings
Distributed by	Metro-Goldwyn-Mayer
Release date(s)	November 17, 1995
Running time	130 min
Country	United Kingdom United States
Budget	$US 58,000,000

Worldwide gross	$US $352,194,034 [1]
Preceded by	*Licence to Kill*
Followed by	*Tomorrow Never Dies*

GoldenEye is the seventeenth spy film in the James Bond series, and the first to star Pierce Brosnan as the fictional MI6 agent James Bond. Released in 1995, the film was directed by Martin Campbell and unlike previous Bond films, is the first film to not take any story elements from the works of novelist Ian Fleming.[2] The story was conceived and written by Michael France, with later collaboration by other writers. In the film, Bond fights to prevent an arms syndicate from using the GoldenEye satellite weapon against London in order to cause a global financial meltdown.

GoldenEye was released in 1995 after legal disputes forced a six-year hiatus in the series, during which Timothy Dalton resigned from the role of James Bond and was replaced by Pierce Brosnan. M was also recast, with actress Judi Dench becoming the first woman to portray the character, replacing Robert Brown. *GoldenEye* was the first Bond film made after the dissolution of the Soviet Union and the end of the Cold War, which provided a background for the plot.

The film accumulated a worldwide gross of $US 350.7 million - considerably better than Dalton's films, without taking inflation into account.[3] Some critics viewed the film as a modernization of the series, and felt Brosnan was a definite improvement over his predecessor.[4] [5] [6] The film also received award nominations for "Best Achievement in Special Effects" and "Best Sound" from the British Academy of Film and Television Arts.[7]

Plot

In 1986, MI6 agents 007 (James Bond, played by Pierce Brosnan) and 006 (Alec Trevelyan, played by Sean Bean), infiltrate an illicit Soviet chemical weapons facility at Arkhangelsk and plant explosive charges. Alec is captured and shot dead by Colonel Arkady Ourumov (Gottfried John), but Bond steals an airplane and escapes from the facility as it explodes.

Nine years later (1995), Bond arrives in Monte Carlo to follow Xenia Onatopp (Famke Janssen), a suspected member of the Janus crime syndicate, who has formed a suspicious relationship with a Canadian Navy admiral. She murders the admiral to allow Ourumov (now a General) to steal his identity. The next day, they steal a prototype Eurocopter Tiger helicopter that can withstand an electromagnetic pulse, despite Bond's efforts to stop them. They fly it to a bunker in Severnaya, where they massacre the staff and steal the control disk for the dual GoldenEye satellite weapons. The two program one of the GoldenEye satellites to destroy the complex with an electromagnetic pulse, and escape with genius programmer Boris Grishenko (Alan Cumming). The pulse also destroys three Russian MiG-29 aircraft dispatched to check on the facility; causing one to crash into the complex, utterly devastating it. Natalya Simonova (Izabella Scorupco), the lone survivor, contacts Boris and arranges to meet him in St. Petersburg, where he betrays her to Janus.

In London, M (Judi Dench) assigns Bond to investigate the attack due to circumstantial evidence. She also tells 007 to not go out for revenge against Ourumov when he is found (for Trevelyan's death) and he flies to St. Petersburg to meet CIA agent Jack Wade (Joe Don Baker). He suggests Bond meet Valentin Zukovsky (Robbie Coltrane), a Russian Mafia head and business rival of Janus. After Bond gives him a tip on a potential heist, Zukovsky arranges a meeting between Bond and Janus. Xenia is sent to meet Bond at his hotel. She attempts to kill him but he overpowers her and she takes him to Janus after which he proceeds to knock her out cold. Bond meets Janus in a statue graveyard, who reveals himself as Alec Trevelyan (now badly scarred from the explosion from the Arkhangelsk facility). A descendant of those Cossack clans who did collaborate with the Nazi forces in WWII, Trevelyan faked his death, having vowed revenge against Britain for their involvement in his parents' deaths. 007 is about to shoot Alec when he is shot with a tranquilizer dart by an unknown associate of Alec.

Bond awakens tied up with Natalya in the Tiger helicopter programmed to self-destruct, from which the two escape using its ejection system. They are immediately arrested by the Russian police and interrogated by the Russian Minister of Defence, Dmitri Mishkin (Tchéky Karyo), in a military archives building in St. Petersburg. Just as Natalya reveals the existence of a second satellite and Ourumov's involvement in the massacre at Severnaya, Ourumov bursts into the room, shooting Mishkin. As Ourumov calls for his guards, Bond punches him and escapes into the archives with Natalya, where a firefight ensues. Simonova is captured and is dragged into a car by Ourumov. Bond steals a T-54/55 tank and pursues Ourumov through St. Petersburg to Janus' armoured train, where he kills Ourumov as Trevelyan escapes, locking Bond in the train with Simonova. As the train's self-destruct countdown begins, Bond cuts through the floor with a laser watch while Simonova locates Grishenko's satellite dish in Cuba using a computer. The two escape just before the train explodes.

In Cuba, Bond and Natalya meet Jack Wade and trade Bond's car for Wade's airplane. Whilst flying over jungle Bond and Simonova are shot down. As they stumble out of the wreckage, Onatopp rappels down from a helicopter and attacks Bond. As she has Bond in a stranglehold, he manages to use her weapon to shoot the helicopter down. Still attached to the rappel cord, Onatopp is crushed against a tree and dies. Minutes later, he and Natalya watch a lake being drained of its water, uncovering the dish. They infiltrate the control station, where Bond is captured. Trevelyan reveals his plan to steal money from the Bank of England before erasing all of its financial records with the remaining GoldenEye, concealing the theft and destroying Britain's economy.

Meanwhile, Simonova programs the satellite to initiate atmospheric reentry and destroy itself. As Trevelyan captures Simonova and orders Grishenko to save the satellite, Bond triggers an explosion with his Parker Jotter pen grenade provided by Q, and escapes to the antenna cradle. Bond sabotages the antenna, preventing Boris from regaining control of the satellite, before turning and having a fistfight with Trevelyan. The two end up in a very precarious position on the antenna platform, five hundred feet above the dish, and Bond eventually manages to kick Trevelyan off the side of the platform. He grabs him before he falls, but releases him anyway, acknowledging that unlike most kills, this one is personal. Trevelyan survives the fall but is paralyzed. In the meantime, Simonova manages to commandeer a helicopter, onto which Bond jumps just prior to the cradle catching fire, exploding and collapsing, crushing Trevelyan in the process. Grishenko survives momentarily before being frozen to death by exploding tanks of liquid nitrogen. On the surface, Bond and Natalya are rescued by Wade and a team of Force Recon Marines, who take them off to Guantanamo Bay Naval Base by Marine helicopters.

Cast

- Pierce Brosnan as James Bond (007): An MI6 Agent assigned to stop the Janus crime syndicate from acquiring "GoldenEye," a clandestine satellite weapon designed and launched by the Soviets during the Cold War.
- Sean Bean as Alec Trevelyan (006)/Janus: Main antagonist. Initially another double-0 Agent and Bond's friend, he fakes his death at Arkangel and then establishes the Janus crime syndicate in the following nine years. Alec Trevelyan, was originally named Augustus Trevelyan, and written as a much older character and a former mentor of Bond. The producers were keen to hire Anthony Hopkins for the part, but he turned it down. Alan Rickman also turned down the role, stating that he was tired of playing villains. Finally, Sean Bean was cast after the part was rewritten.
- Izabella Scorupco as Natalya Simonova: The only survivor and eyewitness of the attack of GoldenEye on its own control center at Severnaya. A skilled programmer, she helps Bond in his mission and follows him to Cuba to disarm the GoldenEye. Paulina Porizkova and Eva Herzigova were offered the role of Natalya but turned it down.
- Famke Janssen as Xenia Onatopp: A Georgian lust murderer and Trevelyan's henchwoman. A sadomasochist, she enjoys torturing her enemies between her strong thighs.
- Joe Don Baker as Jack Wade: A veteran CIA agent on the same mission as Bond. He later appears in *Tomorrow Never Dies*.
- Dame Judi Dench as M: The strict head of MI6.

- Gottfried John as General Ourumov: A renegade Russian general who nefariously misuses his authority and position for helping Janus gain access to the GoldenEye.
- Robbie Coltrane as Valentin Dmitrovich Zukovsky: A Russian gangster and ex-KGB agent through whom Bond uses to arrange a meeting with Janus (Trevelyan). Zukovsky made his final appearance in *The World Is Not Enough.*
- Alan Cumming as Boris Grishenko: A computer programmer at Severnaya secretly affiliated to Janus.
- Tchéky Karyo as Defence Minister Dmitri Mishkin: The Russian Defence Minister and the person to whom Ourumov had to report. Ourumov shoots him when Simonova reveals the events at Severnaya.
- Desmond Llewelyn as Q: The head of Q Branch (research and development division of the British Secret Service). Llewelyn was the only actor to reprise a role from a previous Bond film.
- Samantha Bond as Miss Moneypenny: M's secretary. Samantha Bond made her first of four appearances as Moneypenny.
- Minnie Driver as Irina: The untalented mistress of Valentin Dmitrovich Zukovsky.

Production

Prelude

Licence to Kill had underperformed at the American box office and was the worst domestic grossing movie of the James Bond films.[8] Also, in 1989, MGM/UA was sold to the Australian based broadcasting group Qintex, which wanted to merge the company with Pathé. Danjaq, the Swiss based parent company of EON Productions, sued MGM/UA because the Bond back catalogue was being licensed to Pathé, who intended to broadcast the Bond series on television in several countries across the world without the approval of Danjaq.[9] These legal disputes delayed the film for several years.[10]

While the legal disputes went on, Timothy Dalton was still expected to play Bond in the new film (rumoured to be *The Property of a Lady*), as he had originally signed up for a three-film contract. Pre-production work began in May 1990 with a story draft written by Alfonso Ruggiero Jr. and Michael G. Wilson. Production was set to start in 1990 in Hong Kong for a release in late 1991. However, the legal disputes meant that these dates slipped.[11] In an interview in 1993, Dalton said that Michael France was writing the story for the film, which was due to begin production in January or February 1994.[12] However, the deadline passed, and in April 1994, Dalton officially resigned from the role.[13] [14] To replace Dalton, the producers cast Pierce Brosnan, who had been prevented from succeeding Roger Moore in 1986 because of his contract to star in the *Remington Steele* series.[15] [16] Judi Dench was cast as M, thus making *GoldenEye* the first film of the series featuring a female M. The decision is widely believed to be inspired by Stella Rimington becoming head of MI5 in 1992.[17] [18]

GoldenEye was produced by Albert R. Broccoli's EON Productions. With Albert Broccoli's health deteriorating (he died seven months after the film's release), his daughter Barbara Broccoli described him as taking "a bit of a back seat" in film's production.[19] In his stead, Barbara and Michael G. Wilson took the lead roles in production while Albert Broccoli oversaw the production of GoldenEye as consulting producer but is credited as presenter.[20] [21] [22] Metro-Goldwyn-Mayer approached John Woo to make *GoldenEye*, but Woo turned down the opportunity despite being honored with the offer.[23] The producers then chose New Zealander Martin Campbell as the director. Brosnan later described Campbell as "warrior-like in his take on the piece" and that "there was a huge passion there on both our parts".[24] Campbell would go on to direct *Casino Royale* in 2006. The producers had originally chosen not to use Richard Maibaum, long-time writer for the series; he died in 1991.[9] [25] After Michael France wrote the original screenplay, Jeffrey Caine was brought in to rewrite it.[26] Caine kept many of France's ideas but added the prologue prior to the credits. Kevin Wade polished the script and Bruce Feirstein added the finishing touches.[27] In the film, the writing credit was shared by Caine and Feirstein, while France was credited with only the story, an arrangement he felt was unfair,[28] particularly as he believed the additions made were not an improvement on his original version.[28] Wade did not receive an official credit, but was acknowledged in the naming of Jack Wade, the CIA character he created.

While the story was not based on a work by Ian Fleming, the title *GoldenEye* traces its origins to the name of Fleming's Jamaican estate where he wrote the Bond novels.[29] Fleming gave a number of origins for the name of his estate, including Carson McCullers' *Reflections in a Golden Eye*[30] and Operation Goldeneye, a contingency plan Fleming himself developed during World War II in case of a Nazi invasion through Spain.[31] [32]

Since the release of *Licence to Kill*, the world had changed drastically. *GoldenEye* was the first James Bond film to be produced since the fall of the Berlin Wall and the collapse of the Soviet Union. This cast doubt over whether James Bond was still relevant in the modern world, as many of the previous films pitted him against Soviet villains trying to take advantage of the Cold War.[33] Much of the film industry felt that it would be "futile" for the Bond series to make a comeback, and that it was best left as "an icon of the past".[34] However, when released, the film was viewed as a successful revitalization and it effectively adapted the series for the 1990s.[5] [35] One of *GoldenEye's* innovations was the casting of a female M. In the film, the new M quickly establishes her authority, remarking that Bond is a "sexist, misogynist dinosaur" and a "relic of the Cold War". This is an early indication that Bond is portrayed as far less tempestuous than Timothy Dalton's Bond from 1989.[36]

Liam Neeson, Pierce Brosnan and Mel Gibson were suggested for the role of James Bond. Sam Neill, who wanted to play James Bond, and had screen tested for the role prior to *The Living Daylights*, was also considered. There were rumors that Gibson could play James Bond, but Gibson refused to do a screen test. Pierce Brosnan was named the "new James Bond" in a press conference on June 7, 1994.

Filming

Principal photography for the film began on January 16, 1995 and continued until June 6.[37] The producers were unable to film at Pinewood Studios, the usual location for Bond films, because it had been reserved. Instead, an old Rolls-Royce factory at the Leavesden Aerodrome in Hertfordshire was converted into a new studio.[38] The producers later said Pinewood would have been too small.[19]

The bungee jump was filmed at the Verzasca Dam in Ticino, Switzerland. The film's casino scenes and the Tiger helicopter's demonstration were shot in Monte Carlo. Reference footage for the tank chase was shot on location in St. Petersburg and matched to the studio at Leavesden. The climactic scenes on the satellite dish were shot at Arecibo Observatory in Puerto Rico.[39] The actual MI6 headquarters were used for external views of M's office.[40] Some of the scenes in St. Petersburg were actually shot in London — the Epsom Downs Racecourse doubled the airport — to reduce expenses and security concerns, as the second unit sent to Russia required bodyguards.[41]

The French Navy provided full use of the frigate FS *La Fayette* and their newest helicopter, the Eurocopter Tiger to the film's production team. The French government also allowed the use of Navy logos as part of the promotional campaign for the film. However, the producers had a dispute with the Ministry of Defence over Brosnan's opposition to French nuclear weapons testing and his involvement with Greenpeace; as a result, the French premiere of the film was cancelled.[42]

The sequences involving the armoured train were filmed on the Nene Valley Railway, near Peterborough in the UK. The train was composed of a British Rail Class 20 diesel-electric locomotive and a pair of BR Mk 2 coaches, all three heavily disguised to resemble a Soviet armoured train.[43] [44]

Arecibo Observatory plays a prominent role in the film: Alec Trevelyan uses the dish to communicate with a Russian satellite to fire an electromagnetic pulse at London. (The use of Arecibo to communicate with an earth-orbiting satellite is nonsensical from a technical standpoint.) The dish and the ground below it were covered with water to conceal it as a lake. Additionally, the two main characters, Agents 007 and 006 (rogue agent Trevelyan), fight on the antenna platform in the final scenes of the movie.

Effects

GoldenEye was the last film of special effects supervisor Derek Meddings, to whom the film was dedicated. Meddings' major contribution were miniatures.[45] It was also the first Bond film to use computer generated imagery.[41]

GoldenEye's opening title sequence featured a woman destroying the hammer and sickle.

Among the model effects are most external shots of Severnaya, the scene where Janus' train crashes in to the tank, and the lake which hides the satellite dish, since the producers could not find a round lake in Puerto Rico. The climax in the satellite dish used scenes in Arecibo, a model built by Meddings' team and scenes shot with stuntmen in England.[41]

Stunt car coordinator Rémy Julienne described the car chase between the Aston Martin DB5 and the Ferrari F355 as between "a perfectly shaped, old and vulnerable vehicle and a racecar." The stunt had to be meticulously planned as the cars are vastly different. Nails had to be attached to the F355 tires to make it skid, and during one take of the sliding vehicles, both cars collided.[46]

The largest stunt sequence in the film was the tank chase, which took around six weeks to film, partly on location in St. Petersburg and partly at Leavesden.[47] A Russian T-54/55 tank, on loan from the East England Military Museum, was modified with the addition of fake explosive reactive armor panels.[37] In order to avoid destroying the pavement on the city streets of St. Petersburg, the steel off-road tracks of the T-54/55 were replaced with the rubber-shoed tracks from a British Chieftain tank.

A rectangular viewport was cut in the glacis plate and covered with tinted Perspex, allowing a trained driver to maneuver the tank from a prone position inside the driver's compartment while Pierce Brosnan sat in the (modified) driver's seat with his head protruding from the driver's hatch, creating the illusion he was driving the tank "unbuttoned".[48] The filming at Leavesden also called for the destruction of a number of Lada cars, so many that the production company were unable to provide all of them and were reduced to flagging down vehicles in the vicinity of their offices and offering the owners cash for their vehicles so that they may be used in filming.

For the confrontation between Bond and Trevelyan inside the antenna cradle, director Campbell decided to take inspiration in Bond's fight with Red Grant in *From Russia with Love*. Pierce Brosnan and Sean Bean did all the stunts themselves, except for one take where one is thrown against the wall. Brosnan injured his hand while filming the part in the extending ladder, making producers delay his scenes and film the ones in Severnaya earlier.[41]

The opening 220 m (720 ft) bungee jump at Archangel, shot at the Verzasca Dam in Switzerland and performed by Wayne Michaels, was voted the best movie stunt of all time in a 2002 Sky Movies poll, and set a record for the highest bungee jump off a fixed structure.[49] [50]

The fall of communism in Russia is the main focus of the opening titles, designed by Daniel Kleinman (who took over from Maurice Binder after his death in 1991). They show the collapse and destruction of several structures associated with the Soviet Union, such as the red star and hammer and sickle. In an interview, Kleinman said they were meant to be "a kind of story telling sequence" showing that "what was happening in Communist countries was Communism was falling down".[51] According to producer Michael G. Wilson, some Communist parties protested against "Socialist symbols being destroyed not by governments, but by bikini-clad women", especially the Indian one, which threatened to boycott the film.[41]

Product placement

GoldenEye was the first film bound by BMW's three picture deal,[52] so the producers were offered BMW's latest roadster, the BMW Z3. It was featured in the film months before its release, and a limited edition "007 model" sold out within a day of being available to order. As part of the car's marketing strategy, several Z3's were used to drive journalists from a complimentary meal at the Rainbow Room restaurant to *GoldenEye's* premiere at Radio City Music Hall.[53] For the film, a convertible Z3 is equipped with the usual Q refinements, including a self-destruct feature and Stinger missiles behind the headlights.[54]

The Z3 does not have much screentime and none of the gadgets are used, which Martin Campbell attributed to the deal with BMW coming in the last stages of production.[41] The Z3's appearance in *GoldenEye* is thought to be the most successful promotion through product placement in 1995.[55] Ten years later, *The Hollywood Reporter* listed it as one of the most successful product placements in recent years. The article quoted Mary Lou Galician, head of media analysis and criticism at Arizona State University's Walter Cronkite School of Journalism and Mass Communication, as saying that the news coverage of Bond's switch from Aston Martin to BMW "generated hundreds of millions of dollars of media exposure for the movie and all of its marketing partners."[56]

In addition, all computers in the film were provided by IBM, and in some scenes (such as the pen grenade scene towards the end), the OS/2 Warp splash screen can be seen on computer monitors.

Music

The theme song, "GoldenEye", was written by Bono and The Edge, and was performed by Tina Turner.[57] As the producers did not collaborate with Bono or The Edge, alternate versions of the song did not appear throughout *GoldenEye*, as was the case in previous James Bond films.[58]

The soundtrack to *GoldenEye* was composed and performed by Éric Serra. Prolific Bond composer John Barry said he was offered it by Barbara Broccoli, but turned it down.[59] Serra's score has been heavily criticised: Richard von Busack, in *Metro*, wrote that it was "more appropriate for a ride on an elevator than a ride on a roller coaster",[60] and Filmtracks said Serra "failed completely in his attempt to tie Goldeneye to the franchise's past."[61]

Later, John Altman provided the music for the tank chase in St. Petersburg. Serra's original track for that sequence can still be found on the soundtrack as "A Pleasant Drive In St. Petersburg".[62] Serra composed and performed a number of synthesizer tracks, including the version of the James Bond Theme that plays during the gun barrel sequence,[63] while John Altman and David Arch provided the more traditional symphonic music.[64]

Release and reception

GoldenEye premiered on November 13, 1995, at the Radio City Music Hall in New York City, and went on general release in the USA on November 17, 1995. The UK premiere, attended by Prince Charles, followed on November 22 at the Odeon Leicester Square, with general release two days later.[65] Brosnan boycotted the French premiere to support Greenpeace's protest against the French nuclear testing program, causing the premiere to be abrogated.[66] The film was later released in a further 31 countries, under three alternate titles.[67]

The film earned over $US26 million during its opening across 2,667 theaters in the USA. Its worldwide sales were around the equivalent of $US350 million.[68] It had the fourth highest worldwide gross of all films in 1995[69] and, was the most successful Bond film since *Moonraker*, taking inflation into account.[3]

GoldenEye was edited in order to be guaranteed a PG-13 rating from the MPAA and a 12 rating from the BBFC. The cuts included the visible bullet impact to Trevelyan's head when he is shot in the prologue, several additional deaths during the sequence in which Onatopp guns down the workers at the Severnaya station, more explicit footage and violent behaviour in the Admiral's death, extra footage of Onatopp's death, and Bond giving her a rabbit punch in the car.[38] In 2006, the film was remastered and re-edited for the James Bond Ultimate Edition DVD in which some of the BBFC cuts—including headbutts and violent sound effects—were restored, causing the rating to be changed to

15. However, the original MPAA edits still remain.[70]

Reviews

The critical reception of the film was mostly positive. Film review collection website *Rotten Tomatoes* holds it at an 80% Fresh approval rating,[71] while a similar site, *Metacritic*, holds it at 65%.[72] In the *Chicago Sun-Times*, Roger Ebert gave the film 3 stars out of 4, and said Brosnan's Bond was "somehow more sensitive, more vulnerable, more psychologically complete" than the previous ones, also commenting on Bond's "loss of innocence" since previous films.[73] James Berardinelli described Brosnan as "a decided improvement over his immediate predecessor" with a "flair for wit to go along with his natural charm", but added that "fully one-quarter of *Goldeneye* is momentum-killing padding."[74]

Several reviewers lauded M's appraisal of Bond as a "sexist, misogynist dinosaur",[5] [75] [76] with Todd McCarthy in *Variety* saying *GoldenEye* "breathes fresh creative and commercial life" into the series.[5] John Puccio of DVD Town said that *GoldenEye* was "an eye and ear-pleasing, action-packed entry in the Bond series" and that the film gave Bond "a bit of humanity, too".[77] Ian Nathan of *Empire* said that *GoldenEye* "revamps that indomitable British spirit" and that the *Die Hard* movies "don't even come close to 007". Tom Sonne of the *Sunday Times* considered *GoldenEye* the best Bond film since *The Spy Who Loved Me*. Jose Arroyo of *Sight & Sound* considered the greatest success of the film in modernising the series.[35]

GoldenEye was also ranked high in Bond-related lists. IGN chose it as the fifth best movie,[78] while *Entertainment Weekly* ranked it 8th,[79] and Norman Wilner of MSN as 9th.[80] *ET* also voted Xenia Onatopp as the 6th most memorable Bond Girl,[81] while IGN ranked Natalya as 7th in a similar list.[82]

However, the film received several negative reviews. Richard Schickel of *Time* wrote that after "a third of a century's hard use", Bond's conventions survived on "wobbly knees",[83] while in *Entertainment Weekly*, Owen Gleiberman thought the series had "entered a near-terminal state of exhaustion."[84] Dragan Antulov said that *GoldenEye* had a predictable series of scenes,[85] and Kenneth Turan of the *Los Angeles Times* said that the film was "a middle-aged entity anxious to appear trendy at all costs".[86] David Eimer of *Premiere* wrote that "the trademark humour is in short supply" and that "Goldeneye isn't classic Bond by any stretch of the imagination."[35] Madeleine Williams said that "there are plenty of stunts and explosions to take your mind off the plot."[87]

Awards

GoldenEye was nominated for two BAFTAs, Best Sound and Special Effects.[7] Éric Serra won a BMI Film Award for the soundtrack and the film also earned nominations for Best Action Film and Actor at the Saturn Awards and Best Fight Scene at the MTV Movie Awards.[88] [89] [90]

Appearances in other media

GoldenEye was the second and final Bond film to be adapted to a novel by novelist John Gardner. The book closely follows the film's storyline, but Gardner added a violent sequence prior to the opening bungee jump in which Bond kills a group of Russian guards, a change that the video game *GoldenEye 007* retained.[91]

The Bunker Level of the N64 *GoldenEye 007*, similar to the film's story.

In late 1995, Topps Comics began publishing a three-issue comic book adaptation of *GoldenEye*. The script was adapted by Don McGregor with art by Rick Magyar. The first issue carried a January 1996 cover date.[92] For unknown reasons, Topps cancelled the entire adaptation after the first issue had been published, and to date the adaptation has never been released in its entirety.[93]

The film was the basis for *GoldenEye 007*, a successful video game for the Nintendo 64 developed by Rare (known at the time as Rareware) and published by Nintendo.[94] [95] In January 2000, readers of the British video game magazine *Computer and Video Games* listed *GoldenEye 007* in first place in a list of "the hundred greatest video games".[96] In *Edge's* 10th anniversary issue in 2003, the game was included as one of their top ten shooters of all time,[97] . It is based upon the film, but many of the missions were extended or modified.[98]

The only released screenshot of the cancelled Virtual Boy version of *GoldenEye 007*.

GoldenEye 007 was modified into a racing game intended to be released for the Virtual Boy console. However, the game was cancelled before release.[99] In 2004, Electronic Arts released *GoldenEye: Rogue Agent*, the first game of the James Bond series in which the player does not take on the role of Bond. Instead, the protagonist is an aspiring Double-0 agent Jonathan Hunter, known by his codename "GoldenEye" recruited by a villain of the Bond universe, Auric Goldfinger.[100] Except for the appearance of Xenia Onatopp, the game was unrelated to the film, and was released to mediocre reviews.[101] [102] [103] It was excoriated by several critics including Eric Qualls for using the name "GoldenEye" as an attempt to ride on the success of Rare's game.[104] [105]

Nintendo announced a remake of the original *GoldenEye 007* game at their E3 press conference on June 15, 2010. The remake will be similar to the original, though Pierce Brosnan is being replaced by Daniel Craig. The game is being developed by Eurocom to be published by Activision for the Wii.[106]

References

[1] According to Box Office Mojo <http://www.boxofficemojo.com>

[2] "The James Bond Films - 1994-2002" (http://www.bbc.co.uk/dna/h2g2/A817823). *BBC News*. 2002-11-10. . Retrieved 22 October 2007.

[3] "Box Office History for James Bond Movies" (http://www.the-numbers.com/movies/series/JamesBond.php). *The Numbers*. Nash Information Service. . Retrieved 18 October 2007.

[4] James Kendrick. "GoldenEye" (http://www.qnetwork.com/?page=review&id=348). Qnetwork. . Retrieved 27 April 2007.

[5] Todd McCarthy (1995-11-15). "GoldenEye" (http://www.variety.com/review/VE1117904690.html?categoryid=31&cs=1). Variety. . Retrieved 18 November 2006.

[6] Christopher Null. "GoldenEye" (http://web.archive.org/web/20071013021650/http://www.filmcritic.com/misc/emporium.nsf/ddb5490109a79f598625623d0015f1e4/9503ab99be3b464086256275001adc5a?OpenDocument).Filmcritic.com. Archived from the original (http://www.filmcritic.com/misc/emporium.nsf/ddb5490109a79f598625623d0015f1e4/9503ab99be3b464086256275001adc5a?OpenDocument) on October 13, 2007. . Retrieved 27 April 2007.

[7] "Film Nominations 1995" (http://www.bafta.org/awards/film/nominations/?year=1995). British Academy of Film and Television Arts. . Retrieved 5 April 2008.

[8] "James Bond" (http://www.boxofficemojo.com/franchises/jamesbond/adjusted.htm). *Box Office Mojo*. . Retrieved 16 November 2008.

[9] "Production Notes - GoldenEye" (http://www.mi6.co.uk/sections/movies/ge_production.php3). MI6.co.uk. . Retrieved 19 May 2007.

[10] "GoldenEye - The Road To Production" (http://www.mi6.co.uk/sections/articles/ge_roadtoproduction.php3).mi6.co.uk. 2003-06-23. . Retrieved 4 January 2007.

[11] "Bond 17 - History" (http://www.mi6.co.uk/sections/articles/bond_17_intro.php3). *MI6 - The Home of James Bond*. . Retrieved 28 January 2008.

[12] "Interview with Dalton". *The Daily Mail*.1993-08-06.

[13] Michael G. Wilson, Martin Campbell, Pierce Brosnan, Judi Dench, Desmond Llewelyn. (1999). *The Making of 'GoldenEye': A Video Journal*. [DVD]. MGM Home Entertainment.

[14] "Biography: Timothy Dalton" (http://web.archive.org/web/20021213051853/www.ianfleming.org/mkkbb/guide/timothydalton/). IanFleming.org. . Retrieved 7 May 2007.

[15] Maggie Fox (1994-06-08). "Pierce Brosnan Is New James Bond" (http://www.klast.net/bond/ge_news2.html). Reuters. . Retrieved 12 November 2006.

[16] Kimberly Last (1995). "Pierce Brosnan's Long and Winding Road To Bond" (http://www.klast.net/bond/pb_road.html). *GoldenEye (magazine)*. . Retrieved 12 November 2006.

[17] Jay MacDonald. "Her majesty's not-so-secret service" (http://www.bookpage.com/0502bp/stella_rimington.html). BookPage. . Retrieved 14 November 2006.

[18] Nigel Morris (2002-04-30). "Woman tipped to head MI5 in footsteps of Stella Rimington" (http://web.archive.org/web/20071013210329/http://www.findarticles.com/p/articles/mi_qn4158/is_20020430/ai_n12622913). *Independent, The (London)*. Archived from the original (http://www.findarticles.com/p/articles/mi_qn4158/is_20020430/ai_n12622913) on October 13, 2007. . Retrieved 14 November 2006.
[19] Richard Ashton (1995). "Richard Ashton Interview Michael G. Wilson" (http://www.hmss.com/films/mgw/mgw95.html). Her Majesty's Secret Servant. . Retrieved 12 November 2006.
[20] "Familia Broccoli" (http://www.archivo007.com/index.php?option=com_content&task=view&id=53&Itemid=110). Archivo 007. . Retrieved 2010-05-23.
[21] http://www.imdb.com/title/tt0113189/fullcredits#cast
[22] "James Bond 007 - Goldeneye" (http://www.007.info/FactfileGE.asp). 007.info. 1995-11-13. . Retrieved 2010-05-23.
[23] Heard, Christopher (1999). "8". *Ten Thousand Bullets: The Cinematic Journey of John Woo*. Doubleday Canada Limited. pp. 138–139. ISBN 0385257317.
[24] Richard Jobson (2003-03-18). "'My heavens, I haven't been found out yet'" (http://film.guardian.co.uk/interview/interviewpages/0,,922395,00.html). *The Guardian*. . Retrieved 11 December 2006.
[25] "Hollywood mogul puts $US200m price on James Bond's head; Albert "Cubby" Broccoli". *The Sunday Times*. 1990-08-12.
[26] Nick Birren (2005-09-30). "The Spirit of the Story: The Constant Gardener's Jeffrey Caine" (http://www.creativescreenwriting.com/csdaily/trenches/9_30_05_Caine.html). *CreativeScreenwriting* (accessdate = 12 November 2006). .
[27] Kerry Douglas Dye (1999-11-15). "His Word is Bond: An Interview With 007 Screenwriter Bruce Feirstein" (http://www.leisuresuit.net/Webzine/articles/bruce_feirstein.shtml). LeisureSuit.net. . Retrieved 12 November 2006.
[28] Reg Seeton and Dayna Van Buskirk. IGN title = Screenwriting Punishment with Michael France. http://uk.movies.ign.com/articles/424/424582p1.html. Retrieved 12 November 2006.
[29] "Two profiles: Ian Fleming & Boris Johnson" (http://www.tenerifenews.com/index.php?option=com_content&view=article&id=8140:two-profiles-ian-fleming-a-boris-johnson&catid=64:features&Itemid=26). Fortnightly Tenerife News. 2008-05-11. . Retrieved 16 December 2008.
[30] Pearson, John (1966). *The Life of Ian Fleming*. p. 137 publisher = Vintage/Ebury. ISBN 0-224-61136-4.
[31] "The Real James Bond" (http://www.channel4.com/history/microsites/R/real_lives/james_bond.html). Channel 4. . Retrieved 19 November 2006.
[32] Andrew Lycett (2006-11-05). "Adultery, Cambridge spies, a Jamaican idyll — Ian Fleming's biographer Andrew Lycett traces the origins of James Bond" (http://www.timesonline.co.uk/article/0,,2101-2432127,00.html). London: The Times. . Retrieved 19 November 2006.
[33] Edward P. Comentale; Stephen Watt, Skip Willman (2005). *Ian Fleming and James Bond* (http://books.google.com/?id=NpkbHkuxYTUC&dq=Edward+P.+Comentale). Indiana University Press. ISBN 978-0253345233. . Retrieved 21 August 2007.
[34] Lee Pfeiffer; Worrall, Dave (2003) [1998]. "*GoldenEye*". *The Essential Bond: The Authorized Guide to the World of 007*. Boxtree. p. 169. ISBN 0752215620.
[35] "GoldenEye - Premiere & Press" (http://www.mi6.co.uk/sections/articles/ge_premiere.php3?t=ge&s=ge). MI6.co.uk. . Retrieved 28 May 2007.
[36] "GoldenEye" (http://notcoming.com/reviews.php?id=417). Notcoming.com. . Retrieved 28 April 2007.
[37] Garth Pearce (1995-10-31). *The Making of GoldenEye*. Boxtree. ISBN 978-1852834845.
[38] Peter Aston, Pierce Brosnan, Martin Campbell. (1995-12-26). *GoldenEye: The Secret Files*. [TV Documentary]. Carlton Television.
[39] Michael G. Wilson, Andrew Ackland-Snow, Peter Lamont, Chris Corbould. (2006-07-17). *Location Scouting with Peter Lamont: GoldenEye*. [TV Documentary]. Cloverland Productions.
[40] Lee Pfeiffer; Worrall, Dave (2003) [1998]. "*GoldenEye*". *The Essential Bond: The Authorized Guide to the World of 007*. Boxtree. p. 171. ISBN 0752215620.
[41] Martin Campbell, Michael G. Wilson. *GoldenEye audio commentary*. MGM Home Entertainment.
[42] Lang, Kirsty (1995-12-03). "Bond drops a bomb". *The Sunday Times*.
[43] Lee Pfeiffer; Worrall, Dave (2003) [1998]. "*GoldenEye*". *The Essential Bond: The Authorized Guide to the World of 007*. Boxtree. p. 176. ISBN 0752215620.
[44] Andrew Wright (May 4, 2006). "Licensed to Thrill" (http://www.swanagerailway.co.uk/news298.htm). *Historic James Bond Diesel Locomotive to star in evocative branch line weekend*. Swanage Railway. . Retrieved 23 June 2007.
[45] *Making It Small In Pictures: Derek Meddings*. MGM Home Entertainment.
[46] *Driven to Bond: Remy Julienne*. MGM Home Entertainment.
[47] "Interview - Steve Street (Part 1)" (http://www.mi6.co.uk/sections/articles/interview_steve_street1.php3?t=&s=articles). MI6.co.uk. 2003-08-26. . Retrieved 11 December 2006.
[48] ""T55 Main Battle Tank - The "Goldeneye Tank"" (http://www.tanks4hire.co.uk/T55armouredmilitarytank.html). Tanks For Hire Inc. . Retrieved 11 February 2007.
[49] "Amazing Bond stunt wins top award" (http://news.bbc.co.uk/cbbcnews/hi/tv_film/newsid_2486000/2486357.stm). CBBC Newsround. 2002-11-17. . Retrieved 15 November 2008.
[50] "007's bungee jump tops best movie stunt poll". Breaking News. 2002-11-17.
[51] "Opening Sequence W/ Daniel Kleinman" (http://web.archive.org/web/20060204162919/http://www.jamesbond.com/bond20/newsflash/newsflash_27.php). Metro-Goldwyn-Mayer Studios Inc.. Archived from the original (http://www.jamesbond.com/bond20/

newsflash/newsflash_27.php) on 2006-02-04. . Retrieved 18 January 2007.

[52] Michael G. Wilson, Barbara Broccoli, Martin Campbell, Chris Corbould, Pierce Brosnan, Famke Janssen, Izabella Scorupco, Peter Lamont. (1994). *GoldenEye: Building a Better Bond*. [Theatrical Teaser]. MGM Home Entertainment.

[53] Lee Pfeiffer; Worrall, Dave (2003) [1998]. "*GoldenEye*". *The Essential Bond: The Authorized Guide to the World of 007*. Boxtree. p. 177. ISBN 0752215620.

[54] "BMW Z3" (http://www.jamesbondmm.co.uk/vehicles/bmw-z3-roadster.php). James Bond multimedia. . Retrieved 3 January 2007.

[55] Lance Kinney; Barry Sapolsky (1994), *Product Placement*, University of Alabama, Florida State University

[56] "A look at some of the biggest hits in film and TV product placement" (http://www.hollywoodreporter.com/thr/film/feature_display.jsp?vnu_content_id=1000901395). The Hollywood Reporter. 2005-04-28. . Retrieved 12 November 2007.

[57] "Tina Turner performs theme song to new James Bond movie, 'GoldenEye.'" (http://www.findarticles.com/p/articles/mi_m1355/is_n2_v89/ai_17755938). Jet. 1995-11-20. . Retrieved 20 November 2006.

[58] Lee Pfeiffer; Worrall, Dave (2003) [1998]. "*GoldenEye*". *The Essential Bond: The Authorized Guide to the World of 007*. Boxtree. p. 175. ISBN 0752215620.

[59] Robert Hoshowsky (November 1996). "John Barry The Gstaad Memorandum" (http://www.filmscoremonthly.com/features/barry.asp). Film Score. . Retrieved 18 November 2006.

[60] Richard von Busack (1995-11-22). "Bond for Glory" (http://www.metroactive.com/papers/metro/11.22.95/bond-9547.html). Metro. . Retrieved 19 November 2006.

[61] "Filmtracks Editorial Review" (http://www.filmtracks.com/titles/goldeneye.html). *filmtracks.com*. . Retrieved 19 November 2006.

[62] *GoldenEye*. [Audio CD]. London: Virgin Records. 1995. Event occurs at 26 minutes.

[63] *GoldenEye*. [Audio CD]. London: EMI Capitol. 2003-02-25.

[64] (2003) Album notes for *EMI proudly presents: GoldenEye*. EMI Capitol (72435-41423-2-1).

[65] "GoldenEye - Première & Press" (http://www.mi6.co.uk/sections/articles/ge_premiere.php3?t=ge&s=ge). MI6.co.uk. 2003-11-13. . Retrieved 15 November 2006.

[66] "Pierce Brosnan boycotts French premiere of GoldenEye to support Greenpeace protests" (http://www.klast.net/bond/ge_news3.html#boycott). PRNewswire. 1995-12-01. . Retrieved 16 November 2006.

[67] "Release Information - GoldenEye" (http://www.mi6.co.uk/sections/movies/ge_releases.php3?t=ge&s=ge).MI6.co.uk. . Retrieved 26 May 2007.

[68] "GoldenEye" (http://www.boxofficemojo.com/movies/?page=main&id=goldeneye.htm). Box Office Mojo. . Retrieved 15 November 2006.

[69] "1995 Worldwide Grosses" (http://www.boxofficemojo.com/yearly/chart/?view2=worldwide&yr=1995&p=.htm).Box Office Mojo. . Retrieved 24 November 2006.

[70] (PAL, Widescreen) *GoldenEye: James Bond Ultimate Edition Region 2*. [DVD]. Mgm Home Ent. 2006-07-17. ASIN: B000FIF5KC.

[71] "GoldenEye (1995)" (http://uk.rottentomatoes.com/m/goldeneye/).*rottentomatoes.com*. . Retrieved 16 November 2006.

[72] "GoldenEye" (http://www.metacritic.com/video/titles/goldeneye). *metacritic.com*. . Retrieved 24 November 2006.

[73] Roger Ebert (1995-11-17). "GoldenEye" (http://rogerebert.suntimes.com/apps/pbcs.dll/article?AID=/19951117/REVIEWS/511170303/1023). *Chicago Sun-Times*. . Retrieved 16 November 2006.

[74] James Berardinelli (1995). "GoldenEye" (http://www.reelviews.net/movies/g/goldeneye.html). *www.reelviews.net*. . Retrieved 16 November 2006.

[75] Hal Hinson (1995-11-17). "14-Karat 'GoldenEye': A Polished New Bond" (http://www.washingtonpost.com/wp-srv/style/longterm/movies/videos/goldeneye.htm#hinson). *Washington Post*. . Retrieved 18 November 2006.

[76] Peter Stack (1995-11-17). "New Bond More Action Than Style" (http://www.sfgate.com/cgi-bin/article.cgi?f=/c/a/1995/11/17/DD71044.DTL). *San Francisco Gate*. SFGate.com. . Retrieved 18 November 2006.

[77] John J. Puccio. "DVD review of GoldenEye" (http://web.archive.org/web/20070928051344/http://www.dvdtown.com/reviewspec.asp?reviewid=505). DVD Town. Archived from the original (http://www.dvdtown.com/reviewspec.asp?reviewid=505) on September 28, 2007. . Retrieved 20 May 2007.

[78] "James Bond's Top 20" (http://movies.ign.com/articles/746/746573p4.html). IGN. 2006-11-17. . Retrieved 5 April 2008.

[79] Benjamin Svetkey, Joshua Rich (2006-11-15). "Ranking the Bond Films" (http://www.ew.com/ew/article/0,,1560072_15,00.html). . Retrieved 5 April 2008.

[80] Norman Wilner. "Rating the Spy Game" (http://web.archive.org/web/20080119210839/http://movies.sympatico.msn.ca/features/ArticleNormanWilner.aspx?cp-documentid=436189). MSN. Archived from the original (http://movies.sympatico.msn.ca/features/ArticleNormanWilner.aspx?cp-documentid=436189) on 2008-01-19. . Retrieved 4 March 2008.

[81] "The 10 Best Bond Girls" (http://www.ew.com/ew/article/0,,1557446_6,00.html). Entertainment Weekly. 2007-03-30. . Retrieved 5 April 2008.

[82] "Top 10 Bond Babes" (http://stars.ign.com/articles/746/746292p1.html). IGN. 2006-11-15. . Retrieved 5 April 2008.

[83] Richard Schickel (1995-11-27). "Shaky, Not Stirring" (http://www.time.com/time/magazine/article/0,9171,983763,00.html). *Time*. . Retrieved 18 November 2006.

[84] Owen Gleiberman (1995-11-18). "GoldenEye" (http://www.ew.com/ew/article/review/movie/0,6115,299672_1).*Entertainment Weekly*. . Retrieved 18 November 2006.

[85] Dragan Antulov (2002). "Retrospective: GoldenEye (1995)" (http://groups.google.com/group/rec.arts.movies.reviews/msg/2de00780acc1af5d). Retrospective. . Retrieved 28 April 2007.

[86] Kenneth Turan (1995-11-17). "GoldenEye - Movie Review" (http://web.archive.org/web/20070929141604/http://www.calendarlive.com/movies/reviews/cl-movie960406-47,0,1420920.story). *Los Angeles Times*. Archived from the original (http://www.calendarlive.com/movies/reviews/cl-movie960406-47,0,1420920.story) on September 29, 2007. . Retrieved 28 April 2007.

[87] "GoldenEye film review" (http://www.cinematter.com/movie.php3?goldeye). *Cinematter.com*. . Retrieved 25 July 2007.

[88] "Awards for Eric Serra" (http://www.imdb.com/name/nm0785385/awards). The Internet Movie Database. . Retrieved 15 November 2008.

[89] *MTV Movie Awards*. Burbank, CA: Walt Disney Studios. 1996-06-13.

[90] "Awards and nominations for GoldenEye (1995)" (http://www.imdb.com/title/tt0113189/awards). Internet Movie Database. . Retrieved 5 April 2008.

[91] *Goldeneye 007 Official Player's Guide*. Nintendo Power. 1997. ASIN: B000B66WKA.

[92] Don McGregor (January 1996) [1995]. *James Bond 007: GoldenEye*. Artwork by Rick Magyar and Claude St. Aubin; Cover art by Brian Stelfreeze. New York City: Topps Comics. Direct Sales 61114 00257.

[93] John Cox (2005-05-19). "When Bond Battled Dinosaurs" (http://web.archive.org/web/20071008130905/http://commanderbond.net/cw.cgi?action=Story&SID=2744). commanderbond.net. Archived from the original (http://commanderbond.net/cw.cgi?action=Story&SID=2744) on October 8, 2007. . Retrieved 10 November 2006.

[94] "GoldenEye 007 Reviews" (http://www.gamerankings.com/htmlpages2/197462.asp). gamerankings.com. . Retrieved 29 November 2006.

[95] "Microsoft Acquires Video Game Powerhouse Rare Ltd" (http://www.rareware.com/company/press-microsoft1.html).Microsoft. 2002-09-24. . Retrieved 13 May 2006.

[96] "100 Greatest Games Of All Time". *Computer and Video Games* (218): 53–67. January 2000.

[97] "Ten Top Tens: Shooters". *Edge* (128): 73. October 2003.

[98] Martin Hollis (2004-09-02). "The Making of GoldenEye 007" (http://www.zoonami.com/briefing/2004-09-02.php).Zoonami. . Retrieved 13 May 2006.

[99] "The Lost GoldenEye Videogame" (http://www.mi6.co.uk/sections/articles/gaming_goldeneye_virtual_boy.php3?t=&s=articles). MI6.co.uk. 2007-01-11. . Retrieved 27 April 2007.

[100] *Golden Eye: Rogue Agent (Prima Official Game Guide)*. Roseville, California: Prima Games. November 23. ISBN 0761546332.

[101] "Reviews of GoldenEye: Rogue Agent (PS2)" (http://www.metacritic.com/games/platforms/ps2/goldeneyerogueagent?q=goldeneye rogue agent). Metacritic. . Retrieved 5 April 2008.

[102] "Reviews of GoldenEye: Rogue Agent (Gamecube)" (http://www.metacritic.com/games/platforms/cube/goldeneyerogueagent?q=goldeneye rogue agent). Metacritic. . Retrieved 15 November 2008.

[103] "Reviews of GoldenEye: Rogue Agent (Xbox)" (http://www.metacritic.com/games/platforms/xbx/goldeneyerogueagent?q=goldeneye rogue agent). Metacritic. . Retrieved 15 November 2008.

[104] Eric Qualls. "GoldenEye: Rogue Agent" (http://xbox.about.com/od/reviews/fr/goldeneyerarev.htm). *About.com: Xbox Games*. The New York Times Company. . Retrieved 21 January 2007.

[105] Benjamin Turner. "GoldenEye: Rogue Agent (PS2)" (http://ps2.gamespy.com/playstation-2/james-bond-007-goldeneye-2/568337p1.html). GameSpy. . Retrieved 21 January 2007.

[106] Keith Stewart (17 June 2010). "E3 2010: GoldenEye first look" (http://www.guardian.co.uk/technology/gamesblog/2010/jun/17/e3-2010-goldeneye). The Guardian. . Retrieved 24 June 2010.

External links

- *GoldenEye* (http://www.imdb.com/title/tt0113189/) at the Internet Movie Database
- *GoldenEye* (http://www.allmovie.com/work/135622) at Allmovie
- *GoldenEye* (http://www.rottentomatoes.com/m/goldeneye/) at Rotten Tomatoes
- *GoldenEye* (http://www.boxofficemojo.com/movies/?id=goldeneye.htm) at Box Office Mojo
- MGM's official *GoldenEye* website (http://www.mgm.com/view/movie/757/Goldeneye)

Jack and Sarah

Jack and Sarah	
 Original film poster (US)	
Directed by	Tim Sullivan
Produced by	Simon Channing-Williams Pippa Cross Janette Day
Written by	Tim Sullivan
Starring	Richard E. Grant Samantha Mathis
Music by	Simon Boswell
Cinematography	Jean-Yves Escoffier
Editing by	Lesley Walker
Studio	PolyGram Filmed Entertainment Le Studio Canal + Granada Productions
Distributed by	Gramercy Pictures (USA)
Release date(s)	June 2, 1995
Running time	110 mins.
Country	France United Kingdom
Language	English
Gross revenue	$218,626 (USA) (sub-total) $2,492,000 (UK) (sub-total)

Jack and Sarah is a 1995 British romantic comedy film written and directed by Tim Sullivan. The film was originally released in the UK on 2 June 1995.

Plot

Jack (Richard E. Grant) and Sarah (Imogen Stubbs) are expecting a baby together, but a complication during the birth leads to the death of Sarah. Jack, grief stricken, goes on an alcoholic bender, leaving his daughter to be taken care of by both his and Sarah's parents, until they decide to take drastic action: they return the baby to Jack whilst he is asleep, leaving him to take care of it. Although initially struggling, he eventually begins to dote on the child, and names her Sarah.

Despite this, he nevertheless finds it increasingly difficult to juggle bringing up the baby with his high-powered job, and though both sets of the child's grandparents lend a hand (along with William (Ian McKellen), a dried out ex-alcoholic who, once sober, proves to be a remarkably efficient babysitter and housekeeper), he needs more help. Amy (Samantha Mathis), an American waitress he meets in a restaurant who takes a shine to Sarah, takes up the role as nanny, moving in with Jack after one meeting.

Although clashing with William and the grandparents - especially Jack's mother, Margaret (Judi Dench), Jack and Amy gradually grow closer - but Jack's boss has also taken an interest in him.

The theme song in this film is Stars by British pop group Simply Red.

Cast

- Jack – Richard E. Grant
- Amy – Samantha Mathis
- Margaret – Judi Dench
- Phil – Eileen Atkins
- Anna – Cherie Lunghi
- Sarah – Imogen Stubbs
- William – Ian McKellen
- Baby Sarah – Bianca Lee & Sophia Lee
- Baby Sarah (as a toddler) – Sophia Sullivan

External links

- *Jack and Sarah* [1] at the Internet Movie Database
- *Jack and Sarah* [2] at Allmovie

Behaving Badly (TV serial)

Behaving Badly	
 DVD cover	
Approx. run time	200 minutes
Genre	Drama
Written by	Catherine Heath Moira Williams Based on the novel by Catherine Heath
Directed by	David Tucker
Produced by	Humphrey Barclay Moira Williams
Starring	Judi Dench
Music by	Stephen Oliver
Country	United Kingdom
Language	English
Original channel	Channel 4
Original run	20 February – 13 March 1989
No. of episodes	4

Behaving Badly is a 1989 British television serial directed by David Tucker. The teleplay by Catherine Heath and Moira Williams is based on Heath's novel of the same name. It was initially broadcast by Channel 4. The series was released on DVD in 2005.

The plot focuses on Bridget Mayor, a middle-aged housewife and part-time teacher who is forced to re-evaluate her life when her husband of twenty years abandons her for a younger woman.

Episode summaries

- *The Tale of the Turbot* (Originally broadcast on February 20, 1989)

Five years after her divorce, Bridget is living in a small flat purchased for her by her ex-husband Mark and seeking to improve her life by participating in a variety of evening adult education programs, including a pottery class. At the request of her local clergyman, she attends services at a predominantly black parish in Croydon, where she is unsettled by young pastor Daniel, who regards her as an intruder. She unintentionally departs with a Bible borrowed from one of the congregants. Frieda, her aging, demanding, and sharp-tongued ex-mother-in-law who detests her son's second wife Rebecca and makes every effort to destroy their marriage, is left alone when the couple take a weekend holiday in France. When they return, they discover Bridget not only has moved back into the house she once shared with Paul, but is determined to stay indefinitely.

- *Home Fires* (Originally broadcast on February 27, 1989)

Mark desperately tries to find someone who can convince Bridget to return to her own home, while at the same time she and Rebecca begin to bond. Bridget and Paul's daughter Phyllida sees a photograph of Daniel on the church newsletter tucked into the Bible her mother took and, finding his looks appealing, decides to return it to him. At first he resists her obvious flirting but soon finds himself attracted to her as well, although he is conflicted in his feelings, certain his community would disapprove of a relationship with a white woman.

- *Seize the Day* (Originally broadcast on March 6, 1989)

Phyllida, who shares a flat with bisexual Giles, straight Jonathan, and Serafina, a teacher on the verge of a nervous breakdown, finds her home life disrupted when Giles' crotchety grandfather Herbert is unceremoniously dumped on their doorstep. Although estranged from her father and his wife, Phyllida opts to move in with them to escape the overcrowded conditions, whereupon Bridget takes her daughter's place in the Battersea flat. She finds herself enjoying her unofficial role of mother and caretaker.

- *The Horse May Talk* (Originally broadcast on March 13, 1989)

Bridget finds herself increasingly attracted to the considerably younger Giles, who proposes they move to San Diego, where he was born, and start a new life there together. He wavers in his decision when he realizes he can't leave his grandfather, but that obstacle is removed when the elderly man dies from an overdose of sleeping pills fed to him by an exasperated Serafina, who is fed up with his chronic complaining and constant demands. Bridget and Giles board a British Airways flight; she notices him cruising another male passenger, and as the plane takes off she is left wondering how successful this new relationship will be.

Cast

- Judi Dench ..... Bridget Mayor
- Ronald Pickup ..... Mark Mayor
- Francesca Folan ..... Phyllida
- Frances Barber ..... Rebecca
- Douglas Hodge ..... Giles
- Maurice Denham ..... Herbert
- Hugh Quarshie ..... Daniel
- Gwen Watford ..... Frieda
- Joely Richardson ..... Serafina
- Guy Scantlebury ..... Jonathan

Awards and nominations

Judi Dench was nominated for the BAFTA TV Award for Best Actress.

External links

- *Behaving Badly* at the Internet Movie Database [1]
- *Behaving Badly* at MemorableTV.com [2]

Henry V (1989 film)

Henry V	
 Theatrical release poster	
Directed by	Kenneth Branagh
Produced by	Bruce Sharman
Written by	Kenneth Branagh William Shakespeare (play)
Narrated by	Derek Jacobi
Starring	Kenneth Branagh Brian Blessed Paul Scofield Emma Thompson Michael Maloney Richard Briers Robbie Coltrane Judi Dench Ian Holm Robert Stephens Christian Bale Geraldine McEwan
Editing by	Michael Bradsell
Release date(s)	November 8, 1989
Running time	137 min
Country	United Kingdom
Language	English

Henry V is a 1989 film directed by Kenneth Branagh, based on William Shakespeare's play *The Life of Henry the Fifth* about the famous English king. Branagh stars in the title role, and wrote the screenplay. The film was highly acclaimed on its release.

Style

Branagh's film is frequently compared with the 1944 film of the play directed by and starring Laurence Olivier. The visual style of Branagh's film is grittier and more realist than that of Olivier's. For example, his film avoids Olivier's use of stylized sets, and, where Olivier staged the Battle of Agincourt on a sunlit field, Branagh's takes place amid rain-drenched mud and gore.

Adaptation

The text of the play is heavily cut. In addition, Branagh incorporated flashbacks using extracts from *Henry IV, Part 1* and *Part 2* in which Henry interacts with the character of Falstaff, who, in Shakespeare's *Henry V*, is never seen, merely announced to be deathly ill in Act 2 Scene 1, and dead in Act 2 scene 3. The scenes involve a brief summary of Henry's denouncement of Falstaff primarily with lines from Act 2, Scene 4 of *Henry IV part 1* and a brief though important utterance of Henry's final repudiation of Falstaff in *Part 2*, "I know thee not, old man." The movie also uses Falstaff's line "do not, when thou art King, hang a thief" from Henry IV Part 1 but gives it to Bardolph, in order to highlight the poignancy when Henry later has Bardolph executed.

Casting

The cast includes many well-known actors: Derek Jacobi as the Chorus, Brian Blessed as Exeter, Ian Holm as Fluellen, Christian Bale as the Boy, Paul Scofield as the King of France, Judi Dench as Mistress Quickly, Richard Briers as Bardolph, Robert Stephens as Pistol and Emma Thompson as Princess Katherine. The actor Michael Williams plays the character "Michael Williams". Robbie Coltrane appears in a cameo performance as Falstaff.

Production

The film was produced by Bruce Sharman with the British Broadcasting Corporation and Branagh's company Renaissance Films. The film's budget was $9 million.

The music is by first-time composer Patrick Doyle, which was performed by the City of Birmingham Symphony Orchestra and conducted by Simon Rattle.

Reception

Henry V received near-universal critical acclaim for Branagh's Oscar-nominated performance and direction, for the accessibility of its Shakespearean language and particularly for its music.

The film grossed $10 million in the U.S. and at the time of its widest release played on 134 U.S. screens.

Phyllis Dalton won the Academy Award for Best Costume Design and Kenneth Branagh, in his directorial debut, was nominated for Best Director as well as Best Actor in a Leading Role.

In popular culture

In the *Star Trek: The Next Generation* episode "The Defector", aired on New Years' Day 1990, when the film was still in theaters, the character of Data performs a sequence from Act 4, Scene 1, as Henry, and subsequently cites Branagh's performance as one of those he wishes to study closely.

Full Cast

- Chorus - Derek Jacobi
- Henry V of England - Kenneth Branagh
- Duke of Gloucester Brother to the King - Simon Shepherd
- Duke of Bedford Brother to the King - James Larkin
- Duke of Exeter, Uncle to the King - Brian Blessed
- Westmoreland - Paul Gregory
- Archbishop of Canterbury - Charles Kay
- Bishop of Ely - Alec McCowen
- Earl of Cambridge, Traitor - Fabian Cartwright
- Lord Scroop [sic], Traitor - Stephen Simms
- Sir Thomas de Grey, Traitor - Jay Villiers
- Sir Thomas Erpingham, Officer in King Henry's Army - Edward Jewesbury
- Fluellen, Officer in King Henry's Army - Ian Holm
- Gower, Officer in King Henry's Army - Daniel Webb
- Jamy, Officer in King Henry's Army - Jimmy Yuill
- Macmorris, Officer in King Henry's Army - John Sessions
- Bates, Soldier in King Henry's Army - Shaun Prendergast
- Court, Soldier in King Henry's Army - Pat Doyle
- Williams, Soldier in King Henry's Army - Michael Williams
- Bardolph - Richard Briers
- Nym - Geoffrey Hutchings
- Pistol - Robert Stephens
- Sir John Falstaff - Robbie Coltrane
- Boy - Christian Bale
- Mistress Quickly - Judi Dench
- Charles VI of France - Paul Scofield
- Louis, the Dauphin - Michael Maloney
- Duke of Burgundy - Harold Innocent
- Duke of Orleans - Richard Clifford
- Grandpre, French Lord - Colin Hurley
- Constable - Richard Easton
- Mountjoy, a French Herald - Christopher Ravenscroft
- Katharine, Daughter to Charles and Isabel - Emma Thompson
- Alice, a Lady attending on Katharine - Geraldine McEwan
- Governor of Harfleur - David Lloyd Meredith
- Messenger - David Parfitt
- Warwick - Nicholas Ferguson
- John Talbot, 1st Earl of Shrewsbury - Tom Whitehouse
- Duke of Berry - Nigel Greaves
- Bretagne - Julian Gartside

- 1st Soldier - Mark Inman
- 2nd Soldier - Chris Armstrong
- Child - Calum Yuill

See also

- List of historical drama films

External links

- *Henry V* [1] at the Internet Movie Database
- *Henry V (1989 film)* [2] at the TCM Movie Database
- *Henry V (1989 film)* [3] at Allmovie
- *Henry V* [4] at Box Office Mojo
- *Henry V* @ Rotten Tomatoes [5]
- *Henry V* on Film [6]
- *Henry V* Unofficial Page [7]
- A Word from Kenneth Branagh [8]

A Handful of Dust

A Handful of Dust	

Author	Evelyn Waugh
Country	United Kingdom
Language	English
Genre(s)	Novel
Publisher	Chapman and Hall (UK)
Publication date	1934
Media type	Print (Hardback & Paperback)
Pages	308 pp (1st edition hardcover)
ISBN	NA

A Handful of Dust is a novel by Evelyn Waugh published in 1934. It is included in Modern Library List of Best 20th-Century Novels,[1] and was chosen by *TIME* magazine as one of the one hundred best English-language novels from 1923 to present.[2] The title is an allusion to T. S. Eliot's 1922 poem *The Waste Land*:

> I will show you something different from either
>
> Your shadow at morning striding behind you
>
> Or your shadow at evening rising to meet you;
>
> I will show you fear in a handful of dust.

The novel was originally called *A Handful of Ashes*, but, after a dispute with his American publishers, the quotation from *The Waste Land* was chosen. Christopher Sykes, Waugh's biographer, notes that "the title was not apposite".

Plot

In *A Handful of Dust* Waugh satirises the British landed gentry and mercantile class. The novel is set in the 1930s, and focuses on the breakdown of the marriage of Tony and Brenda Last. Tony is preoccupied with the maintenance of Hetton Abbey, an example of unfashionable Victorian Gothic architecture. John Beaver, a self-interested and impoverished social climber, invites himself to Hetton for the weekend, and soon after begins an affair with Brenda.

After the Lasts' son, also called John, dies in a riding accident, Brenda decides that she wants a divorce. In order to avoid any scandal for his wife, Tony agrees to go through the sham of creating appropriate grounds for divorce. Their agreement on the divorce falls apart when Brenda's brother reveals that Brenda's family will not adhere to her initial agreement on a monetary settlement, but instead will insist on a sum so large as to require Tony to sell Hetton; Tony then refuses to grant or file for a divorce. Instead, he participates in an expedition to Brazil. Stranded in the jungle, Tony falls ill, and his expedition companion, Dr. Messinger, dies while attempting to retrieve help. Tony wanders, delirious, until he stumbles into an isolated tribal village. Once there, he is held captive by a Mr. Todd, who insists that Tony remain forever, reading the works of Charles Dickens to him. Brenda's relationship with John Beaver has fallen apart, and shortly after Tony is assumed dead she marries the couple's mutual friend, Jock Grant-Menzies. The novel ends with obscure relatives of Tony taking over Hetton.

In an alternative ending for the novel, required by Waugh's American publishers who did not approve of the bleakness of the original, Tony returns from Brazil and to his relationship with Brenda.

Waugh wrote of how the novel came to be written:

> "I had just written a short story about a man trapped in the jungle, ending his days reading Dickens aloud. The idea came quite naturally from the experience of visiting a lonely settler of that kind and reflecting how easily he could hold me prisoner [...] eventually the thing grew into a study of other sorts of savages at home and the civilized man's helpless plight among them." (Gallagher, 303).

The short story referred to is "The Man Who Liked Dickens".

Adaptations

The novel was filmed in 1988 by Charles Sturridge, and starring James Wilby as Tony Last, Kristin Scott Thomas as Brenda Last, Judi Dench as Mrs Beaver, and Rupert Graves as John Beaver. It also starred Alec Guinness as Mr Todd, and Anjelica Huston as Mrs Rattery. Carlton Towers was used as the location of Hetton.

References

- Gallagher, Donat, editor. *The Essays, Articles, and Reviews of Evelyn Waugh.* London: Methuen, 1983.

[1] The Modern Library | 100 Best | Novels (http://www.randomhouse.com/modernlibrary/100bestnovels.html)

[2] http://www.time.com/time/2005/100books/the_complete_list.html

External links

- Detailed notes on the novel (http://www.vanderbilt.edu/AnS/english/English151W-03/handful.htm).

84 Charing Cross Road (film)

84 Charing Cross Road	
 Original poster	
Directed by	David Hugh Jones
Produced by	Mel Brooks Geoffrey Helman
Written by	Hugh Whitemore Based on the play by James Roose-Evans adapted from the book by Helene Hanff
Starring	Anne Bancroft Anthony Hopkins
Music by	George Fenton
Cinematography	Brian West
Editing by	Chris Wimble
Studio	Brooksfilms
Distributed by	Columbia Pictures
Release date(s)	February 13, 1987 (United States) April 30, 1987 (Australia)
Running time	100 minutes
Country	United Kingdom/United States
Language	English
Gross revenue	$1,083,486 (US)

84 Charing Cross Road is a 1987 British/American drama film directed by David Hugh Jones. The screenplay by Hugh Whitemore is based on a play by James Roose-Evans, which itself was an adaptation of the 1970 epistolary memoir of the same name by Helene Hanff, a compilation of letters between herself and Frank Doel dating from 1949 to 1968. Although the play has only two characters, the dramatis personae for the film were expanded to include Hanff's Manhattan friends, the bookshop staff, and Doel's wife Nora.

Plot

In 1949 Helene Hanff, in search of obscure classics and British literature titles she has been unable to find in New York City, notices an ad placed by antiquarian booksellers Marks & Co located at the titular address in London in the *Saturday Review of Literature*. She contacts the shop and manager Frank Doel fulfills her requests. A long distance friendship evolves over time, not only between the two but between Hanff and other staff members as well, including birthday gifts, holiday packages, and food parcels to compensate for post-World War II food shortages in England. Their correspondence includes discussions about topics as diverse as the sermons of John Donne, how to make Yorkshire Pudding, the Brooklyn Dodgers, and the coronation of Queen Elizabeth II.

Hanff postpones visiting her English friends until too late: Doel dies in December 1968 and the bookshop eventually closes. She finally visits Charing Cross Road and the vacant shop in the summer of 1971.

Principal cast

- Anne Bancroft as Helene Hanff
- Anthony Hopkins as Frank Doel
- Judi Dench as Nora Doel
- Maurice Denham as George Martin
- Eleanor David as Cecily Farr
- Mercedes Ruehl as Kay
- Daniel Gerroll as Brian
- Wendy Morgan as Megan Wells
- Ian McNeice as Bill Humphries
- J. Smith-Cameron as Ginny

Production

The film was shot on location in London and New York City. London settings include Buckingham Palace, Soho Square, Trafalgar Square, St James's, Westminster, White Hart Lane in Tottenham, and suburban Richmond. Manhattan settings include Central Park, Madison Avenue, and Saint Thomas Church. Interiors were filmed at Lee International Studios and Shepperton Studios in Surrey.

Critical reception

In his review in the *New York Times*, Vincent Canby called it "a movie guaranteed to put all teeth on edge . . . a movie of such unrelieved genteelness that it makes one long to head for Schrafft's for a double-gin martini, straight up, and a stack of cinnamon toast from which the crusts have been removed."[1]

Roger Ebert of the *Chicago Sun-Times* observed, "The film is based on a hit London and New York play, which was based on a best-selling book. Given the thin and unlikely subject matter, that already is a series of miracles. And yet there are people who are pushovers for this material. I should know. I read the book and I saw the play and now I am reviewing the movie, and I still don't think the basic idea is sound . . . Miss Fiske . . . was the librarian at the Urbana Free Library when I was growing up . . . She never had to talk to me about the love of books because she simply exuded it and I absorbed it. She would have loved this movie. Sitting next to her, I suspect, I would have loved it, too. But Miss Fiske is gone now, and I found it pretty slow-going on my own."[2]

Variety described it as "an appealing film on several counts, one of the most notable being Anne Bancroft's fantastic performance in the leading role . . . [She] brings Helene Hanff alive in all her dimensions, in the process creating one of her most memorable characterizations."[3]

Box office

In its opening weekend in the U.S. the film grossed $24,350 at one theater. The total U.S. box office was $1,083,486.[4]

Awards and nominations

Anne Bancroft won the BAFTA Award for Best Actress in a Leading Role. Judi Dench was nominated for the BAFTA Award for Best Actress in a Supporting Role, and Hugh Whitemore for BAFTA Award for Best Adapted Screenplay. At the Moscow International Film Festival, Anthony Hopkins was named Best Actor, and David Hugh Jones was nominated for the Golden Prize for his direction. Whitemore and Helene Hanff shared the first USC Scripter Award for their contributions to the screenplay.

References

[1] *New York Times* review (http://movies.nytimes.com/movie/review?res=9B0DE1D6113DF930A25751C0A961948260)

[2] *Chicago Sun-Times* review (http://rogerebert.suntimes.com/apps/pbcs.dll/article?AID=/19870327/REVIEWS/703270301/1023)

[3] *Variety* review (http://www.variety.com/review/VE1117790662.html?categoryid=31&cs=1&p=0)

[4] *84 Charing Cross Road* at BoxOfficeMojo.com (http://www.boxofficemojo.com/movies/?id=84charingcrossroad.htm)

External links

- *84 Charing Cross Road* (http://www.imdb.com/title/tt0090570/) at the Internet Movie Database

A Room with a View (film)

A Room with a View	
 Theatrical release poster	
Directed by	James Ivory
Produced by	Ismail Merchant
Written by	Ruth Prawer Jhabvala Novel: E.M. Forster
Starring	Maggie Smith Helena Bonham Carter Denholm Elliott Julian Sands Daniel Day Lewis Judi Dench
Music by	Richard Robbins (score) Giacomo Puccini (sung by Kiri Te Kanawa)
Cinematography	Tony Pierce-Roberts
Editing by	Humphrey Dixon
Studio	Merchant Ivory Productions
Distributed by	Curzon (UK) Cinecom (US)
Release date(s)	United Kingdom: December, 1985 (premiere) 11 April 1986 (wide) United States: 7 March 1986 (NYC) 23 May 1986
Running time	117 minutes
Country	United Kingdom
Language	English
Budget	$3,000,000

Gross revenue	$20,966,644

A Room with a View is a 1985 British drama film, with a screenplay by Ruth Prawer Jhabvala. The film was directed by James Ivory and produced by Ismail Merchant. The film is a close adaptation of E. M. Forster's novel of the same name (but for its unequivocally happy ending), and even uses his chapter titles to divide the film into sections.

It stars Helena Bonham Carter as a young woman in the restrictive Edwardian culture of turn-of-the century England and her love for a free-spirited young man. Maggie Smith, Denholm Elliott, Julian Sands, Simon Callow, Judi Dench, Daniel Day-Lewis, and Rupert Graves round out the main cast. Both Denholm Elliott and Maggie Smith was nominated for Academy Award for Best Supporting Actor and Academy Award for Best Supporting Actress, but both lost to Michael Caine and Dianne Wiest from *Hannah and Her Sisters*.

Plot

Miss Lucy Honeychurch is on holiday in Italy with her cousin and chaperone, Charlotte Bartlett. Both Lucy and Charlotte are conventionally English in contrast with the more free-thinking and free-spirited backdrop of Italy. It is at a small *pensione* in Italy that Lucy meets elderly Mr. Emerson and his handsome son, George. These men, although also English, represent the forward-thinking ideals of the turn-of-the-century, seeking to leave behind the repression and caution that was the norm in Victorian times. At first, the two Emerson men seem strange and unfamiliar to Lucy and Charlotte. However, as Lucy begins her journey to maturity, she finds herself drawn to the men, especially the handsome George.

In an unguarded moment, George embraces and passionately kisses Lucy as she approaches him to ask a question in a rural barley field. Charlotte sees the act and quickly stops it. George's unrestrained passion shocks Lucy, but also lights a secret desire and romance in her heart.

Upon returning to England, Lucy forgets the incident. She accepts a marriage proposal from an uptight, but respectable and wealthy man named Cecil Vyse, assuming that she will never see George again. However, she soon learns that both George and his father have moved to her small village and will be her neighbours. The appearance of George soon disrupts her plans and forces her to make a choice.

At this point in the movie, there is a swimming scene with continuous male frontal nudity and a chase scene that surprises the women main characters, who are surprised by seeing three nude men running through the woods.

After a while, the Emerson men decide that they do not fit in with the locals. They make plans to move to a more open-minded place. Lucy has already broken her ties to Cecil, and wants to travel for a while. She yearns to separate herself from the antics of her brother, Freddy, as well as the sweet-yet-tiresome older neighbours (including Charlotte and Lucy's own mother). Just as she is about to leave Windy Corner to set out on an independent adventure, she elopes with George to Florence.

Cast

In Florence

- Maggie Smith - Charlotte Bartlett
- Helena Bonham-Carter - Lucy Honeychurch
- Denholm Elliott - Mr. Emerson
- Julian Sands - George Emerson
- Simon Callow - The Reverend Mr. Beebe
- Patrick Godfrey - The Reverend Mr. Eager, Chaplain of the Anglican Church in Florence
- Judi Dench - Eleanor Lavish, a novelist
- Fabia Drake - Miss Catharine Alan
- Joan Henley - Miss Teresa Alan

- Amanda Walker - The Cockney Signora

In England

- Daniel Day-Lewis - Cecil Vyse
- Maria Britneva - Mrs Vyse, Cecil's mother
- Rosemary Leach - Mrs Honeychurch, Lucy's mother
- Rupert Graves - Freddy Honeychurch, Lucy's brother
- Peter Cellier - Sir Harry Otway, a landlord
- Mia Fothergill - Minnie Beebe

Other cast

- Kitty Aldridge - New Lucy
- Brigid Erin Bates - Maid at Windy Corner
- Isabella Celani - Persephone
- Luigi Di Fiore - Murdered Youth
- Matyelok Gibbs - New Charlotte
- Mirio Guidelli - Santa Croce Guide
- Freddy Korner - Mr. Floyd
- Patty Lawrence - Mrs. Butterworth
- Elizabeth Marangoni - Miss Pole
- Peter Munt - Coachman
- Lucca Rossi - Phaeton
- Stefano Serboli - Fighting Youth
- Phillida Sewell - Lady at Sir Harry's Garden Party
- Margaret Ward - Lady at Sir Harry's Garden Party

Cameos

- Richard Robbins - Party Guest
- James Wilby - Party Guest

Awards

Wins

- Academy Awards: *Best Art Direction* (Brian Ackland-Snow), *Best Costume Design* (Jenny Beavan), *Best Adapted Screenplay* (Ruth Prawer Jhabvala)[1]
- BAFTAs: *Best Actress* (Maggie Smith), *Best Supporting Actress* (Judi Dench), *Best Costume Design* (Jenny Beavan), *Best Film* (James Ivory), *Best Production Design* (Brian Ackland-Snow)[2]
- Evening Standard British Film Awards: *Best Film* (James Ivory), *Best Technical/Artistic Achievement* (Tony Pierce-Roberts)[2]
- Golden Globes: *Best Supporting Actress* (Maggie Smith)[3]
- Kansas City Film Critics Circle Awards: *Best Supporting Actor* (Denholm Elliott), *Best Supporting Actress (Maggie Smith)*[2]
- London Critics Circle Film Awards: *Best Film* (James Ivory)[4]
- National Board of Review: *Best Film*, *Best Supporting Actor* (Daniel Day-Lewis)[5]
- New York Film Critics Circle Awards: *Best Cinematography* (Tony Pierce-Roberts), *Best Supporting Actor* (Daniel Day-Lewis)[6]
- Writers Guild of America: *Best Adapted Screenplay* (Ruth Prawer Jhabvala)[7]

Nominations

- Academy Awards: *Best Supporting Actor* (Denholm Elliott), *Best Supporting Actress* (Maggie Smith), *Best Picture* (Ismail Merchant), *Best Cinematographer* (Tony Pierce-Roberts), *Best Director* (James Ivory)[8]
- BAFTAs: *Best Supporting Actor* (Simon Callow), (Denholm Elliott), *Best Supporting Actress* (Rosemary Leach), *Best Cinematography* (Tony Pierce-Roberts), *Best Director* (James Ivory), *Best Editing* (Humphrey Dixon), *Best Score* (Richard Robbins), *Best Adapted Screenplay* (Ruth Prawer Jhabvala), *Best Sound*[9]
- Directors Guild of America: *Outstanding Directorial Achievement in Motion Pictures* (James Ivory)[10]
- Golden Globes: *Best Director* (James Ivory), *Best Motion Picture - Drama*[11]

Soundtrack

1. "O mio babbino caro" (from *Gianni Schicchi* by Puccini) - Kiri Te Kanawa with London PO, conducted by Sir John Pritchard
2. "The Pensione Bertollini"
3. "Lucy, Charlotte, and Miss Lavish See the City"
4. "In the Piazza Signoria"
5. "The Embankment"
6. "Phaeton and Persephone"
7. "Chi il bel sogno di Doretta" (from *La Rondine*, Act One by Puccini) - Kiri Te Kanawa with London PO, conducted by Sir John Pritchard
8. "The Storm"
9. "Home, and the Betrothal"
10. "The Sacred Lake"
11. "The Allan Sisters"
12. "In the National Gallery"
13. "Windy Corner"
14. "Habanera"
15. "The Broken Engagement"
16. "Return to Florence"
17. "End Titles"

- Music Composed by Richard Robbins
- Soundtrack Album Produced by Simon Heyworth
- Arrangements by Frances Shaw and Barrie Gurad
- Music Published by Filmtrax PLC

See also

- Baedeker, a travel guide mentioned several times in the film
- Chiddingstone Castle, used as a location for the film

References

[1] "The 1987 Oscar Winners - RopeofSilicon.com Award Show Central" (http://www.ropeofsilicon.com/award_show/oscars/1987). Ropeofsilicon.com. . Retrieved 21 August 2010.

[2] (http://www.imdb.com/title/tt0091867/awards)

[3] "The 1987 Golden Globe Award Winners - RopeofSilicon.com Award Show Central" (http://www.ropeofsilicon.com/award_show/golden_globe_awards/1987). Ropeofsilicon.com. . Retrieved 21 August 2010.

[4] (http://www.imdb.com/Sections/Awards/London_Critics_Circle_Film_Awards/1987)

[5] "National Board of Review of Motion Pictures :: Awards" (http://www.nbrmp.org/awards/past.cfm?year=1986).Nbrmp.org. . Retrieved 21 August 2010.

[6] "New York Film Critics Circle: 1986 Awards" (http://nyfcc.com/awards.php?year=1986). Nyfcc.com. . Retrieved 21 August 2010.

[7] (http://www.imdb.com/Sections/Awards/Writers_Guild_of_America_USA/1987)
[8] (http://www.imdb.com/Sections/Awards/Academy_Awards_USA/1987)
[9] (http://www.imdb.com/Sections/Awards/BAFTA_Awards/1987)
[10] (http://www.imdb.com/Sections/Awards/Directors_Guild_of_America_USA/1987)
[11] (http://www.imdb.com/Sections/Awards/Golden_Globes_USA/1987)

External links

- Merchant Ivory Production (http://merchantivory.com/roomview.html)
- *A Room with a View* (http://www.imdb.com/title/tt0091867/) at the Internet Movie Database

Wetherby (film)

Wetherby	

Directed by	David Hare
Produced by	Simon Relph
Written by	David Hare
Starring	Vanessa Redgrave Ian Holm Tim McInnerny Judi Dench Joely Richardson Tom Wilkinson Stuart Wilson Suzanna Hamilton
Music by	Nick Bicât
Cinematography	Stuart Harris
Distributed by	MGM/UA Classics
Release date(s)	19 July 1985
Running time	102 min.
Country	UK
Language	English
Gross revenue	$1,299,985

Wetherby is a 1985 British drama film written and directed by playwright David Hare.

Plot synopsis

Set in the town of Wetherby in West Yorkshire, the film focuses on Jean Travers, a middle-aged spinster schoolteacher. One evening, she invites married friends for a dinner party, only to have some terrible repressions and past traumas dredged up when guest John Morgan expresses his emotional pain. The strange young man arrives at Jean's cottage the next morning with a gift of pheasants. While sitting at the kitchen table waiting for tea, he puts the barrel of a gun in his mouth and kills himself.

From this point onward, the film's story is told in chronologically discrete, interlocking flashbacks to the recent and distant past, showing actions and events as seen and experienced from various points of view. The central mystery of Morgan's suicide is the fulcrum around which the narrative turns. The narrative construction of the film resembles a jigsaw puzzle and, in keeping with Hare's style of exposition, frequently appears to have key pieces missing.

There are further scenes of the dinner party as well as scenes of the police investigation into the suicide. We learn Morgan had not been an invited guest — he walked in with others who assumed he was an acquaintance of Jean's, and Jean assumed that her friends had brought him with them.

An aloof and peculiar young woman named Karen Creasy — a former classmate of Morgan's — is delivered from the funeral to Jean's doorstep by Mike Langdon, one of the policemen conducting the inquest. For several weeks after, the girl insinuates herself into Jean's life and home and shows no intention of leaving. Sullen, self-centered, and seemingly devoid of motivation, Karen is curiously unmoved by John's death and is even hostile to his memory. It is later explained that Morgan had developed an obsession with Karen when they were both students at the University of Essex, and she had harshly rebuffed his attempts to initiate a relationship with her. It is implied this rejection may have been the precipitating factor in his decision to leave Essex for Yorkshire with the intention of committing suicide.

When Jean suggests to Karen she may have been responsible for John's decision to kill himself, the young woman angrily denies that her behavior was — or *is* — in any way provocative. She makes it clear that she resists — and resents — having any kind of emotional involvement with people, including Jean, and promptly leaves Wetherby for good.

In addition to the events occurring in the present day, there are flashbacks of Jean and her lifelong friend, Marcia, as teenagers in 1953. These scenes reveal Jean had been engaged to airman, Jim Mortimer, and that she failed to stop him from going away on active service in southeast Asia. In a cruel twist of fate, Jim was senselessly murdered in a gambling den during the anti-imperial uprisings in British Malaya.

As these episodes from the past and present criss-cross and overlap, Jean begins to understand the dull resentment and lonely despair that drove Morgan to take his life. She also seems to gain some insight into the restlessness and self-destructive impulses of the younger generation. In a related incident, she tries to get one of her female students to see the value of continuing her education. At the end of the film, Jean is told that the girl has dropped out of the sixth form to run away to London, presumably with a boyfriend.

Jean is likewise affected by the diminished hopes of her contemporaries, who deplore the state of the country under Thatcherism. She regularly discusses these current matters with Stanley Pilborough, Marcia's husband and the town solicitor, who is often purposefully drunk. She observes the unhappy marriages of her middle-aged friends, particularly the endless bickering that goes on between Roger and Verity Braithwaite. Even lonely, despondent Mike Langdon confesses the failure of his relationship with his mistress, Chrissie, who eventually leaves him to return to her sheep farmer husband.

In the end, it seems that Jean no longer needs to mourn for the life she might have had — and the person she might have become — had she not allowed her fiancé to make his fatal departure for Malaya three decades earlier. She will make the best of what she has — and what is — in the here and now.

Principal cast

- Vanessa Redgrave ..... Jean Travers
- Ian Holm ..... Stanley Pilborough
- Judi Dench ..... Marcia Pilborough
- Tim McInnerny ..... John Morgan
- Stuart Wilson ..... Mike Langdon
- Suzanna Hamilton ..... Karen Creasy
- Tom Wilkinson ..... Roger Braithwaite
- Marjorie Yates ..... Verity Braithwaite
- Joely Richardson ..... Young Jean
- Katy Behean ..... Young Marcia
- Robert Hines ..... Jim Mortimer

Critical reception

Wetherby has an overall approval rating of 80% on Rotten Tomatoes.[1]

In her review in the *New York Times*, Janet Maslin observed the film was written "with a playwright's ear for elegant dialogue and a playwright's portentous sense of symmetry. While the former is certainly welcome on the screen, the latter is less at home, and it serves to make *Wetherby* a peculiar hybrid not entirely suited to either medium . . . the film's momentum varies unpredictably, with a rhythm that is sometimes abrupt, sometimes languid. Equally uneven is the acuteness of the dialogue, with passages that are particularly pointed interspersed with those whose bearing is at best indirect . . . However, Mr. Hare has assembled a superb cast, and its ensemble work is very fine . . . Miss Redgrave's warm, credible performance is very much the heart of the film. She brings to the character a crisp intelligence and a very deep compassion, while still managing to make every movement a surprise."[2]

Roger Ebert of the *Chicago Sun-Times* called it "a haunting film, because it dares to suggest that the death of the stranger is important to everyone it touches - because it forces them to decide how alive they really are."[3]

Time Out London notes, "Redgrave's performance is superb and she's ably supported by Holm, Dench, and Hamilton in particular."[4]

Awards and nominations

- Berlin International Film Festival Golden Bear for Best Motion Picture (winner, tie with *Die Frau und der Fremde*)
- Berlin International Film Festival C.I.C.A.E. Award (David Hare, winner)
- Berlin International Film Festival Interfilm Award - Honorable Mention (David Hare, winner)
- BAFTA Award for Best Actress in a Supporting Role (Judi Dench, nominee)
- National Society of Film Critics Award for Best Actress (Vanessa Redgrave, winner)
- Boston Society of Film Critics Award for Best Supporting Actor (Ian Holm, winner)

References

[1] "Rotten Tomatoes" (http://www.rottentomatoes.com/m/wetherby/). . Retrieved 2010-09-05.
[2] *New York Times* review (http://movies.nytimes.com/movie/review?res=9E03EEDF1538F93AA25754C0A963948260)
[3] *Chicago Sun-Times* review (http://rogerebert.suntimes.com/apps/pbcs.dll/article?AID=/19850927/REVIEWS/509270303/1023)
[4] *Time Out London* review (http://www.timeout.com/film/reviews/64387/Wetherby.html)

External links

- *Wetherby* at the Internet Movie Database (http://www.imdb.com/title/tt0090310/)
- *Wetherby* (http://www.allmovie.com/work/53975) at Allmovie

The Angelic Conversation (film)

The Angelic Conversation	

DVD cover	
Directed by	Derek Jarman
Produced by	James Mackay
Written by	William Shakespeare (Sonnets)
Narrated by	Judi Dench
Starring	Paul Reynolds Phillip Williamson
Music by	Coil
Cinematography	Derek Jarman and James Mackay
Editing by	Peter Cartwright Derek Jarman Cerith Wyn Evans
Release date(s)	• February 28, 1987
Running time	78 min.
Country	United Kingdom
Language	English

The Angelic Conversation is a 1985 arthouse drama film directed by Derek Jarman. Its tone is set by the juxtaposition of slow moving photographic images and Shakespeare's sonnets read by Judi Dench. The film consists primarily of images of homosexuality and opaque landscapes through which two men take a journey into their own desires.

Jarman himself described the film as:

> "a dream world, a world of magic and ritual, yet there are images there of the burning cars and radar systems, which remind you there is a price to be paid in order to gain this dream in the face of a world of violence."

[1]

The soundtrack to the film was composed and performed by Coil, and it was released as an album of the same title. In 2008 Peter Christopherson of Coil (with David Tibet and Ernesto Tomasini) performed a new live soundtrack to the movie during a special screening at the Turin Lesbian and Gay Film Festival.

Shakespeare's sonnets

14 sonnets the film features are:

- Sonnet LVII

  Being your slave, what should I do but tend

  Upon the hours and times of your desire?
- Sonnet XC

  Then hate me when thou wilt, if ever, now,

  Now, while the world is bent my deeds to cross,
- Sonnet XLIII

  When most I wink, then do mine eyes best see,

  For all the day they view things unrespected;
- Sonnet LIII

  What is your substance, whereof are you made,

  That millions of strange shadows on you tend?
- Sonnet CXLVIII

  O me, what eyes hath love put in my head,

  Which have no correspondence with true sight!
- Sonnet CXXVI

  O thou, my lovely boy, who in thy power

  Dost hold Time's fickle glass, his sickle hour,
- Sonnet XXIX

  When, in disgrace with fortune and men's eyes,

  I all alone beweep my outcast state,
- Sonnet XCIV

  They that have power to hurt and will do none,

  That do not do the thing they most do show
- Sonnet XXX

  When to the sessions of sweet silent thought

  I summon up remembrance of things past,
- Sonnet LV

  Not marble nor the gilded monuments

  Of princes shall outlive this powerful rhyme,
- Sonnet XXVII

  Weary with toil, I haste me to my bed,

  The dear repose for limbs with travel tired
- Sonnet LXI

  Is it thy will, thy image should keep open

  My heavy eyelids to the weary night?
- Sonnet LVI

Sweet love, renew thy force; be it not said
Thy edge should blunter be than appetite,

- Sonnet CIV

To me, fair friend, you never can be old,
For as you were when first your eye I ey'd

DVD release

The BFI have released The Angelic Conversation on DVD.

Cast

- Dave Baby
- Timothy Burke
- Simon Costin
- Christopher Hobbs
- Philip McDonald
- Toby Mott
- Steve Randall
- Robert Sharp
- Tony Wood
- Judi Dench (Narrator)
- Paul Reynolds
- Phillip Williamson

References

[1] Jarman, Derek (1997). *Kicking the pricks*. ISBN 978-0-87-951844-8

External links

- *The Angelic Conversation* (http://www.imdb.com/title/tt0088722/) at the Internet Movie Database
- *The Angelic Conversation* (http://www.allmovie.com/work/2381) at Allmovie
- *The Angelic Conversation (film)* (http://www.screenonline.org.uk/film/id/441285/) at the British Film Institute's Screenonline

Langrishe, Go Down (film)

Langrishe, Go Down, the novel by Aidan Higgins (1966), was adapted for the screen by Harold Pinter, directed by David Jones, filmed for BBC Television in association with Raidió Teilifís Éireann, and first broadcast in September 1978 as a 90-minute *BBC2 Play of the Week*.[1] On July 17, 2002, *Langrische, Go Down* was re-released as a theatrical 16mm feature film,[2] after being shown in The Spaces Between the Words: A Tribute to Harold Pinter, by the Film Society of Lincoln Center, as part of the Harold Pinter Festival of the Lincoln Center Festival 2001, held at Lincoln Center for the Performing Arts, in New York City, from July 21 to July 31, 2001.[3]

Credits

- Screenplay: Harold Pinter, from the novel by Aidan Higgins
- Director: David Jones
- Original score: Carl Davis
- Photography: Elmer Cossey
- Sound Recordist: Graham Hare

Cast

- Imogen Langrishe: Judi Dench
- Otto Beck: Jeremy Irons
- Helen Langrishe: Annette Crosbie
- Lily Langrishe: Susan Williamson
- Maureen Layde: Margaret Whiting
- Barry Shannon: Harold Pinter

Setting

The setting is a fading Irish mansion in the ((Kilkenny)) countryside, in the late 1930s, and also includes some locations in Dublin.

Plot synopsis

Three spinster sisters, Imogene (Dench), Helen (Crosby), and Lily Langrische (Williamson), lose their equanimity - and in the case of Imogene her virginity - when a mature German student (Jeremy Irons) rents lodging from them while he works on his thesis.

Notes

[1] Leslie Halliwell and Philip Purser (1986). *Halliwell's Television Companion* (3rd ed. ed.). London: Grafton. ISBN 0246128380.

[2] "Langrische, Go Down (limited theatrical release)" (http://www.rottentomatoes.com/m/langrishe_go_down/). *Rotten Tomatoes*. 2002-07-17. . Retrieved 2008-09-26.

[3] "Harold Pinter Festival" (http://www.haroldpinter.org/home/lincolnfestival.shtml) (Web). *Lincoln Center Festival, New York, USA, 2001. HaroldPinter.org* (Official Website). . Retrieved 2008-09-26.

External links

- *Langrische Go Down* (http://www.imdb.com/title/tt0077830/) at the Internet Movie Database.

Dead Cert (film)

Dead Cert	
Directed by	Tony Richardson
Written by	John Oaksey Tony Richardson
Starring	Scott Antony
Release date(s)	May 1974
Running time	99 min.
Country	United Kingdom
Language	English

Dead Cert is a 1974 crime film directed by Tony Richardson. It is an adaptation of the novel with the same name by Dick Francis.[1]

References

[1] LeVasseur, Andrea. "Overview:Dead Cert" (http://allmovie.com/work/dead-cert-88892). *Allmovie*. . Retrieved August 26, 2010.

External links

- *Dead Cert* (http://www.imdb.com/title/tt0071394/) at the Internet Movie Database

Luther (1973 film)

Luther	

Directed by	Guy Green
Produced by	Ely Landau
Written by	Edward Anhalt Script John Osborne Play
Starring	Stacy Keach Julian Glover Maurice Denham Judi Dench Patrick Magee Hugh Griffith Robert Stephens
Cinematography	Freddie Young
Distributed by	AFT Distributing Corporation
Release date(s)	1973 April 1976
Running time	111 min.
Language	English

Luther is the 1973 film of John Osborne's biographical play, presenting the life of Martin Luther. It was one of eight in the first season of the American Film Theater's series of plays made into films. It was produced by Ely Landau, directed by British director Guy Green, and filmed at Shepperton Studios, England. Martin Luther with all of his historical significance is presented for the world to challenge and assess.

Synopsis

The time span covered by the film is 1506-1526: from Luther's completion of his novitiate in the Order of Eremites of St. Augustine in Erfurt to a time just after the birth of his first son Hans (b. June 7, 1526[1]). It is narrated by Julian Glover, who portrays a young knight in the tradition of Ulrich von Hutten and Franz von Sickingen. He takes Luther to task for failing to complete his "revolution" by supporting the peasants in their uprising: "You could have done it, Martin." Luther is confronted in the course of the film six other times, giving him the opportunity to defend himself in his own words. The metaphor of constipation and flatulence is employed to indicate Luther's progression from insecurity to confidence in life.

Plot

To the pealing of church bells Luther begins to ascend into his pulpit to preach, but he is hindered by stomach cramps. It is 1525 at the time of the Peasants' Revolt. He looks out facing the camera and sees a wounded knight wheeling in a hand cart that holds the body of a fallen comrade. The knight sardonically regales Luther with some of his accomplishments but then accuses him of abandoning those who got his reformation for him. Luther denies this, and the knight dips his right hand into his comrade's blood and wipes it across Luther's white surplice, telling him he now looks like a butcher. Luther stares silently. The film will return to this scene at this very point after the presentation of all the events of the story that precede it (1506-1525).

The scene shifts to the Augustinian cloister in Erfurt in 1506, when Luther becomes a full-fledged monk of the Order of Eremites of St. Augustine at the completion of his novitiate. Following the vesting of the new monk the young knight takes on the role of narrator and commentator for the rest of the film, explaining that Luther had become a monk to protect his soul from demonic attack and that he sought to outdo his brothers in the "counsels of perfection" in order to suppress internal murmurings of doubt. Luther is shown serving his brothers in the refectory, cleaning the cloister's latrines, washing the dishes, shivering in cold as he tries to sleep in his cell, and pacing back and forth in prayer. An important line of Luther's at this point is, "I am afraid of the darkness and the hole in it ... and there's no bottom to it!" He is so overwhelmed by his own sinfulness that he all but bursts open when he is making his confession. In a daily office he leaves the stalls where his brother monks are chanting a psalm, and he collapses in a fit before the altar. The knight reports that he suffered in that way for months but that he was able to cope with his doubts by "dropping them" from out of his head and into his bowels, i.e., becoming constipated.

Luther is then shown in his cell just before his first mass. His friend Brother Weinand comes in to tell him that his father has come to attend. In the course of vesting Luther, Weinand has him confess the Apostles' Creed, repeating twice the article, "the forgiveness of sins" to bring home to Luther that he is expected to believe that his sins are forgiven if he confesses this creed. This is the first time in the film that Luther is confronted. In this confrontation Weinand ends by telling Luther, "God isn't angry with you. It is you that are angry with him."

When Weinand leaves, Luther imagines he sees Jesus Christ as a fearful judge seated on a rainbow with a sword poised to punish him. This image takes him into the saying of his first mass, which he does poorly by seeming to forget the words of the liturgy. He then faces his father at the reception in the refectory. When father and son are left alone, Hans Luther scolds his son for failing to keep the commandment to honor father and mother when he left the study of law to enter the convent. He also tells him that he believes that Luther is murdering himself in the convent. This is the second confrontation. Luther defends himself by affirming that he did see a vision in the thunderstorm that moved him to make a promise to St. Anne to become a monk. He also shares how he felt closest to his father.

The knight begins the next segment with the statement: "So the praising ended, and the blasphemy began." Johann Tetzel is portrayed preaching indulgences with great pomp and circumstance. He makes the bold claim that his indulgences would even provide forgiveness for one who offered violence to the Virgin Mary. In the next scene Luther comes upon his mentor Vicar General Johann von Staupitz as he dozes under a pear tree. Staupitz confronts Luther for a third time with the accusation that he resents authority and makes it look ridiculous by his meticulous observance of his monastic rule. Staupitz urges Luther to articulate his position among his peers in Latin rather than in the vernacular German that would encourage the peasants and young knights to revolt.

Luther then is shown preaching a sermon on the eve of All Saints' Day, 1517, in which he graphically tells how he discovered the gospel of justification by faith alone while sitting on the latrine. He declares that someone has to "bell the cat," and with that he goes out to post his *Ninety-five Theses*. Luther is then confronted for the fourth time by Tetzel and Thomas Cardinal Cajetan de Vio at Augsburg in the fall of 1518. Cajetan warns Luther that if he does not retract his "errors and sermons" that the unity of Christendom would be sundered. Luther refuses, and Cajetan concludes, "That man hates himself, and if he goes to the stake, Tetzel, you can inscribe it: 'he could only love others.'"

The next scene shows Luther burning the bull *Exsurge Domine* in defiance of the pope. He then falls to the ground in a fit for a second time in the film. In a prayer he reminds God that the cause he is fighting is God's not his. He wonders if God is dead, concluding that God cannot die but only hide himself.

The famous session of the Diet of Worms is portrayed when Luther appears for the second time. The inquisitor is portrayed as Johann Eck. Luther is now confronted for the fifth time by Eck, who interrupts his "Here I Stand" speech with the warning that the common man is so greedy as to be incited to revolt if he does not recant. Luther refuses, and the momentousness of that action is emphasized in the film. The young knight exults in the moment: if Luther wanted to he could have led a successful revolt against established authority. The knight breaks off his ardor by disgustedly stating that Luther issued a plea for the extermination of the rebels, his *Against the Murderous, Thieving Hordes of Peasants.* Luther is portrayed as standing before the emperor and the princes declaiming a portion of his notorious tract. The emperor and the princes walk past Luther with their swords drawn to put down the peasants.

Luther is then shown wandering through a devastated marketplace where peasants had been slaughtered. He is brought once again to where he had been confronted by the young knight, who wipes blood across his surplice: Luther is confronted for the fifth time. Luther defends himself with the assertion: "God is the butcher. Address your abuse to him." Luther then tells the story of the Sacrifice of Issac by Abraham, concluding that God gives life when nothing seems imminent but death.

Luther is confronted for the seventh and final time by old Staupitz who has come to visit Martin and his wife Katie. Luther admits that the peasants had just cause but that as a mob they were against Christ. Staupitz is relieved to hear that Luther was not sure when he took his stand at Worms. Luther prays, "Help my unbelief." Katie comes in with their infant son Hans, who cannot get to sleep. Luther repeats his superstition that passing air in the devil's face wards him off: going from being anal retentive to being anal expulsive shows one has overcome one's doubts and fears. In the final scene Luther takes the baby into his pulpit and assures him that "the dark isn't quite as thick as all that," that they should hope that Christ will be true to his word, "A little while and you'll not see me, and then again a little and you shall see me" (John 16:16).

Historical inconsistencies

- Johann Tetzel is wrongly represented as being present at Luther's meeting in 1518 with Cardinal Cajetan (de Vio) at Augsburg. He was never present at this meeting.
- Johann Eck is represented as Luther's interrogator at the Diet of Worms in 1521 when, in reality, he was not.
- Johann von Staupitz is represented as alive in 1526 when, in reality, he had died in 1524.

Cast

(in order of appearance)

- Peter Cellier as Prior
- Leonard Rossiter as Brother Weinand
- Stacy Keach as Martin Luther
- Patrick Magee as Luther's father
- Thomas Heathcote as [Lucas, a] friend [of Luther's father]
- Julian Glover as Knight
- Matthew Guinness as reading monk
- Hugh Griffith as John Tetzel
- Maurice Denham as Johann von Staupitz, Vicar General
- Alan Badel as Cardinal Cajetan de Vio
- Robert Stephens as Johann von Eck
- Bruce Carstairs as Duke Frederick, Elector of Saxony
- Malcolm Stoddard as Emperor Charles the Fifth
- Judi Dench as Luther's wife

External links

- *Luther (1973)* [2] at the Internet Movie Database

Notes

[1] Martin Brecht, *Martin Luther*, 3 vols., (Minneapolis: Fortress Press, 1985-1993), 2:203.

A Midsummer Night's Dream (1968 film)

A Midsummer Night's Dream	
 Theatrical release poster	
Directed by	Peter Hall
Written by	William Shakespeare (play)
Starring	Derek Godfrey Ian Holm Helen Mirren Barbara Jefford Diana Rigg David Warner Michael Jayston
Release date(s)	September 1968
Running time	124 minutes
Country	United Kingdom
Language	English

A Midsummer Night's Dream is a 1968 film of William Shakespeare's play *A Midsummer Night's Dream*, directed by Peter Hall. It was the first live-action film version in color of the play, unless one counts the 1966 film version of the New York City Ballet George Balanchine adaptation.

It stars Derek Godfrey as Theseus, Barbara Jefford as Hippolyta, Diana Rigg as Helena, Helen Mirren as Hermia, Ian Holm as Puck, Ian Richardson as King Oberon, Judi Dench as Queen Titania, and Paul Rogers as Bottom, as well as other members of the Royal Shakespeare Company.

The film premiered in theatres in Europe in September 1968. In the U.S. it premiered on television on the night of February 9, 1969. It was shown on CBS (with commercials).

The film runs two full hours and is quite faithful to the play, with few unusual gimmicks, except for all the fairies wearing green body paint. They do not appear or disappear gradually as in the 1935 film version of the play; instead, they literally pop in and out.

Cast

- Derek Godfrey as Theseus
- Ian Holm as Puck, or Robin Goodfellow
- Judi Dench as Titania
- Helen Mirren as Hermia
- Paul Rogers as Bottom
- Diana Rigg as Helena
- Ian Richardson as Oberon
- David Warner as Lysander
- Michael Jayston as Demetrius
- Sebastian Shaw as Quince
- Bill Travers as Snout
- Clive Swift as Snug
- Donald Eccles as Starveling
- John Normington as Flute
- Barbara Jefford as Hippolyta
- Nicholas Selby as Egeus
- Hugh Sullivan as Philostrate

References

External links

- *A Midsummer Night's Dream* (http://www.imdb.com/title/tt0063297/) at the Internet Movie Database
- Screenonline - more information (http://www.screenonline.org.uk/tv/id/564686/index.html)

He Who Rides a Tiger

He Who Rides a Tiger	
Directed by	Charles Crichton
Produced by	David Newman
Written by	Trevor Peacock
Starring	Tom Bell Judi Dench Paul Rogers
Music by	Alexander Faris
Cinematography	John von Kotze
Distributed by	British Lion Films
Release date(s)	1965
Running time	103 mins
Country	United Kingdom
Language	English

He Who Rides a Tiger is a 1965 British crime drama directed by Charles Crichton, and starring Tom Bell and Judi Dench.[1]

Cast

- Tom Bell as Peter Rayston
- Judi Dench as Joanne
- Paul Rogers as Superintendent Taylor
- Kay Walsh as Mrs. Woodley
- Ray McAnally as Orphanage superintendent
- Jeremy Spenser as The Panda
- Peter Madden as Peepers Woodley
- Inigo Jackson as Detective Sergeant Scott
- Annette Andre as Julie
- Edina Ronay as Anna
- Nicolette Pendrell as Ellen
- Ralph Michael as Carter
- Frederick Piper as Mr. Steed
- Rita Webb as Flower seller
- Robin Hughes as Detective Sergeant Crowley

References

[1] http://ftvdb.bfi.org.uk/sift/title/36317

External links

- *He Who Rides a Tiger* (http://www.imdb.com/title/tt0060492/) at the Internet Movie Database
- http://www.goldonian.org/mem_sub_pages/films/terry_cain_hwrat.htm

A Study in Terror

A Study in Terror	

Directed by	James Hill
Produced by	Herman Cohen Michael Klinger Henry E. Lester
Written by	Arthur Conan Doyle Derek Ford Donald Ford
Starring	John Neville Donald Houston John Fraser Anthony Quayle Robert Morley Barbara Windsor Adrienne Corri Judi Dench
Music by	John Scott
Cinematography	Desmond Dickinson
Editing by	Henry Richardson
Distributed by	Columbia Pictures
Release date(s)	Jan. 1966
Running time	95 minutes
Country	United Kingdom
Language	English

A Study in Terror is a 1965 British thriller film directed by James Hill and starring John Neville as Sherlock Holmes and Donald Houston as Dr. Watson. It was filmed at Shepperton Studios, London, with some location work at Osterley House in Middlesex.

Synopsis

Although it is based on Conan Doyle's characters, the story is an original one, which has the famous detective on the trail of Jack the Ripper. In the dark alleys of nineteenth century London, the notorious Jack the Ripper committed a series of gruesome murders. The story of *A Study in Terror* challenges Sherlock Holmes to solve these horrific crimes. This leads Holmes through a trail of aristocracy, blackmail, and family insanity. Unlike Scotland Yard, and the real-life story, Holmes exposes the identity of the Ripper.

Cast

- John Neville — Sherlock Holmes
- Donald Houston — Dr. Watson
- John Fraser — Lord Carfax
- Anthony Quayle — Doctor Murray
- Barbara Windsor — Annie Chapman
- Adrienne Corri — Angela Osborne
- Frank Finlay — Inspector Lestrade
- Judi Dench — Sally Young
- Charles Régnier — Joseph Beck (as Charles Regnier)
- Cecil Parker — Prime Minister
- Barry Jones — Duke of Shires
- Robert Morley — Mycroft Holmes
- Dudley Foster — Home Secretary

Post-release history

In 1966, the film was novelized by Ellery Queen and Paul W. Fairman. The novelization is unusual in that it adds a framing story wherein Ellery Queen reads a manuscript that re-tells the actions of the film. The framing story was written by Ellery Queen and the novelization of the film itself by Fairman. Several plot points, including most notably the identity of the murderer, were altered for the novelization.

The Holmes-Ripper idea was later taken up in *Murder by Decree* (1978), in which Frank Finlay reprised his role as Lestrade and Anthony Quayle once again had an important part (though this time as Sir Charles Warren of Scotland Yard).

The film inspired the writing of *Sherlock Holmes's War of the Worlds*, blending the story of Sherlock Holmes and the world of H.G Wells' science fiction novel *The War of the Worlds*.

Soundtrack

"A Study in Terror" (1965) composed by John Scott conducting the Hollywood Symphony Orchestra (HSO 333)

External links

- *A Study in Terror* [1] at the Internet Movie Database
- *A Study in Terror* [2] at Allmovie
- *A Study in Terror* [3] at the TCM Movie Database

The Third Secret (film)

The Third Secret

Original poster

Directed by	Charles Crichton
Produced by	Robert L. Joseph Hugh Perceval
Written by	Robert L. Joseph
Starring	Stephen Boyd Pamela Franklin
Music by	Richard Arnell
Cinematography	Douglas Slocombe
Editing by	Frederick Wilson
Distributed by	20th Century Fox
Release date(s)	February 1964
Running time	103 minutes
Country	Great Britain
Language	English

The Third Secret is a 1964 British drama film directed by Charles Crichton. The screenplay by Robert L. Joseph focuses on an American newscaster who investigates the mysterious death of his psychoanalyst. According to the film there are three kind of secret; the First Secret you keep from strangers, the Second Secret you keep from your family and the Third Secret you keep from yourself.

Plot

Prominent London psychoanalyst Dr. Leo Whitset is discovered injured from a gunshot wound in his home by his housekeeper, and as he lies dying he whispers, "Blame no one but me." These words lead the coroner to rule the death a suicide, a verdict questioned by Alex Stedman, a popular American news commentator for British television who has been in therapy since the deaths of his wife and daughter. The dead man's fourteen-year-old daughter Catherine is certain he was murdered and enlists Alex's aid in finding the killer in order to preserve her father's reputation.

Catherine provides Alex with the names of three other patients. Sir Frederick Belline is a respected judge, Alfred Price-Gorham runs a prestigious art gallery with his assistant Miss Humphries, and Anne Tanner is a corporate secretary. As Alex investigates their backgrounds, he discovers each of the three, like himself, harbors a secret known only by the murdered man. Hoping to find more clues, Alex goes to the doctor's country home to search his files. There he learns Catherine was under her father's care, and when he confronts her she admits she killed the doctor when he threatened to send her to an institution to be treated for schizophrenia. While re-enacting the crime, Catherine stabs Alex and consequently is confined to a psychiatric hospital. Recovered from his wound, Alex visits her and promises to stay in touch.

Cast

- Stephen Boyd as Alex Stedman
- Pamela Franklin as Catherine Whitset
- Jack Hawkins as Sir Frederick Belline
- Richard Attenborough as Alfred Price-Gorham
- Diane Cilento as Anne Tanner
- Judi Dench as Miss Humphries
- Peter Copley as Dr. Leo Whitset

Production

Patricia Neal was cast as one of the doctor's patients, but all her scenes were cut from the film before it was released.[1]

Critical reception

Howard Thompson of *The New York Times* said the film "is recommended only to practitioners, patients and other moviegoers with a wry sense of humor. For in probing Freudian motivations and behavior to solve a crime, the picture obliquely strings out like a strand of loose spaghetti." He added, "[It] uncoils and meanders so deviously and pretentiously, and the dialogue slips into such metaphorical mishmash that the result is more often exasperating than entertaining — or convincing. The music, telegraphing dire things to come, is an atonal teaser." He concluded, "[It] presses so hard for conversational effect and mood that simple suspense occurs only toward the end. The denouement is a good, logical shocker — unsurprising if you study the smoothest talker of the lot."[2]

Variety called the film "an engrossing, if not altogether convincing, mystery melodrama of the weighty psychological school."[3]

TV Guide rated the film 2½ out of four stars and commented, "The episodic, talky drama has some moments that overcome the script's deficiencies, but the film tends to be pretentious and deliberately obtuse. The performances are only adequate. Franklin is particularly good, however, as the troubled young girl."[4]

Home media

The film was released on DVD in Region 1 on May 22, 2007. It is in anamorphic widescreen format with audio tracks and subtitles in English and Spanish. Bonus features include the original trailer, a stills gallery, and a second gallery featuring the film's original press book.

References

[1] AllMovie.com (http://www.allmovie.com/work/the-third-secret-113324)
[2] *New York Times* review (http://movies.nytimes.com/movie/review?res=9404EFDC1030E033A2575AC2A9629C946591D6CF)
[3] *Variety* review (http://www.variety.com/review/VE1117795638.html?categoryid=31&cs=1&p=0)
[4] *TV Guide* review (http://movies.tvguide.com/secret/review/111223)

External links

- *The Third Secret* (http://www.imdb.com/title/tt0058649/) at the Internet Movie Database

Article Sources and Contributors

Judi Dench *Source*: http://en.wikipedia.org/w/index.php?oldid=389936731 *Contributors*: "Jerk, Beefy!", *drew, 12 Basti, 23skidoo, 4meter4, 6afraidof7, A. Carty, AJ24, AKR619, Abbyvp, Achilles17, AdorableRuffian, Agiseb, Aiken drum, Ajbpearce, AlbertSM, AlexOvShaolin, Alientraveller, All Hallow's Wraith, Ameliorate!, Amoammo, Anark, AndTheCrowdGoesWild, Andrewwworth, Angmering, Angr, Angusmclellan, Arichikunoarikuto, Armeria, Art LaPella, Astorknlam, Autodidactyl, Awjvail, AxG, Azucar, BD2412, Balko Kabo, Bdesham, Belovedfreak, Ben davison, Berks105, Bigger digger, Billbert12, Bjones, Bluemover9999, BobPeck (rename), Bongwarrior, Boothferry, Bradley0110, Brandubh Blathmac, Brian1979, BrianFennell, BudMann9, Camboxer, Cambrant, Cambyses, Camembert, Candice, Carcharoth, Cburnett, Cccphd, Ccherry, Charlie White, Chienlit, Choess, Chris j wood, Cjc13, Cliffb, ColinFine, Collier626, Colonel Cow, Colonies Chris, Cookie90, Coolhawks88, Craigy144, Crazycomputers, CrossHouses, Crumbsucker, Crypticfirefly, CybDarla, Czyrko, D6, DJ Clayworth, DMacks, DStoykov, DTOx, Dale Arnett, Dashwortley, Davemcarlson, David crozer, DavidCane, DavidFarmbrough, Davis 11, Dbf.lib, Dcrossle, Deb, Deiz, Dell9300, Demiurge, Diet, DionysosProteus, Dizzy hiss, Djbj16, DocWatson42, DoctorWorm, DrBob, Drum guy, Dudesleeper, Duffman, Eagle Owl, Edgarde, Ejfetters, Elliemt, Emerson7, Emperor001, Erik16, Erolos, Eskimosfury, Euchiasmus, Evenmadderjon, ExRat, ExpressingYourself, FMAFan1990, Faigl.ladislav, Favonian, Ferrie, Fifty7, Figaro, Finzi03, Flyboysama, Forteblast, Fourthhorseman, Fratrep, Fschoenm, Gabbe, Garion96, GazzaStrips, Ghaly, Gimme danger, Gnowor, Goya.jolie, Gr8lyknow, GraceKat1981, Greg Godwin, Grstain, Guat6, Haemo, Haipa Doragon, Haldraper, Hamilton365, Hamiltonian, Handicapper, Happenstance, Harkey Lodger, Hatcrazy, Henry Merrivale, Heslopian, HexaChord, HornetMike, Hugh Mason, Ibagli, Icairns, Indialindy, Indyandnorbert, Ingolfson, Iridescent, Isis, Isopropyl, J Milburn, J-boogie, JJJJust, JP8543, Jack Cox, Jack O'Lantern, JackO'Lantern, JackofOz, Jaker5, Jamirocrazy, Jamquinbon, JanSuchy, Jason11MAFIABOY, Jay-W, Jdforrester, Jeff G., Jekman, Jevitop, Jihg, Jimknut, Jimmy Pitt, Jimregan, Jlittlet, JmT, Jmcd88, Joey80, Johann Wolfgang, John Thaxter, Joshuapaquin, Jpbowen, JuPitEer, Justme89, Jwalte04, Jzummak, K1Bond007, Kaly99, Kameyama, Katefan0, Kbthompson, Kchishol1970, Keith D, Kevin Steinhardt, Kilfoylea, Knavesdied, Kuru, Kyorosuke, LJade728, LaVidaLoca, Lang rabbie, Lauren, Le baron, Litalex, LiteraryMaven, Llowe2008, Lord Cornwallis, Ltrustno1l, Luk, Luke4545, Lukobe, Lumos3, MC MasterChef, MDCollins, Marcsin, Marek69, MarnetteD, MassimoAr, Mauitunes, Mav, MaxHund, Mayaw 99, Maziotis, Mebden, Merinda, Merlis4, Mfkirk, Mhkay, Michaelsbll, Mike309, Minnesotajohn29, Monnitewars, MovieMadness, Mrsdelahunty, Mrwojo, Muhgcee, Namzie11, Nandesuka, Necrothesp, Neddyseagoon, Nehrams2020, Neilbeach, NigelJ, Noboyo, Notheruser, Notjudyskid, October1990, Okino, Old Moonraker, Orbicle, Ottens, OverlordQ, Pa-merynaten, Pantaallou, Pascal.Tesson, Patrickmcg, Paul Carpenter, Pauljonlevy, Pcpcpc, Pdb781, Pegship, Philip Cross, Philthecow, Pianistdave, Piccadilly, Pperos, Prodego, Proteus, Pumplesmoo, Quadell, Quentin X, RBBrittain, RUL3R, Rachel1, Radiopathy, Rama's Arrow, Rebecca, Redrocketboy, Reguy3, Retroviseur, Rhindle The Red, Rhwsisson, Richardcarroll1981, Righty007, Rjwilmsi, Rms125a@hotmail.com, RobertG, Rogerd, Rosenknospe, Rossrs, Roundhouse0, RunningAway, RyanGerbil10, Rypcord, SDS, SP-KP, Saa19952, Saguamundi, Sam 1123, Savolya, Scog, Scottrb, Shantavira, ShelfSkewed, Shoaler, SkeletorUK, SkidzKid, Slawojarek, SmileyN, Smnafe1, Sophie, Stephenb, Steveking 89, Stoa, Stone, Sugarfish, Super Mario, Supercoop, TA-ME, Tad Lincoln, Talia679, Tassedethe, Tb240904, Teaberries123, Teapotgeorge, Textbook, The Almighty Creator, The Giant Puffin, The Madras, The Man in Question, The lake district, The28wall, Thegman99, Theoldgoat, Thismightbezach, Tide rolls, Tim!, Timbralls, Timdownie, Timrollpickering, Tinton5, Titocavalera, Tobin Richard, Tommy2010, TommyP, Tommyt, Tone, TonyW, Traxs7, Treybien, Tsango, Twix1875, Ulric1313, Ultraviolet scissor flame, UpDown, Varlaam, Veemonkamiya, Veledan, Vincej, Virek, WBardwin, Wai Hong, Who, WikiFlier, Wildhartlivie, Willhsmit, Willthacheerleader18, Woohookitty, Xevior, Xezbeth, Xover, Yamla, YeshuaDavid, Ygrasil, Yllosubmarine, Youtuberay, Yurik, Zerbey, Zoe, Zooweee, Zutopiaa, Zzyzx11, 478 anonymous edits

My Week with Marilyn *Source*: http://en.wikipedia.org/w/index.php?oldid=389807955 *Contributors*: Bbb23, Bovineboy2008, Lord Cornwallis, 2 anonymous edits

Jane Eyre (2011 film) *Source*: http://en.wikipedia.org/w/index.php?oldid=386172981 *Contributors*: Agiseb, Auntof6, Beemer69, Cirt, Katherinemusgrave, Lynskeyium, PollyAhn, TheMovieBuff, Vikeke, 2 anonymous edits

Nine (film) *Source*: http://en.wikipedia.org/w/index.php?oldid=389703716 *Contributors*: AbsoluteGleek92, AchimP, Adavidw, Ajd, Ajquioc, All Hallow's Wraith, Angel caboodle, Angelic-alyssa, AnmaFinotera, Artkopit, Artoasis, AyaK, BLGM5, BelzerBall, Benatfleshofthestars, Bender235, Bovineboy2008, Boxofficeguy, Ccacsmss, Cinemaniac86, Ckatz, Colfer2, Commander Shepard, Correogsk, Courcelles, Cybercobra, Daedalus969, Dan6hell66, David Rush, Dawi, Deanb, Djbj16, Djistus, DocWatson42, Donmike10, Doub95, Dylancraigboyes, EEMIV, Eastendersfreak, Emjaybee, EoGuy, Erianna, ExpressingYourself, Faithlessthewonderboy, Fierce Beaver, Freikorp, GDallimore, Gimmetoo, Greekboy, HamburgerRadio, Hullaballoo Wolfowitz, Hyju, IceUnshattered, Ilovemusicals, ItsTheClimb17, Jack Merridew, Jal11497, Jamamik, JamesLucas, Jamesbanesmith, Jason.cinema, JeanColumbia, Jo-pelrojta, JohnBlackburne, Johnny1971, Kernitou, Kiwiboy121, Konczewski, Krazycev13, Krisallenno1fanindaworld, Levibep92, Lewiscb, Lightmouse, LilHelpa, Marccontini, Marek69, MarkusBJoke, MartinVillafuerte85, Master Deusoma, MatthewWaller, MegaSloth, MiTfan3, Midhav Ravindran, MikeAllen, Movieguru2006, Music + Pageants, NewEnglandYankee, Nymf, ObsessiveJoBroDisorder, P. S. Burton, Paride81, Patrick, Pernelldh, Phaeton23, PoeticVerse, Polishedcamille808, PrisonMan, Quentin X, Quoth, Red-Blue-White, Roger McCoy, Romarth, Ron whisky, Rossrs, Secret Saturdays, Semari1, Sevilledade, SkyWalker, Smond359, Snottywong, Teatreez, Tethet2Tethet, TheMovieBuff, Tide rolls, Tkotw12, Trivialist, Trogga, Tvfreak1, Ulric1313, Urcolors, Valadius, Wikibarista, Woohookitty, Xandgood, Xcentaur, Yllosubmarine, Zombie433, 569 anonymous edits

Rage (2009 film) *Source*: http://en.wikipedia.org/w/index.php?oldid=385442673 *Contributors*: Darrenhusted, Firsfron, FrankRizzo2006, GMTX, Horkana, Ragethemovie, Robert100chat, Saa19952, SkyWalker, Tim!, Wakeyjamie, Wik4, Wildhartlivie, 18 anonymous edits

Quantum of Solace (film) *Source*: http://en.wikipedia.org/w/index.php?oldid=260425328 *Contributors*: -5-, 007-Goldeneye, 007Fan, 16@r, 23skidoo, 24JackBauer, 2D, 2T, 762b3918, 97198, A Nobody, AEMoreira042281, ANGGUN, Ab1, Ablahblahblah, Abomasnow, Acaeton, Acebloo, Achybreakyheart, AdamDeanHall, Adi39, Adrian Parratt, Aerodynamicnikobellick2009, Agent007ravi, Agentsands, Agrumer, Ahoerstemeier, Akyoyo94, Alanraywiki, Alansohn, Aleksa Lukic, Alex Gabriel, Alex.muller, Alex250P, AlexLevyOne, Alexanderkg, Alienautic, Alientraveller, Almost Anonymous, Amatulic, Amyreelz, Anaxial, AndrewHowse, Andrewdyt, Andrzejbanas, Andy, Animum, Anirvan, Anna Lincoln, Anonymi, Anonymous Dissident, Anshuk, Antonio Prates, Apparition11, Apstyle, Arbero, Arknascar44, Aronnp, Asteriks, AtheWeatherman, Augustburns007, Auric, Autonova, Avala, AxG, BD2412, Badgernet, Bagaaak, Banano03, Bart-16, Beardscratcher, Beautiful so ur, Belinrahs, Bencey, Benchrispicklaw, Benjamintchip, Bennish, Betty Logan, Bgtgwazi, Bhalli619, Bigbmc26, Bignole, Bigpatpunisher, Bihco, Billyrageguy, Blacwainwright, Blolz, BloodDoll, Blueboy96, Bobo192, Bobtedvoom001, Bombayspeaks, Bond212223, Bondfanforever, Bonding for Today, Bonduk7, Boombaard, BorgQueen, Borgx, Bovineboy2008, Brandon, Breakinguptheguy, Brinkeguthrie, Broncopaul, Broncostar, Bronks, BrownHairedGirl, BrownHornet21, Buckaroo54, Butterscotch, C+C, C.byron, CPTGbr, Cablebfg, Cadabena, Caiaffa, Camo111, Canterbury Tail, Capricorn42, Captain panda, Caralho, Carta025, Cat Tricks, Cavie78, Charlotte Potnoodle, Chee-sen, Cheesechinch, Chelseageorge, Chensiyuan, Cherylweedy, Chris 42, Chris Halpin (2nd), Chris huh, Christianster45, CieloEstrellado, CillanXC, Ckatz, Clarince63, Clarityfiend, Clashfrankcastle, Classicpolo, Cliff smith, Cloudbound, Clpo13, Coffin, ColdFusion650, Comicist, Commander Shepard, ContinuityOrder, Cooldude3240, Cop 663, Coquimbano, Count aj, Cperrott wiki, Crappertay, Croctotheface, Cst17, Cyclone49, CzechOut, D4tis, DHN, DaDogG, Dakwithaps3, Dale Arnett, Damian Thorne, Danbarnesdavies, Dancter, Daniel 1992, Danlev, Danno uk, Darrenhusted, Darryl.matheson, Darth Panda, Davedash, Daveyjones182, David A McIntee, David Gerard, Db099221, DeWaine, Decltype, Del91, Dell9300, Dentren, Dergel, Deus257, Digata200, Dirtyharry1994, Disco Volante, Discospinster, Dithridge, Dlr192, DocYako, Doczilla, Don-Don, DonQuixote, Donmike10, DoubleBlue, Douken, Dpaajones, Dr. Blofeld, DrKiernan, DrOxacropheles, Dravecky, Drjayphd, Dryranm, Dspradau, Duncancumming, DurinsBane87, Dvyuk, Dynesclan, EVula, Ealgian, Eddie6705, Editor510, EditorGuy07, Edlitz36, Edmund XXIII, Eeekster, Eickenberg, El Beno Returns, El Greco, Elassint, Ellamosi, Elsonlau, Em-jay-es, Emancipator, Emperor001, Empty2005, Emurphy42, EncMstr, Engelberg, Englishrockgirl, Epbr123, Eqdoktor, Eric-Wester, Erik, EscapingLife, Esp rus2, Eugene-elgato, Evans1982, Evening Times, Excirial, Extraordinary, Falcon9x5, Fastily, Fearlessfool, Fethers, FightTheDarkness, Fightingirish, Fish and karate, Fish1941, Fitzochris, Flashpenny, Foolsfoolsfoolsfools, Fourthhorseman, Fram, Frank980, FrankCM, FrankRizzo2006, Frankie0607, FreeMorpheme, Funnyman79, Gaia Octavia Agrippa, Gaius Cornelius, Galahaut, Gamer007, Garik, Garik 11, Gary King, Gatolanudo, Gaunt, Ged UK, GeneralBelly, Generic, Gerrardperrett, Gilliam, Glane23, GlassCobra, GlobetrottingAussie, GoatGod, Gogo Dodo, Goyo1980, Gpsov, GraemeLeggett, Gran2, Granpuff, Grayjay90, Graymornings, Gregory j, Grsz11, Gsamit, Gunslinger, GuruAskew, Gwernol, Haji11, Hammersfan, Harkers007, Hateless, Hawaiian717, Hbdragon88, Head & Munky, Hektor, HenryPage23, Hereford, HexaChord, Highfields, Hiphats, Holmes3000, Holzy1139, Huangdi, Hubier, Huckwhitney, Hugochiva93, Hymie8, II MusLiM HyBRiD II, IW.HG, Ibbn, Icarus Warrior, Idontknow324, Igoldste, Igordebraga, Impala2009, ImperatorExercitus, Imthemonsta, Inanimate photographer, Inmateofcomedy41, Inqvisitor, Invincible Ninja, Iridescent, Irishguy, It Is Me Here, Italian5talli0n5, J.delanoy, J4m35 80nd, JCRendle, JFSanta, JForget, JJGoldenEye, JQF, JRRobinson, Jabbasi, Jackaman, Jake Wartenberg, James Emtage, James086, JamesBHunt, JamesBWatson, JamesR, Jamesontai, Jan eissfeldt, Japanscot, Jason.cinema, Jatopian, Jay-r101, JayPenn, Jbird669, Jc-SOCO, Jedi Striker, JettaMann, Jezzabr, Jfdarmo, Jhsounds, Jimbracks, Jjmoore, Jkp1187, Jmcd88, Jnate19, Jogers, John Kenneth Fisher, Johnnyvilay, Johnuniq, Jojhutton, Jollypanda123, Jom, Jordancelticsfan, Jordybhoy, Jose the Jalapeno, Joshdboz, JulianHensey, Junafani, Jusdafax, JuventusGamer, Jwmoreau, K1Bond007, Karan9005, Karaokequeen3, Karatemanchan37, Kartikey12, Keilana, Kelvinc, Keraunoscopia, Kevin, Kevin Tod Haug, Keysthird22, Khoikhoi, Khunglongcon, Kierant, Kieranthompson, Kingdrakarthik, Kingscorp1712, Kjmathew, Klapper, KnightRider, Ko.S.ystem.OV@, Koavf, Kollision, Konczewski, Ktalon, Kuralyov, Kuru, Kuruvi949, KyotoKobe, LGreen29, Lamro, Latics, LeaW, LeaveSleaves, Leemorrison, Legend83, Leo11, Leonidas23, Leonsbuddydave, Lesonyra, Leuqarte, Lineface, LiteraryMaven, Ljastangs21, Locke Cole, Lofty, Londo06, Lord Cornwallis, Lordz, Losha Master, Love.of.bond.of.love, Lowellian, Lt. penguin, Lugnuts, M-2, MAdaXe, MJisnotmylover, Mac Davis, Madchester, Madeem99, Maestro25, Mallanox, Maniahmed, Manofthings, Marc-Olivier Pagé, Marcd30319, Mark83, Markczel, Markemory, Markhh, Markwpowell64, Martarius, Martin451, Martiniminister, Marwood, Math Champion, Mathew shires, Mathewshires, Mattlaabs, McSly, Melesse, MementoVivere, Messy Thinking, MetalHeadMat, MetroPlayer, Mhking, MickMacNee, Mikeo, Milkshake6789, Millahnna, Mineros, Minusf, Monzonda, Morrad, Movieguru2006, Mr-susans, Mr. Beans69, Mr. Laser Beam, Mr. Nick46, Mr. diddlydooskins, MrClarkWithoutRemorse, MrMagoo, Mrjbond007, Msa1701, Mtmelendez, Muso99, Myscrnnm, Mzmadmike, NateDan, Naughtkelvin, NavarroJ, NawlinWiki, Nearly famous writer, Necronaut, Neelix, Nehrams2020, Nellynel7619, Newkirk Plaza David, Nick72, NickD531, Nikku BR, Nintendere, NotMuchToSay, Nsign, NuclearWarfare, Nw adelman, Nytimes19992000, Ohconfucius, Oi bizatchnitch, Ojjy27, Oldmanuk, Omegium, Onebravemonkey, Onesius, Oonacchaplin, Oosh, Oscarthecat, P. Buasuwan, Painjoiker, Palfrey, Paste, Patar knight, Patrickneil, Patrickrox11, PaulLargo, Pedro thy master, Philip Trueman, Piano non troppo, Plastikspork, Po8crg, Polylerus, Poptartz13, Possecomitatus, Powerofjuju, Pp60, Ppntori, PranksterTurtle, Prem555, PrimeHunter, Princeajb 007, ProfJebus, Prolog, Ps3sonyrules, Pyrrhus16, Qoscoolqos, QuasiAbstract, Quentin X, RJNeb2, RKAvatar, RKSony12, RKcoolo, Radon210, Radvideogamer, RainbowOfLight, Rambo14392, RandomXYZb, Rc52, Rdhinakar, ReWinD, Redranger241, Remurmur, Renegade Raconteur, Rettetast, Revelian, Reza 2638, Rich Farmbrough, Richard Arthur Norton (1958-), Richard j uk, Richardpcox, Righty007, Riksweeney, RingbearerNZ, Rishoutfield, Rjeong, Rjwilmsi, Rkunreal, Roaring Siren, RobertMfromLI, Robertcoolo, Rocky stallone, Rockysmile11, Ron B. Thomson, Rotring, Rrburke, RunningAway, Ryankat25, Ryanthedon, S@bre, SVG, Sachinkilkile, Sam26681, Samil20, Sammyd487,

Sanford34, Sanfranman59, Saurabh523, Scarian, Sceptre, Scjessey, Scoutersig, Screen42, Seaphoto, Seattle Skier, SecretAgentBond, Severo, Shadowman99, Shagojyo1, Shoito, Signalhead, SilkTork, Sillywalker, Simon Beavis, SimpleJYouTube, Sina, Sionus, Skomorokh, SkyWalker, Slaja, SluggoOne, Slyraccoon007, SmallPotatoes, Smithx123, Snowybeagle, Sohailstyle, Some guy, SomeGuy11112, SpOnGeFaN818, Spartan4077, Spcleddy, SpecialWindler, Speedboy Salesman, Spellcast, SpiderJon, SpikeToronto, Spock2266, Spoonkymonkey, Sportomanokin, Squishy Vic, Staffwaterboy, Staka, Statostatostato, Steel, Stephaniexoxo, Steve, Steven Evens, Stevo1000, Stormek, Stwalkerster, Styrofoam1994, Subhaan123, Sumahoy, SuperMarioMan, Supergeek Mike, Supermanjovi, Swpb, Synchronism, T1v37r, TDogg310, TG193, TMC1982, TaerkastUA, Tassedethe, TaylorLaabs, Tds247, Tedbun, Telecineguy, Tellyaddict, Tewfik, The Anome, The C of E, The Dark Apocalypse, The Evil Spartan, The Giant Puffin, The Real Jean-Luc, The Thing That Should Not Be, The undertow, TheCharmingMan, TheCosmicFrog, TheMovieBuff, TheRealFennShysa, Thefourdotelipsis, TheologyJohn, ThinkBlue, Tilefish, Timeineurope, Timrollpickering, Tiswaser, Tobogganoggin, Tobyink, Tocamak, Tom, Tommyt, Tomypaika, Tony Sidaway, Tony1, Tonytam, Tonywiki, Topperray, Touch Of Light, Tphi, TracyLinkEdnaVelmaPenny, Treybien, Trident13, TriiipleThreat, True Pagan Warrior, Tschow, Tsunamishadow, TubularWorld, Tukogbani, TutterMouse, Twitty666, Txomin, Typ932, Typhoon966, U, UKER, UNK222, Ultraviolet scissor flame, Universal Hero, Useight, VKemyss, Victory93, Vid26, VisitBritain, Viva Chile, Walkiped, Warlordwolf, Watsona.2, Weatherman15, Websurfer246, Wendroa, Wheel Bound, Whiley2008x, Whitmore 8621, WickerGuy, Widgett, WikiTome, Wikieditor06, Wikinator ME, WikipedianMarlith, Wikispirit 99, Wikiteur, William Flowers, WilliamJE, Wimt, Wneedham02, Woodsyblue, WookieInHeat, Wordsmith, World Cinema Writer, X201, Xhienne, Xxxsacheinxxx, Yachtsman1, Yankeyfan315, Yerpo, YesMapRadio, Ylee, Yorkshiresky, Youlittlehandsomeguy, Youwillnotgortea, Z11100, ZZninepluralZalpha, Zain1987, Zaop-d, Zatch908, Zeality, Zencato, Zik2, Zolotros, Zr2d2, Zzzsleepzzz, 2374 anonymous edits

Go Inside to Greet the Light *Source*: http://en.wikipedia.org/w/index.php?oldid=334109622 *Contributors*: Dravecky, GregorB, Lugnuts, Mebden

Notes on a Scandal (film) *Source*: http://en.wikipedia.org/w/index.php?oldid=390554652 *Contributors*: 8474tim, AJ42, AN(Ger), Absurdtrousers, Abtinb, Acc78, Albalb, AlbertSM, Allie cabab, Amphytrite, Andrzejbanas, Angr, Anonymous from the 21st century, Araker, Arbero, Ashleyy osaurus, BillSung, Carabinieri, Carter.charles, Casliber, Chris the speller, Chubbles, Cliffb, Commander Shepard, DagnyB, Danielba894, Darkieboy236, Davemcarlson, David Gerard, Dawkeye, Dcrossle, Deb, Doub95, Dr. Blofeld, Dude 0 man, EamonnPKeane, Eilraet, Electrosaurus, Enpitsu, Erik, Evanreyes, Exploding Boy, FMAFan1990, Fieryrogue, Fuxx, Fxcastellanos, Haiduc, Haldraper, Hapleworth, Harrigan, Henning M, Ianacts, Ilesmark, Ilikedietcola, Irk, It Is Me Here, Jaqen, Jevitop, Jsl83, Keimzelle, KenelmJames, Kitfaustus, Kpetrov, Light Bulb, Lucian C., MartinPoulter, Monday Addams, Morpose, Moshe Constantine Hassan Al-Silverburg, Mr pand, NWill, Naniwako, Nehrams2020, Ngc1976, Nick Number, NorthernThunder, Nqnpipnr, Orbicle, Patrick, Pegship, Phantomsnake, Pricer1980, Quentin X, Redl@nds597198, ReeseM, Rjgibb, Rjwilmsi, Rmannion, Rosalbissima, Rosebud953, SGGH, Sgporsche48, Sprky182, Supertigerman, SurvivorGuy99, TTTV, Tassedethe, Teatreez, Tellerman, Theangelofdarkness, Tony Sandel, Tpbradbury, Treybien, Turkeyphant, User0529, WarthogDemon, Xinoph, Zzuuzz, 134 anonymous edits

Casino Royale (2006 film) *Source*: http://en.wikipedia.org/w/index.php?oldid=390731636 *Contributors*: *Kat*, -Majestic-, .:Alex:., 2.7182V, 2005, 23skidoo, 4sure, 5ko, 6afraidof7, 790, 97198, A Kiwi, A Nobody, A man alone, A380 Fan, Aardark, AaronCBurke, Acaeton, Accountforthesolepurposeofvandalising, Achle, Achmelvic, Adam Brink, AdamDeanHall, Adb91, Agent007ravi, Agentsands, Agustinaldo, Ahs4y, Alan smithee, Alaric Deschain, Alex earlier account, Alex43223, Alientraveller, AlistairMcMillan, Allstarecho, Alsotop, Ambrozd, Anaxial, Andres, AndrewHowse, Andrewferrier, Andrzejbanas, Andy, Andymarczak, Anetode, Angmering, Angryxpeh, Anirbans, Anirudhmylaster, AnonEMouse, Another Believer, Anothertruthteller, Apoltix, Arathon, Arbero, Argash, Arjun01, Arman88, Armchair info guy, Arojr, ArtistScientist, Asado, AskFranz, Asphyxx, Assassin Droid, Astonmartin, Atlan, Atlastawake, Avala, Averette, Axem Titanium, Ayrshire--77, Azfan, Azucar, BQZip01, Backpackadam, Banaticus, Bap07, Bart-16, Bballindil32, Beano73, Beardo, Beetstra, Belovedfreak, Bergsten, Betty Logan, Bhumiya, Bibliomaniac15, Bigger Boss, Bignole, Bihco, Biiru, Billydeeuk, Binadot, Bjones, BlackDevil, Blacksqr, BlaiseFEgan, Blolz, Bluepea, Boadrummer, BobTheMad, Bobmack89x, Boffy b, Bonding for Today, Bonduk7, Bongopinky, BorgQueen, Bovineboy2008, Boxing245, Boyar, BrainBlessed, BrckoGOS, Brian Welch, Brighterorange, Brockfreak007, Broncopaul, Bsiatadshmia, Bushcarrot, C Ronald, C.byron, CO, CR85747, Calbookaddict, Calliopejen1, Calmer Waters, Camcallister, Camembert, Canadian-Bacon, Canterbury Tail, CapDac, Capedia, Capricorn42, Carbon-16, CartmanUK26, Casino royale casino royale, Caspar esq., Cbarbry, Cbrown1023, Cburnett, CharlotteWebb, Chensiyuan, Chicago103, Chicagofan01, Cholmes75, Chris 42, Chris huh, Chris the speller, Chrism, Christian75, Christopher Kraus, Chucky Cosmo, Cinemaretro, Cjung89, Ck lostsword, Ckatz, Clarityfiend, Cliff smith, Clinevol98, Clq, Cmdrjameson, Cobaltcigs, Codenamecuckoo, Col3h, ColdFusion650, Collinf, Comicman345, Commander Keane, Connerybond1962, Connorhays, ConradKilroy, Cooldude3240, Corms, Count de Ville, Cowcow, CrazyInSane, Creepy Crawler, Croctotheface, Cruz-iglesia, Crzycheetah, Cshay, Cubs Fan, Cueball8384, Cunard, CyberSkull, Cyclone49, CyclopsScott, D4thking, DEastman, DTM, DVD Smith, Dabomb199620, Dale Arnett, Damien Shiest, Dan100, DanJ, Dancter, DanielHawking, Danner578, Dannyg007, Darrenhusted, Dave3141592, David A McIntee, David Edgar, David Gerard, Davidhorman, Davidkazuhiro, Dcarrano, Dct, DeWaine, Deagle AP, Del91, Dell9300, Delldot, Deltabeignet, Designbooth, Desk Jockey, Dexxa, Dhp1080, Diablo1024, Diberri, Directormtb, Disco Volante, Dismas, Dispenser, Dmondom, DoctorWho42, Dominicbillings, Donald McKinney, Donarreiskoffer, Donmike10, Dopefish, Dorftrottel, DoubleBlue, DoubleCross, DougM, Douna, DownwardSpiralV1, Dpaajones, Dr who1975, Dr. Blofeld, DrKiernan, Dramagirlforjesus, Dreaded Walrus, Drmies, Drwhotheinvasion, Dudesleeper, Duffman, Duja, Duncancumming, Dungodung, Dunph, DurinsBane87, Dynesclan, EJBanks, Ealgian, Easchiff, Eboli, Ebyabe, Ed, Ed Fitzgerald, Ed g2s, EdGl, EdTrist, Edcolins, Edlitz36, Efe foksy, Eggman183, Ekedolphin, El Destructeso, El Greco, Elil, Eloipfeiffer, Elysdir, Emperor001, Empoor, Energyboy, EnsRedShirt, Epbr123, Epf, Epolk, Eqdoktor, Erc, Erik, Esaborio, Etcwebb, EternalWashuFanboy, Ethikos, Evagfan, Evanmc, Evanreyes, Extraordinary, Extraordinary Machine, F McGady, F15 sanitizing eagle, FMAFan1990, FT2, Fanboyz87, Father McKenzie, FayssalF, FeldBum, Ffgamera, Fhb3, Fhqwhgads000, Films addicted, Finiteyoda, Fireaxe888, Fistjedi, Flashpenny, FlashpointDFW, Flex2008, Florian BAY, Folksong, Fordmadoxfraud, Formeruser-81, Formeruser-82, Forteblast, Fourthhorseman, Franck Drake, FrankRizzo2006, Fratrep, Freddiegirlmercury, Fredler Brave, Fredrik, Freemarket, Freshh, Fro81, Fvasconcellos, Fxer, G.bargsnaffle, GMc, GagHalfrunt, Gaius Cornelius, Ganglandboss, Garik 11, Gavjudge, Geniac, Georgebrind, Gero, Gerph, Ghirlandajo, Gideondev, Gifford924, Ginsengbomb, Girolamo Savonarola, Gnarlodious, Gogo Dodo, GoldDragon, Goodge Street, Goodnightmush, Govontario, GraemeL, Granpuff, Graveenib, Greatrobo76, Greg321, Gregfitzy, GroundZ3R0 002, Grunners, Gubarenko, Gunmetal Angel, Gunslinger, GuruAskew, Gurudata, Guy14, Gwernol, Gzkn, H2g2bob, Hal987, Halsteadk, Hammersfan, Hammett9, Hanswaarle, Harimau, Harleytarantina, Harro5, HarryKG, Harryboyles, Hateless, Havarhen, HawkeAnyone, Hbdragon88, Heart Like a Wheel, Hektor, Helixblue, Hereford, Hig Hertenfleurst, Hiphats, Hippi ippi, Hnsampat, Hobbies.nes, Hofro, Holocron, Holynightfever, Hu12, Hubier, Hughezy, Husky, Hypnosifl, IAMTrust, IKato, Iamhungey, Ian Rose, Ianhurley, Icarus of old, Igordebraga, Imacphee, Imgroup, Impala2009, Imperatore, Indigodelta, Infection123, Info@pinewoodshepperton.com, Inkypinky, Inqvisitor, Ipi2m2n, Irishguy, IronGargoyle, IstvanWolf, IvanLanin, J Milburn, J.delanoy, JBK405, JBond5, JCRendle, JHFTC, JLaTondre, JP Watrin, JPX7, JQF, JRRobinson, Jackyan, Jacoplane, JadailyTCU, Jake0711, Jalabi99, Jalans, James Emtage, James2006789, JamesNK, Jamesgibbon, Jamyskis, Jason One, Jay-W, Jayden54, Jcating12, Jeb69, Jedd the Jedi, Jedi Striker, Jellypuzzle, Jeremypnet, Jeysaba, Jgoulden, Jimbracks, Jimknut, Jimmy Bond of Royale, Jkelly, Jmca567, JobSmee, JoeHillen, Joelvanatta, Johann Schlinker, John254, Jonathan.s.kt, Jorburn993, Jordancelticsfan, Joshafina, Jovianeye, Jp.bc, JuJube, Julesd, Juliancolton, Justin Herbert, Jwk3, K. Annoyomous, K1Bond007, Ka'Jong, Kaaveh Ahangar, Kablammo, Kahar5, Kalaong, Karl eichholtz 13, KarlFrei, Katana314, Kawayama, Kbdank71, Kbolino, Kbthompson, KeithB, KenL, Kennedy, 007, Kerowyn, Kesla, Kevin Myers, Kicking222, Kieranthompson, Kisssule4ka, Kitkatcrazy, Kizor, Kollision, Kostantino888Z, Krabs514, Krabs515, Kschreck0105, Kubrickfan83, Kuddenchristo, Kuralyov, Kuru, Kvasir, Kvkhozein, KyraVixen, Kzollman, LORD17712772, Lady Aleena, Lamro, Laonoodlekeemow, Latin Guy, Lauriem804, Lavenderbunny, LeChiffre, LeaW, LeaveSleaves, Len Raymond, Leon..., Lfh, Lgl6spears, Liam Skoda, Liamabob, Life of Riley, Lightmouse, Ligulem, Linas, Lincolnshep, Liontamer, Liquidous Snake, Lloydpick, Logitec007, Londo06, Longquando, Lordz, Lowellian, Lproven, Ltrustno1l, Lugnuts, Luigibob, Luk, LukeTheSpook, Luna Santin, Lynch9000s, MAG1, MER-C, Macfrugal, Madchester, Maelwys, Maestro25, Magister Mathematicae, Magyar14, Mallanox, Mandarax, Mang0es, Mankar Camoran, Marc-Olivier Pagé, Mark5677, Mark83, MarkBA, Markczel, Marktreut, MarnetteD, Marquis De Carabas, Marskell, MartinP1983, MartinSFSA, Martpol, Mashedpotatowithsomegravy, Master Deusoma, Mathew shires, Mattberk26, Mattgenne, MatttiMatti0000, Mausy5043, MaxPowar, Mbsteger82, McLeod1, McSly, Mchowdhury234, Mclean007, Mclentch, Mcwebeditor, MegX, Megan1967, Meheller, Mel Etitis, Melly42, Mentality, Mervyn, Mezigue, Mgiganteus1, Mhambster, Mhking, Mhous616, MiAnRo, MiLo28, Michael Devore, Michael Zimmermann, Michaelas10, MickO'Bants, Mike Payne, Mike Selinker, Mikeyickey, Minghong, Mister macphisto, Misterwindupbird, Misza13, Mitsukai, Mlaffs, Mlibby, Mm 202, Momusufan, Moneyfink, Monsieur Belanger, Mooman95, Morrad, Mount Molehill, Moviefan1, Mpj17, Mr. Blake, Mr. XYZ, MrClarkWithoutRemorse, MrMagoo, Mrjbond007, Mrmiscellanious, Mrowland92, Myscrnnm, Mzmadmike, NaBUru38, NastalgicCam, Natalya, Nathparkling, Nehrams2020, NeilUK, Neilc, Netoholic, Newone, Neznanec, Nich148 9, Nick, Nick R, Nick San, Nickptar, Nickycaulfield, Nicolas suszczyk, Night Gyr, Nije bitno..., Nishkid64, Norkus007, Norm mit, NotMuchToSay, Noz92, Nsayer, Nsign, OOODDD, OPaul, Oatmeal batman, Obi-WanKenobi-2005, ObiWan353, Odie5533, Oedii, Olexandr Kravchuk, Omnijohn, Omphaloscope, Onimaster, Onionmon, Online casino Casino royale, Orphan Wiki, Osaboramirez, Oscar Sanchez, Oscarthecat, Otherone, Ou tis, Ouishoebean, Owen, PBP, Pabouk, Pank 619, ParisianBlade, Passive, Paste, Patrick, Paul A, PaulLargo, PaxEquilibrium, Pd THOR, Pedroagpt, Pegship, Peppage, Pepperoniann, Peter Harriman, PhantomObserver, Phantomsnake, Phil500, Philipwhiuk, Picaroon, Picoy, Pkapitola, Plange, Plasticspork, Plasticup, Plm209, Pmj, Pogokidd, Pogu, Possecomitatus, Ppntori, Preacherdoc, Prem555, President David Palmer, Presuming Ed, Prince Godfather, Princeajb 007, Prodego, ProhibitOnions, Prolog, Purealex, Q8-falcon, Quadell, Quentin X, Quiddity, R Bartholomew, R'n'B, RKAvatar, RKcoolo, RWyn, Rackstraw, Radagast, Rahulswarnkar, Rait, Raul654, Raven4x4x, RazorICE, Rdsmith4, Rdunn, RealityTelevisionFan, Redeeming Light, Republic of China, Retired username, Rettetast, RevelationDirect, Rex1 wiki*, Reywas92, Rhindle The Red, RicJac, Rich Farmbrough, Richard D. LeCour, RichiH, Riley Jenkins, Rillian, RiseDarthVader, River4, Rje, Rjwilmsi, Roastytoast, RobWill80, Robaato, RobertG, Robferny, Robin Kerrison, Rock God162, Rocky143, Roger Roger, Rollingstonesfan99, Ross angus, Rotring, RoyBoy, Rpab, Rray, Rrburke, Rtcpenguin, RunningAway, Ruud Koot, Ryan-D, Ryankat25, Ryanthedon, S25E, S@bre, SD6-Agent, SG03, ST47, Salgueiro, Sam Blacketer, Sam Hocevar, Sam Li, SamKey uk, SandyGeorgia, Sarolite, Sasuke3, Saxonviolence, Scarythought12, Sceptre, Schizobullet, Scorpion0422, Seanmilloy, Seaphoto, Sebastian Goll, Sedian, Ser Amantio di Nicolao, Seraph 31, Sfnhltb, Shadowjams, Shanes, Sheed92, ShelfSkewed, Shiyang, Shoemortgage, Shulzi, Sietse Snel, Sillygostly, Sim0n20, Simon Beavis, Simon porkpie, Simonte2006, SimpleJYouTube, Sin-man, Sina, Sintonak.X, Sir Jimmy, Sir-john, SkerHawx, Skier Dude, Skrooball, SkyWalker, Skypurevis, Slipperyweasel, Smith03, Smp63, Smukles, Smurrayinchester, Snigbrook, Sniper 99, Socrates2008, Soheilm3, Sojin, Soupy12345, Sparklingjacket, SpecialWindler, Splamo, Spookyadler, Springhill40, Squeezeweasel, Standaboveitmanyoyo2, Stebbins, Steffie Laurent, Steh-fan, Stemonitis, StephenBuxton, Stephenb, SteveCrook, Stevepalmer101, Steveweiser, Storytellershrink, Str1977, Su.iss, Sugar Bear, Sujayt, Sumahoy, SunDragon34, SuperEddieZ, Superman8012, Susfele, Susurrus, Swainstonation, Swat671, SymiLover, SynergyBlades, T1980, TFOWR, TG193, TKD, TMC1982, Tailkinker, Tanthalas39, Taufiq2u, Taylor27nufc, Tcncv, Tcpekin, Tech77jp, Teddylayne, Telecineguy, Telephon, Templarion, Tenpoundnote, Teresa44, Tetzcatlipoca, The Anome, The Filmaker, The Giant Puffin, The JPS, The Last Act, The Man in Question, The Moving Finger Writes, The lastquincy, The monkeyhate, The time reaper, TheLateDentarthurdent, TheMovieBuff, TheRealFennShysa, TheSeer, Theflamehaired1, Thefourdotelipsis, Thename'sdante, Theprecious, Thethug89, Thetravellinggourmet, ThisIsJustASagaNow, Thomas Connor, ThomasCrown76, Threeafterthree, Thricecube, Thunderwing, Ticonderoga, Tilefish, Timc, Timothy Titus, Timrollpickering, Tms92, Tnoren, Tom, Tommy2010, Tommy23, Tommyt, Tomsalinsky, Tomtheman5, Tomtre, TonicBH, Tonster, Tony1, Tonywalton, Tpbradbury, Tpoore1, Treisijs, TrevorX, Trident13, TriiipleThreat, Trivialist, Triwbe, Truthiness Jones, Turlo Lomon, Tvarnoe, Typhoon966, UKER, Ulflarsen, Ultraviolet scissor flame, Uranium grenade, Utcursch, Uucp, VK35, VLynd, Vald, Valleyraver13, Valters, VanDenVan, Vanderdecken, Vapour, Vaughan Pratt, Vaughtton, VectorD, Veinor, Verne Equinox, Victory93, VikingLAB79, Viper Daimao, VodkaJazz, VolatileChemical, Voldemore, Voomby, Voracious reader, Voyagerfan5761, WCityMike, WIKI-GUY-16, Wahkeenah, Wai Hong, Waleed Baig, Wantsshort, Watsona.2, Websurfer246, Whataboutbob, WhisperToMe, Whitchurch,

Whitmore 8621, WickerGuy, Wiki Greek Basketball, Wiki Raja, Wiki07, Wikiburger, Willbonsmann, Willkm, Wimt, Winter04, WoodElf, Woohookitty, Wordsmith, World Cinema Writer, Wprlh, Wrad, Wwoods, Wythong, X201, Xaurtmj, Xezbeth, Xinoph, Xlyr, Xmas1973, XxAvalanchexX, Xxxsacheinxxx, YUL89YYZ, Yamla, Ybk33, Yellow Ant, Yeyewa, Yiazmat, Ylee, Yorkshiresky, YourMessageHere, Yuri Kenobi, Z3u2, ZRetro, ZZninepluralZalpha, Zahid Abdassabur, ZaidAhmed, Zeality, Zencato, ZeroOne, ZimZalaBim, Zingi, Zmost22, Zoe, Zondor, Zootm, Zotdragon, Zumbo, Zzyzx11, 2607 anonymous edits

The Magic Roundabout (film) *Source*: http://en.wikipedia.org/w/index.php?oldid=380235179 *Contributors*: (jarbarf), 031586, 041744, AVM, Adaobi, Addicktt, Aeusoes1, Ahoerstemeier, Alex43223, Alphachimp, Altzinn, AmbroseBChirp, Andrzejbanas, Andrés D., Andyman123, Ann Stouter, Bakilas, Beardo, Bigel977, Birger Fricke, Blackbone 5000, Bluerules, Bobet, BubbleDude22, Carinemily, Carlwev, Cat's Tuxedo, Chris Bainbridge, Clairebray79, Clayclayclay, Cooksey, Corvidae682, Cwitty, DJ Clayworth, Dadude3320, Damonkeyman889944, Darkness2005, David Gerard, DigitalCatalyst, Djrobgordon, Downwards, Efyoo, Electricbassguy, Esn, Fang Aili, Flowerparty, Fourohfour, Getcrunk, GrahamHardy, Granpuff, Grstain, HalfShadow, Harmony Melody Guy, Harryboyles, Hitrish, IKR1, Immblueversion, Invincible Ninja, Jay-W, Jean-Jacques Georges, Josh Parris, Jumping cheese, JustAGal, Kassjab, Kazvorpal, Kc007, Kelly Martin, Kicking222, Killing Vector, Koavf, Kollision, Korg, Krazykillaz, Kwsn, Lemuria13, Leolaursen, Lightwing1988, Lovely Head, Lumos3, Martpol, Master of Puppets, McGeddon, MegX, Menzies7, Mewtwowimmer, Mike Peel, Movingimage, Mrstonky, Musicinfluence, Nathen, Nehrams2020, Nejee16, Nekura, Nick, NrDg, Oatmeal batman, Olivier, PMDrive1061, Pafcool2, Pattar, Pizzahutpanpizza, Poopdeck, Pricer1980, Promus Kaa, Quentin X, RP9, Randalllin, Rje, Rossrs, Rspeed, Sagaciousuk, Scorpion0422, Scorpionman, Scottandrewhutchins, Secret Saturdays, Sidonuke, Skudrafan1, Snicker, Snideology, Sugarcaddy, SuperHuman10, Syxx, TBH, TMC1982, Tabercil, Tanthalas39, The Rogue Penguin, TheLH, Tim!, Timc, Tktktk, Tpbradbury, Tregoweth, Tyciol, UBERPITTAY, UberMan5000, Ulric1313, Underneath-it-All, Urbane Legend, Varlaam, Wafulz, WhisperToMe, Wiarthurhu, Wsxccc, XLerate, Xb2u7Zjzc32, Xp54321, 266 anonymous edits

Mrs Henderson Presents *Source*: http://en.wikipedia.org/w/index.php?oldid=368337952 *Contributors*: A. Carty, Amoammo, AnemoneProjectors, Awostrack, Azucar, Bejnar, Big Smooth, Blake-, Bobo192, Bovineboy2008, Brad, Brequinda, Cattona, Circeus, Count de Ville, Darkieboy236, Darkness2005, David Gerard, Deror avi, ESkog, Elbeonore, Erik, Funky Monkey, Grstain, Gurch, Haham hanuka, Hullaballoo Wolfowitz, JackieAnn, Jason.cinema, Jay-W, MKaiserman, Madchester, MarnetteD, MichaelSkinsFan, NWill, Nikon32, Patrick, Quentin X, R4949, RadioKirk, Radosław10, Reginmund, Sceptre, SimonP, Ssilvers, Tapir2001, TheMovieBuff, Thomas Blomberg, Tim!, Treybien, Trogga, Volatile, Wisekwai, 43 anonymous edits

Pride & Prejudice (2005 film) *Source*: http://en.wikipedia.org/w/index.php?oldid=389742107 *Contributors*: *drew, 3Tigers, AKGhetto, Aardvarkleg, Ace Class Shadow, After Midnight, AlexAlexa, Ambonne, Amoammo, Angmering, Arnie587, Astorknlam, Awadewit, Bab dz, BilCat, Bovineboy2008, BrOnXbOmBr21, Brazucs, Bwilkins, C19, CalJW, Caladonia, Carioca, CarolGray, CatBallew, Cheekywee, Cheesy Yeast, Chefington, Circeus, Clamster5, Classicfilms, Cobain, ConCompS, ContiAWB, Cyde, DXRAW, Dammit, Davemck, David Gerard, DearPrudence, Dirgni1986, Durin, Dyl, ESkog, Elbeonore, Electric Storm89, Emc2, Erik, Everyking, FMAFan1990, Fallon6, FloridaGirl90, Fmbpwyhd, FrankRizzo2006, Funguy06, Gabbe, George cowie, Ginny11, Godardesque, Grenavitar, Greyhood, Grstain, Grsz11, Hapleworth, Hede2000, Hegria66, HollywoodDarling, Iane, ImperialJaneite, Insouciance, Jajhill, Jake Role, JaneEyreRules, Janibanani, Jason.cinema, JayKeaton, Jbeans, Jeff Fries, Jmccl50, Julygenie, Jumping cheese, Justi521, Kabir Shah, Kartano, Kernitou, Lady Aleena, Lanky101, Lepetitvagabond, Limetolime, LizHas, Lugnuts, Maestro25, Magicfairy, MarnetteD, Michael Hardy, MikeVitale, Mreesa, Mrmerlot, NWill, Neddyseagoon, Nedrutland, Oberschlesien, Orbicle, Oxymoron83, PM800, Patrick, Paul A, PeaceNT, Philip Taron, PhotoBox, Pinkgoanna, Plange, Plau, Ppntori, RainingOnSunday, RayBirks, Reminiscent, Rjd0060, Rjwilmsi, Rodhullandemu, Rogerd, Sgeureka, SimonP, Sylviaa, TSP, Tassedethe, Teenwriter, The 80s chick, The Priyatyel, TheMovieBuff, Thedevmhs, Tim bates, Tom Worthington, Treybien, TubularWorld, Turnteeth, Ume, Vina, Vorobyaninov, W3stfa11, WOSlinker, White Shadows, Wolfer68, Wwoods, Xtreambar, ZeroJanvier, Zwatkins, 266 anonymous edits

Ladies in Lavender *Source*: http://en.wikipedia.org/w/index.php?oldid=384906956 *Contributors*: *drew, David Gerard, Draggleduck, ExpressingYourself, Fratrep, Gilliam, GrahamHardy, Grstain, Hal Raglan, IBAmyB, Jamyskis, KnightRider, Kubrick, MaxSem, MovieMadness, Nigelhess, Notmicro, Patrick, Pokrajac, Rachel1, Rigaudon, Rjwilmsi, Sander Moholi, Saxophobia, Seven coins, Sgeureka, Shantavira, Skarl the Drummer, SkyWalker, Sreejithk2000, SteinbDJ, Suruena, Tabletop, Thomas Blomberg, Thu, Treybien, Ufinne, 41 anonymous edits

The Chronicles of Riddick *Source*: http://en.wikipedia.org/w/index.php?oldid=388541429 *Contributors*: A Nobody, Abmac, Adraeus, Advent child, Alphonsus, Altenmann, Amicon, Andrzejbanas, Animedude360, AnmaFinotera, Ar-wiki, Arbero, Arctic.gnome, Arguss, Arrowned, Ashthecat3, Aznph8playa2, BD2412, BUF4Life, Bellagio99, BenOKZ, Bentley4, Benwford, Beyond My Ken, Bilalc, Blackmetalbaz, Blemm, Bosco13, Bounce1337, Boyar, Buchanan-Hermit, Burschik, Caeruleancentaur, Cancub, Canterbury Tail, CaptainMorgan, Carerejoe, Cburnett, CelticJobber, Crevaner, DarkestSinsHeartofGold, DaveJB, David Gerard, Davodd, Dee15gon, DennisTheTiger, DepressedPer, Dessydes, Dibbity Dan, Direvus, Djrobgordon, Dk pdx, Doczilla, Doubledice, Downwards, Doze, Dp76764, Drazzib, Ed Fitzgerald, Elatanatari, Erik, Erik9, Euyyn, Exit2DOS2000, FMAFan1990, Feureau, Firsfron, FrankRizzo2006, Friedfish, GENtLe, GSGSGSG, Gabbe, Gabmonta, Gaius Cornelius, Geracudd, Gh5046, GodGell, Grandpafootsoldier, Grtmp, Hebrides, Henryong, Hmoul, Huangdi, Hydrargyrum, Icairns, Iceness, Identification01, Irishguy, IstvanWolf, Izno, Jackal Killer, Jason Palpatine, Jennica, JetLover, John-1107, Jonbry97, Jredd, Justin Eiler, KGV, KHUUHKKUHHK, KajiTetsushi, King kong92, King of Hearts, Kintetsubuffalo, Kjaer, Klptyzm, KnowledgeOfSelf, Kuru, Lady Vaako, Laterensis, Laura Anglin, Levent, Lgl6spears, Liftarn, M.S.K., MakeRocketGoNow, MarcK, Marcus Brute, Martarius, MasterGreenLantern, Matharvest, Matthew hk, Maury Markowitz, Mavericstud9, Mhking, Mika1h, Mintleaf, Moeron, MoopDooPoo, Morven, Mptb3, Mvuijlst, Nanduterabandhu, NawlinWiki, Nemeses9, Nicole122, Nikai, No substitute for you, Noirish, Notmicro, Nowordneeded, Odst Rocker, PatPeter, Pegship, PeteFord, Petr Kopač, Peytonio, Piet Delport, Pinkadelica, Pipedreamergrey, Quentin X, Qzenguardito, RadicalBender, Radiooperator, Rainbow87, Rann Star, Razzfan, Rcswifto, RedWolf, Rernst, Riotgear, Ronhjones, Roxas13066, Sasquatch, Savolya, Scraimer, ScudLee, Shuffdog, SiobhanHansa, Sir Rhosis, Skyraider, Slakr, Soetermans, Sofa jazz man, Soulpopped, Southsloper, Sugar Bear, Suhdfuishd, Swift as an Eagle, TK421, TMC1982, Tavilis, Template namespace initialisation script, The Rogue Penguin, The7thdr, TheAL, TheBeaver, TheCoffee, TheMovieBuff, Theripper42, Thesis4Eva, Tom, Tombomp, TotalTommyTerror, Tremor27, Treybien, Tshannon0, Two Bananas, Uucp, Vapour, Vendettax, Vidkun, WatchAndObserve, Websurfer246, Who, Wikinerdy12346, Wikipelli, Wnt, Xezbeth, Xnuiem, Xsamix, Xsmasher, Year 2144, Yoman650, ZPM, Zanimum, Zetawoof, Zidane tribal, Zombie433, 375 anonymous edits

Home on the Range (film) *Source*: http://en.wikipedia.org/w/index.php?oldid=384477614 *Contributors*: *drew, AKR619, Adityachalla, Al3xil, Alansohn, Alison9, AmDrag21, Apple1013, B Touch, Bazzargh, Bdrischbdemented, Beeblebrox, Benzy19, BoulderDrop, Bovineboy2008, Brian Kendig, BuilderQ, Bw1979, CanisRufus, Cartoon Boy, Celestra, Charlotteswoe2, Chovain, Chris1219, Coasttocoast, Coffee, Darkness2005, David Gerard, Delirium, Deoxys-ex, Dieschwarzetur, Disneyhater, DroEsperanto, Dt128, Dynesclan, Einsteinewton, Eirik, Empoor, Erik9, Esn, Espresso Addict, Estrose, Everyking, Evil Monkey, Extraordinary Machine, Flair Girls, Frog47, FrozenPurpleCube, FuriousFreddy, Gabbe, Garion96, Geonarva, Germ, Gigamaligabyte, Gnrlotto, Granpuff, GrimGrinningGuest, Harley Quinn hyenaholic, Hayfordoleary, Headstrong neiva, Hektor, Hitsandmisses, Hotwiki, Ianblair23, Jedi94, Jeffman52001, JethroElfman, Jojhutton, Jvsett, KF, Kombinatorik, LaukkuTheGreit, LeaveSleaves, Lifterus, LilHelpa, Machchunk, Mafmafmaf, Maxis ftw, Mentifisto, Mickeymousechen, Mohojohn, Mtwstudios, Mütze, NawlinWiki, Neilc, Nelliebellie, Nemeses9, NewYorkMan2210, Nhrenton, Nk18, No substitute for you, Okita2, Oldnick11, Once in a Blue Moon, PMDrive1061, Paul A, Pegorex2, Pink Koala, Pro66, Rakaha, Ramminges, RedWolf, Rhindle The Red, Rockskeeper, Ronhjones, SMOKELESSPOT, SWatsi, ScudLee, Shsilver, SkyWalker, Slgrandson, SpikeJones, Squids and Chips, Squidvillanueva, Supernumerary, TALeopold, TAnthony, Tanthalas39, Tartan, Tfine80, The 80s chick, The Colclough, TheValentineBros, Tregoweth, VML, Vanished User 1004, Varlaam, Wafulz, Will Barks, Wolfcruiser, Workinghorn, Wsultzbach, Wsxccc, Ye Olde de la Man, 195 anonymous edits

Angelina Ballerina *Source*: http://en.wikipedia.org/w/index.php?oldid=388589748 *Contributors*: 54ggg, Aaron Kwajo Kyereh Mireku, Aff123a, Alansohn, Atysn, AussieLegend, Azumanga1, Baa, BarkerJr, Bigg3469, Bunnyhop11, Canley, ChangedDaily, Cholmes75, Cleo Pike, Codymooseandzee, Colonies Chris, Crazy-dancing, Crystallina, Dwanyewest, Enilegna, Freeleet, GMc, GVnayR, Gladys j cortez, Gods10rules, GregorB, Gunnar Guðvarðarson, HalfShadow, Honbicot, Hqb, Isgisgll, J04n, Juhachi, Lord Matt, Mrschimpf, Nelljohn, Nesw, No1lakersfan, Pegship, Pink1Kitty1Cat, Rainbowsunshine86, Rich Farmbrough, ScottNestle, Scoty6776, Shimalay, Sjones23, Slgrandson, SummerPhD, The All New Improved Sim12, The Mingler, Thepangelinanpost, WikHead, Wmahan, 257 anonymous edits

Die Another Day *Source*: http://en.wikipedia.org/w/index.php?oldid=388400117 *Contributors*: 123andy321noodle, 23Elliott, 23skidoo, A man alone, AarnKrry, AdamDeanHall, Addshore, Aerion, Alexis Mane, Alientraveller, AlphaDogma, Andre Engels, Andrewlp1991, Anthony Fok, Antonio Lopez, Anville, Ap, Apoltix, Applejaxs, Arbero, Arthur Ellis, Asasa64, AskFranz, Asmaybe, Aurigas, Avengerx, Avjoska, Aycan, Azure Haights, B. Fairbairn, BW52, Backslash Forwardslash, Bantosh, Beautifulstranger, Bgnuf, Bignole, Bigpatpunisher, BigrTex, Bihco, Blackcarr, Bob Castle, BobTheMad, Boduke343, Boki11080, BorgQueen, Bovineboy2008, Bratsche, Brilliant trees, Brisky, Brockfreak007, Broncopaul, Bryan Derksen, Bryan Seecrets, CR85747, CSWarren, Caissa's DeathAngel, Camembert, Canadian-nerdy-guy, CanisRufus, Canley, Canterbury Tail, Carrie2002, Cburnett, ChibiKareshi, Chilr0y, Chris Croy, Chris huh, Chris the speller, Chrysalis, Chuunen Baka, Cinemaniac, Clancy60, Cocoapropo, Codenamecuckoo, ColdFusion650, Colorfulharp233, Commander Shepard, ContiAWB, Coreycubed, Crazysim, Creepzerg3, Cremepuff222, Cyclone49, Cynical, D.wine, Dale Arnett, Dalejenkins, Dan100, Darrell37, DaveJB, David Gerard, David Kernow, David Pro, DavidA, DeWaine, Debresser, Del91, Derek.Evans82, Dickens10, Dine club, Dismas, Djmckee1, Dopefish, Dorftrottel, Douglasnicol, Dr. Blofeld, Dvenkov, EOTU, Eaglestorm, Ed g2s, Ekedolphin, El Greco, Elephant Talk, Elockid, Emmetlovesmadonna, Epbr123, Eqdoktor, Esn, Evanreyes, FMAFan1990, Fanthrillers, Fatzdaddy, FederSim, FetchcommsAWB, FightTheDarkness, Fightingirish, Flup, Fonzy, Fourthhorseman, Francolee01, FrankRizzo2006, Frecklefoot, Fred Bradstadt, Fred FuManchu, Fredrick day, Freemarket, Fys, Gabbe, Garcilaso, Gfoley4, Giga Wizard, Glane23, GoatGod, Golbez, Granpuff, GreatWhiteNortherner, GregorB, Guidod, Guinness2702, Gyre, H1523702, Hammersfan, Hanfuzzy, Harley500, HashiriyaGDB, Hawaiian717, Hellmark, Henry Flower, Hereford, Hestemand, Hig Hertenfleurst, Hiphats, HipsterDad, Hmains, HolyT, Hppl, Hubier, Iamjosh, Iancaddy, Igordebraga, Ikescs, Inqvisitor, Invincible Ninja, Iridescent, Irishguy, Israeljamesbond, Ixfd64, J-Star, JHT25, JLdesAlpins, JRRobinson, JSpung, Jacobncfc, Jagarin, James Emtage, Jammy0002, Japanese Searobin, Jason One, Jay-W, Jc iindyysgvxc, Jersyko, Jimknut, Jimmy Bond of Royale, Jogers, Johnleemk, Johnnyfog, Joowwww, Jordancelticsfan, Joshua alvara, Juan Cruz, Jusjih, Jóhann Heiðar Árnason, K1Bond007, KF, Karl gregory jones, Keimzelle, KelleyCook, KenL, Keno, Kieranthompson, Kozuch, Kross, Kuralyov, Kuvopolis, L Kensington, Lady Aleena, Lambdoid, Laurabennett14, Lear's Fool, Legolas2186, Lightmouse, Ligulem, Little Professor, Lord Cornwallis, Lords tracy, LovesMacs, Ludraman, M baptiste, MCBastos, MECU, Mabersold, MachoCarioca, Magnificator, Mahjong705, Mallanox, Man vyi, Marcklar, Mark83, Marktreut, McLeod1, Mclay1, MegX, Mel Etitis, Mic, Michael Devore, Michael Hardy, Migospia, Mike Payne, Mikeo, Mikeyeulett, Mintguy, Mipadi, Misterkillboy, Mmdoogie, Monzonda, Moralis, Mr Maestrom, MrMagoo, Mygerardromance, Myscrnnm, N5iln, Nadavspi, Ncusa367, Neddyseagoon, Netoholic, Netsnipe, Neutral arbiter, New matt, Newkirk Plaza David, Nich148 9, Nick R, Nicknackrussian, Nihiltres, Nishkid64, Niteowlneils, Nomorenonotnever, Noogz, Nualran, Nv8200p, O Fenian, Olivier, Orfen, PRRfan, PS2pcGAMER, Packinheat2u, Paul A, Pcb21, Pd THOR, Phil Boswell, Philwelch, Pichpich, Pierzz, Plasticspork, Plumpurple, PoliceChief, Possecomitatus, Prolog, Puffy1632, Quackquack32, Quentin X, RFBailey, RKAvatar, RKcoolo, Racklever, RadioBroadcast, Raymondc0, ReToOcS, Redeagle688, Redfenril, Redranger241, Redrocket, Refillpad, Riana, RicJac, Rich Farmbrough, Rich257, Rjwilmsi, Rkb669, Robert Merkel, RobertG,

Roger Roger, Roke, Rosenknospe, Rotring, Rrburke, RunningAway, Runsiva, RussNelson, SakotGrimshine, SamSim, Savestheday16, Sbpat21, Scarian, Sceptre, Scott 110, SeanEB, Septegram, Sesshomaru, Sheavsey33, Signinstranger, Simon Beavis, Simon lock, SimonP, SimpleJ YouTube, Sir Nicholas de Mimsy-Porpington, Skeejay, Skhare2012, Skipratl01, Smart guy39, Snooker, Soapergem, Solidusspriggan, Sparklingjacket, Sparrowgoose, SpecialWindler, Starman15317, Steelbeard1, Steinninn, Stephaniesoftball, SteveCrook, Stombs, Str1977, Stygian23, Su.iss, Swainstonation, SymiLover, TARDIS, TJuk, TMC1982, TTMSHU, Tapir2001, Template namespace initialisation script, Teresa44, TerriersFan, The Anome, The Giant Puffin, The Man in Question, The Pink Oboe, The Transhumanist, The Wild West guy, The time reaper, TheMovieBuff, TheRealFennShysa, TheValentineBros, Thefourdotelipsis, Thomast, ThuranX, Tilefish, Timeineurope, Tommy2010, Tommyt, TonicBH, Tony1, Tonywiki, TopAce, TrakTonik, Trident13, Tuesdaily, Tyler Goble, Ultraviolet scissor flame, Vargklo, Victor Mazowski, Victory93, Voldemort, Warpozio, Watsona.2, Wbfergus, WesUGAdawg, WesleyDodds, WhiteFireTwin, Whkoh, Wiki Greek Basketball, Wiki alf, Winchelsea, Wireless Keyboard, Wolf530, Woohookitty, Wwoods, X201, Xcentaur, Xezbeth, Y2kcrazyjoker4, Yashman21, ZRetro, Zakolantern, Ztsmart, Zzyzx11, 720 anonymous edits

The Importance of Being Earnest (2002 film) *Source*: http://en.wikipedia.org/w/index.php?oldid=388783807 *Contributors*: AN(Ger), AbsoluteGleek92, Aericanwizard, Alientraveller, Alitheblond, All Hallow's Wraith, Amcbride, Aruffo, Avistor, Balm oral winds or sand ring ham, Biruitorul, Bobo192, BomBom, Colonies Chris, Count de Ville, Darev, El Cubano, Elbeonore, Ever wonder, Galaxia92, Grandpafootsoldier, Jpkeates, Kbdank71, Ktlynch, Lugnuts, MarnetteD, MartinDK, NathanDahlin, Norm mit, Nsrodrig11, Orbicle, Pegship, Retroviseur, Rich Farmbrough, Rigadoun, Rray, Seansinc, Tagilbert, Talented Mr Miller, Tatwell, Tesseran, The Singing Badger, TheBigA, TheMovieBuff, Tide rolls, Treybien, TubularWorld, Ume, UpDown, Whoosher, Woohookitty, Yohan euan o4, Zadcat, ZeroJanvier, 41 anonymous edits

The Shipping News (film) *Source*: http://en.wikipedia.org/w/index.php?oldid=386475852 *Contributors*: Commander Shepard, Dgmoran, Easchiff, Edward, Ekabhishek, Espresso Addict, Gardener of Geda, Glysiak, Henry M J Sedgeley, MattFisher, Mausy5043, Murocan, NWill, Noebse, Plasticspork, Rockfan.by, Santryl, Shawn in Montreal, Smetanahue, Stevebritgimp, The Transhumanist, TheMovieBuff, Treybien, Yllosubmarine, 18 anonymous edits

Iris (2001 film) *Source*: http://en.wikipedia.org/w/index.php?oldid=181696190 *Contributors*: *drew, Ajshm, Angusmclellan, Arbero, Bencherlite, Carbonix, Catamorphism, Cburnett, Danny, Darkieboy236, DuncanHill, Essexgirlbecky, Gail, Garynine, Gtrmp, Hapleworth, Jay-W, Jpbowen, JzG, K1Bond007, MH154, Martynelmy, NWill, NickW557, Pegship, Phoe, Pjoef, Purplewoman, RicJac, Rosalbissima, Sagitario68, Staffwaterboy, Supernumerary, Tassedethe, Teknolyze, The Transhumanist, Tkynerd, Treybien, Twix1875, Versus22, Vlad, Wasted Sapience, Whomp, Yashveer r, 35 anonymous edits

Chocolat (2000 film) *Source*: http://en.wikipedia.org/w/index.php?oldid=386145376 *Contributors*: 32X, 97198, AbsoluteGleek92, AgnosticPreachersKid, Andrew Spinner, Andycjp, Aphaia, Arniep, Atlant, Autiger, Biiru, Bobet, CLW, Cactus.man, Caster23, Cburnett, Commander Shepard, CommonsDelinker, Cossy, Cwphd97, D6, David Gerard, Dbenbenn, Dissonance2009, Dohanlon, Drumguy8800, Dutzi, Easchiff, Ecco1983, Emilyrader, Epbr123, Erik, Esradekan, Etloben, Eurosong, Extraordinary Machine, FMAFan1990, Goustien, Grandpafootsoldier, Huda sa3eed, IRP, ItsTheClimb17, Ixfd64, Jackaranga, Jennifairy, Kenshin, Khitrenovich, KintetsubuffaIo, Kollision, Lady Aleena, Liftarn, Limetolime, LinkTiger, MachoCarioca, MasterOfHisOwnDomain, Micahbrwn, MisterHand, Morio, NWill, Newcotoberissue, OGoncho, Omicronpersei8, P-Chan, PM800, PTSE, Plastikspork, Pokrajac, Powerofjuju, Ppntori, Qutezuce, Rockhopper10r, RoyBoy, RyanGerbil10, SISLEY, Sealman, Signalhead, Silverhorse, Sligocki, Smetanahue, SpNeo, SpankyMac, Spiritia, Steinsky, Steviec112, Talia679, Ted Wilkes, The JumpStation, The Transhumanist, TheMovieBuff, Thingg, Thirdeyeopen33, Tlsmith124, Tony Sidaway, Toussaint, Treybien, Truman Burbank, Tyrane, Visceraeyes, Vmarshall51, Wiltshireway, Witchbaby, Xyzzyva, Zec, 122 anonymous edits

The Last of the Blonde Bombshells *Source*: http://en.wikipedia.org/w/index.php?oldid=385345611 *Contributors*: Azumanga1, Bluemover9999, Crstsk, DanMS, David Gerard, Felix Folio Secundus, Iridescent, Mareino, Mrblondnyc, Ndgp, Onapproval, Orbicle, Philip Cross, REVUpminster, Ronhjones, Slysplace, Sreejithk2000, Talopine, Tenbitbob, TheMovieBuff, Torve, Trident13, Tuesdaily, 11 anonymous edits

Into the Arms of Strangers: Stories of the Kindertransport *Source*:http://en.wikipedia.org/w/index.php?oldid=388166108 *Contributors*: Ameliorate!, Andrzejbanas, Bovineboy2008, Cop 663, Donmike10, Dudeman5685, Elan26, GHcool, Gareth Aus, GwydionM, Luctor IV, Lugnuts, MetaManFromTomorrow, Pegship, Pjoef, Sagredo, Shawn in Montreal, Snefreely, TRoethke, Tewfik, Thismightbezach, Tim1357, Tool2Die4, YUL89YYZ, 6 anonymous edits

The World Is Not Enough *Source*: http://en.wikipedia.org/w/index.php?oldid=385913793 *Contributors*: 10metreh, 23skidoo, 293.xx.xxx.xx, A. Carty, Acegikmo1, AdamDeanHall, AlbertSM, Alexius08, Alexwberg, Alientraveller, Andrzejbanas, AntOvns, Antrophica, Asasa64, AtilimGunesBaydin, Atlan, BattlePete20, Bd84, Beefyt, Bellagio99, Ben King, Bhalli619, Bignole, Biiru, Bkell, Bobert1358, Bolman Deal, Bond fan original, BorgQueen, Bovineboy2008, Bratsche, Breakinguptheguy, Brockfreak007, Brossow, BryanEkers, C. Foultz, CSWarren, Cake taken, Calabraxthis, Calmer Waters, Calton, Camembert, Cast, Cbradshaw, CharlieRCD, Chouchoupette, Chris G, Chucky Cosmo, Cjc13, Clemmy, Cliff smith, Cocoapropo, Coder Dan, ColdFusion650, Commander Shepard, ContiAWB, Cooldude3240, Copyeditor42, Cyclone49, Dale Arnett, Dan100, Darkieboy236, Darkness2005, David Gerard, Davidhorman, Dawkeye, Dbenbenn, Dmn, Dopefish, Dorftrottel, Dr. Blofeld, Dvavasour, Easchiff, Edwardsully, Egoistka69, El Greco, Elf, Elyu, Emperor001, Environnement2100, EoGuy, Epbr123, Eqdoktor, Flexcoupling, Flurry, Fourthhorseman, Frecklefoot, Fschoenm, GOBLUE56, Gabbe, Ganfon, Gcollinsii@aol.com, GeneralYin, Geodyde, Glacier109, Gogo Dodo, GoingBatty, Gold Stur, Gran2, Granpuff, GreatWhiteNortherner, GroovySandwich, Guiseppi, Guy14, H1523702, Hadinho, Hammersfan, Harleytarantina, Hawaiian717, Hereford, Herong, HexaChord, Himalayan Explorer, Hiphats, Hogyn Lleol, Hubier, Igordebraga, Indrek, Inqvisitor, Insomniacpuppy, Iridescent, Izno, JHunterJ, JP Godfrey, JYi, Jahnavi7, Japanese Searobin, Jason One, Jay-W, Jersyko, JoeSmack, Jogers, John254, JohnSawyer, Johnfos, Johnnyfog, Jonghyunchung, Jonnychadwick, Jordancelticsfan, Jusjih, K1Bond007, Kallemax, Kanonkop, Karaboom, KenL, Kieranthompson, Konstantin, Krasniy, Kuralyov, Kwekubo, LGagnon, Lady Aleena, LeCorrector, Lear's Fool, Leuqarte, Lightmouse, LilHelpa, Lotje, M.nelson, MECU, MaGioZal, MachoCarioca, Macphisto12, Makalp, Mallanox, Mamour, Marek69, Mark83, Markdurrant, Marktreut, Martarius, Mattsm, Mav, Mel Etitis, Mgiganteus1, Mic, Michael Devore, Mikeo, Mr.Jackal95, MrMagoo, Msa1701, Mystache, N5iln, Netoholic, Nevermore27, Nicknackrussian, Nightcrawler1089, NoMoon, Notreallydavid, Nv8200p, Nytimes19992000, Olivier, PBP, Parsecboy, Paul A, Paulbrock, Phil Boswell, Phil Ken Sebben, Politepunk, Possecomitatus, Prolog, Pterre, RadioBroadcast, RapidAssistant, Redfenril, RicJac, Rich Farmbrough, RichardBond, Rioux15, Rjwilmsi, Ronald King, Rrburke, RunningAway, Sannse, Sc3499a, Sceptre, Scott Sanchez, SeanEB, Sheitan, Signinstranger, SimpleJYouTube, Sjorford, Skorpionas, SmartyBoots, Sniper 99, SoulOfHamlet, Sparrowgoose, SpecialWindler, Spellcast, Splamo, Splash, Spongefrog, Spoonkymonkey, Starman15317, SteveCrook, TMC1982, Tapir2001, Template namespace initialisation script, Teutonic Tamer, The Giant Puffin, Thefirstchoice, Thefourdotelipsis, ThomasK, Tommyt, Tony1, Tonyho, Trans4mers, Trebor, Treybien, Tuxedo junction, Ultraviolet scissor flame, Vanished user 03, Vclaw, Vespristiano, Voyager, Ward3001, Watsona.2, Whorchatasoto, Wiki Greek Basketball, Wireless Keyboard, Wwoods, X201, Xnacional, Y2kcrazyjoker4, Ylee, Youngvariety, Yurik, Zeichman, ~Viper~, 382 anonymous edits

Tea with Mussolini *Source*: http://en.wikipedia.org/w/index.php?oldid=390333761 *Contributors*: *drew, AbsoluteGleek92, Angmering, Angr, Bbb23, BrownHairedGirl, CarysOx, Che829, Comrade009, Diberri, Dodge Dude, Dyl, Eagle Owl, Easchiff, Fredrik, GTBacchus, Gugganij, Horseagle, JasonAQuest, Jeff3000, John Nevard, Jreferee, Kusma, LJade728, Lilapavza,
MarnetteD, MegX, Megan1967, Ohconfucius, Opera hat, Polylerus, Retraité, Rich Farmbrough, Rockstar Barbie, Rohmerin, Sandstein, Sir Hester, Softlavender, Sonnyandcherfan, Sreejithk2000, T-borg, TheMadBaron, TheMovieBuff, Tiger Marc, Tim!, Treybien, Vikas Kumar Ojha, Vlsimon, WBardwin, Waggers, Whomp, Yossarian, 67 anonymous edits

Shakespeare in Love *Source*: http://en.wikipedia.org/w/index.php?oldid=388721222 *Contributors*: 2bornot2b, ARGOU, Abe Lincoln, AbsoluteGleek92, Abu badali, Acather96, Actryan, Ahoerstemeier, Aitias, Ameliorate!, Andokool12, Andrzejbanas, AndyJones, Andycjp, Angie Y., Aquila89, ArkansasTraveler, Asianchick, B0OP, Barney Jenkins, Beardo, Becky Sayles, Belovedfreak, Bill shannon, Blahaccountblah, Bluerasberry, Bomac, Bongwarrior, Bovineboy2008, Bryan Derksen, Bzuk, CGrahamT, CKarnstein, CanisRufus, Capmango, Captain Tomorrow, Cburnett, Clarityfiend, Cop 663, Cue the Strings, DJ Clayworth, Daeker, Daekharel, Darkness2005, Dbenbenn, DesmondRavenstone, Dharmabum420, Domp18, Douglast86, Dr. Blofeld, DuaneThomas, Eamapelli, Easchiff, Ebyabe, Ed Poor, El Cid, Elbeonore, Emorog, Erik9, Estiv, Excirial, ExpatEgghead, FMAFan1990, Fantasy, Ferrischan, Filmfluff, Films addicted, Fuhghettaboutit, GHcool, Gabbe, Gamaliel, GateKeeper, Gaveston66, Grafen, Gravidef, Gurch, Hapleworth, Henrymrx, Hullaballoo Wolfowitz, Humorousbehavior89, Inliten, Irk, Isis, JHMM13, JP Godfrey, Ja 62, Jesbadio, Jess0501, Jessica2266, Jezzabr, Jmlk17, Jni, Joey80, Jordgubbe, Juicyluvr4life, Jzummak, KJS77, Karl-Henner, Kbdank71, Ketil, Khatru2, Kierant, Kjdamrau, KnightRider, Knovlian, Knyght27, Kungcow12, LGagnon, Lacrimosus, Lee M, Levineps, LinkTiger, LtMuldoon, M samadi, M1ss1ontomars2k4, MER-C, MachoCarioca, Madhero88, Majicwand, Mallanox, Mandel, MarkSutton, MarnetteD, MartinDK, MartinVillafuerte85, Marychan41, Massimo Macconi, Materialscientist, Matt Deres, Mattcolville, Mav, Maximus Rex, Melaen, Merinda, Mervyn, MikeAllen, MileyDavidA, MishaPan, Modeha, Mona, Nadim.alex, Nandt1, Neddyseagoon, Nedrutland, Neo-Jay, Ner102, Niall Guinan, Nimakha, Niteowlneils, Noirish, Notmicro, ONEder Boy, Old Moonraker, Onthewiki, Optiguy54, PNW Raven, PallyP, Patar knight, Paul Barlow, Phbasketball6, Philip Trueman, Polylerus, ProhibitOnions, Protonk, Queenmomcat, Qxz, RBBrittain, RMHED, Rachel1, Radosław10, Raemie, Rainyskies713, RattleandHum, Reaper89, Redhotwheels, Remurmur, Rico402, Robert K S, Robert Merkel, RobertG, Ronstew, Rutherfordjigsaw, ST47, Sam, Savidan, ScottDavis, Sergeiarias, Shoy, Shubho122, SimonP, SlowwwwMoses, Smalljim, SouthernNights, Sreejithk2000, Stanleykubrick224, StefanoC, Stefanomione, Stephen e nelson, SteveW, Stratman07, Supertigerman, Sverdrup, Swordsmankirby, TAnthony, Tabletop, TallulahBelle, Tarquin, Ted Wilkes, Tenorcnj, Texboy, The Bread, The Duke of Waltham, The Famous Movie Director, The Thing That Should Not Be, TheAznSensation, TheLastAmigo, TheMovieBuff, Tide rolls, Tony Sidaway, Tony414, Tool2Die4, Treybien, TrustTruth, UZiBLASTER7, Ulric1313, UnicornTapestry, Varlaam, W.Ross, Weedle McHairybug, Wickedxjade, Wildhartlivie, Witchy2006, Wolfch, Wwestarwars, Wwoods, Xchristinecandyx, Xezbeth, Xover, YeshuaDavid, Ylee, Zec, ZeroJanvier, Zhurnaly, Zotdragon, Zzyzx11, 349 anonymous edits

Tomorrow Never Dies *Source*: http://en.wikipedia.org/w/index.php?oldid=386786126 *Contributors*: 23skidoo, 6afraidof7, Accaldwell, AdamDeanHall, AdultSwim, Alientraveller, Anakata, Andrzejbanas, Angmering, Atlan, Avjoska, BalticPat22, Ben King, Bencey, Bender235, Betty Logan, Bignole, Bigs slb, Biiru, Bovineboy2008, Breakinguptheguy, Bubbleboys, C777, CALR, CLW, CMG, Cathal Toomey, Cbradshaw, Charmed88, Citius Altius Fortius, Cliff smith, ColdFusion650, D.wine, DHN, Dabomb87, Dale Arnett, Darkness2005, DeWaine, Delta-2030, Dmastrovich, Dmn, Dorftrottel, Dr. Blofeld, Drbreznjev, Dunhere, Echuck215, Edlitz36, Ekedolphin, El Greco, Elockid, Emperor001, Eqdoktor, Eurocopter, Favonian, Fightingirish, Finlay McWalter, Firetrap9254, Floydgeo, Fortdj33, Fourthhorseman, Fox, Francs2000, Fredrick day, Fyyer, Gabbe, Garion96, GoldDragon, GoldenGoose100, Granpuff, GreatWhiteNortherner, Gregmce, Griffinn, H1523702, H92, HADRIANVS, Hadinho, Halsteadk, Hammersfan, Harleytarantina, HenryLi, Hereford, Hig Hertenfleurst, Hiphats, Hubier, I Helfrich, IAmTheCoinMan, Ian Pitchford, Ianblair23, Iceberg3k, Igordebraga, Incrediblehunk, Inqvisitor, Ioavves, Iridescent, JB988, JHunterJ, JLdesAlpins, Jac16888, Jackwiliamsteiner, James Callahan, JamesHenstridge, Jamesgibbon, Japanese Searobin, Jason One, Jay-W, Jb007ltkill, Jedd the Jedi, Jellyfish dave, Jersyko, Jiang, Joffeloff, John, John Smith's, Jthotshot, Jwy, K1Bond007, Kchisholl1970, Kdkeller,

KenL, KenWalker, Kevin W., Kieranthompson, Koavf, Kuralyov, Kusma, Kwamikagami, LGagnon, LeCire, Lear's Fool, Lindell005, Localzuk, LonelyBeacon, Lots42, Lowellian, LuciferMorgan, M-Storbeck, Ma'ame Michu, Magnus Manske, Mallanox, Mark83, MarnetteD, Martarius, Martin.Bock, Mathew shires, Mattgirling, Matthew R Dunn, Maximus Rex, Mel Etitis, Mic, Missionary, Mokus, Monedula, Montrose Patriot, Mr. Laser Beam, MrMagoo, Msa1701, Msl5046, Myominane, Myscrnnm, Nae'blis, Neddyseagoon, Nehrams2020, Netoholic, Noogz, Notreallydavid, NuclearWarfare, Nv8200p, O Fenian, Olivier, Papman1, Pardy, ParisianBlade, Patrick Bernier, Patrickbowman, Paul A, Pherdy, Phil Boswell, Piano non troppo, PoliceChief, Possecomitatus, Prolog, QueenCake, Racklever, RadioBroadcast, RaseaC, Rbrwr, Red marquis, Redfenril, Renata3, RevRagnarok, Rich Farmbrough, Richhoncho, Rknobbe, Ro308, RobJ1981, Runsiva, Ryanbstevens, SDC, SJrX10, Savolya, Scohoust, Ser Amantio di Nicolao, Sgeureka, ShadowLaguna, ShakataGaNai, ShaunMacPherson, Shirik, Showtime2009, Signinstranger, SimpleJ YouTube, Sledgeh101, Sparklingjacket, SpecialWindler, StAnselm, Starman15317, SteveCrook, Stu-Rat, Suomi Finland 2009, SynergyStar, TJ Spyke, TMC1982, Template namespace initialisation script, Th1rt3en, The Giant Puffin, The JPS, The Moving Finger Writes, Thefourdotelipsis, Thingg, Tkynerd, Tom Black, Tommyt, Tompie913, TonicBH, Tony1, Toquinha, Trebor, Treybien, Ultraviolet scissor flame, Unmitigated Success, Victory93, Voxparadox, Voyager, Watsona.2, Websurfer246, Werty1234, Whataboutbob, Wiki Greek Basketball, Wimt, Wmlschlotterer, Woohookitty, Wwoods, X201, Xhienne, Y2kcrazyjoker4, Ytcracker, ZS, Zachera, Zzyzx11, 369 anonymous edits

Mrs. Brown *Source*: http://en.wikipedia.org/w/index.php?oldid=389533185 *Contributors*: 23skidoo, AN(Ger), Ahoerstemeier, Aldis90, Andrzejbanas, Arcadian, Arthena, Asbl, Asfarer, Belovedfreak, CanisRufus, Canley, Cburnett, Chris the speller, Dcs315, Ddlfan, Donreed, Elbeonore, EoGuy, FeanorStar7, Good Olfactory, GusF, Gwguffey, Hobbesy3, Jamiecampbell, Jay-W, Jcw69, Jevansen, JohnG62, JuliaVictoria, Kablammo, Karen Johnson, Karin127, Khatru2, Khukri, King Cobb, Lee M, Little Miss Might Be Wrong, Lugnuts, Magioladitis, MarnetteD, Mister BV, MrTAToad, NWill, Neddyseagoon, Nick Cooper, Niteowlneils, Notmicro, PainMan, Paul A, Pinethicket, Polylerus, Radosław10, Rich Farmbrough, Rockvee, SDC, SimonP, Sreejithk2000, SuperDude115, The FinalWord, The Wednesday Island, TheMovieBuff, Tim!, Treybien, Voyager640, WOSlinker, Wool Mintons, Yllosubmarine, Zoe, 63 anonymous edits

Hamlet (1996 film) *Source*: http://en.wikipedia.org/w/index.php?oldid=390612599 *Contributors*: Ajplmr, Ajshm, AlbertSM, AndyJones, Ann77, Ausir, Azucar, Brain, CJMylentz, Catamorphism, Chris the speller, Comicist, Cthuljew, Cubs Fan, Deltabeignet, Doc glasgow, Donald McKinney, Downstage right, Ed Poor, Esn, Fmbpwyhd, Gabbort, Generica, Girolamo Savonarola, Hal 10000.0, JHFTC, Jevon Tompkins, Jogers, Jordancelticsfan, Josh Parris, Judesba, JudgePat, Julle, KarenViceroy, Kitch, Korny O'Near, Kuralyov, Lachatdelarue, Leedsrhino, LinkTiger, Lugnuts, Lupin, M.nelson, MER-C, MarnetteD, Matthew Auger, Mav, Mdiamante, Meta faye, Mike R, Mikeo, Montecarlocars, Nevilley, Oneiros, Patriarch, Paul A, Paul Barlow, Paul441391, Pfistermeister, Pufferfish101, Quilche, RedWolf, RicJac, Robertbyme, Sbpat21, ScottMHoward, SeanEB, Sesesq, Stevekeiretsu, Supernumerary, Swordman182, TFNorman, Tassedethe, The Drama Llama, TheFeds, TheMovieBuff, Thebdj, ThuranX, Tim!, Tintazul, Towzzer, Tregoweth, Trivialist, Ushionna, VolatileChemical, VonV, Websurfer246, Wrad, Wysdom, Xover, YUL89YYZ, Yworo, Zigger, 97 anonymous edits

GoldenEye *Source*: http://en.wikipedia.org/w/index.php?oldid=389603757 *Contributors*: 23skidoo, A bit iffy, AarHan3, Ab113fm, AcademicMatt1989, Acegikmo1, AdamDeanHall, Adrian Parratt, Ajuk, Alai, Alcoved id, Alientraveller, Alvis, Amatulic, Anaisfirewalkwithme, Andrevan, AndrewT, Andrzejbanas, Andymarczak, Angmering, AnonMoos, Anynobody, Arguss, Arpingstone, Asams10, Avjoska, Axem Titanium, Azucar, AzureCitizen, BarretBonden, Bathawes, Batmanand, Bavaria, Beardo, Bensin, Bentley4, BigHairRef, Bignole, Bigs slb, Biiru, Billcosby, Bob Castle, Bob6, Bobblehead, BorgQueen, Bouyeeze, Bovineboy2008, Brettsky1202, Brianboulton, Brownsteve, Bullzeye, Bwmartin, CLW, CRKingston, Cancatan, CapDac, CaptainVindaloo, Cbrown1023, Cflm001, CharlotteWebb, Chase92, Chem-awb, ChipDoran, Chombawomba, Clampton, Cliff smith, Cloudbound, Cochise6, CodyKhaos, ColdFusion650, Comander Bond, Commander Keane, Corilof, Ctempire, D Boland, DJFairborne77, DONOVAN, Dale Arnett, Dark Kubrick, Darkness2005, DarthScorcho, Dashmast3r, David Graham, Davidhorman, Deniserogue, Diaa abdelmoneim, Dmn, Don't give an Ameriflag, Donmike10, Dorftrottel, Doughnut540, Dr Jonty, Dr. Blofeld, Dudeface, Dudtz, EJBanks, Ebyabe, EdJogg, Eekerz, Egon Eagle, El Greco, Elockid, Ender qa, Eptin, Eqdoktor, Erik, EwkRocks, Falcon9x5, Ferdinand Pienaar, Finduilas 09, Finetooth, Fireaxe888, Floydgeo, Fourohfour, Fourthhorseman, Fox, FrankRizzo2006, Frap, Fredrik, Fvw, Gabbe, Gabrielkat, Gaius Cornelius, Garion96, GavSalkeld, Geniac, Ghiraddje, Gimboid13, Giraffedata, Goldeneye Mission 1-2, Goustien, Granpuff, GreatWhiteNortherner, GregorB, Grendelkhan, Grillo, Guidod, Gökhan, H1523702, Hammerite, Hammersfan, Harleytarantina, HarryKG, Harryboyles, Headbomb, Henning Blatt, Hereford, Heycos, Hh, Hig Hertenfleurst, Hiphats, Hmains, Holkstemwo, HonestTom, Hubier, Hurricanehink, Ian Pitchford, Igordebraga, Imacphee, Impala2009, Indon, Inqvisitor, Iridescent, J Greb, JHCC, JTSchreiber, Jamesbanesmith, Jamesgibbon, Jason One, Jay-W, JayEsJay, Jc iindyysgvxc, Jealousagain38, Jedd the Jedi, Jeff Muscato, Jeff3000, Jersyko, Jetro, Jmcollier, Joe123451, John Broughton, John-1107, JonathanDP81, Jordanceltiscfan, K1Bond007, Kdkeller, Kelapstick, KenL, Kieranthompson, Kingpin13, Kintetsubuffalo, Kirachinmoku, Kitch, Kjp993, KnightRider, Koavf, Koffieyahoo, Kozuch, Kristbg, Kuralyov, Kusma, Kwekubo, LGagnon, Lady Aleena, Lang rabbie, Le Cleaner, Lear's Fool, Lenin and McCarthy, Lightmouse, Lightsup55, LilHelpa, Ling.Nut, LittleSmall, Lradrama, Ls883, Lvprice, MI6agent, MachoCarioca, MadJulle, Maestrodagod, Magic Window, Magister Mathematicae, Magnificator, Mallanox, Marblespire, Marc Shepherd, Mark83, MarnetteD, Martarius, Martin451, Master of Puppets, Mazaru, Mdmday, Mel Etitis, Mic, Michael Devore, MightyJordan, Mikeo, Millard73, Minesweeper, Minjamonkeyw00t, Modster, Momusufan, Monowi, MrMagoo, Mrmiscellanious, Myscrnnm, Mzajac, NKSCF, NcSchu, Nehrams2020, Neptunius, Netoholic, Nick Cooper, Nick R, Nicknackrussian, Nk, Noeticsage, Nono64, Nubbie44, Nv8200p, O Fenian, Obehave, Olivier, Oni no Akuma, Onkel Tuca, Ophois, Optichan, Oscarthecat, ParisianBlade, Parsecboy, Paul A, Paulita1292, Peter Isotalo, Peter-lavalle, Phil Boswell, Pichpich, Pirate2000, Plasticup, Prolog, PsyMar, Puckly, Punitpankaj, PureLegend, Quadzilla99, Quentin X, Quincel99, Racklever, RadioBroadcast, Rajah, RattleandHum, Reagar, RealityTelevisionFan, RedEyesMetal, RedWolf, Redvers, Regushee, RevRagnarok, Rhindle The Red, Rich Farmbrough, Rjwilmsi, Rl, Robert K S, RockMFR, Roger Roger, Romclef007, RossPatterson, SCARECROW, SPKx, SandyGeorgia, Savolya, Scienceman123, SeanEB, ShadowUltra, Shafi4uf, Sietse Snel, Signinstranger, SimpleJ YouTube, Slady, Slimdavey, Smurrayinchester, Sniper 99, Solidusspriggan, Soulxlight, Spangineer, Sparklingjacket, SpecialWindler, Spongefrog, Stalin's Smile, Starman15317, Stenun, Stephen Shaw, Suomi Finland 2009, SuperTank17, SupermanReturns, Suruena, TDogg310, TMC1982, Tassedethe, Template namespace initialisation script, Tenebrous, The Filmaker, The Giant Puffin, The Rogue Penguin, TheMovieBuff, Thefourdotelipsis, Theman008, Thunderbrand, Timrollpickering, Tom, Tommyt, Tompw, Tony Myers, Tony1, Tonytam, Trachtemacht, Trebor, TreyGeek, TubularWorld, Ty123, Ultraviolet scissor flame, Upthera23, Ustas, Vague Rant, VampWillow, Victor Mazowski, Victory93, Viper h, Voorlandt, W.M. O'Quinlan, Warhol13, Watsona.2, Wendroa, Whataboutbob, WhiskyWhiskers, WhisperToMe, Whitmore 8621, Wiki Greek Basketball, Wiki alf, Wikiborg, WilliamH, WyvernOne, X201, Xhienne, Xmnemonic, Y2kcrazyjoker4, Yashman18, Yomangani, ZanderZ, Zeality, Zelmerszoetrop, Zimnick, Zombie433, 744 anonymous edits

Jack and Sarah *Source*: http://en.wikipedia.org/w/index.php?oldid=385477241 *Contributors*: Angmering, Belovedfreak, Bradley0110, David Gerard, Donald McKinney, Erik, Furryleopard, Joseph Q Publique, Kumagoro-42, Luckyles, Mallanox, Onebravemonkey, Orbicle, Paddyman1989, PoostivalHello, Quentin X, Robsteadman, Treybien, Violetriga, 15 anonymous edits

Behaving Badly (TV serial) *Source*: http://en.wikipedia.org/w/index.php?oldid=283017933 *Contributors*: Arch dude, Bradley0110, LiteraryMaven, MovieMadness

Henry V (1989 film) *Source*: http://en.wikipedia.org/w/index.php?oldid=390178379 *Contributors*: Andrzejbanas, Ausir, Average Earthman, Azucar, Bardolator601, Bertaut, CJMylentz, CalvertdeGrey, CambridgeBayWeather, Catamorphism, Cburnett, D, DLand, Danismint, Danny, Deb, Deltabeignet, Donfbreed, Downstage right, Easchiff, Estrose, Fdewaele, Geniac, GoodDay, GrahamHardy, Grandpafootsoldier, Grifter84, Grutness, Gurch, Hebrides, Invisifan, Ironsnail, JamesAM, Jason Palpatine, Jay-W, Jeanne boleyn, Jihg, Joost 99, Kate, Larphenflorp, Lugnuts, Lupin, Maolmhuire, Marieblasdell, MarnetteD, Mhacdebhandia, Mholland, Moshe Constantine Hassan Al-Silverburg, Neal777, Neddyseagoon, OliverH, Paul A, Paulatthehug, RB1956, Respice, Ron whisky, Sottolacqua, Spaceflower, Sreejithk2000, Tassedethe, Ten-pint, The Filmaker, TheMovieBuff, Thefourdotelipsis, Tim!, Tomwhite56, Trappist the monk, Tuckerresearch, Vox Rationis, Wjemather, Woohookitty, XinJeisan, Zoe, 50 anonymous edits

A Handful of Dust *Source*: http://en.wikipedia.org/w/index.php?oldid=377539043 *Contributors*: AlainV, Andycjp, Astrowob, Bielle, Brian0918, Citarac, Cnwb, Commander Keane, Danny, Deb, Drbuzzard, Erik Kennedy, Gamaliel, Garrit, Gizzakk, Hayford Peirce, Henry Merrivale, Iron Ghost, Jask99, Jimdscottesq, Jlittlet, KF, Kevinalewis, Kx1186, LGagnon, Luokehao, Mandel, Maproom, Mel Etitis, MikeBriggs, Misza13, MrDarcy, Mwanner, PeaceNT, Pearle, Quuxplusone, Rjwilmsi, Simonides, SofiePedersen, Str1977, Supergee, Thewikiman, Tonyfuchs1019, Varlaam, 35 anonymous edits

84 Charing Cross Road (film) *Source*: http://en.wikipedia.org/w/index.php?oldid=386232855 *Contributors*: AN(Ger), Cjc13, EraserGirl, Foofbun, Hapleworth, Jordancelticsfan, MarnetteD, MovieMadness, Nehrams2020, Nice poa, Pegship, Plasticspork, Royalcello, TheBearPaw, TheMovieBuff, Treybien, Tyrenius, Wildhartlivie, 7 anonymous edits

A Room with a View (film) *Source*: http://en.wikipedia.org/w/index.php?oldid=390022696 *Contributors*: AN(Ger), Ahoerstemeier, Astor, Azucar, C0r, Che829, Clarityfiend, Classicfilms, Cop 663, CutOffTies, DanielVovak, Daxmaryrussel, Delta 51, Drbreznjev, Esyleeicats, Flowerkiller1692, Garion96, Grstain, Gökhan, Hapleworth, Hegria66, Inner City Teacher, Irishguy, JackofOz, Jake Wildstrom, Jay-W, Karin127, Kckoch, Koavf, Kusma, Lady Aleena, Lightmouse, Lugnuts, MachoCarioca, Max scott61, Ohconfucius, Olivier, OwenBlacker, Passitivity, Pegship, Phbasketball6, Ppntori, Radon210, Rich Farmbrough, Rnt20, SaxTeacher, Shortride, Shotwell, SilkTork, Skier Dude, Smb1001, Spaceflower, Surréalatino, TIY, Tassedethe, The Singing Badger, Thismightbezach, Tim!, Treybien, Ume, Ume3, WikiKingOfMishawaka, 34 anonymous edits

Wetherby (film) *Source*: http://en.wikipedia.org/w/index.php?oldid=383198209 *Contributors*: Ameliorate!, Belovedfreak, CBM, Camptown, Chanheigeorge, Cop 663, Handsome Jack, Lugnuts, MovieMadness, Mtaylor848, Philip Cross, Ronhjones, RottenPotato, Thismightbezach, Tony Sidaway, Treybien, 21 anonymous edits

The Angelic Conversation (film) *Source*: http://en.wikipedia.org/w/index.php?oldid=385900661 *Contributors*: Belovedfreak, Camelotrose, Cheesemite, JamesBFI, Jamesmackay44, Lugnuts, Masem, PC78, SilkTork, TAnthony, Teppei Aita, Tim!, Treybien, User0529, Wikignome0529, 5 anonymous edits

Langrishe, Go Down (film) *Source*: http://en.wikipedia.org/w/index.php?oldid=386835928 *Contributors*: A. Carty, Cgingold, John Thaxter, NYScholar, Rms125a@hotmail.com, 4 anonymous edits

Dead Cert (film) *Source*: http://en.wikipedia.org/w/index.php?oldid=381156098 *Contributors*: Aardvarkzz, Andrzejbanas, Fratrep, TheMovieBuff

Luther (1973 film) *Source*: http://en.wikipedia.org/w/index.php?oldid=379793377 *Contributors*: Daisyabigael, Drboisclair, Drpickem, Kathleen.wright5, Philip Cross, Rogerd, Soenke Rahn, Tim1357, Woohookitty, Yachtsman1, 3 anonymous edits

A Midsummer Night's Dream (1968 film) *Source*: http://en.wikipedia.org/w/index.php?oldid=382098222 *Contributors*: After Midnight, AlbertSM, Alexkin, AndrewHowse, Dino, Dr timebomb, Goustien, Jevansen, Lightmouse, MarnetteD, Pegship, Reginmund, Rich Farmbrough, Rjwilmsi, SilkTork, Skier Dude, Sue Wallace, Wool Mintons, Wysdom, 7 anonymous edits

He Who Rides a Tiger *Source*: http://en.wikipedia.org/w/index.php?oldid=385038525 *Contributors*: A. Carty, McDoobAU93, Yoenit

A Study in Terror *Source*: http://en.wikipedia.org/w/index.php?oldid=387660319 *Contributors*: A. Carty, Accounting4Taste, Andrew777, Andrzejbanas, Beardo, Belovedfreak, Cayla, ColumbiaClassics, Cooksey, Count de Ville, David L Rattigan, Djrobgordon, Epbr123, Fvw, Jack1956, Jay-W, Johnbeal, Kchisholl1970, Kuralyov, LeaveSleaves, Lord Cornwallis, Lugnuts, MER-C, MarnetteD, Owen, Paul Barlow, Pegship, Pfistermeister, Ralphmerridew, Rpab, Savolya, Schmiteye, Skier Dude, Tassedethe, Thismightbezach, Threegee, TomorrowWeDie, Treybien, Wildhartlivie, 19 anonymous edits

The Third Secret (film) *Source*: http://en.wikipedia.org/w/index.php?oldid=374835906 *Contributors*: Andrzejbanas, Draggleduck, LiteraryMaven, Nehrams2020, Pinnaclekl, Thefourdotelipsis, 3 anonymous edits

Image Sources, Licenses and Contributors

File:Judi Dench at the BAFTAs 2007.jpg *Source*:http://en.wikipedia.org/w/index.php?title=File:Judi_Dench_at_the_BAFTAs_2007.jpg *License*: Creative Commons Attribution 3.0 *Contributors*: Caroline Bonarde Ucci at http://flickr.com/photos/caroline_bonarde/

File:NineA ver4.jpg *Source*: http://en.wikipedia.org/w/index.php?title=File:NineA_ver4.jpg *License*: unknown *Contributors*: Quentin X

File:Rage_filmposter.jpg *Source*: http://en.wikipedia.org/w/index.php?title=File:Rage_filmposter.jpg *License*: unknown *Contributors*: Calmer Waters, Nehrams2020, Saa19952, Sreejithk2000

File:Qos-teaser.jpg *Source*: http://en.wikipedia.org/w/index.php?title=File:Qos-teaser.jpg *License*: unknown *Contributors*: AEMoreira042281, Alientraveller, David Pro, Debresser, Grandpafootsoldier, MJisnotmylover, S@bre, Skier Dude, 10 anonymous edits

File:Quantum Of Solace Shelter Bay.jpg *Source*:http://en.wikipedia.org/w/index.php?title=File:Quantum_Of_Solace_Shelter_Bay.jpg *License*: Public Domain *Contributors*: User:MAdaXe

File:Paranal camp.jpg *Source*:http://en.wikipedia.org/w/index.php?title=File:Paranal_camp.jpg *License*: GNU Free Documentation License *Contributors*: Rivi

File:BregenzToscaBühnenbild4.JPG *Source*:http://en.wikipedia.org/w/index.php?title=File:BregenzToscaBühnenbild4.JPG *License*: Creative Commons Attribution-Sharealike 2.5 *Contributors*: User:Böhringer

File:AstonMartinDBSCC08.jpg *Source*: http://en.wikipedia.org/w/index.php?title=File:AstonMartinDBSCC08.jpg *License*: Creative Commons Attribution-Sharealike 3.0 *Contributors*: User:Nehrams2020

File:CA1208cover-James Bond.jpg *Source*: http://en.wikipedia.org/w/index.php?title=File:CA1208cover-James_Bond.jpg *License*: unknown *Contributors*: Benning79, 1 anonymous edits

File:Notes on a Scandal.jpg *Source*:http://en.wikipedia.org/w/index.php?title=File:Notes_on_a_Scandal.jpg *License*: unknown *Contributors*: Myanw, Nehrams2020, 3 anonymous edits

File:Casino_Royale_3.jpg *Source*:http://en.wikipedia.org/w/index.php?title=File:Casino_Royale_3.jpg *License*: unknown *Contributors*: Alientraveller, Collard, Fit for purpose, Jeandré du Toit, Kieranthompson, Llywrch, Nehrams2020, Quentin X, Videmus Omnia, Wiki alf, 4 anonymous edits

Image:Daniel Craig on Venice yacht crop w Wilson.jpg *Source*:http://en.wikipedia.org/w/index.php?title=File:Daniel_Craig_on_Venice_yacht_crop_w_Wilson.jpg *License*: Creative Commons Attribution 2.0 *Contributors*: Flickr user wonderferret

File:Magic Roundabout-one-sheet.jpg *Source*:http://en.wikipedia.org/w/index.php?title=File:Magic_Roundabout-one-sheet.jpg *License*: unknown *Contributors*: Quentin X, Shimgray, Skier Dude, TheLH

File:Mrs. Henderson Presents poster.jpg *Source*:http://en.wikipedia.org/w/index.php?title=File:Mrs._Henderson_Presents_poster.jpg *License*: unknown *Contributors*: Brad, NWill, Sfan00 IMG

File:Prideandprejudice-movieposter.jpg *Source*:http://en.wikipedia.org/w/index.php?title=File:Prideandprejudice-movieposter.jpg *License*: unknown *Contributors*: Gsl, RainingOnSunday, Skier Dude

Image:Pride & Prejudice London Bus.jpg *Source*:http://en.wikipedia.org/w/index.php?title=File:Pride_&_Prejudice_London_Bus.jpg *License*: GNU Free Documentation License *Contributors*: User:Corcoran

File:Ladies in Lavender Poster.jpg *Source*:http://en.wikipedia.org/w/index.php?title=File:Ladies_in_Lavender_Poster.jpg *License*: unknown *Contributors*: ExpressingYourself

File:Chronicles of riddick ver2.jpg *Source*:http://en.wikipedia.org/w/index.php?title=File:Chronicles_of_riddick_ver2.jpg *License*: unknown *Contributors*: User:Grandpafootsoldier

File:homerangeposter.jpg *Source*:http://en.wikipedia.org/w/index.php?title=File:Homerangeposter.jpg *License*: unknown *Contributors*: Chris1219, Melesse, ST47, Skier Dude, Speedway

Image:Grace, Mrs Calloway & Maggie.JPG *Source*:http://en.wikipedia.org/w/index.php?title=File:Grace,_Mrs_Calloway_&_Maggie.JPG *License*: unknown *Contributors*: DarkFalls, KF, LordBleen, Melesse, Rhindle The Red, Sfan00 IMG, Sherool, 2 anonymous edits

file:Home_on_the_range_soundtrack_cover.jpg *Source*:http://en.wikipedia.org/w/index.php?title=File:Home_on_the_range_soundtrack_cover.jpg *License*: unknown *Contributors*: Nemeses9, Skier Dude

File:Star full.svg *Source*: http://en.wikipedia.org/w/index.php?title=File:Star_full.svg *License*: Public Domain *Contributors*: User:Conti, User:RedHotHeat

File:Star empty.svg *Source*: http://en.wikipedia.org/w/index.php?title=File:Star_empty.svg *License*: Creative Commons Attribution-Sharealike 2.5 *Contributors*: User:Conti, User:RedHotHeat

File:007DAD1.jpg *Source*: http://en.wikipedia.org/w/index.php?title=File:007DAD1.jpg *License*: unknown *Contributors*: DarkFalls, Fastfission, Joaquin008, K1Bond007, Kieranthompson, Nehrams2020, Nv8200p

Image:Dad2002.jpg *Source*: http://en.wikipedia.org/w/index.php?title=File:Dad2002.jpg *License*: Attribution *Contributors*: BigrTex, Dr. Blofeld, MachoCarioca, Ultraviolet scissor flame

Image:Diefencing.jpg *Source*: http://en.wikipedia.org/w/index.php?title=File:Diefencing.jpg *License*: unknown *Contributors*: Dr. Blofeld

Image:Die Another Dayintro.jpg *Source*: http://en.wikipedia.org/w/index.php?title=File:Die_Another_Dayintro.jpg *License*: unknown *Contributors*: Dr. Blofeld

Image:Jökulsárlón April 07-3.JPG *Source*: http://en.wikipedia.org/w/index.php?title=File:Jökulsárlón_April_07-3.JPG *License*: Attribution *Contributors*: Martin Peeks

Image:Die another day jaguar xkr.jpg *Source*:http://en.wikipedia.org/w/index.php?title=File:Die_another_day_jaguar_xkr.jpg *License*: Creative Commons Attribution-Sharealike 2.0 *Contributors*: robadob

File:Ernestposter.jpg *Source*: http://en.wikipedia.org/w/index.php?title=File:Ernestposter.jpg *License*: Attribution *Contributors*: Grandpafootsoldier

File:The Shipping News film.jpg *Source*:http://en.wikipedia.org/w/index.php?title=File:The_Shipping_News_film.jpg *License*: unknown *Contributors*: *drew, For An Angel, Rettetast, Sfan00 IMG, Skier Dude

File:Iris poster.jpg *Source*: http://en.wikipedia.org/w/index.php?title=File:Iris_poster.jpg *License*: unknown *Contributors*: Blathnaid, NWill

File:Chocolat_sheet.jpg *Source*: http://en.wikipedia.org/w/index.php?title=File:Chocolat_sheet.jpg *License*: unknown *Contributors*: Avy, Baird, Crstsk, Ecco1983

File:The Last of the Blonde Bombshells.jpg *Source*:http://en.wikipedia.org/w/index.php?title=File:The_Last_of_the_Blonde_Bombshells.jpg *License*: unknown *Contributors*: Crstsk, Skier Dude

File:Flag of the United States.svg *Source*:http://en.wikipedia.org/w/index.php?title=File:Flag_of_the_United_States.svg *License*: Public Domain *Contributors*: User:Dbenbenn, User:Indolences, User:Jacobolus, User:Technion, User:Zscout370

File:Flag of the United Kingdom.svg *Source*:http://en.wikipedia.org/w/index.php?title=File:Flag_of_the_United_Kingdom.svg *License*: Public Domain *Contributors*: User:Zscout370

File:Kindertransport film.jpg *Source*: http://en.wikipedia.org/w/index.php?title=File:Kindertransport_film.jpg *License*: unknown *Contributors*: Cop 663, Roninbk File:World-is-not-enoughposter.jpg *Source*:http://en.wikipedia.org/w/index.php?title=File:World-is-not-enoughposter.jpg *License*: unknown *Contributors*: Dr. Blofeld

Image:ChathamHDSubmarine0083.JPG *Source*:http://en.wikipedia.org/w/index.php?title=File:ChathamHDSubmarine0083.JPG *License*: Creative Commons Attribution 2.5 *Contributors*: Clem Rutter, Rochester Kent

Image:PierceBMW99.jpg *Source*: http://en.wikipedia.org/w/index.php?title=File:PierceBMW99.jpg *License*: Attribution *Contributors*: Dr. Blofeld, Ultraviolet scissor flame

Image:QBoatThames.jpg *Source*: http://en.wikipedia.org/w/index.php?title=File:QBoatThames.jpg *License*: Attribution *Contributors*: Dr. Blofeld

File:Tea with Mussolini film.jpg *Source*:http://en.wikipedia.org/w/index.php?title=File:Tea_with_Mussolini_film.jpg *License*: unknown *Contributors*: *drew, Nehrams2020, Quentin X, Sfan00 IMG

File:Shakes-in-love-mov-poster.jpg *Source*: http://en.wikipedia.org/w/index.php?title=File:Shakes-in-love-mov-poster.jpg *License*: unknown *Contributors*: *drew, Dr. Blofeld, Melesse, MykReeve, Nehrams2020, Pearle, Sfan00 IMG

File:007TNDposter.jpg *Source*: http://en.wikipedia.org/w/index.php?title=File:007TNDposter.jpg *License*: unknown *Contributors*: Fastfission, K1Bond007, Kieranthompson, Quentin X, Rettetast, Skier Dude

Image:007-BMW.jpg *Source*: http://en.wikipedia.org/w/index.php?title=File:007-BMW.jpg *License*: Creative Commons Attribution-Sharealike 3.0 *Contributors*: User:F30

Image:JB HALO.png *Source*: http://en.wikipedia.org/w/index.php?title=File:JB_HALO.png *License*: unknown *Contributors*: Dr. Blofeld, Haemo, Lindell005

Image:TomorrowNeverDiesNovel.jpg *Source*: http://en.wikipedia.org/w/index.php?title=File:TomorrowNeverDiesNovel.jpg *License*: unknown *Contributors*: User:23skidoo

File:Mrsbrownposter.jpg *Source*:http://en.wikipedia.org/w/index.php?title=File:Mrsbrownposter.jpg *License*: unknown *Contributors*: Skier Dude, Yllosubmarine

File:Hamlet_1996_poster.jpg *Source*:http://en.wikipedia.org/w/index.php?title=File:Hamlet_1996_poster.jpg *License*: unknown *Contributors*: Alientraveller, Donald McKinney, Erik, N. Harmonik, Nehrams2020, Patriarch, Sfan00 IMG, VolatileChemical

Image:Hamlet1996cameos.jpg *Source*: http://en.wikipedia.org/w/index.php?title=File:Hamlet1996cameos.jpg *License*: unknown *Contributors*: Cubs Fan, 1 anonymous edits

File:007GEposter.jpg *Source*: http://en.wikipedia.org/w/index.php?title=File:007GEposter.jpg *License*: unknown *Contributors*: Fastfission, K1Bond007, Kieranthompson, Pekaje, Riana, Skier Dude

Image:Kleinman titlecredits.jpg *Source*: http://en.wikipedia.org/w/index.php?title=File:Kleinman_titlecredits.jpg *License*: unknown *Contributors*: User:K1Bond007

Image:Goldeneyeemulated4lw.jpg *Source*: http://en.wikipedia.org/w/index.php?title=File:Goldeneyeemulated4lw.jpg *License*: Attribution *Contributors*: Alphachimp, Anetode, Diaa abdelmoneim, Icey, Igordebraga, N. Harmonik, Pagrashtak, Renegadeviking, Threedots dead

Image:GE-Virtual-Boy-screenshot-1.png *Source*: http://en.wikipedia.org/w/index.php?title=File:GE-Virtual-Boy-screenshot-1.png *License*: Attribution *Contributors*: Ultraviolet scissor flame

File:Jack and sarah.jpeg *Source*: http://en.wikipedia.org/w/index.php?title=File:Jack_and_sarah.jpeg *License*: unknown *Contributors*: Orbicle

File:Flag of France.svg *Source*: http://en.wikipedia.org/w/index.php?title=File:Flag_of_France.svg *License*: Public Domain *Contributors*: User:SKopp, User:SKopp, User:SKopp, User:SKopp, User:SKopp, User:SKopp

File:BehavingBadlyDVD.JPG *Source*: http://en.wikipedia.org/w/index.php?title=File:BehavingBadlyDVD.JPG *License*: unknown *Contributors*: Bradley0110, MovieMadness

File:Henry v post.jpg *Source*: http://en.wikipedia.org/w/index.php?title=File:Henry_v_post.jpg *License*: Attribution *Contributors*: Grandpafootsoldier

Image:Dust300.jpg *Source*: http://en.wikipedia.org/w/index.php?title=File:Dust300.jpg *License*: unknown *Contributors*: Evelyn Waugh

File:84 Charing Cross Road poster.jpg *Source*:http://en.wikipedia.org/w/index.php?title=File:84_Charing_Cross_Road_poster.jpg *License*: unknown *Contributors*: EraserGirl, Fuzzy510, NWill, Skier Dude

File:Room_with_a_view.jpg *Source*: http://en.wikipedia.org/w/index.php?title=File:Room_with_a_view.jpg *License*: unknown *Contributors*: David Pro, MachoCarioca, Skier Dude, 1 anonymous edits

File:Wetherby.jpg *Source*: http://en.wikipedia.org/w/index.php?title=File:Wetherby.jpg *License*: unknown *Contributors*: Cop 663

File:Angelic conversation.jpg *Source*: http://en.wikipedia.org/w/index.php?title=File:Angelic_conversation.jpg *License*: unknown *Contributors*: Belovedfreak

File:Flag of Japan.svg *Source*: http://en.wikipedia.org/w/index.php?title=File:Flag_of_Japan.svg *License*: Public Domain *Contributors*: Various

File:Luther 1973 film DVD cover.jpg *Source*:http://en.wikipedia.org/w/index.php?title=File:Luther_1973_film_DVD_cover.jpg *License*: unknown *Contributors*: Drboisclair

Image:Flag of the United States.svg *Source*:http://en.wikipedia.org/w/index.php?title=File:Flag_of_the_United_States.svg *License*: Public Domain *Contributors*: User:Dbenbenn, User:Indolences, User:Jacobolus, User:Technion, User:Zscout370

Image:Flag of the United Kingdom.svg *Source*:http://en.wikipedia.org/w/index.php?title=File:Flag_of_the_United_Kingdom.svg *License*: Public Domain *Contributors*: User:Zscout370

File:A Midsummer Nights Dream (1968 film).jpg *Source*:http://en.wikipedia.org/w/index.php?title=File:A_Midsummer_Nights_Dream_(1968_film).jpg *License*: unknown *Contributors*: Melesse, Sue Wallace

File:Study in terror43.jpg *Source*: http://en.wikipedia.org/w/index.php?title=File:Study_in_terror43.jpg *License*: unknown *Contributors*: Skier Dude, Thismightbezach

File:ThirdSecretPoster.jpg *Source*: http://en.wikipedia.org/w/index.php?title=File:ThirdSecretPoster.jpg *License*: unknown *Contributors*: LiteraryMaven

License

on can be obtained at www.ICGtesting.com
/00006B/2/P